LIBERTY

Isaiah Berlin was born in Riga, capital of Latvia, in 1909. When he was six, his family moved to Russia; there in 1917, in Petrograd, he witnessed both Revolutions – Social Democratic and Bolshevik.

In 1921 his family came to England, and he was educated at St Paul's School and Corpus Christi College, Oxford. At Oxford he was a Fellow of All Souls, a Fellow of New College, Professor of Social and Political Theory and founding President of Wolfson College. He also held the Presidency of the British Academy. In addition to *Liberty* and the simultaneously published *Freedom and its Betrayal*, his main published works are *Karl Marx*, *Russian Thinkers*, *Concepts and Categories*, *Against the Current*, *Personal Impressions*, *The Crooked Timber of Humanity*, *The Sense of Reality*, *The Proper Study of Mankind*, *The Roots of Romanticism*, *The Power of Ideas* and *Three Critics of the Enlightenment*. As an exponent of the history of ideas he was awarded the Erasmus, Lippincott and Agnelli Prizes; he also received the Jerusalem Prize for his lifelong defence of civil liberties. He died in 1997.

Henry Hardy, a Fellow of Wolfson College, Oxford, is one of Isaiah Berlin's Literary Trustees. He has edited several other books by Berlin, and is currently preparing his letters and his remaining unpublished writings for publication.

For further information about Isaiah Berlin visit
http://berlin.wolf.ox.ac.uk/

Also by Isaiah Berlin

*

KARL MARX
THE AGE OF ENLIGHTENMENT

Edited by Henry Hardy and Aileen Kelly

RUSSIAN THINKERS

Edited by Henry Hardy

CONCEPTS AND CATEGORIES
AGAINST THE CURRENT
PERSONAL IMPRESSIONS
THE CROOKED TIMBER OF HUMANITY
THE SENSE OF REALITY
THE ROOTS OF ROMANTICISM
THE POWER OF IDEAS
THREE CRITICS OF THE ENLIGHTENMENT
FREEDOM AND ITS BETRAYAL

Edited by Henry Hardy and Roger Hausheer

THE PROPER STUDY OF MANKIND

LIBERTY

ISAIAH BERLIN

Incorporating *Four Essays on Liberty*

Edited by Henry Hardy

With an essay on Berlin and his critics
by Ian Harris

OXFORD
UNIVERSITY PRESS

OXFORD

UNIVERSITY PRESS

Great Clarendon Street, Oxford OX2 6DP

Oxford University Press is a department of the University of Oxford.
It furthers the University's objective of excellence in research, scholarship
and education by publishing worldwide in

Oxford New York

Athens Auckland Bangkok Bogotá Bombay Buenos Aires
Cape Town Chennai Dar es Salaam Delhi Florence Hong Kong Istanbul
Karachi Kolkata Kuala Lumpur Madrid Melbourne Mexico City Mumbai
Nairobi Paris São Paolo Shanghai Singapore Taipei Tokyo Toronto Warsaw

with associated companies in Berlin Ibadan

Oxford is a registered trade mark of Oxford University Press
in the UK and in certain other countries

Published in the United States
by Oxford University Press Inc., New York

British Library Cataloguing in Publication Data

Data available

Library of Congress Cataloguing in Publication Data

Data available

ISBN 0-19-924988-1 (hbk)   ISBN 0-19-924989-x (pbk)

Typeset in Monotype Garamond
by Deltatype Ltd, Birkenhead, Merseyside

Printed in Great Britain
by T. J. International, Padstow, Cornwall

To the memory of Stephen Spender
1909–1995

The essence of liberty has always lain in the ability to choose as you wish to choose, because you wish so to choose, uncoerced, unbullied, not swallowed up in some vast system; and in the right to resist, to be unpopular, to stand up for your convictions merely because they are your convictions. That is true freedom, and without it there is neither freedom of any kind, nor even the illusion of it.

Isaiah Berlin, *Freedom and its Betrayal*[1]

[1] London and Princeton, 2002, pp. 103–4. The lectures that comprise *Freedom and its Betrayal* were delivered in 1952. (Berlin uses the words 'freedom' and 'liberty' interchangeably.)

CONTENTS

Illustrations   viii
The Editor's Tale   ix

FIVE ESSAYS ON LIBERTY

Introduction   3
Political Ideas in the Twentieth Century   55
Historical Inevitability   94
Two Concepts of Liberty   166
John Stuart Mill and the Ends of Life   218
From Hope and Fear Set Free   252

OTHER WRITINGS ON LIBERTY

Liberty   283
The Birth of Greek Individualism   287
Final Retrospect   322

AUTOBIOGRAPHICAL APPENDICES

The Purpose Justifies the Ways   331
A Letter to George Kennan   336
Notes on Prejudice   345

Berlin and his Critics by Ian Harris   349
Concordance to Four Essays on Liberty   367
Index   371

ILLUSTRATIONS

A page from the proofs of *Four Essays on Liberty*   xviii

The front cover of the first impression of
    Four Essays on Liberty   xxiii

The source of the title 'Five Essays on Liberty'   xxxiv

Berlin's notes for 'My Intellectual Path'   282

Berlin aged twelve, Arundel House School, July 1921   329

The first page of the manuscript of
    'The Purpose Justifies the Ways'   330

The first page of the typescript of 'Political Ideas in the
    Romantic Age'   348

The end of the bibliography from the Isaiah Berlin Virtual
    Library, *http://berlin.wolf.ox.ac.uk/*, October 2001   365

THE EDITOR'S TALE

Liberty is the only true riches.

William Hazlitt[1]

IN THE YEAR that Isaiah Berlin died, I was invited by *The Times Higher Education Supplement* to contribute to their 'Speaking Volumes' series, in which readers write briefly about the book that has influenced them most. I had no hesitation in choosing Berlin's *Four Essays on Liberty*, which not only bowled me over when I first read it, but also set me on course towards becoming Berlin's editor, and so led, thirty years on, to the publication of this expanded edition of the book.

My *THES* piece was written just before Berlin's death, and published shortly thereafter.[2] Part of what I said seems to me to bear repeating in the present context:

> I had no idea when I joined Oxford's Wolfson College as a graduate student in 1972 that I was about to discover my eventual occupation. The College's President was Isaiah Berlin. It was clear as soon as I met him (at a scholarship interview for which I arrived late after a car accident, and during which he repeatedly went to the window to see if a taxi had arrived to take him to a lunch appointment) that he was a remarkable man; but I had never read any of his work, and knew next to nothing about him.
>
> I asked where I should start, and was rightly directed to *Four Essays on Liberty*, published three years earlier. I took it with me on a visit with friends to a remote Exmoor cottage during a University vacation, and was transfixed. Berlin liked to refer to the unmistakable sensation

[1] From 'Common Places' (1823): vol. 20, p. 122, in *The Complete Works of William Hazlitt*, ed. P. P. Howe (London and Toronto, 1930–4).

[2] Issue dated 21 November 1997, p. 21. Berlin died on 5 November. The article is also available on line at *http://berlin.wolf.ox.ac.uk/*, under 'Writing about Berlin'. I have slightly adapted the extract used here.

of 'sailing in first-class waters', and this was the sensation I experienced. Quite apart from the persuasiveness of the propositions contained in the book, here was obviously a man of rare insight into human nature, a man plentifully endowed with that 'sense of reality' that he welcomed when he found it in others. There was room for disagreement on this or that point, but on the large issues one felt in safe hands.

The central plank in the book is Berlin's value pluralism, his belief that the values humans pursue are not only multiple but sometimes irreconcilable, and that this applies at the level of whole cultures – systems of value – as well as between the values of a particular culture or individual. It is an essential characteristic of the great monistic religions and political ideologies to claim that there is only one way to salvation, one right way to live, one true value-structure. This is the claim which, when it is given fanatical expression, leads to fundamentalism, persecution and intolerance. Pluralism is a prophylactic against such dangers. It is a source of liberalism and toleration – not just the unstable kind of toleration that waits for the mistaken to see the light, but the deep, lasting toleration that accepts and welcomes visions of life irretrievably different from those we ourselves live by.

Four Essays is full of other gold, including the devastating critique of historicism and determinism in 'Historical Inevitability', the famous discussion of 'positive' and 'negative' freedom in 'Two Concepts of Liberty', and the examination of the tensions in Mill's views in 'John Stuart Mill and the Ends of Life'. It is one of the richest and most humane books I have ever read, and it has deservedly become a classic.

This said, it may seem *lèse-majesté* to tamper with it now, but, as will soon become clear, the first stage of expansion was devoutly wished for by the author himself, and I see myself as taking the process further towards its logical conclusion.

I do not apologise for having put pluralism rather than liberalism centre stage in my comments on *Four Essays*, though others would invert this priority. Berlin's pluralism seems to me the deeper and more original thesis – which is not to deny the indispensability of his version of liberalism, or of the view of humanity that lies at its heart, a view in which freedom of choice among incommensurably multiple possibilities is central. Indeed pluralism and liberalism, the two leading components of Berlin's philosophical outlook (sometimes aptly called 'liberal pluralism'), are mutually interdependent and supportive,[1] and I have at times thought of giving this

---

[1] In this view I differ, in company with others, from John Gray, author of the

collection a title such as *Freedom and Diversity*; but the Occamist imperative, reinforced by the pragmatic desirability of echoing the well-known earlier title, won out.

FIVE ESSAYS ON LIBERTY

The time has come said Linnet to Stallworthy to talk about Berlin again.

> Oxford University Press memo from Catherine Linnet,
> New York, to Jon Stallworthy, London, 21 June 1967

Berlin's *oeuvre* has been described by Ira Katznelson, somewhat sweepingly but quite understandably, as 'both correct and bold':[1] the luminous, settled, assured qualities of Berlin's writing are widely recognised and appreciated. But there is a paradoxical relationship between these undoubted attributes and the tortuous and tortured route by which his publications came to take the form they do. The 'correctness' is not achieved at the first attempt, nor even at the nineteenth; and the boldness is not matched by an equivalent self-confidence. As Berlin wrote to Karl Popper in gratitude for his approval of *Two Concepts of Liberty*, 'I have little confidence in the validity of my own intellectual processes.'[2] Although he commanded the stage, he trembled in the wings.

The genesis of *Four Essays on Liberty*[3] was just as chaotic and prolonged as that of the other compilation of his essays that Berlin published before I became his editor, namely *Vico and Herder*.[4] The Oxford University Press file on the book is a treasure-house of anecdote: frustration, misunderstanding, tergiversation, indecisiveness, prevarication, unrealistic expectations abound. The whole

---

excellent *Isaiah Berlin* (London, 1995), who believes that Berlin's pluralism narrows the field for the justification of his liberalism: see Gray's chapter 6, 'Agonistic Liberalism'.

[1] 'Why is it so intuitively true that Berlin's work is both correct and bold?' he asks in 'Isaiah Berlin's Modernity': Arien Mack (ed.), *Liberty and Pluralism* [*Social Research* 66 No 4 (Winter 1999)], 1079–101, at 1079.

[2] Letter of 16 March 1959.

[3] Published by OUP in London and New York in 1969. Bibliographies often state, misleadingly, that the book was published in Oxford.

[4] I offer a brief version of the saga of this later (1976) volume in Berlin's *Three Critics of the Enlightenment: Vico, Hamann, Herder* (London, 2000: Chatto and Windus; Princeton, 2000: Princeton University Press), pp. vii–viii.

proceedings, year after year, are accompanied by frantic re-
schedulings on the part of OUP, as well as complementary and
conflicting discussions of other projects, which appear out of the
fog and then recede. OUP become increasingly desperate as time
slips by, and some of the wry internal memoranda make excellent
reading. I say all this not to poke fun, though the file is
undoubtedly fun to read, but because we learn much about Berlin
the man by having the complex process of creation of his famous
and important book – in his view, his most important book – laid
bare in such comprehensive detail. I hope it is clear, too, from my
opening remarks that the spirit in which I tell the story of the
book's gradual emergence is one of affection rather than censure,
for all that Berlin's conduct, benign but gloriously unprofessio-
nal,[1] caused justifiable exasperation on the part of his publisher.
The path was stony, but the destination fully worth the journey,
and not to be reached by a more direct route.

Here I can only skim off the cream of the story. The file opens in
November 1953 with a letter from the New York office of Berlin's
literary agent, then as now Curtis Brown, to Oxford University
Press, Inc., New York, who had taken the lead in the commission-
ing of the book. At this point only the first two of the four essays
had been written, though a book of essays 'on political topics' was
already under discussion. 'I will try to obtain a list of essays from
Mr Berlin as quickly as I can,' writes John Cushman of Curtis
Brown. What would he have said, we may speculate, had he known
that it would be sixteen years before the book finally appeared?

At that time OUP had two publishing offices in the UK, one in
Oxford (the academic Clarendon Press) and one in London, at
Amen House. Amen House was responsible for publications aimed
at a general readership, including Oxford Paperbacks, the series in
which the UK edition of the book was to appear. The London
Publisher, Geoffrey Cumberledge, was interested but pessimistic:
'Berlin ... is brilliant but his output is very small and his
performance is worse than his promise.'

In 1958 Berlin gave his celebrated inaugural lecture as Chichele
Professor of Social and Political Theory in Oxford, 'Two Concepts
of Liberty', and in 1959 his Robert Waley Cohen Memorial
Lecture, 'John Stuart Mill and the Ends of Life'. Both of these

---

[1] The manner of the book's creation would surely have been roundly censured
in a Research Assessment Exercise.

thereafter start to appear as constituents of the volume, by 1960 hyperbolically if provisionally entitled 'Collected Writings' by the New York office.

In reply to an enquiry from New York early that year about progress, Colin Roberts, Secretary (that is, head) of OUP, writing from the Clarendon Press, quotes a letter from Berlin, the first communication from him represented in the file:

> Alas, my Introduction to the paperback on liberty is not just a question of a willing typist – I wish it were – last-minute corrections are my *métier* as you know too well, but it is not that that is delaying me. I should like to write a preface – more a postface – in the way of discussing and, so far as I can, replying to the various points and objections which all three essays[1] have encountered one way and another – not indeed by name and address, but in fairly general terms. This I cannot do for a while – I am a slow worker – and hope to do in summer.

In March 1961 Amen House writes to OUP's Deputy Secretary, Dan Davin, at the Clarendon Press: 'Is there the vaguest possible chance that Berlin might even have begun to work on the prefaces which he insists are necessary?' A letter from Berlin reported by Davin later that month announces that

> The Three Essays have now become four – Mill being added ... As to the Introduction, I shall write it in the summer in July and August, it will have to be in the nature of a general reply to all the many and fierce objections that have been made to these essays, and are still being made in current publications, so that the Press in New York must not think they are losing something with every new reference in my reply to the critics. They will acquire at least one new potential reader (the latest onslaught is in a magazine called *Dissent*, which arrived yesterday)[2] – so long as my opinions to my own astonishment provide a live horse for the critics to flog, it will not be too late to re-issue the essays.

Answering an enquiry from John Brown (Cumberledge's successor), Berlin's typist Olive Sheldon writes on his behalf in September that he is at work on the Introduction to a book to be

---

[1] The essay on Mill had not yet been added. At this stage the work is usually referred to as 'Three Essays on Liberty'.

[2] David Spitz, 'The Nature and Limits of Freedom', *Dissent* 8 (1961–2), 78–86.

called 'Essays on Liberty' or 'Against the Current' or 'Against the Stream'. Through her he expresses doubts about the value of the essays on J. S. Mill and on twentieth-century political ideas and suggests that they be sent to a referee. The Introduction is promised for January 1962. In November Harold Beaver of Amen House writes to Catherine Linnet in New York: 'I feel sure that Berlin is merely flapping when he wishes his material to be read.' Read it was, however, by Adam Ulam, Professor of Government at Harvard, who reported favourably, as expected, prefacing his remarks with this sound observation: 'I am not entirely in sympathy with the custom of sending the work of a reputable scholar which has a style and point of view of its own to be picked and hacked at by somebody else.'

In January 1962 Berlin writes a letter to John Brown that is worth quoting in full:

I am oppressed by feelings of guilt about the Introduction to the paperback containing my various essays on liberty and generally related topics. I do not believe I shall achieve this Introduction before the Summer. The reasons for this are: (1) that since it involves reading the accumulated criticisms of the various ingredients of this volume – that was the point of the new Introduction – [it] needs a good deal of time and deliberation and careful drafting of answers to objections. Critical reviews seem never to cease although I am prepared to draw a line at 1 January 1962 and take into consideration nothing that appears thereafter.

(2) Living the life that I do, I deliver too many lectures outside my Oxford curriculum, sit on too many committees, and generally scatter such energies as I possess in a highly uneconomic and indeed often absurd manner. In my lucid moments I regret this very much and make constant resolutions to resist invitations by undergraduate societies, and to lead a rational, i.e. more concentrated, life. But all these excellent resolutions break against the barrier, and the feeling that as a Professor I cannot refuse to tell the truth to those who make quite a good show of appearing to want to hear it. As for the committees, since they are my only excuse for going to London or abroad, I secretly cling to them even though I recognise their time-eating and energy-destroying properties.

These things being so, I know myself well enough to realise that I cannot write this Introduction in term-time – in April I shall be away both lecturing and functioning on my committees – but I shall write my piece in May or June, and you shall have it by mid-July. I felt it to be only fair to you to let you know how the matter stands – if this delays publication, then, so far as I am concerned, I shall shed no tears, but I sincerely hope that it will not interfere with your publishing plans too much.

This generates a note from Beaver to Linnet: 'Isaiah Berlin, the great cunctator, has again put off supplying the preface.'

In May Bud MacLennan of Curtis Brown asks John Brown for an advance of £100, and in his absence a colleague tells her that they can pay £50 or £75, 'but I do not think we can go beyond this figure'. (One wonders what OUP's estimate was of the likely sales of the book, which has remained in print and in constant demand ever since.) The contract for what was now to be called *Four Essays on Liberty* was signed in July, replacing an earlier contract of July 1959 with New York for *Three Essays*. In October John Brown writes to Sheldon Meyer in New York: 'I think we have got everything satisfactorily tied up, provided only that Berlin will produce the copy.'

Berlin writes to John Brown in February 1963 that 'the Introduction for *Four Essays on Liberty* is a ... complicated matter', partly because he was giving priority to another project (which, like many others, did not materialise), a book based on the 1962 Storrs Lectures at Yale, 'Three Turning-Points in the History of Political Thought'.

In March 1964 Jon Stallworthy of Amen House, by then in charge of Oxford Paperbacks, writes to Curtis Brown that 'it is over a year since we last corresponded about the Introduction for Sir Isaiah Berlin's *Four Essays on Liberty* and I wonder whether you could give us any news of progress on this?' The reply is that the piece will not be ready for at least another year, and OUP are asked if they wish to cancel the contract. Stallworthy writes to Peter Sutcliffe in Oxford: 'The Preface has been promised us for the best part of four years, and I think everyone – including perhaps even Berlin – realises that we shall never see it now.' Stallworthy asks Curtis Brown for permission to go ahead without it. Richard Simon of Curtis Brown replies that Berlin will definitely produce the Introduction for April 1966, and that, if he doesn't, OUP may publish without it. This arrangement is accepted by Stallworthy.

Needless to say, this deadline slipped, ostensibly because Berlin was ill. Stallworthy secured permission to typeset the four essays before the arrival of the Introduction.[1] Before sending the typescript to the printer, he consulted Berlin about two possible forms of typesetting – hot metal and Monophoto – and explained that, if there were to be changes, it was vital to opt for hot metal. Berlin undertook to make no changes, and Stallworthy, rashly believing him, opted for Monophoto.[2] The Introduction was re-promised for the end of August, again on the understanding that the book would appear without it if it were not ready in time.

A further reversal occurred when Berlin wrote in the following terms to Stallworthy four days short of the new deadline, in a letter signed on his behalf in his absence by his secretary, Baillie Knapheis:

> [. . .] I should like to hasten, in the first place, to thank you for your extremely considerate and patient treatment of me – beyond my deserts. I know that the Oxford Press in New York must regard me as a highly unsatisfactory client – because of all these delays – but one of the secret causes of this is my suspicion that the works which they kindly wish to reprint as a paperback are in some cases scarcely worth it; I have looked through 'Historical Inevitability' again, and I find that there are all kinds of things wrong with it, and I should certainly be ashamed if it appeared in an unaltered form. I have gone through the disagreeable task of reading through the nastier criticisms of it – such as I have kept – the more violent and ephemeral I mislaid or lost almost at once – and it appears to me that what some of the critics said is true, and that, in the interests of the readers and general integrity, the text cannot be left wholly intact. Consequently I have introduced corrections – though far less radical ones than were perhaps required – and hope to make up for this in the Introduction, which I propose to prepare next week. In the meanwhile I do hope that the corrections will not reduce the Press to despair: I realise that there is something for the printers to do,[3] and if this is regarded as financially awkward, I am so anxious for this labour to be done – that is, for the corrections to be introduced (I should be ashamed – and indeed could not conceive the prospect – of letting the texts go out unaltered), that I should be prepared to consider reimbursing the Press for these

[1] This is why roman numerals are used to paginate the Introduction in *Four Essays*.

[2] It seems he had not studied the file for 'Two Concepts of Liberty', where, with impressive self-restraint, Colin Roberts writes to Berlin on 6 November 1958: 'You have certainly had a field day with the proofs.' The lecture had to be completely reset.

[3] One of the great understatements of our time: in the end the whole book had to be reset.

unexpected expenses. In fact the only prospect I could not contemplate was for the corrections not to be incorporated.

I hope you will forgive me for being such a nuisance. I know all authors are, and am perhaps not the worst among them; nevertheless, unlike some authors, I do possess a genuine conscience with regard to publishers and do not regard them as mere philistine adversaries to be sparred with, but as genuine intellectual collaborators, particularly the Press. Consequently I do hope that you will once again be patient with me, again beyond my proper deserts – for I am quite clear that if the only condition for publication is that the texts should go out unaltered, I would rather nothing were published at all, and that these essays continued to dwell in their present decent obscurity [. . .]

Mercy, rather than justice, is, I suppose, what I am asking for: but I truly cannot see how you could deny it to me. You must have had authors far more tiresome than even myself. Perhaps what I am asking for is not so terribly unreasonable. At any rate, I am very grateful.

Page proofs of the four essays arrived at the end of November, but there was still no Introduction. This finally arrived in May 1967, but was immediately put on hold because Berlin wanted comments from Stuart Hampshire and Herbert Hart. In the meantime he continued to correct the essays themselves heavily, despite his promise not to do so. This elicited the following comment from between Stallworthy's gritted teeth:

I think I should mention [a tactful substitution for 'remind you'] that the book has been set up by a Monophoto machine that produces a page not of lead but of film negative. Every correction involves a delicate operation not unlike that for the removal of a cataract from a human eye; the skin of the negative has to be cut and a new line or letter grafted on. Such corrections are very expensive.

Berlin finally returned the corrected proofs of the four essays in August. A month later he sent OUP a revised text of his Introduction, writing in his covering note: 'Owing to the devastating criticisms it has received, I have altered it, not nearly as much as the critics wish, but still, perhaps sufficiently to avoid howling errors (or perhaps not).' At this point an internal OUP note from Stallworthy reads: 'Despite all my explanations about the cost of correcting a filmset text, my suggestions, pleas, further explanations, further suggestions, and further pleas, Berlin has made extensive corrections.' If only the book had been published in the days of word processors and modern typesetting technology.

were established as an accepted truth, our world would be transformed far more radically than was the teleological world of the
classical and middle ages by the triumphs of mechanistic principles or those of natural selection. Our words—our modes
of speech and thought—would be transformed in literally unimaginable ways; the notions of choice, of voluntary action, of
responsibility, freedom, are so deeply embedded in our outlook,
that our new life, as creatures in a world genuinely lacking in these
concepts, can, I should maintain, be conceived by us only with
the greatest difficulty. But there is, as yet, no need to alarm ourselves unduly. We are speaking only of pseudo-scientific ideals;
the reality is not in sight. The evidence for a thoroughgoing
determinism is not to hand; and if there is a persistent tendency
to believe in it in some theoretical fashion, that is surely due far
more to the lure of a 'scientistic' or metaphysical ideal, or a
on the part of those who desire to change society, to believe that
the stars in their courses are fighting for them. Or it may be due
to a longing to lay down moral burdens, or minimize individual
responsibility and transfer it to impersonal forces which can be
safely accused of causing all our discontents, than to any increase
in our powers of critical reflection or any improvement in our
scientific techniques. Belief in historical determinism of this
type is, of course, very widespread, particularly in what I should
like to call its 'historiosophical' form, by which I mean metaphysico-theological theories of history, which attract many who
have lost their faith in older religious orthodoxies. Yet perhaps
this attitude, so prevalent recently, is ebbing; and a contrary
trend is discernible today. Our best historians use empirical tests
in sifting facts, make microscopic examinations of the evidence,
deduce no patterns, and show no false fear in attributing responsibility to individuals. Their specific attributions and analyses may
be mistaken, but both they and their readers would be surprised
to be told that their very activity had been superseded and
stultified by the advances of sociology, or by some deeper metaphysical insight, like that of oriental stargazers by the dis-

As for the attempt to 'reinterpret' these notions so as to bring them into conformity
with determinism, this can be achieved only at the cost of altering their meaning of such
concepts beyond applicability to our normal experience. Cf. p. , footnote.

In November Stallworthy sent Berlin a long list of queries about the final text of the Introduction, but it was February 1968 before Berlin replied. In his letter (reproduced on page 2 below) he wrote:

I see that gradually but inexorably I am becoming if not your most intolerable (though I may be that too) certainly your most time-consuming author. At the risk of inflicting a blow upon you which may seriously endanger your health – such health and optimism as you may have regained during your recent holiday – I propose to inflict yet another hideous blow upon you [. . .] It has been represented to me by kind friends (for once genuinely kind) that the book might be improved by the inclusion in it of yet another essay on the same subject, namely my Presidential Address to the Aristotelian Society a few years ago, the title of which was 'From Hope and Fear Set Free'. This would make a fifth essay in the book and the title could be altered from 'Four Essays on Liberty' either to 'Five Essays on Liberty' or simply 'Essays on Liberty', since five essays perhaps begin to deserve that title. The piece in question is not the worst that I have written, and I should like it included.

He enclosed the necessary small changes to the first paragraph of the Introduction, and added in a covering manuscript note: 'I do indeed grovel before you: I cannot operate any differently from the way that I do: but why should you (or the printer) suffer? Determinism & the helplessness of man must be true after all.'

Stallworthy's reply on the fifth essay was this:

Tempted as we are by the thought of a fifth essay, I'm very much afraid that it is now too late to include this. We have advertised 'Four Essays' in numerous catalogues, have made a block for the cover, have

---

(*opposite*) A page from the proofs of *Four Essays on Liberty*: see pp. 161–2 below. Berlin's long correction, which was not incorporated into the finished book in this form, reads as follows: 'Some thinkers seem to feel no intellectual discomfort in interpreting such concepts as responsibility, culpability, etc. in conformity with strict determinism. I must own that while the notion of uncaused choice, which is nevertheless not something out of the blue, is one of which I know of no adequate analysis, its opposite, a choice fully attributable to antecedent causes mental or physical, and yet regarded as entailing responsibility and therefore subject to moral praise or blame, seems to me even less intelligible. This difference, which has so deeply divided opinion, is the crux of the matter: a puzzle which has exercised some thinkers for more than two thousand years: while others either fail to see it, or have regarded it as a mere confusion. The present state of controversy seems to me much the same as in the days of the Greeks who first began it.'

worked out a published price on the basis of the present length, and – not last and not least – have set up as headline on every other page 'Four Essays on Liberty'.

Berlin replied:

I am naturally disappointed that you should consider it too late to include 'From Hope and Fear Set Free'. I am afraid that no further collection of essays on philosophical topics by myself will ever materialise [...] But this essay belongs as of right to the original collection which you are about to publish and, if not included there, can never be reprinted at all. This may seem to you (and, on reflection, to myself) not to be an appreciable loss to anyone; nevertheless, I should like to make a final plea, and beg you to consider whether perhaps it could not be substituted at the last moment for 'Political Ideas in the Twentieth Century', to which it is vastly superior. The changes required will, after all, not be very grave. It will mean the loss of one appendix[1] and one, by now, ancient piece – that really could reappear, if it were thought worthy, in some other collection. I do not underestimate the trouble to which I am putting you, but, for once, my desire to improve the volume – as this substitution undoubtedly would do – is much stronger than even my easily disturbed guilt about all this tiresome chopping and changing for which I have been responsible. Would you give the matter another thought? Could you attempt to soften the (by now) savage breast of your New York colleagues? I do beg you to consider this once again.

Far from softening a savage New York breast, this hardened an Oxford heart. Deciding that the time had come for straight speaking, Stallworthy asked Berlin to come and see him. He now takes up the story in his own words:

Berlin countered with an invitation to lunch in All Souls. 'Thank you, but no,' I replied. There had to be a show-down and I wanted the territorial advantage of my own corral. Berlin, recognising the strategy, proposed other meeting-places, pleaded pressure of work, but I said No: there would be no further progress on the book until we had met – at the Press – to discuss the situation. He prevaricated for some weeks, but finally agreed.

I waited for him that morning wearing my darkest suit, my darkest frown.

'Sir Isaiah ...'

He interrupted my frontal attack with a raised hand and a rapid

---

[1] This now appears as note 1 to p. 69 below.

diversionary manoeuvre: 'They tell me you're translating Blok.[1] Greatest poet of the Revolution. Did you know his wife? No? I met her. MUST tell you about her.' And he did – brilliantly.

'Sir Isaiah . . .'

Again the raised hand – and now the diversionary manoeuvre cunningly changed course: 'I know I've been tiresome, but I've been so busy, so distracted by this new College for homeless lecturers.' Thirty-four years later, as a Fellow of that College, I am amused to remember the old magician's revolutionary peroration: 'I will take them from the highways and byways. They will be the sweepings of the streets, but they will inherit the earth!'

He was irresistible. I stuck to my guns over the fifth essay, but weakly agreed to have reset – at OUP expense – the four he had so outrageously revised.

The fifth essay was not, however, banished from the book for all time. In his next letter Stallworthy wrote: 'We are agreed that when a new edition is called for we will add "From Hope and Fear Set Free".' The Stallworthy Treaty of 1968 is being honoured in 2002.

Berlin, by his own admission, over-corrected the proofs of the Introduction 'as usual'. He asked Stuart Hampshire to write a footnote answering the criticisms of his views.[2] He observes to Stallworthy that E. H. Carr would be happy to do the same, 'my God! if let. But the whole piece must not consist of attributions of views (mainly my own) furiously disowned by their putative holders.' Stallworthy replies, having suggested a reduction of the corrections: 'I think it is no exaggeration to say that the present corrections would require the resetting of nearly half the Introduction.' (In the end the whole of it was reset.) In his reply to Stallworthy's pleas, Berlin says that he has endeavoured to make changes that occupy the same space as what they replace. He adds: 'So now we can go – I should like to say full steam ahead, except that I feel that I have held the engine up so long, I cannot complain

---

[1] 'They' must have been Maurice Bowra, who had introduced me to the work of the Russian poet Alexander Blok (1880–1921), and Max Hayward, with whom I was then translating the title-poem of what would become Alexander Blok, *The Twelve and Other Poems*, trans. Jon Stallworthy and Peter France (London, 1970). J.S.

[2] This appears as note 1 to p. 18 below. Hampshire comments when he sends in the note: 'the alien footnote is a new literary genre' (deployed again in the previous note). Not to be outdone, I have made use of another rare genre – the alien interpolation – by asking Jon Stallworthy to add the preceding passage on his memory of his definitive meeting with Berlin.

if it seizes up or moves backwards.' A later letter, answering final queries on the proofs, concludes: 'My doctrines are attacked so ferociously in this year's B.Phil. examination in Politics that I anticipate storms, not from embattled students only, but from every possible quarter, when my unpopular doctrines are published: that or chilly silence, broken by a few mildly contemptuous dismissals in the *TLS* and the like. To all this I am resigned, or at least suppose myself to be.'

From now on it is more or less downhill all the way, though there is still a series of minor hitches. In September Stallworthy tells Linnet: 'Berlin continues to fight a harassing rearguard action, but we shall overcome.' The following month a memo from Linnet ventures: 'We are toying with the idea of listing this book in the next seasonal catalog.' When Berlin saw the final proofs in October, supplied only so that he could answer some questions about page references in the index, he noticed that there were still a number of errors in the text; the survival of some of these in the finished book is an additional minor justification for a new edition.

An advance copy was eventually sent to Berlin in March 1969, together with the information that the publication date would be 15 May. As had been intended from the start, the book was published only in paperback, as part of the Oxford Paperbacks series. This strategy, in my view (perhaps aided by hindsight), was a mistake, at best a premature publishing experiment, since it played its part in ensuring the noticeably meagre review coverage the book received: the established custom of literary editors, visible even to this day, was to take hardbacks more seriously than original paperbacks.[1] The book may have improved the profile of Oxford Paperbacks, but its manner of publication, possibly reinforced by its somewhat self-effacing title, damaged its early fortunes.

Berlin's reaction to the advance copy includes the following:

I was naturally horrified to see my own likeness upon the cover – I had not been warned about this and it set me back a good deal. Is this

---

[1] In New York, however, a hardback edition was published in 1970. In 1979, too, when I was myself an editor at OUP, I bound up part of a reprint of the Oxford Paperback in hard covers in an attempted rearguard action, but because of the low-quality paper used for the series at that time this was an unsatisfactory hybrid. Only now is the book being given the kind of physical incarnation it has always deserved.

The front cover of the first UK impression of *Four Essays on Liberty* (1969)

absolutely indispensable? However, it is done and I must not cry over what seems to me a slight lapse in taste (do you not agree? secretly). As for the rest, the book looks very nicely done. Now I expect terrible brickbats, though it seems to me about the worst moment for preaching the sentiments for which I do not feel ashamed and which I do not wish to withdraw, but which are regarded by young and old as singularly 'irrelevant' to their preoccupations. However, never mind, perhaps posterity will be kinder or perhaps there will be no posterity to have to be kind. Perhaps it will all be justifiably forgotten – book, author, reactions and all.

He also provided lists of people, nearly 200 in all, to whom he wished copies to be sent at his expense, commenting: 'I expect these are about the only persons who will in fact wish to buy the book – however, never mind.'

Stallworthy replies: 'I was sorry to learn that you are now not happy with the cover. You will remember, I am sure, that Carol Buckroyd called at your house one Sunday morning with a proof. You did not then like the yellow lettering and chose from the books on your shelves a light blue to replace it.' And in its light blue livery, bound with rapidly crumbling glue, the book now finally entered the public domain.

*

For 'Five Essays on Liberty' – the second edition of *Four Essays* with which this new collection begins – I have added, for reasons that will already be apparent, 'From Hope and Fear Set Free', finally removing the quotation marks that signalled the Swinburnian origin of its title,[1] since the accurate but perhaps pedantic punctuation ' "From Hope and Fear Set Free" ' (just as in the case of ' "The Purpose Justifies the Ways" ') has seemed to cause more difficulties than enlightenment. I have also edited the text of the original four essays and their Introduction, breaking up some long sentences and paragraphs in line with wishes Berlin had expressed too late to OUP, adding and correcting references, quotations and translations as necessary, reinstating a handful of late alterations overruled by OUP for the first edition on practical grounds, and generally ironing out wrinkles – without, of course, making any

---

[1] A line from Swinburne's *The Garden of Proserpine*.

alterations of substance.[1] 'Two Concepts of Liberty' and 'Historical Inevitability' had already received most of this treatment for their inclusion in the one-volume selection from Berlin's writings published in 1997 as *The Proper Study of Mankind*, and have not been significantly further revised here. But because *Four Essays* has been so widely cited in the literature, I have provided a concordance showing where the page numbers of the first edition began, so that references to that edition can easily be looked up in this one.

OTHER WRITINGS ON LIBERTY

> The reprinting of already published articles is in principle to be reprobated, but in this case there are extenuating circumstances.
>
> A. H. M. Jones, *Athenian Democracy* (Oxford, 1960), p. v

I have also added a number of other writings that bear on the same subject, so that they can all be conveniently consulted together in one place. Indeed, the essay on the Greeks has not hitherto been collected, and the penultimate appendix not previously published. The inclusion of 'Liberty' and of the excerpts from 'My Intellectual Path' entitled 'Final Retrospect' breaches my general rule that the same material should not appear in more than one collection edited by myself:[2] but as these are short items the duplication is perhaps venial, and they do so evidently belong here. 'From Hope and Fear Set Free' is another such exception, of course, since it has already appeared in *Concepts and Categories* (1978); but the special reasons that apply here have already been made clear. I have wavered about also adding 'Herzen and Bakunin on Individual Liberty' from *Russian Thinkers* (1978), since it does throw a good deal of light on the topic of the present volume; but it is another full-length piece, and since its approach is more prosopographical, its inclusion here seemed in the end not essential. The other obvious candidate would have been Berlin's 1952 lecture series, *Freedom and its Betrayal*: this, however, is being published by Chatto and Windus

---

[1] There are, however, some necessary alterations of detail, especially in quotations and references, and readers who are concerned with accuracy at this level should use this revised edition in preference to, or alongside, the original edition. In particular, some quotations were attributed by Berlin, usually following inaccurate accounts by earlier writers, to the wrong author.

[2] Excluding *The Proper Study of Mankind*, which is an anthology drawn from earlier collections.

and by Princeton University Press as a separate volume at the same time as *Liberty*.

Remarks on each of the additional items now follow seriatim.

Liberty

This short summary of Berlin's views on liberty provides a useful orienteering guide for the newcomer. Berlin drafted it in preparation for his appearance in 1962 in an Associated Television film on freedom of speech, the first of a series of five (*sic*) programmes collectively entitled *The Four Freedoms*, presented by Bamber Gascoigne. What Berlin actually said in the film is very different from the remarks he prepared in advance, as usually happened; and out of nearly ten minutes of recorded material (a transcript survives) only two minutes were used in the broadcast.

In 1993 Ted Honderich invited Berlin to contribute an article on liberty to a volume he was editing, *The Oxford Companion to Philosophy*. Berlin did not feel able to write a new piece. He had written nothing substantial since 1988, when he published his intellectual *credo*, 'On the Pursuit of the Ideal', a response to the award of the first Agnelli Prize for his contribution to ethics.[1] Although his intellect was undiminished, and he continued to compose short occasional pieces, it seemed clear that – reasonably enough in his eighties – he had in effect laid down his authorial pen.

He asked me, however, whether there was anything among his papers that could be made use of; I offered him this short item, which he had dismissed as nugatory when I first drew it to his attention. Slightly to my surprise, therefore, he now found it 'not bad', revised it, and offered it to Honderich, who happily accepted it as it stood.

The Birth of Greek Individualism

It was also in 1993 that Jeffrey Perl, the editor of *Common Knowledge*, told Berlin, in a letter inviting him to contribute an article, that the journal had been set up under the influence of his

---

[1] This piece was published in the *New York Review of Books* in 1988, and is also included in *The Crooked Timber of Humanity* (1990) and *The Proper Study of Mankind*.

work, especially on the subject of pluralism. In his reply Berlin ventured a degree of scepticism about this assertion, but allowed that he felt 'profoundly flattered by the possibility, let alone the probability', of its truth. He also regretfully declined the invitation to write for the journal, partly because of his general disinclination – mentioned above – to undertake new writing, but also because he did not believe he was equipped to deal with the specific topic suggested by Professor Perl.

Not long after Berlin's death I came across this exchange of letters among his papers, and told Perl that, in the light of his original invitation, Berlin's Literary Trustees would be happy to offer him one of Berlin's unpublished pieces. I selected this particular essay because it deals with a topic not covered except in passing in any of Berlin's other publications, and because Berlin himself had told me that he thought something might one day be made of it.

The essay is an edited version of the text Berlin prepared as a basis for the first of his three Storrs Lectures at Yale in 1962; as mentioned above, these were entitled 'Three Turning-Points in the History of Political Thought'. The second and third turning-points – Machiavelli and romanticism – are well covered in his other published essays, especially 'The Originality of Machiavelli', reprinted in both *Against the Current* (1979) and *The Proper Study of Mankind*, and 'The Romantic Revolution', which appears in *The Sense of Reality* (1996). There is also now, of course, *The Roots of Romanticism* (1999).

Final Retrospect

The two excerpts included under this heading are taken from 'My Intellectual Path', a retrospective autobiographical survey written towards the end of Berlin's life. In February 1996, in his eighty-seventh year, he received a letter from Ouyang Kang, Professor of Philosophy at Wuhan University in China, inviting him to provide a summary of his ideas for translation into Chinese and inclusion in a volume designed to introduce philosophers and students of philosophy in China to contemporary Anglo-American philosophy, hitherto largely unavailable to them in their own language.

Despite his *de facto* authorial retirement, the Chinese project caught his imagination; he regarded this new readership as important, and felt an obligation to address it. He told the Professor that he would try to write something. With a single sheet of notes before him, he dictated a first draft on to cassette. The transcript was at times rough-hewn, and stood in need of the editing he invited, but scarcely any intellectual additives were needed to produce a readable text. When he had approved my revised version, making a few final insertions and adjustments, he said, with his characteristic distaste for revisiting his work, that he did not wish to see the piece again. It was to be the last essay he wrote. It was published in the *New York Review of Books* in the year after his death, and also in *The Power of Ideas* (2000). I have included the two most directly relevant sections here because they bring up to date, albeit more briefly, the view of his critics which occupies much of the Introduction to 'Five Essays on Liberty'. It would have been possible to add other sections, especially those on monism, pluralism and the pursuit of the ideal, but it seemed best to mirror the structure of that Introduction more narrowly.

AUTOBIOGRAPHICAL APPENDICES

All central beliefs on human matters spring from a personal predicament.

Berlin to Jean Floud, 5 July 1968

The Purpose Justifies the Ways

Berlin first came to England, as an immigrant, in early 1921, aged eleven, with virtually no English. This story (untitled in the manuscript), which, he told me, won 'a hamper of tuck' in a children's magazine competition, was written in February 1922, when he was twelve.[1] As far as is known, it is his earliest surviving piece of writing, as well as his only story, and shows how far his

---

[1] The story is written on headed notepaper from the Royal Palace Hotel, Kensington, where the Berlins stayed while waiting to move to a new address; the sheets have been sewn together, presumably by Berlin's mother. At the top of the first page there is an inscription in another hand, apparently the author's own at a later date: 'I. Berlin. February 1922. (author being $12\frac{1}{2}$ years of age)'. At the end of the manuscript appears the signature 'I Berlyn'. The Harmsworth weekly magazine *The Boy's Herald* ran a 'Tuck Hamper Competition' for 'storyettes' at the time, but Berlin is not listed among the prize-winners in early 1922, frustratingly. However, the 'storyettes' are merely humorous anecdotes of around a hundred words: perhaps Berlin was awarded an *ex gratia* hamper for an impressive contribution in the wrong genre.

English had developed after just a year, as well as his general precociousness.[1]

It is a fictional story about a real person, Moise Solomonovich Uritsky, Commissar for Internal Affairs in the Northern Region Commune of Soviet Russia, and Chairman of the Petrograd Cheka, who was in fact murdered by a Socialist Revolutionary named Leonid Kannegiesser on 31 August 1918. I chose Uritsky's 'motto' as the title because the story so clearly points forward to Berlin's repeated later insistence that present suffering cannot be justified as a route to some imaginary future state of bliss. In this sense the story is the first recorded step on his intellectual journey through life, a journey summarised in 'My Intellectual Path', written seventy-four years later.

Berlin always ascribed his lifelong horror of violence, especially when ideologically inspired, to an episode he witnessed at the age of seven during the February Revolution in Petrograd in 1917: while out walking he watched a policeman loyal to the Tsar, white-faced with terror, being dragged off by a lynch mob to his death. This story surely vividly reflects the power of this early experience, and reveals one of the deepest sources of his mature liberalism.

Letter to George Kennan

Berlin's papers include a mass of often detailed correspondence about the contents of *Four Essays on Liberty*, both before and after its constituent essays were collected in that volume. Much of this material will in due course be published in its proper chronological place among Berlin's other letters, but there is one letter in particular that stands out from the rest as a powerful statement of the personal vision that lies behind Berlin's work in this area. Berlin liked to allude[2] to a passage in Bertrand Russell's *History of Western Philosophy* where Russell says that, if we are to understand a philosopher's views, we must 'apprehend their imaginative background':

---

[1] I have normalised the somewhat wayward spelling, punctuation and layout of the original manuscript, but otherwise, apart from a few insignificant adjustments to ease the reader's passage, have followed what the young Berlin wrote exactly. These changes were not made when the story was first published, in 1998 (see p. xxxii below); I have made them now because they seemed appropriate in this more disproportionately grown-up company.

[2] e.g. on pp. 245–6, 288 below.

Every philosopher, in addition to the formal system which he offers to
the world, has another, much simpler, of which he may be quite
unaware. If he is aware of it, he probably realises that it won't quite
do; he therefore conceals it, and sets forth something more sophisticated, which he believes because it is like his crude system, but which
he asks others to accept because he thinks he has made it such as
cannot be disproved. The sophistication comes in by way of refutation
of refutations, but this alone will never give a positive result: it shows,
at best, that a theory *may* be true, not that it *must* be. The positive
result, however little the philosopher may realise it, is due to his
imaginative preconceptions, or what Santayana calls 'animal faith'.[1]

One might discuss the extent to which this picture fits Berlin's own
case: for example, Berlin was certainly not unaware of his own
'imaginative preconceptions'. At all events, the letter to Kennan
vividly expresses the character of one of the main rooms in Berlin's
own 'inner citadel', to use his own metaphor.[2] For this reason I
decided to include this letter here in advance of its publication as
part of Berlin's correspondence. It was written in response to a
warmly appreciative letter from George Kennan about 'Political
Ideas in the Twentieth Century', and surely speaks for itself.

Notes on Prejudice

Another room in the citadel is brought to life equally vividly, if
more briefly, in some hurried notes Berlin wrote for a friend (who
prefers not to be identified) in 1981. His friend was due to give a
lecture, and wrote to Berlin to ask for suggestions as to how he
might treat his theme. Berlin had to go abroad early the day after
he received the request, and wrote the notes quickly, in his own
hand, without time for revision or expansion. The result is
somewhat breathless and telegraphic, no doubt, but it conveys with
great immediacy Berlin's opposition to intolerance and prejudice,
especially fanatical monism, stereotypes and aggressive nationalism. It was to have appeared here for the first time, but it spoke so
clearly to the events of 11 September 2001 that I published it in the
first issue of the *New York Review of Books* to appear thereafter.[3]

[1] *History of Western Philosophy* (New York, 1945; London, 1946), p. 226.
[2] See pp. 246, 288 below. Berlin also uses 'inner citadel' in a rather different
sense, as on pp. 181–2, 306 below.
[3] *New York Review of Books*, 18 October 2001, 12. The editors made a few

Berlin and his Critics

As Berlin indicates in 'Final Retrospect', the literature stimulated by the two central essays in *Four Essays on Liberty* has been large. Indeed, the rate of growth of the secondary literature has increased rather than diminishing as the years have passed. I have attempted to keep a tally of it on the official website of the Isaiah Berlin Literary Trust,[1] and I hope this resource will continue to be updated. The publication of *Liberty* provides an opportunity to supplement this bare list with a brief critical vade-mecum that will assist readers to find their way through the growing volume of articles and books discussing Berlin's ideas: the main focus, given this book's rationale, is on the discussion of liberty. This guide – beyond the capability of a mere editor – has kindly been provided by Dr Ian Harris of Leicester University, himself the author of a valuable article on 'Two Concepts'.[2]

Index

The index to *Four Essays on Liberty* is somewhat unsatisfactory – adequate in its coverage of names but too sparing of concepts. Accordingly, I have turned again to Douglas Matthews, sometime Librarian of the London Library, and faithful indexer of almost all my collections of Berlin's work, and invited him to start again from scratch.

Sources and acknowledgements

The original publication details of the pieces included in *Liberty* are as follows:

Five Essays on Liberty
Introduction: in *Four Essays on Liberty* (London and New York, 1969: Oxford University Press)
'Political Ideas in the Twentieth Century': *Foreign Affairs* 28 No 3 (April 1950)

adjustments not included in this volume, where Berlin's manuscript is reproduced in a direct transcript (underlinings are indicated by italics), with only tiny corrections of slips of the pen. I have omitted material relevant only to the specific occasion in question.

[1] See p. ix above, note 2.   [2] See p. 357 below, note 14.

'Historical Inevitability': delivered on 12 May 1953 under the title 'History as an Alibi'[1] at the London School of Economics and Political Science as the first Auguste Comte Memorial Trust Lecture (London, 1954: Oxford University Press); repr. in *Auguste Comte Memorial Lectures 1953–1962* (London, 1964: Athlone Press)

'Two Concepts of Liberty': Inaugural Lecture as Chichele Professor of Social and Political Theory, Oxford University, delivered on 31 October 1958 (Oxford, 1958: Clarendon Press)

'John Stuart Mill and the Ends of Life': Robert Waley Cohen Memorial Lecture 1959, delivered on 2 December 1959 at County Hall, London (London, 1959: Council of Christians and Jews)

'From Hope and Fear Set Free': Presidential Address to the Aristotelian Society, delivered on 14 October 1963 at 21 Bedford Square, London WC1, *Proceedings of the Aristotelian Society* 64 (1963–4)

Other writings on liberty

'Liberty': in Ted Honderich (ed.), *The Oxford Companion to Philosophy* (Oxford, 1995: Oxford University Press); repr. in Berlin's *The Power of Ideas* (London, 2000: Chatto and Windus; Princeton, 2000: Princeton University Press)

'The Birth of Greek Individualism': as 'A Turning-Point in Political Thought', *Common Knowledge* 7 No 3 (Winter 1998)

'Final Retrospect': excerpts from 'My Intellectual Path', published with 'The Purpose Justifies the Ways' as 'The First and the Last', *New York Review of Books*, 14 May 1988; repr. in *The First and the Last* (New York, 1999, New York Review of Books; London, 1999: Granta), and in *The Power of Ideas* (see under 'Liberty' above)

Autobiographical appendices

'The Purpose Justifies the Ways' (1922): published with 'My Intellectual Path' as 'The First and the Last' (see under 'Final Retrospect' above), without the editorial adjustments introduced for the present volume (see p. xxix above, note 1)

A Letter to George Kennan (1951): published here for the first time

'Notes on Prejudice' (1981): see p. xxx above, note 3

I am grateful to Tim Barton, my successor at OUP, for allowing me to revisit the files on *Four Essays*, though he knew that I was not certain to be unfailingly diplomatic about what I found there. His colleagues Angela Griffin and Jo Stanbridge have shown great professionalism, courtesy and restraint as the book has assumed physical form. I should like to repeat my thanks to Roger

---

[1] At one stage, in proof, it was called 'History as the Culprit'.

Hausheer, Leofranc Holford-Strevens (who also contributed elsewhere) and Christopher Taylor for help in preparing the somewhat problematic text of 'The Birth of Greek Individualism' for publication. Help with individual problems was kindly provided by Chimen Abramsky, Terrell Carver, Joshua Cherniss, Timothy Day, Steffen Groß, Roger Hausheer (who remains a perpetual, patient source of sage counsel), Jeremy Jennings, Leszek Kolakowski, Mary Pickering, Hans Poser, Helen Rappaport, Mario Ricciardi, Philip Schofield, Marshall Shatz, Steven B. Smith and Manfred Steger. Betty Colquhoun keyboarded the whole book over a period of years with her usual exemplary dependability, and Serena Moore has masterminded the subsequent administrative processes, as well as suggesting several editorial improvements and an excellent metaphor. Samuel Guttenplan has supplied moral support and sensible advice, as well as providing, with Jennifer, a haven where the back of the editorial work was finally broken. Wolfson College and my generous benefactors continue to underpin everything I do.

HENRY HARDY

Wolfson College, Oxford
La Taillède, Laguépie
22 September 2001

John Stallworthy, Esq.,
Oxford University Press,
Ely House,
57, Dover Street,
London, W.1.

            8th February, 1968.
_____

Dear Mr. Stallworthy,

   I see that gradually but inexorably I am becomming
if not your most intolerable (though I may be that too)
certainly your most time consuming author. At the risk
of inflicting a blow upon you which may seriously endanger
your health such health and optimisim as you may have
regained during your recent holiday I proposeto inflict yet
another hideous blow upon you. Before I do this however
let me assure you that I have carefully gone through your
most valuable list of queries and answered them all. I
enclose the answers on separate sheets. I enclose a copy
of your questionaire but the answers have proved somewhat
more extensive than could comfortably be accommodated on
it. Hence the extra sheets which I hope will not be a
nusience.

   The blow is this: it has been represented to me by
kind friends (for once genuinely kind) that the book might
be improved by the inclusion in it of yet another essay on
the same subject namely my Presidential Address to the
Ariscotelian Society a few years ago the title of which was
"From Hope and Fear Set Free". This would make a fifth essay
in the book and the title could be altered from "Four Essays
on Liberty" either to "Five Essays on Liberty" or simply
"Essays on Liberty", since five essays perhaps begin to deserve
that title. The piece in question is not the worst that I
have written, and I should like it included. To ease the
birth pangs I am prepared to make the following promises:

             Contd...

The source of the title 'Five Essays on Liberty'
(typed by one of Berlin's less accomplished secretaries)

FIVE ESSAYS ON LIBERTY

INTRODUCTION

... l'on immole à l'être abstrait les êtres réels; l'on offre au
peuple en masse l'holocauste du peuple en détail.

Benjamin Constant, *De l'esprit de conquête*[1]

I

THE FIRST of these five essays appeared in the mid-century
number of the New York periodical *Foreign Affairs*; the remaining
four originated in lectures. They deal with various aspects of
individual liberty. They are concerned in the first place with the
vicissitudes of this notion during the ideological struggles of our
century; secondly, with the meaning it is given in the writings of
historians, social scientists, and writers who examine the presuppositions and methods of history or sociology; thirdly, with the
importance of two major conceptions of liberty in the history of
ideas; fourthly, with the part played by the ideal of individual
liberty in the outlook of one of its most devoted champions, John
Stuart Mill; and, finally, with the relationship between knowledge
and freedom.

The first, fourth and fifth of these essays evoked little comment.
The second and third stimulated wide and, as it seems to me,
fruitful controversy. Since some of my opponents have advanced
objections that seem to me both relevant and just, I propose to
make it clear where I think that I stand convicted of mistakes or
obscurities; other strictures (as I hope to show) seem to me
mistaken. Some of my severest critics attack my views without
adducing either facts or arguments, or else impute to me opinions
that I do not hold; and even though this may at times be due to my
own lack of clarity, I do not feel obliged to discuss, still less to

---

[1] 'Real beings are sacrificed to an abstraction; individual people are offered up
in a holocaust to people as a collectivity.' *De l'esprit de conquête et de l'usurpation
dans leur rapports avec la civilisation européenne*, part 1, chapter 13, 'De
l'uniformité': p. 169 in Benjamin Constant, *Écrits politiques*, ed. Marcel Gauchet
([Paris], 1997).

defend, positions which, in some cases, appear to me as absurd as they do to those who assail them.[1]

The main issues between my serious critics and myself may be reduced to four heads: firstly, determinism and its relevance to our notions of men and their history; secondly, the place of value judgements, and, in particular, of moral judgements, in historical and social thinking; thirdly, the possibility and desirability of distinguishing, in the realm of political theory, what modern writers have called 'positive' liberty from 'negative' liberty, and the relevance of this distinction to the further difference between liberty and the conditions of liberty, as well as the question of what it is that makes liberty, of either sort, intrinsically worth pursuing or possessing; and finally, the issue of monism, of the unity or harmony of human ends. It seems to me that the unfavourable contrast sometimes drawn between 'negative' liberty and other, more obviously positive, social and political ends sought by men – such as unity, harmony, peace, rational self-direction, justice, self-government, order, co-operation in the pursuit of common purposes – has its roots, in some cases, in an ancient doctrine according to which all truly good things are linked to one another in a single, perfect whole; or, at the very least, cannot be incompatible with one another. This entails the corollary that the realisation of the pattern formed by them is the one true end of all rational activity, both public and private. If this belief should turn out to be false or incoherent, this might destroy or weaken the basis of much past and present thought and activity; and, at the very least, affect conceptions of, and the value placed on, personal and social liberty. This issue, too, is therefore both relevant and fundamental.

Let me begin with the most celebrated question of all as it affects human nature: that of determinism, whether causal or teleological. My thesis is not, as has been maintained by some of my most vehement critics, that it is certain (still less that I can show) that determinism is false; only that the arguments in favour of it are not conclusive; and that if it ever becomes a widely accepted belief and

[1] While I have not altered the text in any radical fashion, I have made a number of changes intended to clarify some of the central points which have been misunderstood by critics and reviewers. I am most grateful to Stuart Hampshire, H. L. A. Hart, Thomas Nagel and Patrick Gardiner for drawing my attention to errors and obscurities. I have done my best to remedy these, without, I feel sure, fully satisfying these distinguished and helpful critics.

enters the texture of general thought and conduct, the meaning and use of certain concepts and words central to human thought would become obsolete or else have to be drastically altered. This entails the corollary that the existing use of these basic words and concepts constitutes some evidence, not, indeed, for the proposition that determinism is false, but for the hypothesis that many of those who profess this doctrine seldom, if ever, practise what they preach, and (if my thesis is valid) seem curiously unaware of what seems, prima facie, a lack of correspondence between their theory and their real convictions, as these are expressed in what they do and say. The fact that the problem of free will is at least as old as the Stoics; that it has tormented ordinary men as well as professional philosophers; that it is exceptionally difficult to formulate clearly; that medieval and modern discussions of it, while they have achieved a finer analysis of the vast cluster of the concepts involved, have not in essentials brought us any nearer a definitive solution; that while some men seem naturally puzzled by it, others look upon such perplexity as mere confusion, to be cleared away by some single powerful philosophical solvent – all this gives determinism a peculiar status among philosophical questions.

I have, in these essays, made no systematic attempt to discuss the problem of free will as such; my focus is on its relevance to the idea of causality in history. Here I can only restate my original thesis that it seems to me patently inconsistent to assert, on the one hand, that all events are wholly determined to be what they are by other events (whatever the status of this proposition),[1] and, on the other, that men are free to choose between at least two possible courses of action – free not merely in the sense of being able to do what they choose to do (and because they choose to do it), but in the sense of not being determined to choose what they choose by causes outside their control. If it is held that every act of will or choice is fully determined by its respective antecedents, then (despite all that has been said against this) it still seems to me that this belief is incompatible with the notion of choice held by ordinary men, and by philosophers when they are not consciously defending a determinist position. More particularly, I see no way

---

[1] It has the appearance of a universal statement about the nature of things. But it can scarcely be straightforwardly empirical, for what item of experience would count as evidence against it?

round the fact that the habit of giving moral praise and blame, of congratulating and condemning men for their actions, with the implication that they are morally responsible for them, since they could have behaved differently, that is to say, need not have acted as they did (in some sense of 'could' and 'need' which is not purely logical or legal, but in which these terms are used in ordinary empirical discourse by both men in the street and historians), would be undermined by belief in determinism. No doubt the same words could still be used by determinists to express admiration or contempt for human characteristics or acts; or to encourage or deter; and such functions may be traceable to the early years of human society. However that may be, without the assumption of freedom of choice and responsibility in the sense in which Kant used these terms, one, at least, of the ways in which they are now normally used is, as it were, annihilated.

Determinism clearly takes the life out of a whole range of moral expressions. Very few defenders of determinism have addressed themselves to the question of what this range embraces and (whether or not this is desirable) what the effect of its elimination on our thought and language would be. Hence I believe that those historians or philosophers of history who maintain that responsibility and determinism are never incompatible with one another are mistaken, whether or not some form of determinism is true;[1] and again, whether or not some form of belief in the reality of moral responsibility is justified, what seems clear is that these possibilities are mutually exclusive: both beliefs may be groundless but both cannot be true. I have not attempted to adjudicate between these alternatives; only to maintain that men have, at all times, taken freedom of choice for granted in their ordinary discourse. And I further argue that if men became truly convinced that this belief was mistaken, the revision and transformation of the basic terms and ideas that this realisation would call for would be greater and more upsetting than the majority of contemporary determinists

---

[1] What kind of incompatibility this is – logical, conceptual, psychological or of some other kind – is a question to which I do not volunteer an answer. The relations of factual beliefs to moral attitudes (or beliefs) – both the logic and psychology of this – seem to me to need further philosophical investigation. The thesis that no relevant logical relationship exists, e.g. the division between fact and value often attributed to Hume, seems to me to be unplausible, and to point to a problem, not to its solution.

seem to realise. Beyond this I did not go, and do not propose to go now.

The belief that I undertook to demonstrate that determinism is false – on which much criticism of my argument has been based – is unfounded. I am obliged to say this with some emphasis, since some of my critics (notably E. H. Carr) persist in attributing to me a claim to have refuted determinism. But this, like another odd view ascribed to me, namely that historians have a positive duty to moralise, is a position that I have never defended or held; this is a point to which I shall have occasion to revert later. More specifically, I have been charged with confusing determinism with fatalism.[1] But this, too, is a complete misunderstanding. I assume that what is meant or implied by fatalism is the view that human decisions are mere by-products, epiphenomena, incapable of influencing events which take their inscrutable course independently of human wishes. I have never attributed this unplausible position to any of my opponents. The majority of them cling to 'self-determinism' – the doctrine according to which men's characters and 'personality structures' and the emotions, attitudes, choices, decisions and acts that flow from them do indeed play a full part in what occurs, but are themselves results of causes, psychical and physical, social and individual, which in turn are effects of other causes, and so on, in unbreakable sequence. According to the best-known version of this doctrine, I am free if I can do what I wish and, perhaps, choose which of two courses of action I shall take. But my choice is itself causally determined; for if it were not, it would be a random event; and these alternatives exhaust the possibilities; so that to describe choice as free in some further sense, as neither caused nor random, is to attempt to say something meaningless. This classical view, which to most philosophers appears to dispose of the problem of free will, seems to me simply a variant of the general determinist thesis, and to rule out responsibility no less than its 'stronger' variant. Such 'self-determinism' or 'weak determinism', in which, since its original formulation by the Stoic sage Chrysippus, many thinkers have come to rest, was described by Kant as a 'miserable subterfuge'.[2]

[1] See A. K. Sen, 'Determinism and Historical Predictions', *Enquiry* (Delhi) 2 (1959), 99–115. Also Gordon Leff in *The Tyranny of Concepts: A Critique of Marxism* (London, 1961), pp. 146–9.

[2] 'Elender Behelf', in the *Critique of Practical Reason: Kant's gesammelte Schriften* (Berlin, 1900–　), vol. 5, p. 96, line 15.

William James labelled it 'soft determinism', and called it, perhaps too harshly, 'a quagmire of evasion'.[1]

I cannot see how one can say of Helen not only that hers was the face that launched a thousand ships but, in addition, that she was responsible for (and did not merely cause) the Trojan War, if the war was due solely to something that was the result not of a free choice – to elope with Paris – which Helen need not have made, but only of her irresistible beauty. Sen, in his clear and moderately worded criticism, concedes what some of his allies do not – that there is an inconsistency between, at any rate, some meanings attached to the contents of ordinary moral judgement on the one hand, and determinism on the other. He denies, however, that belief in determinism need eliminate the possibility of rational moral judgement, on the ground that such judgements could still be used to influence men's conduct, by acting as stimuli or deterrents. In somewhat similar terms, Ernest Nagel, in the course of a characteristically scrupulous and lucid argument,[2] says that, even on the assumption of determinism, praise, blame and assumption of responsibility generally could affect human behaviour – for example, by having an effect on discipline, effort and the like, whereas they would (presumably) not in this way affect a man's digestive processes or the circulation of his blood.

This may be true but it does not affect the central issue. Our value judgements – eulogies or condemnations of the acts or characters of men dead and gone – are not intended solely, or even primarily, to act as utilitarian devices, to encourage or warn our contemporaries, or as beacons to posterity. When we speak in this way we are not attempting merely to influence future action (though we may, in fact, be doing this too) or solely to formulate quasi-aesthetic judgements – as when we testify to the beauty or ugliness, intelligence of stupidity, generosity or meanness of others (or ourselves) – attributes which we are then simply attempting to grade according to some scale of values. If someone praises or condemns me for choosing as I did, I do not always say either 'This is how I am made; I cannot help behaving so', or 'Please go on

[1] William James, 'The Dilemma of Determinism': p. 149 in his *The Will to Believe, and Other Essays in Popular Philosophy* (New York etc., 1897).

[2] *The Structure of Science: Problems in the Logic of Scientific Explanation* (London, 1961), pp. 599–605. Also, by the same author, 'Determinism in History', *Philosophy and Phenomenological Research* 20 (1959–60), 291–317, at 311–16.

saying this, it is having an excellent effect on me: it strengthens [or weakens] my resolution to go to war, or to join the Communist Party.'

It may be that such words, like the prospect of rewards and punishments, do affect conduct in important ways, and that this makes them useful or dangerous. But this is not the point at issue. It is whether such praise, blame and so on are merited, morally appropriate, or not. One can easily imagine a case where we think that a man deserves blame, but consider that to utter it may have a bad effect, and therefore say nothing. But this does not alter the man's desert, which, whatever its analysis, entails that the agent could have chosen, and not merely acted, otherwise. If I judge that a man's conduct was in fact determined, that he could not have behaved (felt, thought, desired, chosen) otherwise, I should regard this kind of praise or blame as inappropriate to his case. If determinism is true, the concept of merit or desert, as these are usually understood, has no application. If all things and events and persons are determined, then praise and blame do indeed become purely pedagogical devices – hortatory and minatory. Or else they are quasi-descriptive – they grade in terms of distance from some ideal. They comment on the quality of men, what men are and can be and do, and may themselves alter it and, indeed, be used as deliberate means towards it, as when we reward or punish an animal; save that in the case of men we assume the possibility of communication with them, which we cannot do in the case of animals.

This is the heart of 'soft' determinism – the so-called Hobbes–Hume–Schlick doctrine. If, however, the notions of desert, merit, responsibility and so forth rested on the notion of choices not themselves fully caused, they would, on this view, turn out to be irrational or incoherent; and would be abandoned by rational men. The majority of Spinoza's interpreters suppose him to have maintained precisely this, and a good many of them think that he was right. But whether or not Spinoza did in fact hold this view, and whether or not he was right in this respect, my thesis is that, however it may be with Spinoza, most men and most philosophers and historians do not speak or act as if they believe this. For if the determinist thesis is genuinely accepted, it should, at any rate to men who desire to be rational and consistent, make a radical difference. Sen, with admirable consistency and candour, does indeed explain that, when determinists use the language of moral

praise and blame, they are like atheists who still mention God, or
lovers who speak of being faithful 'till the end of time';[1] such talk
is hyperbolic and not meant to be taken literally. This does at least
concede (as most determinists do not) that if these words were
taken literally something would be amiss. For my part I see no
reason for supposing that most of those who use such language,
with its implication of free choice among alternatives, whether in
the future or in the past, mean this not literally, but in some
Pickwickian or metaphorical or rhetorical way. Ernest Nagel
points out that determinists, who, like Bossuet, believed in the
omnipotence and omniscience of Providence and its control over
every human step, nevertheless freely attributed moral responsibility to individuals; and that adherents of determinist faiths –
Muslims, Calvinists and others – have not refrained from attribution of responsibility and a generous use of praise and blame.[2]
Like much that Ernest Nagel says, this is perfectly true.[3] But it is
nothing to the issue: the fact that not all human beliefs are coherent
is not novel. These examples merely point to the fact that men
evidently find it perfectly possible to subscribe to determinism in
the study and disregard it in their lives. Fatalism has not bred
passivity in Muslims, nor has determinism sapped the vigour of
Calvinists or Marxists, although some Marxists feared that it might.
Practice sometimes belies profession, no matter how sincerely held.

E. H. Carr goes a good deal further. He declares: 'The fact is that
all human actions are both free and determined, according to the

---

[1] op. cit. (p. 7 above, note 1), p. 114.

[2] *The Structure of Science* (see p. 8 above, note 2), pp. 603–4.

[3] See also a similar but equally unconvincing argument in the inaugural lecture
by Sydney Pollard at Sheffield University, 'Economic History – A Science of
Society?', *Past and Present* 30 (April 1965), 3–22. Much of what Pollard says
seems to me valid and worth saying, but his view, supported by an appeal to
history, that men's professions must be consistent with their practice is to say the
least oddly surprising in a historian. Nagel (*The Structure of Science*, p. 602)
suggests that belief in free will may relate to determinism much as the conviction
that a table has a hard surface relates to the hypothesis that it consists of whirling
electrons; the two descriptions answer questions at different levels, and therefore
do not clash. This does not seem to me an apt parallel. To believe that the table is
hard, solid, at rest etc. entails no beliefs about electrons; and is, in principle,
compatible with any doctrine about them: the levels do not touch. But if I
supposed a man to have acted freely, and am later told that he acted as he did
because he was 'made that way', and could not have acted differently, I certainly
suppose that something that I believed is being denied.

point of view from which one considers them.' And again: 'adult human beings are morally responsible for their own personality'.[1] This seems to me to present the reader with an insoluble puzzle. If Carr means that human beings can transform the nature of their personality, while all antecedents remain the same, then he denies causality; if they cannot, and acts can be fully accounted for by character, then talk of responsibility (in the ordinary sense of this word, in which it implies moral blame) does not make sense. There are no doubt many senses of 'can'; and much light has been shed on this by important distinctions made by acute modern philosophers. Nevertheless, if I literally cannot make my character or behaviour other than it is by an act of choice (or a whole pattern of such acts) which is itself not fully determined by causal antecedents, then I do not see in what normal sense a rational person could hold me morally responsible either for my character or for my conduct. Indeed the notion of a morally responsible being becomes, at best, mythological; this fabulous creature joins the ranks of nymphs and centaurs.

The horns of this dilemma have been with us for over two millennia, and it is useless to try to escape or soften them by the comfortable assertion that it all depends on the point of view from which we regard the question. This problem, which preoccupied Mill (and to which, in the end, he returned so confused an answer), and from the torment of which William James escaped only as a result of reading Renouvier, and which is still well to the forefront of philosophical attention, cannot be brushed aside by saying that the questions to which scientific determinism is the answer are different from those which are answered by the doctrine of voluntarism and freedom of choice between alternatives; or that the two types of question arise at different 'levels', so that a pseudo-problem has arisen from the confusion of these 'levels' (or the corresponding categories). The question to which determinism and indeterminism, whatever their obscurities, are the rival answers is one and not two. What kind of question it is – empirical, conceptual, metaphysical, pragmatic, linguistic – and what schema or model of man and nature is implicit in the terms used are major

---

[1] Edward Hallett Carr, *What is History?* (London, 1961), p. 89 (p. 95 in the paperback edition, Harmondsworth, 1964; page references to this edition are added in parentheses in subsequent notes).

philosophical issues; but it would be out of place to discuss them here.

Nevertheless, if only because some of the sharpest criticisms of my thesis come from philosophers concerned with this central issue, it cannot be entirely passed over. Thus J. A. Passmore[1] urges two considerations against me: (a) That the concept of Laplace's observer, who can infallibly predict the future, since he has all the relevant knowledge of antecedent conditions and laws that he needs for this, cannot in principle be formulated, because the notion of an exhaustive list of all the antecedents of an event is not coherent; we can never say of any state of affairs 'These are all the antecedents there are; the inventory is complete.' This is clearly true. Nevertheless, even if determinism were offered as no more than a pragmatic policy – 'I intend to act and think on the assumption that every event has an identifiable sufficient cause or causes' – this would satisfy the determinist's demand. Yet such a resolve would make a radical difference, for it would effectively take the life out of any morality that works with such notions as responsibility, moral worth and freedom in Kant's sense, and do so in ways and with logical consequences which determinists as a rule either forbear to examine, or else play down.

(b) That the more we find out about a prima facie morally culpable act, the more we are likely to realise that the agent, given the particular circumstances, characters, antecedent causes involved, was prevented from taking the various courses which we think he should have adopted; we condemn him too easily for failing to do or be what he could not have done or been. Ignorance, insensitiveness, haste, lack of imagination darken counsel and blind us to the true facts; our judgements are often shallow, dogmatic, complacent, irresponsible, unjust, barbarous. I sympathise with the humane and civilised considerations which inspire Passmore's verdict. Much injustice and cruelty has sprung from avoidable ignorance, prejudice, dogma and lack of understanding. Nevertheless to generalise this – as Passmore seems to me to do – is to fall into the old *tout comprendre* fallacy in disarmingly modern dress. If (as happens to those who are capable of genuine self-criticism) the more we discover about ourselves the less we are inclined to forgive ourselves, why should we assume that the opposite is valid

[1] 'History, the Individual, and Inevitability', *Philosophical Review* 68 (1959), 93–102.

for others, that we alone are free, while others are determined? To expose the deleterious consequences of ignorance or irrationality is one thing; to assume that these are the sole sources of moral indignation is an illicit extrapolation; it would follow from Spinozist premisses, but not necessarily from others. Because our judgements about others are often superficial or unfair, it does not follow that one must never judge at all; or, indeed, that one can avoid doing so. As well forbid all men to count, because some cannot add correctly.

Morton White attacks my contentions from a somewhat different angle.[1] He concedes that one may not, as a rule, condemn (as being 'wrong') acts which the agent could not help perpetrating (for example, Booth's killing of Lincoln, on the assumption that he was caused to choose to do this, or anyway to do it whether or not he so chose). Or at least White thinks that it is unkind to blame a man for a causally determined action; unkind, unfair, but not inconsistent with determinist beliefs. We could, he supposes, conceive of a culture in which such moral verdicts would be normal. Hence it may be mere parochialism on our part to assume that the discomfort we may feel in calling causally determined acts right or wrong is universal, and springs from some basic category which governs the experience of all possible societies.

White discusses what is implied by calling an act 'wrong'. I am concerned with such expressions as 'blameworthy', 'something you should not have done', 'deserving to be condemned' – none of which is equivalent to 'wrong' or, necessarily, to each other. But even so, I wonder whether White, if he met a kleptomaniac, would think it reasonable to say to him: 'You cannot, it is true, help choosing to steal, even though you may think it wrong to do so. Nevertheless you must not do it. Indeed, you should choose to refrain from it. If you go on, we shall judge you not only to be a wrongdoer, but to deserve moral blame. Whether this deters you or not, you will deserve it equally in either case.' Would White not feel that something was seriously amiss about such an approach, and that not merely in our own society, but in any world in which such moral terminology made sense? Or would he think this very question to be evidence of insufficient moral imagination in the

[1] *Foundations of Historical Knowledge* (New York and London, 1965), pp. 275 ff. I cannot pretend to be able to do justice here to the complex and interesting thesis which White's luminous book expounds. I ask him to forgive me for the summary character of this brief rejoinder.

questioner? Is it merely unkind or unfair to reproach men with what they cannot avoid doing, or, like much cruelty and injustice, irrational too? If you said to a man who betrayed his friends under torture that he should not have done this, that his act was morally wrong, even though you are convinced that, being what he is, he could not help choosing to act as he did, could you, if pressed, give reasons for your verdict? What could they be? That you wished to alter his (or others') behaviour in the future? Or that you wished to ventilate your revulsion?

If this were all, questions of doing him justice would not enter at all. Yet if you were told that in blaming a man you were being unfair or wickedly blind, because you had not troubled to examine the difficulties under which the man laboured, the pressures upon him, and so on, this kind of reproach rests on the assumption that in some cases, if not in all, the man could have avoided the choice that you condemn, only a good deal less easily than you realise, at the price of martyrdom, or the sacrifice of the innocent, or at some cost which your critic believes that you, the moraliser, have no right to demand. Hence the critic rightly reproaches you for culpable ignorance or inhumanity. But if you really thought that it was (causally) impossible for the man to have chosen what you would have preferred him to choose, is it reasonable to say that he should nevertheless have chosen it? What reasons can you, in principle, adduce for attributing responsibility or applying moral rules to him (such as Kant's maxims, which we understand whether or not we accept them) which you would not think it reasonable to apply in the case of compulsive choosers – kleptomaniacs, dipso-maniacs and the like? Where would you draw the line, and why?

If the choices in all these cases are causally determined, however different the causes, in some cases being compatible (or, according to some views, identical) with the use of reason, in others not, why is it rational to blame in one case and not in the other? I exclude the utilitarian argument for praise or blame or threats or other incentives, since White, rightly in my view, ignores it too, to concentrate on the moral quality of blame. I cannot see why it is less unreasonable (and not merely less futile) to blame a man psychologically unable to refrain from it for acting cruelly than a physical cripple for possessing a deformed limb. To condemn a murderer is no more or less rational than to blame his dagger; so reasoned Godwin. At least he was consistent in his fanatical way. Although his best-known book is called *Political Justice*, it is not easy to tell what justice, as a moral concept, would mean to a convinced determinist. I could grade just and unjust acts, like legal and illegal ones, like ripe and unripe peaches. But if a man could not help acting as he did, how much would it mean to say that something 'served him right'? The notion of poetic justice, of just deserts, of moral desert as such, would, if this were the case, not merely have no application, but become scarcely intelligible.

When Samuel Butler in *Erewhon* makes crimes objects of sympathy and pity, but ill health an offence which leads to sanctions, he is set on emphasising not the relativity of moral values, but their irrationality in his own society – the irrationality of blame directed at moral or mental aberrations, but not to physical or physiological ones. I know of no more vivid way of bringing out how different our moral terminology and conduct would be if we were the really consistent scientific determinists that some suppose that we ought to be. The more rigorous sociological determinists do indeed say precisely this, and consider that not only retribution or revenge, but justice too – outside its strictly legal sense – conceived as a moral standard or canon not determined by alterable rules, is a pre-scientific notion grounded in psychological immaturity and error. As against this Spinoza and Sen seem to me to be right. There are some terms which, if we took determinism seriously, we should no longer use, or use only in some peculiar sense, as we speak of witches or the Olympian Gods. Such notions as justice, equity, desert, fairness would certainly have to be re-examined if they were to be kept alive at all and not relegated to the role of discarded figments – fancies rendered harmless by the march of reason, myths potent in our irrational youth, exploded, or at any rate rendered innocuous, by the progress of scientific knowledge. If determinism is valid, this is a price that we must pay. Whether or not we are ready to do so, let this prospect at least be faced.

If our moral concepts belong only to our own culture and society, then what we should be called upon to say to a member of White's unfamiliar culture is not that he was logically contradicting himself in professing determinism and yet continuing to utter or imply moral judgements of a Kantian sort, but that he was being incoherent, that we could not see what reasons he could have for using such terms, that his language, if it was intended to apply to the real world, was no longer sufficiently intelligible to us. Of course the fact that there have been, and no doubt may still be, plenty of thinkers, even in our own culture, who at one and the same time profess belief in determinism, and yet do not feel in the least inhibited from dispensing this kind of moral praise and blame freely, and pointing out to others how they should have chosen, shows only, if I am right, that some normally lucid and self-critical thinkers are at times liable to confusion. My case, in other words, amounts to making explicit what most men do not doubt – namely that it is not rational both to believe that choices are caused, and to consider men as deserving of reproach or indignation (or their opposites) for choosing to act or refrain as they do.

The supposition that, if determinism were shown to be valid, ethical language would have to be drastically revised is not a psychological or a physiological, still less an ethical, hypothesis. It is an assertion about what any system of thought that employs the basic concepts of our normal morality would permit or exclude. The proposition that it is unreasonable to condemn men whose choices are not free rests not on a particular set of moral values (which another culture might reject) but on the particular nexus between descriptive and evaluative concepts which governs the language we use and the thoughts we think. To say that you might as well morally blame a table as an ignorant barbarian or an incurable addict is not an ethical proposition, but one which emphasises the conceptual truth that this kind of praise and blame makes sense only among persons capable of free choice. This is what Kant appeals to; it is this fact that puzzled the early Stoics; before them freedom of choice seems to have been taken for granted; it is presupposed equally in Aristotle's discussion of voluntary and involuntary acts and in the thinking of unphilosophical persons to this day.

One of the motives for clinging to determinism seems to be the fear on the part of the friends of reason that it is presupposed by scientific method as such. Thus Stuart Hampshire tells us that:

> In the study of human behaviour, philosophical superstition might now easily take over the role of traditional religious superstitions as an obstruction to progress. In this context superstition is a confusion of the belief that human beings ought not to be treated as if they were natural objects with the belief that they are not in reality natural objects: one may so easily move from the moral proposition that persons ought not to be manipulated and controlled, like any other natural objects, to the different, and quasi-philosophical, proposition that they cannot be manipulated and controlled like any other natural

objects. In the present climate of opinion a very natural fear of planning and social technology is apt to be dignified as a philosophy of indeterminism.[1]

This strongly worded cautionary statement seems to me characteristic of the widespread and influential feeling I have mentioned that science and rationality are in danger if determinism is rejected or even doubted. This fear appears to me to be groundless; to do one's best to find quantitative correlations and explanations is not to assume that everything is quantifiable; to proclaim that science is the search for causes (whether this is true or false) is not to say that all events have them. Indeed the passage that I have quoted seems to me to contain at least three puzzling elements.

(a) We are told that to confuse 'the belief that human beings ought not to be treated as if they were natural objects with the belief that they are not in reality natural objects' is superstitious. But what other reason have I for not treating human beings 'as if they were natural objects' than my belief that they differ from natural objects in some particular respects – those in virtue of which they are human – and that this fact is the basis of my moral conviction that I should not treat them as objects, that is, solely as means to my ends, and that it is in virtue of this difference that I consider it wrong freely to manipulate, coerce, brainwash them and so on? If I am told not to treat something as a chair, the reason for this may be the fact that the object in question possesses some attribute which ordinary chairs do not, or has some special association for me or others which distinguishes it from ordinary chairs, a characteristic which might be overlooked or denied. Unless men are held to possess some attribute over and above those which they have in common with other natural objects – animals, plants, things – (whether this difference is itself called natural or not), the moral command not to treat men as animals or things has no rational foundation. I conclude that, so far from being a confusion of two different kinds of proposition, this connection between them cannot be severed without making at least one of them groundless; and this is certainly unlikely to forward the progress of which the author speaks.

(b) As for the warning not to move from the proposition that 'persons ought not to be manipulated and controlled' to the

[1] 'Philosophy and Madness', *Listener* 78 (July–December 1967), 289–92, at 291.

proposition that 'they cannot be manipulated or controlled like any other natural object', it is surely more reasonable to suppose that if I tell you not to do it, that is not because I think persons cannot be so treated, but because I believe that it is all too likely that they can. If I order you not to control and manipulate human beings, it is not because I think that, since you cannot succeed, this will be a sad waste of your time and effort; but on the contrary, because I fear that you may succeed all too well, and that this will deprive men of their freedom, a freedom which, if they can only escape from too much control and manipulation, I believe they may be able to preserve.

(c) 'Fear of planning and social technology' may well be most acutely felt by those who believe that these forces are not irresistible; and that if men are not too much interfered with they will have opportunities of choosing freely between possible courses of action, not merely (as determinists believe) of, at best, implementing choices themselves determined and predictable. The latter may in fact be our actual condition. But if one prefers the former state – however difficult it may be to formulate – is this a superstition, or some other case of 'false consciousness'? It is such only if determinism is true. But this is a viciously circular argument. Could it not be maintained that determinism itself is a superstition generated by a false belief that science will be compromised unless it is accepted, and is therefore itself a case of 'false consciousness' generated by a mistake about the nature of science? Any doctrine could be turned into a superstition, but I do not myself see any reason for holding that either determinism or indeterminism is, or need turn into, one.[1]

To return to non-philosophical writers. The writings of those who have stressed the inadequacy of the categories of the natural sciences when applied to human action have so far transformed the question as to discredit the crude solutions of the nineteenth- and twentieth-century materialists and positivists. Hence all serious discussion of the issues must now begin by taking some account of the world-wide discussion of the subject during the last twenty-

---

[1] Hampshire replies: 'The injunction not to treat men as merely objects defines the moral point of view precisely because, being studied from the scientific point of view, men can be so treated. Isaiah Berlin disagrees with me (and with Kant) in regarding the question "Are men only natural objects?" as an empirical issue, while I hold that since no one *can* treat himself as merely a natural object, no one *ought* to treat another as merely a natural object.'

five years. When E. H. Carr maintains that to attribute historical events to the acts of individuals ('biographical bias') is childish, or at any rate childlike, and that the more impersonal we make our historical writing, the more scientific, and therefore mature and valid, it will be, he shows himself a faithful – too faithful – follower of the eighteenth-century dogmatic materialists. This doctrine no longer seemed altogether plausible even in the day of Comte and his followers, or, for that matter, of the father of Russian Marxism, Plekhanov, who, for all his brilliance, in his philosophy of history owed more to eighteenth-century materialism and nineteenth-century positivism than to Hegel or the Hegelian elements in Marx.

Let me give Carr his due. When he maintains that animism or anthropomorphism – the attribution of human properties to inanimate entities – is a symptom of a primitive mentality, I have no wish to controvert this. But to compound one fallacy with another seldom advances the cause of truth. Anthropomorphism is the fallacy of applying human categories to the non-human world. But then there presumably exists a region where human categories do apply: namely the world of human beings. To suppose that only what works in the description and prediction of non-human nature must necessarily apply to human beings too and that the categories in terms of which we distinguish the human from the non-human must therefore be delusive – to be explained away as aberrations of our early years – is the opposite error, the animist or anthropomorphic fallacy stood on its head. What scientific method can achieve, it must, of course be used to achieve. Anything that statistical methods or computers or any other instrument or method fruitful in the natural sciences can do to classify, analyse, predict or 'retrodict' human behaviour should, of course, be welcomed; to refrain from using these methods for some doctrinaire reason would be mere obscurantism. However, it is a far cry from this to the dogmatic assurance that the more the subject-matter of an enquiry can be assimilated to that of a natural science the nearer the truth we shall come. This doctrine, in Carr's version, amounts to saying that the more impersonal and general, the more valid, the more generic, the more grown up; the more attention to individuals, their idiosyncrasies and their role in history, the more fanciful, the remoter from objective truth and reality. This seems to me no more and no less dogmatic than the opposite fallacy – that history is reducible to the biographies of great men and their deeds. To assert that the truth lies somewhere between these extremes, between the equally fanatical positions of Comte and Carlyle, is a dull thing to say, but may nevertheless be closer to the truth. As an eminent philosopher of our time[1] once drily observed, there is no a priori reason for supposing that the truth, when it is discovered, will prove interesting. Certainly it need not prove startling or upsetting; it may or may not; we cannot tell. This is not the place to examine Carr's historiographical views, which seem to me to breathe the last enchantments of the Age of Reason, more rational-ist than rational, with all the enviable simplicity, lucidity and freedom from doubt or self-questioning which characterised this field of thought in its unclouded beginnings, when Voltaire and Helvétius were on their thrones; before the Germans, with their passion for excavating everything, ruined the smooth lawns and symmetrical gardens. Carr is a vigorous and enjoyable writer, touched by historical materialism, but essentially a late positivist, in the tradition of Auguste Comte, Herbert Spencer and H. G. Wells; what Sainte-Beuve called 'un grand simplificateur',[2] un-troubled by the problems and difficulties which have bedevilled the subject since Herder and Hegel, Marx and Max Weber. He is respectful towards Marx, but remote from his complex vision; a master of short ways and final answers to the great unanswered questions.

But if I cannot here attempt to deal with Carr's position with the care that it deserves, I can at least try to reply to some of his severest strictures on my own opinions. His gravest charges against me are threefold: (a) that I believe determinism to be false and reject the axiom that everything has a cause, which, according to Carr, 'is a condition of our capacity to understand what is going on around us',[3] (b) that I 'insist with great vehemence that it is the duty of the historian "to judge Charlemagne or Napoleon or

---

[1] Identified by Berlin elsewhere (the wording varies) as C. I. Lewis. I have not been able to find this remark in Lewis's published writings. Ed.

[2] The phrase 'grand simplificateur' and the word 'simplificateur' itself were coined by Sainte-Beuve to describe Benjamin Franklin in 'Franklin à Passy' (29 November 1852): p. 181 in C.-A. Sainte-Beuve, *Causeries du lundi* (Paris, [1926–42]), vol. 7. (The equally familiar 'terribles simplificateurs', used by Berlin on p. 56 below, note 1 – and cf. p. 290 below – was coined by Jacob Burckhardt in a letter of 24 July 1889 to Friedrich von Preen.) Ed.

[3] op. cit. (p. 11 above, note 1), pp. 87–8 (93–4).

Genghis Khan or Hitler or Stalin for their massacres"',[1] that is, to award marks for moral conduct to historically important individuals; (c) that I believe that explanation in history is an account in terms of human intentions, to which Carr opposes the alternative concept of 'social forces'.[2]

To all this I can only say once again: (a) I have never denied (nor considered) the logical possibility that some version of determinism may, in principle (although, perhaps, only in principle), be a valid theory of human conduct; still less do I hold myself to have refuted it. My sole contention has been that belief in it is not compatible with beliefs deeply embedded in the normal speech and thought of either ordinary men or historians, at any rate in the Western world; and therefore that to take determinism seriously would entail a drastic revision of these central notions – an upheaval of which neither Carr's nor any other historian's practice has, as yet, provided any conspicuous examples. I know of no conclusive argument in favour of determinism. But that is not my point; it is that the actual practice of its supporters, and their reluctance to face what unity of theory and practice in this case would cost them, indicate that such theoretical support is not at present to be taken too seriously, whoever may claim to provide it.

(b) I am accused of inviting historians to moralise. I do nothing of the kind. I merely maintain that historians, like other men, use language which is inevitably shot through with words of evaluative force, and that to invite them to purge their language of it is to ask them to perform an abnormally difficult and self-stultifying task. To be objective, unbiased, dispassionate is no doubt a virtue in historians, as in anyone who wishes to establish truth in any field. But historians are men, and are not obliged to attempt to dehumanise themselves to a greater degree than other men; the topics they choose for discussion, their distribution of attention and emphasis, are guided by their own scale of values, which, if they are either to understand human conduct or to communicate their vision to their readers, must not diverge too sharply from the common values of men.

To understand the motives and outlook of others it is not, of course, necessary to share them; insight does not entail approval; the most gifted historians (and novelists) are the least partisan;

---

[1] ibid., p. 71 (76); cf. p. 163 below.   [2] ibid., p. 38–49 (44–55).

some distance from the subject is required. But while comprehension of motives, moral or social codes, entire civilisations does not require acceptance of, or even sympathy with, them, it does presuppose a view of what matters to individuals or groups, even if such values are found repulsive. And this rests on a conception of human nature, human ends, which enters into the historian's own ethical or religious or aesthetic outlook. These values, particularly the moral values which govern the selection of facts by historians, the light in which they exhibit them, are conveyed, and cannot but be conveyed, by their language as much and as little as are those of anyone else who seeks to understand and describe men. The criteria which we use in judging the work of historians are not, and need not, in principle, be, different from those by which we judge specialists in other fields of learning and imagination. In criticising the achievements of those who deal with human affairs we cannot sharply divorce 'facts' from their significance. 'Values enter into the facts and are an essential part of them. Our values are an essential part of our equipment as human beings.' These words are not mine. They are the words of none other (the reader will surely be astonished to learn) than Carr himself.[1] I might have chosen to formulate this proposition differently. But Carr's words are quite sufficient for me; on them I am content to rest my case against his charges.

There is clearly no need for historians formally to pronounce moral judgements, as Carr mistakenly thinks that I wish them to do. They are under no obligation as historians to inform their readers that Hitler did harm to mankind, whereas Pasteur did good (or whatever they may think to be the case). The very use of normal language cannot avoid conveying what the author regards as commonplace or monstrous, decisive or trivial, exhilarating or depressing. In describing what occurred I can say that so many million men were brutally done to death; or alternatively that they perished; laid down their lives; were massacred; or simply that the population of Europe was reduced, or that its average age was lowered; or that many men lost their lives. None of these descriptions of what took place is wholly neutral: all carry moral implications. What the historian says will, however careful he may be to use purely descriptive language, sooner or later convey his attitude. Detachment is itself a moral position. The use of neutral

[1] ibid., p. 125 (131).

language ('Himmler caused many persons to be asphyxiated') conveys its own ethical tone.

I do not mean to say that severely neutral language about human beings is unattainable. Statisticians, compilers of intelligence reports, research departments, sociologists and economists of certain kinds, official reporters, compilers whose task it is to provide data for historians or politicians, can and are expected to approach it. But this is so because these activities are not autonomous but are designed to provide the raw material for those whose work is intended to be an end in itself – historians, men of action. The research assistant is not called upon to select and emphasise what counts for much, and play down what counts for little, in human life. The historian cannot avoid this; otherwise what he writes, detached as it will be from what he, or his society, or some other culture, regards as central or peripheral, will not be history. If history is what historians do, then the central issue, which no historian can evade, whether he knows this or not, is how we (and other societies) come to be as we are or were. This, *eo facto*, entails a particular vision of society, of men's nature, of the springs of human action, of men's values and scales of value – something that physicists, physiologists, physical anthropologists, grammarians, econometricians or certain sorts of psychologists (like the providers of data for others to interpret) may be able to avoid. History is not an ancillary activity; it seeks to provide as complete an account as it can of what men do and suffer; to call them men is to ascribe to them values that we must be able to recognise as such, otherwise they are not men for us. Historians cannot therefore (whether they moralise or not) escape from having to adopt some position about what matters and how much (even if they do not ask why it matters). This alone is enough to render the notion of a 'value-free' history, of the historian as a transcriber *ipsis rebus dictantibus*,[1] an illusion.

Perhaps this is all that Acton urged against Creighton: not simply that Creighton used artificially non-moral terms, but that in using them to describe the Borgias and their acts he was, in effect, going some way towards exonerating them; that, whether he was right or wrong to do it, he was doing it; that neutrality is also a moral attitude, and that it is as well to recognise it for what it is.

---

[1] 'The things themselves speaking.' The phrase appears to originate in Justinian's *Digest* at I. 2. 2. II. 2.

Acton had no doubt that Creighton was wrong. We may agree with Acton or with Creighton. But in either case we are judging, conveying, even when we prefer not to state, a moral attitude. To invite historians to describe men's lives but not the significance of their lives in terms of what Mill called the permanent interests of man, however conceived, is not to describe their lives. To demand of historians that they try to enter imaginatively into the experience of others and forbid them to display moral understanding is to invite them to tell too small a part of what they know, and to deprive their work of human significance. This is in effect all that I have to say against Carr's moral sermon against the bad habit of delivering moral sermons.

No doubt the view that there exist objective moral or social values, eternal and universal, untouched by historical change, and accessible to the mind of any rational man if only he chooses to direct his gaze at them, is open to every sort of question. Yet the possibility of understanding men in one's own or any other time, indeed of communication between human beings, depends upon the existence of some common values, and not on a common 'factual' world alone. The latter is a necessary but not a sufficient condition of human intercourse. Those who are out of touch with the external world are described as abnormal or, in extreme cases, insane. But so also – and this is the point – are those who wander too far from the common public world of values. A man who declares that he once knew the difference between right and wrong, but has forgotten it, will scarcely be believed; if he is believed, he is rightly considered deranged. But so too is a man who does not merely approve or enjoy or condone, but literally cannot grasp what conceivable objection anyone could have to, let us suppose, a rule permitting the killing of any man with blue eyes, with no reason given. He would be considered about as normal a specimen of the human race as one who cannot count beyond six, or thinks it probable that he is Julius Caesar. What such normative (not descriptive) tests for insanity rest on is what gives such plausibility as they have to doctrines of natural law, particularly in versions which refuse them any a priori status. Acceptance of common values (at any rate some irreducible minimum of them) enters our conception of a normal human being. This serves to distinguish such notions as the foundations of human morality on the one hand from such other notions as custom, or tradition, or law, or manners, or fashion, or etiquette – all those regions in which the

occurrence of wide social and historical, national and local differences and change are not regarded as rare or abnormal, or evidence
of extreme eccentricity or insanity, or indeed as undesirable at all;
least of all as philosophically problematic.

No historical writing which rises above a bare chronicler's
narrative, and involves selection and the unequal distribution of
emphasis, can be wholly *wertfrei*.[1] What then distinguishes
moralising that is justly condemned from that which seems
unescapable from any degree of reflection on human affairs? Not
its overtness: mere choice of apparently neutral language can well
seem, to those who do not sympathise with an author's views, even
more insidious. I have attempted to deal with what is meant by bias
and partiality in the essay on historical inevitability. I can only
repeat that we seem to distinguish subjective from objective
appraisal by the degree to which the central values conveyed are
those which are common to human beings as such, that is, for
practical purposes, to the great majority of men in most places and
times. This is clearly not an absolute or rigid criterion; there is
variation, there are virtually unnoticeable (as well as glaring)
national, local and historical peculiarities, prejudices, superstitions,
rationalisations and their irrational influence. But neither is this
criterion wholly relative or subjective, otherwise the concept of
man would become too indeterminate, and men or societies,
divided by unbridgeable normative differences, would be wholly
unable to communicate across great distances in space and time and
culture.

Objectivity of moral judgement seems to depend on (almost
consist in) the degree of constancy in human responses. This
notion cannot in principle be made sharp and unalterable. Its edges
remain blurred. Moral categories – and categories of value in
general – are nothing like as firm and ineradicable as those of, say,
the perception of the material world, but neither are they as relative
or as fluid as some writers have too easily, in their reaction against
the dogmatism of the classical objectivists, tended to assume. A
minimum of common moral ground – interrelated concepts and
categories – is intrinsic to human communication. What they are,
how flexible, how far liable to change under the impact of what
'forces' – these are empirical questions, in a region claimed by

---

[1] 'Value-free.'

moral psychology and historical and social anthropology, fascinating, important and insufficiently explored. To demand more than this seems to me to wish to move beyond the frontiers of communicable human knowledge.

(c) I am accused of supposing that history deals with human motives and intentions, for which Carr wishes to substitute the action of 'social forces'. To this charge I plead guilty. I am obliged to say once more that anyone concerned with human beings is committed to consideration of motives, purposes, choices, the specifically human experience that belongs to human beings uniquely, and not merely with what happened to them as animate or sentient bodies. To ignore the play of non-human factors; or the effect of the unintended consequences of human acts; or the fact that men often do not correctly understand their own individual behaviour or its sources; to stop searching for causes, in the most literal and mechanical sense, in accounting for what happened and how – all this would be absurdly childish and frivolous (not to say obscurantist), and I did not suggest anything of this kind. But to ignore motives and the context in which they arose, the range of possibilities as they stretched before the actors, most of which never were, and some never could have been, realised; to ignore the spectrum of human thought and imagination – how the world and they themselves appear to men whose vision and values (illusions and all) we can grasp in the end only in terms of our own – would be to cease to write history. One may argue about the degree of difference that the influence of this or that individual made in shaping events. But to try to reduce the behaviour of individuals to that of impersonal 'social forces' not further analysable into the conduct of the men who, even according to Marx, make history is 'reification' of statistics, a form of the 'false consciousness' of bureaucrats and administrators who close their eyes to all that proves incapable of quantification, and thereby perpetrate absurdities in theory and dehumanisation in practice.

There are remedies that breed new diseases, whether or not they cure those to which they are applied. To frighten human beings by suggesting to them that they are in the grip of impersonal forces over which they have little or no control is to breed myths, ostensibly in order to kill other figments – the notion of supernatural forces, or of all-powerful individuals, or of the invisible hand. It is to invent entities, to propagate faith in unalterable patterns of events for which the empirical evidence is, to say the least, insufficient, and which by relieving individuals of the burdens of personal responsibility breeds irrational passivity in some, and no less irrational fanatical activity in others; for nothing is more inspiring than the certainty that the stars in their courses are fighting for one's cause, that 'History', or 'social forces', or 'the wave of the future' are with one, bearing one aloft and forward.

This way of thinking and speaking is one which it is the great merit of modern empiricism to have exposed. If my essay has any polemical thrust, it is to discredit metaphysical constructions of this kind. If to speak of men solely in terms of statistical probabilities, ignoring too much of what is specifically human in men – evaluations, choices, differing visions of life – is an exaggerated application of scientific method, a gratuitous behaviourism, it is no less misleading to appeal to imaginary forces. The former has its place; it describes, classifies, predicts, even if it does not explain. The latter explains indeed, but in occult, what I can only call neo-animistic, terms. I suspect that Carr does not feel anxious to defend either of these methods. But in his reaction against *naïveté*, smugness, the vanities of nationalistic or class or personal moralising, he has permitted himself to be driven to the other extreme – the night of impersonality, in which human beings are dissolved into abstract forces. The fact that I protest against it leads Carr to think that I embrace the opposite absurdity. His assumption that between them these extremes exhaust the possibilities seems to me to be the basic fallacy from which his (and perhaps others') vehement criticism of my real and imaginary opinions ultimately stems.

At this point I should like to reiterate some commonplaces from which I do not depart: that causal laws are applicable to human history (a proposition which, *pace* Carr, I should consider it insane to deny); that history is not mainly a 'dramatic conflict' between individual wills;[1] that knowledge, especially of scientifically established laws, tends to render us more effective[2] and extend our

---

[1] A view attributed to me by Christopher Dawson in his review of *Historical Inevitability*, *Harvard Law Review* 70 (1956–7), 584–8, at 587.

[2] My evident failure to state my view sufficiently clearly is brought home to me by the fact that the opposite of this position – a crude and absurd anti-rationalism – is attributed to me by Gordon Leff, loc. cit. (p. 7 above, note 1), by J. A. Passmore, loc. cit. (p. 12 above, note 1), by Christopher Dawson, op. cit. (see previous note), and by half a dozen Marxist writers: some of these in evident good faith.

liberty, which is liable to be curtailed by ignorance and the illusions, terrors and prejudices that it breeds;[1] that there is plenty of empirical evidence for the view that the frontiers of free choice are a good deal narrower than many men have in the past supposed, and perhaps still erroneously believe;[2] and even that objective patterns in history may, for all I know, be discernible. I must repeat that my concern is only to assert that unless such laws and patterns are held to leave some freedom of choice – and not only freedom of action determined by choices that are themselves wholly determined by antecedent causes – we shall have to reconstruct our view of reality accordingly; and that this task is far more formidable than determinists tend to assume.

The determinist's world may, at least in principle, be conceivable: in it all that Ernest Nagel declares to be the function of human volition will remain intact; a man's behaviour will still be affected by praise and blame as his metabolism (at any rate directly) will not;[3] men will continue to describe persons and things as beautiful or ugly, evaluate actions as beneficial or harmful, brave or cowardly, noble or ignoble. But when Kant said that if the laws that governed the phenomena of the external world turned out to govern all there was, then morality – in his sense – was annihilated; and when, in consequence, being concerned with the concept of freedom presupposed by his notion of moral responsibility, he adopted very drastic measures in order to save it, he seems to me, at the very least, to have shown a profound grasp of what is at stake. His solution is obscure, and perhaps untenable; but although it may have to be rejected, the problem remains. In a causally determined system the notions of free choice and moral responsibility, in their usual senses, vanish, or at least lack application, and the notion of action would have to be reconsidered.

I recognise the fact that some thinkers seem to feel no intellectual discomfort in interpreting such concepts as responsibility, culpability, remorse in strict conformity with causal determination. At most they seek to explain the resistance of those who dissent from them by attributing to them a confusion of causality with some sort of compulsion. Compulsion frustrates my wishes but when I

---

[1] Though not in all situations: see my article 'From Hope and Fear Set Free' [reprinted below].

[2] I state this explicitly on pp. 120, 122, 124–6, 134–5.

[3] See H. P. Rickman, 'The Horizons of History', *Hibbert Journal* 56 (October 1957 to July 1958), January 1958, 167–76, at 169–70.

fulfil them I am surely free, even though my wishes themselves are causally determined; if they are not, if they are not effects of my general tendencies, or ingredients in my habits and way of living (which can be described in purely causal terms), or if these, in their turn, are not what they are entirely as a result of causes – physical, social, psychological – then there is surely an element of pure chance or randomness, which breaks the causal chain. But (the argument continues) is not random behaviour the very opposite of freedom, rationality, responsibility? And yet these alternatives seem to exhaust the possibilities. The notion of uncaused choice as something out of the blue is certainly not satisfactory. But (I need not argue this again) the only alternative permitted by such thinkers – a caused choice held to entail responsibility, desert and the like – is equally untenable.

This dilemma has now divided thinkers for more than two thousand years. Some continue to be agonised or at least puzzled by it, as the earliest Stoics were; others see no problem at all. It may be that it stems, at least in part, from the use of a mechanical model applied to human actions; in one case choices are conceived as links in the kind of causal sequence that is typical of the functioning of a mechanical process; in the other, a break in this sequence, still conceived in terms of a highly complex mechanism. Neither image seems to fit the case at all well. We seem to need a new model, a schema which will rescue the evidence of moral consciousness from the beds of Procrustes provided by the obsessive frameworks of the traditional discussions. All efforts to break away from the old obstructive analogies, or (to use a familiar terminology) the rules of an inappropriate language game, have so far proved abortive. This needs a philosophical imagination of the first order, which in this case is still to seek. White's solution – to attribute the conflicting views to different scales of value or varieties of moral usage – seems to me no way out. I cannot help suspecting that his view is part of a wider theory, according to which belief in determinism or any other view of the world is, or depends on, some sort of large-scale pragmatic decision about how to treat this or that field of thought or experience, based on a view of what set of categories would give the best results. Even if one accepted this, it would not be easier to reconcile the notions of causal necessity, avoidability, free choice, responsibility and the rest. I do not claim to have refuted the conclusions of determinism; but neither do I see why we need be driven towards them. Neither the idea of historical explanation as such, nor respect for scientific method, seems to me to entail them.

This sums up my disagreements with Ernest Nagel, Morton White, E. H. Carr, the classical determinists and their modern disciples.

II

Positive versus negative liberty

In the case of social and political liberty a problem arises that is not wholly dissimilar from that of social and historical determinism. We assume the need of an area for free choice, the diminution of which is incompatible with the existence of anything that can properly be called political (or social) liberty. Indeterminism does not entail that human beings cannot in fact be treated like animals or things; nor is political liberty, like freedom of choice, intrinsic to the notion of a human being; it is a historical growth, an area bounded by frontiers. The question of its frontiers, indeed whether the concept of frontiers can properly be applied to it, raises issues on which much of the criticism directed upon my theses has concentrated. The main issues may here too be summarised under three heads: (*a*) whether the difference I have drawn between (what I am not the first to have called) positive and negative liberty is specious, or, at any rate, too sharp; (*b*) whether the term 'liberty' can be extended as widely as some of my critics appear to wish, without thereby depriving it of so much significance as to render it progressively less useful; (*c*) why political liberty should be regarded as being of value.

Before discussing these problems, I wish to correct a genuine error in the original version of *Two Concepts of Liberty*. Although this error does not weaken, or conflict with, the arguments used in the essay (indeed, if anything, it seems to me to strengthen them), it is, nevertheless, a position that I consider to be mistaken.[1] In the original version of *Two Concepts of Liberty*[2] I speak of liberty as the absence of obstacles to the fulfilment of a man's desires. This is

---

[1] The generous and acute anonymous reviewer [Richard Wollheim] of my lecture in the *Times Literary Supplement* ('A Hundred Years After', 20 February 1959, 89–90) was the first writer to point out this error; he also made other penetrating and suggestive criticisms by which I have greatly profited.

[2] Oxford, 1958: Clarendon Press. See p. xxxii above.

a common, perhaps the most common, sense in which the term is used, but it does not represent my position. For if to be free – negatively – is simply not to be prevented by other persons from doing whatever one wishes, then one of the ways of attaining such freedom is by extinguishing one's wishes. I offered criticisms of this definition, and of this entire line of thought, in the text, without realising that it was inconsistent with the formulation with which I began. If degrees of freedom were a function of the satisfaction of desires, I could increase freedom as effectively by eliminating desires as by satisfying them: I could render men (including myself) free by conditioning them into losing the original desires which I have decided not to satisfy. Instead of resisting or removing the pressures that bear down upon me, I can 'internalise' them. This is what Epictetus achieves when he claims that he, a slave, is freer than his master. By ignoring obstacles, forgetting, 'rising above' them, becoming unconscious of them, I can attain peace and serenity, a noble detachment from the fears and hatreds that beset other men – freedom in one sense indeed, but not in the sense in which I wish to speak of it. When (according to Cicero's account) the Stoic sage Posidonius, who was dying of an agonising disease, said, 'Do your worst, pain; no matter what you do, you cannot make me hate you',[1] thereby accepting, and attaining unity with, 'Nature', which, being identical with cosmic 'reason', rendered his pain not merely inevitable, but rational, the sense in which he achieved freedom is not that basic meaning of it in which men are said to lose freedom when they are imprisoned or literally enslaved. The Stoic sense of freedom, however sublime, must be distinguished from the freedom or liberty which the oppressor, or the oppressive institutionalised practice, curtails or destroys.[2] For once I am happy to acknow-

---

[1] Cicero, *Tusculan Disputations* 2. 61. 'Nihil agis, dolor! quamvis sis molestus, numquam te esse confitebor malum.'

[2] There is an illuminating discussion of this topic by Robert Waelder in 'Authoritarianism and Totalitarianism: Psychological Comments on a Problem of Power': this essay appears in George B. Wilbur and Warner Muensterberger (eds), *Psychoanalysis and Culture: Essays in Honour of Géza Rósheim* (New York, 1951; repr. 1967), pp. 185–95. He speaks of the remoulding of the superego into 'internalising' external pressures, and draws an illuminating distinction between authoritarianism, which entails obedience to authority without acceptance of its orders and claims, and totalitarianism, which entails in addition inner conformity to the system imposed by the dictator; hence totalitarian insistence on education and indoctrination as opposed to mere outward obedience, a sinister process with

ledge the insight of Rousseau: to know one's chains for what they are is better than to deck them with flowers.[1]

Spiritual freedom, like moral victory, must be distinguished from a more fundamental sense of freedom, and a more ordinary sense of victory, otherwise there will be a danger of confusion in theory and justification of oppression in practice, in the name of liberty itself. There is a clear sense in which to teach a man that, if he cannot get what he wants, he must learn to want only what he can get, may contribute to his happiness or his security; but it will not increase his civil or political freedom. The sense of freedom in which I use this term entails not simply the absence of frustration (which may be obtained by killing desires), but the absence of obstacles to possible choices and activities – absence of obstructions on roads along which a man can decide to walk. Such freedom ultimately depends not on whether I wish to walk at all, or how far, but on how many doors are open, how open they are, upon their relative importance in my life, even though it may be impossible literally to measure this in any quantitative fashion.[2] The extent of my social or political freedom consists in the absence of obstacles not merely to my actual, but to my potential, choices – to my acting in this or that way if I choose to do so. Similarly absence of such freedom is due to the closing of such doors or failure to open them, as a result, intended or unintended, of alterable human practices, of the operation of human agencies; although only if such acts are deliberately intended (or, perhaps, are accompanied by awareness that they may block paths) will they be liable to be called oppression. Unless this is conceded, the Stoic conception of liberty ('true' freedom – the state of the morally autonomous slave), which is compatible with a very high degree of political despotism, will merely confuse the issue.

It is an interesting, but perhaps irrelevant, historical question at

which we have become all too familiar. There is, of course, all the difference in the world between assimilating the rules of reason, as advocated by Stoicism, and those of an irrational movement or arbitrary dictatorship. But the psychological machinery is similar.

[1] This point is well made by one of my critics, L. J. Macfarlane, in 'On Two Concepts of Liberty', *Political Studies* 14 (1966), 77–81. In the course of a very critical but fair and valuable discussion Macfarlane observes that to know one's chains is often the first step to freedom, which may never come about if one either ignores or loves them.

[2] See p. 177 below, note 1.

what date, and in what circumstances, the notion of individual liberty in this sense first became explicit in the West. I have found no convincing evidence of any clear formulation of it in the ancient world.[1] Some of my critics have doubted this, but apart from pointing to such modern writers as Acton, Jellinek or Barker, who do profess to find this ideal in ancient Greece, some of them also, more pertinently, cite the proposals of Otanes after the death of pseudo-Smerdis in the account given by Herodotus, and the celebrated paean to liberty in the Funeral Oration of Pericles, as well as the speech of Nikias before the final battle with the Syracusans (in Thucydides), as evidence that the Greeks, at any rate, had a clear conception of individual liberty. I must confess that I do not find this conclusive. When Pericles and Nikias compare the freedom of the Athenian citizens with the fate of the subjects of less democratic States, what (it seems to me) they are saying is that the citizens of Athens enjoy freedom in the sense of self-government, that they are not slaves of any master, that they perform their civic duties out of love for their *polis*, without needing to be coerced, and not under the goads and whips of savage laws or taskmasters (as in Sparta or Persia). So might a headmaster say of the boys in his school that they live and act according to good principles not because they are forced to do so, but because they are inspired by loyalty to the school, by 'team spirit', by a sense of solidarity and common purpose; whereas at other schools these results have to be achieved by fear of punishment and stern measures. But in neither case is it contemplated that a man might, without losing face, or incurring contempt, or a diminution of his human essence, withdraw from public life altogether, and pursue private ends, live in a room of his own, in the company of personal friends, as Epicurus later advocated, and perhaps the Cynic and Cyrenaic disciples of Socrates had preached before him. As for Otanes, he wished neither to rule nor to be ruled – the exact opposite of Aristotle's notion of true civic liberty. Perhaps this attitude did begin to occur in the ideas of unpolitical thinkers in Herodotus' day: of Antiphon the Sophist, for example, and possibly in some moods of Socrates himself. But it remains isolated and, until Epicurus, undeveloped. In other words, it seems to me that the issue of individual freedom,

---

[1] For a fuller treatment by Berlin of liberty in the ancient world see now 'The Birth of Greek Individualism', reprinted below. Ed.

of the frontiers beyond which public authority, whether lay or ecclesiastical, should not normally be allowed to step, had not clearly emerged at this stage; the central value attached to it may, perhaps (as I remarked in the penultimate paragraph of my lecture), be the late product of a capitalist civilisation, an element in a network of values that includes such notions as personal rights, civil liberties, the sanctity of the individual personality, the importance of privacy, personal relations and the like. I do not say that the ancient Greeks did not in fact enjoy a great measure of what we should today call individual liberty.[1] My thesis is only that the notion had not explicitly emerged, and was therefore not central to Greek culture, or, perhaps, to any other ancient civilisation known to us.

One of the by-products or symptoms of this stage of social development is that, for instance, the issue of free will (as opposed to that of voluntary action) is not felt to be a problem before the Stoics; the corollary of which seems to be that variety for its own sake – and the corresponding abhorrence of uniformity – is not a prominent ideal, or perhaps an explicit ideal at all, before the Renaissance, or even, in its full form, before the beginning of the eighteenth century. Issues of this type seem to arise only when forms of life, and the social patterns that are part of them, after long periods in which they have been taken for granted, are upset, and so come to be recognised and become the subject of conscious reflection. There are many values which men have disputed, and for and against which they have fought, that are not mentioned in some earlier phase of history, either because they are assumed without question, or because men are, whatever the cause, in no condition to conceive of them. It may be that the more sophisti-cated forms of individual liberty did not impinge upon the consciousness of the masses of mankind simply because they lived in squalor and oppression. Men who live in conditions where there is not sufficient food, warmth, shelter, or the minimum degree of security, can scarcely be expected to concern themselves with freedom of contract or of the press.

It may make matters clearer if at this point I mention what seems to me yet another misconception – namely the identification of freedom with activity as such. When, for example, Erich Fromm, in

---

[1] A. W. Gomme and others have provided a good deal of evidence for the hypothesis that they did.

virtually all his moving tracts for the times, speaks of true freedom as the spontaneous, rational activity of the total, integrated personality, and is partly followed in this by Bernard Crick,[1] I disagree with them. The freedom of which I speak is opportunity for action, rather than action itself. If, although I enjoy the right to walk through open doors, I prefer not to do so, but to sit still and vegetate, I am not thereby rendered less free. Freedom is the opportunity to act, not the action itself; the possibility of action, not necessarily that dynamic realisation of it which both Fromm and Crick identify with it. If apathetic neglect of various avenues to a more vigorous and generous life – however much this may be condemned on other grounds – is not considered incompatible with the notion of being free, then I have nothing to quarrel with in the formulations of either of these writers. But I fear that Fromm would consider such abdication as a symptom of lack of integration, which for him is indispensable to – perhaps identical with – freedom; while Crick would look upon such apathy as too inert and timid to deserve to be called freedom. I find the ideal advocated by these champions of the full life sympathetic; but to identify it with freedom seems to me conflation of two values. To say that freedom is activity as such is to make the term cover too much; it tends to obscure and dilute the central issue – the right and freedom to act – about which men have argued and fought during almost the whole of recorded history.

To return to concepts of liberty. Much has been made by my opponents of the distinction (regarded by them as specious or exaggerated) that I have tried to draw between two questions: 'By whom am I governed?' and 'How much am I governed?' Yet I confess that I cannot see either that the two questions are identical, or that the difference between them is unimportant. It still seems to me that the distinction between the two kinds of answer, and therefore between the different senses of 'liberty' involved, is neither trivial nor confused. Indeed, I continue to believe that the issue is a central one both historically and conceptually, both in theory and practice.

Let me say once again that 'positive' and 'negative' liberty, in the sense in which I use these terms, start at no great logical distance

[1] In his inaugural lecture to the University of Sheffield in 1966, *Freedom as Politics* (Sheffield, 1966), reprinted in his *Political Theory and Practice* (London, [1972]).

from each other. The questions 'Who is master?' and 'Over what area am I master?' cannot be kept wholly distinct. I wish to determine myself, and not be directed by others, no matter how wise and benevolent; my conduct derives an irreplaceable value from the sole fact that it is my own, and not imposed upon me. But I am not, and cannot expect to be, wholly self-sufficient or socially omnipotent.[1] I cannot remove all the obstacles in my path that stem from the conduct of my fellows. I can try to ignore them, treat them as illusory, or 'intermingle' them and attribute them to my own inner principles, conscience, moral sense; or try to dissolve my sense of personal identity in a common enterprise, as an element in a larger self-directed whole. Nevertheless, despite such heroic efforts to transcend or dissolve the conflicts and resistance of others, if I do not wish to be deceived, I shall recognise the fact that total harmony with others is incompatible with self-identity; that if I am not to be dependent on others in every respect, I shall need some area within which I am not, and can count on not being, freely interfered with by them. The question then arises: how wide is the area over which I am, or should be, master? My thesis is that historically the notion of 'positive' liberty – in answer to the question 'Who is master?' – diverged from that of 'negative' liberty, designed to answer 'Over what area am I master?'; and that this gulf widened as the notion of the self suffered a metaphysical fission into, on the one hand, a 'higher', or a 'real', or an 'ideal' self, set up to rule a 'lower', 'empirical', 'psychological' self or nature, on the other; into 'myself at my best' as master over my inferior day-to-day self; into Coleridge's great I AM over less transcendent incarnations of it in time and space.[2]

A genuine experience of inner tension may lie at the root of this ancient and pervasive metaphysical image of the two selves, the

---

[1] It has been suggested that liberty is always a triadic relation; one can only seek to be free from x to do or be y; hence 'all liberty' is at once negative and positive or, better still, neither. See G. C. MacCallum, jr, 'Negative and Positive Freedom', *Philosophical Review* 76 (1967), 312–34, repr. in Peter Laslett, W. G. Runciman and Quentin Skinner (eds), *Philosophy, Politics and Society*, Fourth Series (Oxford, 1972). This seems to me an error. A man struggling against his chains or a people against enslavement need not consciously aim at any definite further state. A man need not know how he will use his freedom; he just wants to remove the yoke. So do classes and nations.

[2] See Coleridge *Biographia Literaria* (1817), chapter 12, theses 6–7, and chapter 13, antepenultimate paragraph.

influence of which has been vast over language, thought and conduct; however this may be, the 'higher' self duly became identified with institutions, Churches, nations, races, States, classes, cultures, parties, and with vaguer entities, such as the general will, the common good, the enlightened forces of society, the vanguard of the most progressive class, Manifest Destiny. My thesis is that, in the course of this process, what had begun as a doctrine of freedom turned into a doctrine of authority and, at times, of oppression, and became the favoured weapon of despotism, a phenomenon all too familiar in our own day. I was careful to point out that this could equally have been the fate of the doctrine of negative liberty. Among the dualists who distinguished the two selves, some – in particular Jewish and Christian theologians, but also Idealist metaphysicians in the nineteenth century – speak of the need to release the 'higher' or 'ideal' self from obstacles in its path, such as interference by, 'slavery to', the 'lower' self; and some saw this base entity incarnated in institutions serving irrational or wicked passions and other forces of evil likely to obstruct the proper development of the 'true' or 'higher' self, or 'myself at my best'. The history of political doctrines might (like that of some Protestant sects) have taken this 'negative' form. The point, however, is that it did so relatively seldom – as, for example, in early liberal, anarchist and some types of populist writings. But for the most part freedom was identified, by metaphysically inclined writers, with the realisation of the real self not so much in individual men as incarnated in institutions, traditions, forms of life wider than the empirical spatio-temporal existence of the finite individual. Freedom is identified by such thinkers most often, it seems to me, with the 'positive' activity of these institutional ('organic') forms of life, growth and so forth rather than with mere ('negative') removal of obstacles even from the paths of such 'organisms', let alone from those of individuals – such an absence of obstacles being regarded as, at best, a means to, or a condition of, freedom; not as freedom itself.

It is doubtless well to remember that belief in negative freedom is compatible with, and (so far as ideas influence conduct) has played its part in generating, great and lasting social evils. My point is that it was much less often defended or disguised by the kind of specious arguments and sleights-of-hand habitually used by the champions of 'positive' freedom in its more sinister forms. Advocacy of non-interference (like 'social Darwinism') was, of course, used to support politically and socially destructive policies which armed the strong, the brutal and the unscrupulous against the humane and the weak, the able and ruthless against the less gifted and the less fortunate. Freedom for the wolves has often meant death to the sheep. The bloodstained story of economic individualism and unrestrained capitalist competition does not, I should have thought, today need stressing. Nevertheless, in view of the astonishing opinions which some of my critics have imputed to me, I should, perhaps, have been wise to underline certain parts of my argument. I should have made even clearer that the evils of unrestricted laissez-faire, and of the social and legal systems that permitted and encouraged it, led to brutal violations of 'negative' liberty – of basic human rights (always a 'negative' notion: a wall against oppressors), including that of free expression or association, without which there may exist justice and fraternity and even happiness of a kind, but not democracy. And I should perhaps have stressed (save that I thought this too obvious to need saying) the failure of such systems to provide the minimum conditions in which any degree of significant 'negative' liberty can be exercised by individuals or groups, and without which it is of little or no value to those who may theoretically possess it. For what are rights without the power to implement them?

I had supposed that enough had been said by almost every serious modern writer concerned with this subject about the fate of personal liberty during the reign of unfettered economic individu-alism – about the condition of the injured majority, principally in the towns whose children were destroyed in mines or mills while their parents lived in poverty, disease and ignorance, a situation in which the enjoyment by the poor and the weak of legal rights to spend their money as they pleased or to choose the education they wanted (which Cobden and Herbert Spencer and their disciples offered them with every appearance of sincerity) became an odious mockery.

All this is notoriously true. Legal liberties are compatible with extremes of exploitation, brutality and injustice. The case for intervention, by the State or other effective agencies, to secure conditions for both positive, and at least a minimum degree of negative, liberty for individuals, is overwhelmingly strong. Liberals like Tocqueville and J. S. Mill, and even Benjamin Constant (who prized negative liberty beyond any modern writer), were not unaware of this. The case for social legislation or planning, for the

Welfare State and socialism, can be constructed with as much validity from consideration of the claims of negative liberty as from those of its positive brother, and if, historically, it was not made so frequently, that was because the kind of evil against which the concept of negative liberty was directed as a weapon was not laissez-faire, but despotism. The rise and fall of the two concepts can largely be traced to the specific dangers which, at a given moment, threatened a group or society most: on the one hand excessive control and interference, or, on the other, an uncontrolled 'market' economy. Each concept seems liable to perversion into the very vice which it was created to resist. But whereas liberal ultra-individualism could scarcely be said to be a rising force at present, the rhetoric of 'positive' liberty, at least in its distorted form, is in far greater evidence, and continues to play its historic role (in both capitalist and anti-capitalist societies) as a cloak for despotism in the name of a wider freedom.

'Positive' liberty, conceived as the answer to the question, 'By whom am I to be governed?', is a valid universal goal. I do not know why I should have been held to doubt this, or, for that matter, the further proposition, that democratic self-government is a fundamental human need, something valuable in itself, whether or not it clashes with the claims of negative liberty or of any other goal; valuable intrinsically and not only for the reasons advanced in its favour by, for example, Constant – that without it negative liberty may be too easily crushed; or by Mill, who thinks it an indispensable means – but still only a means – to the attainment of happiness. I can only repeat that the perversion of the notion of positive liberty into its opposite – the apotheosis of authority – did occur, and has for a long while been one of the most familiar and depressing phenomena of our time. For whatever reason or cause, the notion of 'negative' liberty (conceived as the answer to the question 'How much am I to be governed?'), however disastrous the consequences of its unbridled forms, has not historically been twisted by its theorists as often or as effectively into anything so darkly metaphysical or socially sinister or remote from its original meaning as its 'positive' counterpart. The first can be turned into its opposite and still exploit the favourable associations of its innocent origins. The second has, much more frequently, been seen, for better and for worse, for what it was; there has been no lack of emphasis, in the last hundred years, upon its more disastrous implications. Hence the greater need, it seems to me, to expose the aberrations of positive liberty than those of its negative brother.

Nor do I wish to deny that new ways in which liberty, in both its positive and its negative sense, can be, and has been, curtailed have arisen since the nineteenth century. In an age of expanding economic productivity there exist ways of curtailing both types of liberty – for example, by permitting or promoting a situation in which entire groups and nations are progressively shut off from benefits which have been allowed to accumulate too exclusively in the hands of other groups and nations, the rich and strong – a situation which, in its turn, has produced (and was itself produced by) social arrangements that have caused walls to arise around men, and doors to be shut to the development of individuals and classes. This has been done by social and economic policies that were sometimes openly discriminatory, at other times camouflaged, by the rigging of educational policies and of the means of influencing opinions, by legislation in the sphere of morals, and by similar measures, which have blocked and diminished human freedom at times as effectively as the more overt and brutal methods of direct oppression – slavery and imprisonment – against which the original defenders of liberty lifted their voices.[1]

---

[1] Not that such open violence has been lacking in our own country, practised at times under the noble banner of the suppression of arbitrary rule and the enemies of liberty and the emancipation of hitherto enslaved populations and classes. I agree with a great deal of what has been said on this subject by A. S. Kaufman ('Professor Berlin on "Negative Freedom"', *Mind* 71 (1962), 241–3). Some of his points may be found in an earlier attack by Marshall Cohen ('Berlin and the Liberal Tradition', *Philosophical Quarterly* 10 (1960), 216–27). Some of Kaufman's objections have, I hope, been answered already. There is one point, however, on which I must take further issue with him. He appears to regard constraint or obstruction not brought about by human means as being forms of deprivation of social or political freedom. I do not think that this is compatible with what is normally meant by political freedom – the only sense of freedom with which I am concerned. Kaufman speaks (op. cit., p. 241) of 'obstructions to the human will, which have nothing to do with a community's pattern of power relations' as obstacles to (political or social) liberty. Unless, however, such obstructions do, in the end, spring from power relations, they do not seem to be relevant to the existence of social or political liberty. I cannot see how one can speak of 'basic human rights' (to use Kaufman's phrase) as violated by what he calls 'non-human . . . interference'. If I stumble and fall, and so find my freedom of movement frustrated, I cannot, surely, be said to have suffered any loss of basic human rights. Failure to discriminate between human and non-human obstacles to freedom seems to me to mark the beginning of the great confusion of types of

Let me summarise my position thus far. The extent of a man's negative freedom is, as it were, a function of what doors, and how many, are open to him; upon what prospects they open; and how open they are. This formula must not be pressed too far, for not all doors are of equal importance, inasmuch as the paths on which they open vary in the opportunities they offer. Consequently, the problem of how an overall increase of liberty in particular circumstances is to be secured, and how it is to be distributed (especially in situations, and this is almost invariably the case, in which the opening of one door leads to the lifting of other barriers and the lowering of still others), how, in a word, the maximisation of opportunities is in any concrete case to be achieved, can be an agonising problem, not to be solved by any hard-and-fast rule.[1]

---

freedom, and of the no less fatal identification of conditions of freedom with freedom itself, which is at the root of some of the fallacies with which I am concerned.

[1] David Nicholls in an admirable survey, 'Positive Liberty, 1880–1914', *American Political Science Review* 56 (1962), 114–28, at 114 note 8, thinks that I contradict myself in quoting with approval Bentham's view that every law is an infraction of liberty (see p. 195 below, note 1), since some laws increase the total amount of liberty in a society. I do not see the force of this objection. Every law seems to me to curtail *some* liberty, although it may be a means to increasing another. Whether it increases the total sum of attainable liberty will of course depend on the particular situation. Even a law which enacts that no one shall coerce anyone in a given sphere, while it obviously increases the freedom of the majority, is an infraction of the freedom of potential bullies and policemen. Infraction may, as in this case, be highly desirable, but it remains infraction. There is no reason for thinking that Bentham, who favoured laws, meant to say more than this.

In his article (at p. 121, note 63) Nicholls quotes T. H. Green's statement (in his 'Lecture on "Liberal Legislation and Freedom of Contract"'): 'the mere removal of compulsion, the mere enabling a man to do as he likes, is in itself no contribution to true freedom ... the ideal of true freedom is the maximum of power for all members of human society alike to make the best of themselves': pp. 199–200 in T. H. Green, *Lectures on the Principles of Political Obligation and Other Writings*, ed. Paul Harris and John Morrow (Cambridge etc., 1986). This is a classical statement of positive liberty, and the crucial terms are, of course, 'true freedom' and 'the best of themselves'. Perhaps I need not enlarge again upon the fatal ambiguity of these words. As a plea for justice, and a denunciation of the monstrous assumption that workmen were (in any sense that mattered to them) free agents in negotiating with employers in his time, Green's essay can scarcely be improved upon. The workers, in theory, probably enjoyed wide negative freedom. But since they lacked the means of its realisation, it was a hollow gain. Hence I find nothing to disagree with in Green's recommendations; I reject only the metaphysical doctrine of the two selves – the individual streams versus the

What I am mainly concerned to establish is that, whatever may be the common ground between them, and whichever is liable to graver distortion, negative and positive liberty are not the same thing. Both are ends in themselves. These ends may clash irreconcilably. When this happens, questions of choice and preference inevitably arise. Should democracy in a given situation be promoted at the expense of individual freedom? Or equality at the expense of artistic achievement; or mercy at the expense of justice; or spontaneity at the expense of efficiency; or happiness, loyalty, innocence at the expense of knowledge and truth? The simple point which I am concerned to make is that where ultimate values are irreconcilable, clear-cut solutions cannot, in principle, be found. To decide rationally in such situations is to decide in the light of general ideals, the overall pattern of life pursued by a man or a group or a society. If the claims of two (or more than two) types of liberty prove incompatible in a particular case, and if this is an instance of the clash of values at once absolute and incommensurable, it is better to face this intellectually uncomfortable fact than to ignore it, or automatically attribute it to some deficiency on our part which could be eliminated by an increase in skill or knowledge, as was done by Condorcet and his disciples; or, what is worse still, suppress one of the competing values altogether by pretending that it is identical with its rival – and so end by distorting both. Yet, it appears to me, it is exactly this that philosophical monists who demand final solutions – tidiness and harmony at any price – have done and are doing still. I do not, of course, mean this as an argument against the proposition that the application of knowledge and skill can, in particular cases, lead to satisfactory solutions. When such dilemmas arise it is one thing to say that every effort must be made to resolve them, and another that it is certain a priori that a correct, conclusive solution must always in principle be discoverable – something that the older rationalist metaphysics appeared to guarantee.

social river in which they should be merged, a dualistic fallacy used too often to support a variety of despotisms. Nor, of course, do I wish to deny that Green's views were exceptionally enlightened; and this holds of many of the critics of liberalism in Europe and America in the last hundred years or so. Nevertheless, words are important, and a writer's opinions and purposes are not sufficient to render the use of a misleading terminology harmless either in theory or in practice. The record of liberalism is no better in this respect that that of most other schools of political thought.

Consequently, when another of my critics, David Spitz,[1] maintains that the frontier falls not so much between positive and negative liberty, but 'in determination of which complex of particular liberties and concomitant restraints is most likely to promote those values that, in Berlin's theory, are distinctively human', and, in the course of his interesting and suggestive review, declares that the issue depends on one's view of human nature, or of human goals (on which men differ), I do not dissent. But when he goes on to say that, in my attempt to cope with the relativity of values, I fall back on the views of J. S. Mill, he seems to me mistaken on an important issue. Mill does seem to have convinced himself that there exists such a thing as attainable, communicable, objective truth in the field of value judgements; but that the conditions for its discovery do not exist save in a society which provides a sufficient degree of individual liberty, particularly of enquiry and discussion. This is simply the old objectivist thesis, in an empirical form, with a special rider about the need for individual liberty as a necessary condition for the attainment of this final goal. My thesis is not this at all; but that, since some values may conflict intrinsically, the very notion that a pattern must in principle be discoverable in which they are all rendered harmonious is founded on a false a priori view of what the world is like.

If I am right in this, and the human condition is such that men cannot always avoid choices, they cannot avoid them not merely for the obvious reasons, which philosophers have seldom ignored, namely that there are many possible courses of action and forms of life worth living, and therefore to choose between them is part of being rational or capable of moral judgement; they cannot avoid choice for one central reason (which is, in the ordinary sense, conceptual, not empirical), namely that ends collide; that one cannot have everything. Whence it follows that the very concept of an ideal life, a life in which nothing of value need ever be lost or sacrificed, in which all rational (or virtuous, or otherwise legiti- mate) wishes must be capable of being truly satisfied – this classical vision is not merely Utopian, but incoherent. The need to choose, to sacrifice some ultimate values to others, turns out to be a permanent characteristic of the human predicament. If this is so, it undermines all theories according to which the value of free choice derives from the fact that without it we cannot attain to the perfect

---

[1] op. cit. (p. xiii above, note 2).

life; with the implication that once such perfection has been reached the need for choice between alternatives withers away. On this view, choice, like the party system, or the right to vote against the nominees of the ruling party, becomes obsolete in the perfect Platonic or theocratic or Jacobin or communist society, where any sign of the recrudescence of basic disagreement is a symptom of error and vice. For there is only one possible path for the perfectly rational man, since there are now no beguiling illusions, no conflicts, no incongruities, no surprises, no genuine, unpredictable novelty; everything is still and perfect in the universe governed by what Kant called the Holy Will.

Whether or not this calm and tideless sea is conceivable or not, it does not resemble the real world in terms of which alone we conceive men's nature and their values. Given things as we know them, and have known them during recorded human history, capacity for choosing is intrinsic to rationality, if rationality entails a normal ability to apprehend the real world. To move in a frictionless medium, desiring only what one can attain, not tempted by alternatives, never seeking incompatible ends, is to live in a coherent fantasy. To offer it as the ideal is to seek to dehumanise men, to turn them into the brainwashed, contented beings of Aldous Huxley's celebrated totalitarian nightmare. To contract the areas of human choice is to do harm to men in an intrinsic, Kantian, not merely utilitarian, sense. The fact that the maintenance of conditions making possible the widest choice must be adjusted – however imperfectly – to other needs, for social stability, predictability, order and so on – does not diminish their central importance. There is a minimum level of opportunity for choice – not of rational or virtuous choice alone – below which human activity ceases to be free in any meaningful sense. It is true that the cry for individual liberty has often disguised desire for privilege, or for power to oppress and exploit, or simply fear of social change. Nevertheless the modern horror of uniformity, conformism and mechanisation of life is not groundless.

As for the issue of relativity and the subjective nature of values, I wonder whether this has not, for the sake of argument, been exaggerated by philosophers: whether men and their outlooks have differed, over wide stretches of space and time, as greatly as has at times been represented. But on this point – how unchanging, how 'ultimate', how universal and 'basic' human values are – I feel no certainty. If values had varied very widely between cultures and periods, communication would have been harder to achieve, and our historical knowledge, which depends on some degree of ability to understand the goals and motives and ways of life at work in cultures different from our own, would turn out to be an illusion. So, of course, would the findings of historical sociology, from which the very concept of social relativity largely derives. Scepticism, driven to extremes, defeats itself by becoming self-refuting.

As for the question of what in fact are the values which we regard as universal and 'basic' – presupposed (if that is the correct logical relation) by the very notions of morality and humanity as such – this seems to me a question of a quasi-empirical kind. That is to say, it seems to be a question for the answer to which we must go to historians, anthropologists, philosophers of culture, social scientists of various kinds, scholars who study the central notions and central ways of behaviour of entire societies, revealed in monuments, forms of life, social activity, as well as more overt expressions of belief such as laws, faiths, philosophies, literature. I describe this as *quasi*-empirical, because concepts and categories that dominate life and thought over a very large portion (even if not the whole) of recorded history are difficult, and in practice impossible, to think away; and in this way differ from the more flexible and changing constructions and hypotheses of the natural sciences.

There is one further point which may be worth reiterating. It is important to discriminate between liberty and the conditions of its exercise. If a man is too poor or too ignorant or too feeble to make use of his legal rights, the liberty that these rights confer upon him is nothing to him, but it is not thereby annihilated. The obligation to promote education, health, justice, to raise standards of living, to provide opportunity for the growth of the arts and the sciences, to prevent reactionary political or social or legal policies or arbitrary inequalities, is not made less stringent because it is not necessarily directed to the promotion of liberty itself, but to conditions in which alone its possession is of value, or to values which may be independent of it. And still, liberty is one thing, and the conditions for it are another. To take a concrete example: it is, I believe, desirable to introduce a uniform system of general primary and secondary education in every country, if only in order to do away with distinctions of social status that are at present created or promoted by the existence of a social hierarchy of schools in some

Western countries, notably my own. If I were asked why I believe this, I should give the kind of reasons mentioned by Spitz,[1] for instance, the intrinsic claims of social equality; the evils arising from differences of status created by a system of education governed by the financial resources or the social position of parents rather than the ability and the needs of the children; the ideal of social solidarity; the need to provide for the bodies and minds of as many human beings as possible, and not only of members of a privileged class; and, what is more relevant here, the need to provide the maximum number of children with opportunities for free choice, which equality in education is likely to increase.

If I were told that this must severely curtail the liberty of parents who claim the right not to be interfered with in this matter – that it was an elementary right to be allowed to choose the type of education to be given to one's child, to determine the intellectual, religious, social, economic conditions in which the child is to be brought up – I should not be ready to dismiss this outright. But I should maintain that when (as in this case) values genuinely clash, choices must be made. In this case the clash arises between the need to preserve the existing liberty of some parents to determine the type of education they seek for their children; the need to promote other social purposes; and, finally, the need to create conditions in which those who lack them will be provided with opportunities to exercise those rights (freedom to choose) which they legally possess, but cannot, without such opportunities, put to use. Useless freedoms should be made usable, but they are not identical with the conditions indispensable for their utility. This is not a merely pedantic distinction, for if it is ignored, the meaning and value of freedom of choice is apt to be downgraded. In their zeal to create social and economic conditions in which alone freedom is of genuine value, men tend to forget freedom itself; and if it is remembered, it is liable to be pushed aside to make room for these other values with which the reformers or revolutionaries have become preoccupied.

Again, it must not be forgotten that even though freedom without sufficient material security, health, knowledge, in a society that lacks equality, justice, mutual confidence, may be virtually useless, the reverse can also be disastrous. To provide for material

[1] ibid., p. 80.

needs, for education, for such equality and security as, say, children have at school or laymen have in a theocracy, is not to expand liberty. We live in a world characterised by regimes (both right- and left-wing) which have done, or are seeking to do, precisely this; and when they call it freedom, this can be as great a fraud as the freedom of the pauper who has a legal right to purchase luxuries. Indeed, one of the things that Dostoevsky's celebrated fable of the Grand Inquisitor in *The Brothers Karamazov* is designed to show is precisely that paternalism can provide the conditions of freedom, yet withhold freedom itself.

A general consideration follows. If we wish to live in the light of reason, we must follow rules or principles; for that is what being rational is. When these rules or principles conflict in concrete cases, to be rational is to follow the course of conduct which least obstructs the general pattern of life in which we believe. The right policy cannot be arrived at in a mechanical or deductive fashion: there are no hard-and-fast rules to guide us; conditions are often unclear, and principles incapable of being fully analysed or articulated. We seek to adjust the unadjustable, we do the best we can. Those, no doubt, are in some way fortunate who have brought themselves, or have been brought by others, to obey some ultimate principle before the bar of which all problems can be brought. Single-minded monists, ruthless fanatics, men possessed by an all-embracing coherent vision do not know the doubts and agonies of those who cannot wholly blind themselves to reality. But even those who are aware of the complex texture of experience, of what is not reducible to generalisation or capable of computation, can, in the end, justify their decisions only by their coherence with some overall pattern of a desirable form of personal or social life, of which they may become fully conscious only, it may be, when faced with the need to resolve conflicts of this kind. If this seems vague, it is so of necessity. The notion that there must exist final objective answers to normative questions, truths that can be demonstrated or directly intuited, that it is in principle possible to discover a harmonious pattern in which all values are reconciled, and that it is towards this unique goal that we must make; that we can uncover some single central principle that shapes this vision, a principle which, once found, will govern our lives – this ancient and almost universal belief, on which so much traditional thought and action and philosophical doctrine rests, seems to me invalid, and at times to have led (and still to lead) to absurdities in theory and barbarous consequences in practice.[1]

The fundamental sense of freedom is freedom from chains, from imprisonment, from enslavement by others. The rest is extension of this sense, or else metaphor. To strive to be free is to seek to remove obstacles; to struggle for personal freedom is to seek to curb interference, exploitation, enslavement by men whose ends are theirs, not one's own. Freedom, at least in its political sense, is coterminous with the absence of bullying or domination. Nevertheless, freedom is not the only value that can or should determine behaviour. Moreover to speak of freedom as an end is much too general. I should like to say once again to my critics that the issue is not one between negative freedom as an absolute value and other, inferior, values. It is more complex and more painful. One freedom may abort another; one freedom may obstruct or fail to create conditions which make other freedoms, or a larger degree of freedom, or freedom for other persons, possible; positive and negative freedom may collide; the freedom of the individual or the group may not be fully compatible with a full degree of participation in a common life, with its demands for co-operation, solidarity, fraternity. But beyond all these there is an acuter issue: the paramount need to satisfy the claims of other, no less ultimate, values: justice, happiness, love, the realisation of capacities to create new things and experiences and ideas, the discovery of the truth. Nothing is gained by identifying freedom proper, in either of its senses, with these values, or with the conditions of freedom, or by confounding types of freedom with one another. The fact that given examples of negative freedom (especially where they coincide with powers and rights) – say the freedom of parents or schoolmasters to determine the education of children, of employers to exploit or dismiss their workers, of slave-owners to dispose of their slaves, of the torturer to inflict pain on his victims – may, in many cases, be wholly undesirable, and should in any sane or decent society be curtailed or suppressed, does not render them genuine freedoms any the less; nor does that fact justify us in so

---

[1] The classical – and still, it seems to me, the best – exposition of this state of mind is to be found in Max Weber's distinction between the ethics of conscience and the ethics of responsibility in 'Politics as a Vocation': see Max Weber, *From Max Weber: Essays in Sociology*, trans. and ed. H. H. Gerth and C. Wright Mills (New York, 1946), pp. 77–128.

reformulating the definition of freedom that it is always represented as something good without qualification – always leading to
the best possible consequences, always likely to promote my
'highest' self, always in harmony with the true laws of my own
'real' nature or those of my society, and so on, as has been done in
many a classical exposition of freedom, from Stoicism to the social
doctrines of our day, at the cost of obscuring profound differences.

If either clarity of thought or rationality in action is not to be
hopelessly compromised, such distinctions are of critical importance. Individual freedom may or may not clash with democratic
organisation, and the positive liberty of self-realisation with the
negative liberty of non-interference. Emphasis on negative liberty,
as a rule, leaves more paths for individuals or groups to pursue;
positive liberty, as a rule, opens fewer paths, but with better
reasons or greater resources for moving along them; the two may
or may not clash. Some of my critics are made indignant by the
thought that a man may, on this view, have more 'negative' liberty
under the rule of an easygoing or inefficient despot than in a
strenuous, but intolerant, egalitarian democracy. But there is an
obvious sense in which Socrates would have had more liberty – at
least of speech, and even of action – if, like Aristotle, he had
escaped from Athens, instead of accepting the laws, bad as well as
good, enacted and applied by his fellow citizens in the democracy
of which he possessed, and consciously accepted, full membership.
Similarly, a man may leave a vigorous and genuinely 'participatory'
democratic State in which the social or political pressures are too
suffocating for him, for a climate where there may be less civic
participation, but more privacy, a less dynamic and all-embracing
communal life, less gregariousness, but also less surveillance. This
may appear undesirable to those who look on distaste for public
life or social activity as a symptom of *malaise*, of a deep alienation.
But temperaments differ, and too much enthusiasm for common
norms can lead to intolerance and disregard for the inner life of
man. I understand and share the indignation of democrats; not
only because any negative liberty that I may enjoy in an easygoing
or inefficient despotism is precarious, or confined to a minority,
but because despotism is irrational and unjust and degrading as
such: because it denies human rights even if its subjects are not
discontented; because participation in self-government, is, like
justice, a basic human requirement, an end in itself. Jacobin
'repressive tolerance' destroys individual liberty as effectively as a

despotism (however tolerant) destroys positive liberty and degrades its subjects. Those who endure the defects of one system tend to forget the shortcomings of the other. In different historical circumstances some regimes grow more oppressive than others, and to revolt against them is braver and wiser than to acquiesce. Nevertheless, in resisting great present evils, it is as well not to be blinded to the possible danger of the total triumph of any one principle. It seems to me that no sober observer of the twentieth century can avoid qualms in this matter.[1]

What is true of the confusion of the two freedoms, or of identifying freedom with its conditions, holds in even greater measure of the stretching of the word 'freedom' to include an amalgam of other desirable things – equality, justice, happiness, knowledge, love, creation and other ends that men seek for their own sakes. This confusion is not merely a theoretical error. Those who are obsessed by the truth that negative freedom is worth little without sufficient conditions for its active exercise, or without the satisfaction of other human aspirations, are liable to minimise its importance, to deny it the very title of freedom, to transfer it to something that they regard as more precious, and finally to forget that without it human life, both social and individual, withers away. If I have been too vehement in the defence of it – only one, I may be reminded, among other human values – and have not insisted as much as my critics demand that to ignore other values can lead to evils at least as great, my insistence upon it in a world in which conditions for freedom may demand an even higher priority does not seem to me to invalidate my general analysis and argument.

Finally one may ask what value there is in liberty as such. Is it a response to a basic need of men, or only something presupposed by other fundamental demands? And further, is this an empirical

---

[1] This, indeed, was the point of the penultimate paragraph of *Two Concepts of Liberty*, which was widely taken as an unqualified defence of 'negative' against 'positive' liberty. This was not my intention. This much criticised passage was meant as a defence, indeed, but of a pluralism based on the perception of incompatibility between the claims of equally ultimate ends, against any ruthless monism which solves such problems by eliminating all but one of the rival claimants. I have therefore revised the text (see pp. 216–17 below) to make it clear that I am not offering a blank endorsement of the 'negative' concept as opposed to its 'positive' twin brother, since this would itself constitute precisely the kind of intolerant monism against which the entire argument is directed.

question, to which psychological, anthropological, sociological, historical facts are relevant? Or is it a purely philosophical question, the solution of which lies in the correct analysis of our basic concepts, and for the answer to which the production of examples, whether real or imaginary, and not the factual evidence demanded by empirical enquiries, is sufficient and appropriate? 'Freedom is the essence of man'; 'Frei sein ist nichts – frei werden ist der Himmel' ('To be free is nothing, to become free is very heaven');[1] 'Every man has a right to life, liberty and the pursuit of happiness.'[2] Do these phrases embody propositions resting on some empirical foundation, or have they some other logical status? Are they propositions or disguised commands, emotive expressions, declarations of intent or commitment? What role, if any, does evidence – historical, psychological, sociological – play in establishing truth or validity in these matters? Could it be the case that if the evidence of the facts should go against us, we should have to revise our ideas, or withdraw them altogether, or at best concede that they – these propositions, if they are propositions – hold only for particular societies, or particular times and places, as some relativists claim?[3] Or is their authority shown by philosoph-

---

[1] Quoted without a reference in German, in the article on Fichte in *Entsiklopedicheskii slovar'* (St Petersburg, 1890–1907), vol. 36, p. 50, col. 2, and in Xavier Léon, *Fichte et son temps* (Paris, 1922–7), vol. 1, p. 47; untraced in Fichte, and possibly not correctly attributed to him. Ed.

[2] A reference to the American Declaration of Independence, which includes among men's 'unalienable rights' 'life, liberty and the pursuit of happiness'. Ed.

[3] Émile Faguet once paraphrased Joseph de Maistre by observing that, when Rousseau asked why it was that men who were born free were nevertheless everywhere in chains, this was like asking why it was that sheep, who were born carnivorous, nevertheless everywhere nibbled grass. Émile Faguet, *Politiques et moralistes du dix-neuvième siècle*, 1st series (Paris, 1899), p. 41 [cf. Maistre: 'What does [Rousseau] mean? ... This mad pronouncement, *Man is born free*, is the opposite of the truth', *Oeuvres complètes de J. de Maistre* (Lyon/Paris, 1884–7), vol. 2, p. 338].
Similarly the Russian radical Alexander Herzen observed that we classify creatures by zoological types, according to the characteristics and habits that are most frequently found to be conjoined. Thus, one of the defining attributes of fish is their liability to live in water; hence, despite the existence of flying fish, we do not say of fish in general that their nature or essence – the 'true' end for which they were created – is to fly, since most fish fail to achieve this and do not display the slightest tendency in this direction. Yet in the case of men, and men alone, we say that the nature of man is to seek freedom, even though only very few men in the long life of our race have in fact pursued it, while the vast majority at most

ical analysis which convinces us that indifference to freedom is abnormal, that is, offends against what we conceive of as being specifically human, or, at least, fully human – whether by human beings we mean the average members of our own culture, or men in general, everywhere, at all times? To this it is sufficient, perhaps, to say that those who have ever valued liberty for its own sake believed that to be free to choose, and not to be chosen for, is an inalienable ingredient in what makes human beings human; and that this underlies both the positive demand to have a voice in the laws and practices of the society in which one lives, and to be accorded an area, artificially carved out, if need be, in which one is one's own master, a 'negative' area in which a man is not obliged to account for his activities to any man so far as this is compatible with the existence of organised society.

I should like to add one final qualification. Nothing that I assert in the essay on two concepts of liberty about the frontiers of individual liberty (and this applies to the liberty of groups and associations too) should be taken to mean that freedom in any of its meanings is either inviolable, or sufficient, in some absolute sense. It is not inviolable, because abnormal conditions may occur, in which even the sacred frontiers of which Constant speaks, for instance those violated by retrospective laws, punishment of the innocent, judicial murder, information laid against parents by children, the bearing of false witness, may have to be disregarded if some sufficiently terrible alternative is to be averted. Macfarlane[1] urges this point against me, correctly, it seems to me. Nevertheless, the exception proves the rule: precisely because we regard such situations as being wholly abnormal, and such measures as abhorrent, to be condoned only in emergencies so critical that the choice is between great evils, we recognise that under normal conditions, for the great majority of men, at most times, in most

times have showed little taste for it, and seem contented to be ruled by others, seeking to be well governed by those who provide them with sufficient food, shelter, rules of life, but not to be self-governed. Why should man alone, Herzen asked, be classified in terms of what at most small minorities here or there have ever sought for its own sake, still less actively fought for? This sceptical reflection was uttered by a man whose entire life was dominated by a single-minded passion – the pursuit of liberty, personal and political, of his own and other nations, to which he sacrificed his public career and his private happiness. A. I. Gertsen, *Sobranie sochinenii v tridsati tomakh* (Moscow, 1954–66), vol. 6, pp. 94–5.

[1] op. cit. (p. 32 above, note 1).

places, these frontiers are sacred, that is to say, that to overstep them leads to inhumanity. Conversely, the minimum area that men require if such dehumanisation is to be averted, a minimum which other men, or institutions created by them, are liable to invade, is no more than a minimum; its frontiers are not to be extended against sufficiently stringent claims on the part of other values, including those of positive liberty itself. Nevertheless the proper concept of degrees of individual liberty still seems to me to consist in the extent of the area in which choices are open. This minimum area may be incompatible with arrangements required by other social ideals, theocratic or aristocratic or technocratic and the like, but this claim is what the demand for individual liberty entails. Least of all does it call for abdication by individuals or groups from democratic self-government of the society, after their own nicely calculated corner has been made secure and fenced in against others, leaving all the rest to the play of power politics. An indefinite expansion of the area in which men can freely choose between various possible courses of action may plainly not be compatible with the realisation of other values. Hence, things being as they are, we are compelled to adjust claims, compromise, establish priorities, engage in all those practical operations that social and even individual life has, in fact, always required.

If it is maintained that the identification of the value of liberty with the value of a field of free choice amounts to a doctrine of self-realisation, whether for good or evil ends, and that this is closer to positive than to negative liberty, I shall offer no great objection; only repeat that, as a matter of historical fact, distortions of this meaning of positive liberty (or self-determination), even by so well-meaning a liberal as T. H. Green, so original a thinker as Hegel, or so profound a social analyst as Marx, obscured this thesis and at times transformed it into its opposite. Kant, who stated his moral and social position a good deal less equivocally, denounced paternalism, since self-determination is precisely what it obstructs; even if it is indispensable for curing certain evils at certain times, it is, for opponents of tyranny, at best a necessary evil; as are all great accumulations of power as such. Those who maintain[1] that such concentrations are sometimes required to remedy injustices, or to increase the insufficient liberties of individuals or groups, tend to ignore or play down the reverse of the coin: that much power (and

---

[1] As do L. J. Macfarlane, ibid., and the majority of democratic theorists.

authority) is also, as a rule, a standing threat to fundamental liberties. All those who have protested against tyranny in modern times, from Montesquieu to the present day, have struggled with this problem. The doctrine that accumulations of power can never be too great, provided that they are rationally controlled and used, ignores the central reason for pursuing liberty in the first place – that all paternalist governments, however benevolent, cautious, disinterested and rational, have tended, in the end, to treat the majority of men as minors, or as being too often incurably foolish or irresponsible; or else as maturing so slowly as not to justify their liberation at any clearly foreseeable date (which, in practice, means at no definite time at all). This is a policy which degrades men, and seems to me to rest on no rational or scientific foundation, but, on the contrary, on a profoundly mistaken view of the deepest human needs.

I have, in the essays that follow, attempted to examine some of the fallacies that rest on misunderstanding of certain central human needs and purposes – central, that is, to our normal notion of what it is to be a human being; a being endowed with a nucleus of needs and goals, a nucleus common to all men, which may have a shifting pattern, but one whose limits are determined by the basic need to communicate with other similar beings. The notion of such a nucleus and such limits enters into our conception of the central attributes and functions in terms of which we think of men and societies.

I am only too fully conscious of some of the difficulties and obscurities which my thesis still contains. But short of writing another book, I could do no more than deal with those criticisms which seemed to me at once the most frequent and the least effective, resting as they do on an over-simple application of particular scientific or philosophical principles to social and political problems. But even here I am well aware of how much more needs to be done, especially on the issue of free will, the solution of which seems to me to require a set of new conceptual tools, a break with traditional terminology, which no one, so far as I know, has yet been able to provide.

POLITICAL IDEAS IN THE
TWENTIETH CENTURY

Anyone desiring a quiet life has done badly to be born
in the twentieth century.

L. Trotsky[1]

I

HISTORIANS OF IDEAS, however scrupulous and minute they may
feel it necessary to be, cannot avoid perceiving their material in
terms of some kind of pattern. To say this is not necessarily to
subscribe to any form of Hegelian dogma about the dominant role
of laws and metaphysical principles in history – a view increasingly
influential in our time – according to which there is some single
explanation of the order and attributes of persons, things, and
events. Usually this consists in the advocacy of some fundamental
category or principle which claims to act as an infallible guide both
to the past and to the future, a magic lens revealing 'inner',
inexorable, all-pervasive historical laws, invisible to the naked eye
of the mere recorder of events, but capable, when understood, of
giving the historian a unique sense of certainty – certainty not only
of what in fact occurred, but of the reason why it could not have
occurred otherwise, affording a secure knowledge which the mere
empirical investigator, with his collections of data, his insecure
structure of painstakingly accumulated evidence, his tentative

This article was written in 1949 at the request of the editor [Hamilton Fish
Armstrong] of the American journal *Foreign Affairs*, for its mid-century issue. Its
tone was to some extent due to the policies of the Soviet regime during Stalin's
last years. Since then a modification of the worst excesses of that dictatorship has
fortunately taken place; but the general tendency with which the issue was
concerned seems to me, if anything, to have gained, if not in intensity, then in
extent: some of the new national states of Asia and Africa seem to show no
greater concern for civil liberties, even allowing for the exigencies of security and
planning which these States need for their development or survival, than the
regimes they have replaced. [1969]

[1] [Untraced.]

approximations and perpetual liability to error and reassessment, can never hope to attain.[1]

The notion of 'laws' of this kind is rightly condemned as a species of metaphysical fantasy; but the contrary notion of bare facts – facts which are nothing but facts, hard, inescapable, untainted by interpretation or arrangement in man-made patterns – is equally mythological. To comprehend and contrast and classify and arrange, to see in patterns of lesser or greater complexity, is not a peculiar kind of thinking, it is thinking itself. We accuse historians of exaggeration, distortion, ignorance, bias or departure from the facts, not because they select, compare and set forth in a context and order which are in part, at least, of their own choosing, in part conditioned by the circumstances of their material and social environment or their character or purpose – we accuse them only when the result deviates too far from, contrasts too harshly with, the accepted canons of verification and interpretation which belong to their own time and place and society. These canons and methods and categories are those of the normal rational outlook of a given period and culture, at their best a sharpened, highly trained form of this outlook, which takes cognisance of all the relevant scientific techniques available, but is itself not one of them. All the criticisms directed against this or that writer for an excess of bias or fancy, or too weak a sense of evidence, or too limited a perception of connections between events, are based not upon some absolute standard of truth, of strict 'factuality', of a rigid adherence to a permanently fixed, ideal method of 'scientifically' discovering the past *wie es eigentlich gewesen*,[2] in contrast with mere theories about it, for there is in the last analysis no meaning in the notion of 'objective' criticism in this timeless sense. They rest rather on the most refined concepts of accuracy and objectivity and scrupulous 'fidelity to the facts' that obtain in a given society at a given period, within the subject in question.

When the great romantic revolution in the writing of history transferred emphasis from the achievements of individuals to the growth and influence of institutions conceived in much less personal terms, the degree of 'fidelity to the facts' was not thereby automatically altered. The new kind of history – the account of the

[1] I do not, of course, attribute this view either to Hegel or to Marx, whose doctrines are both more complex and far more plausible; only to the *terribles simplificateurs* among their followers.
[2] 'As it really was.'

development, let us say, of public and private law, or government, or literature, or social habits during some given period of time – was not necessarily less or more accurate or 'objective' than earlier accounts of the acts and fate of Alcibiades or Marcus Aurelius or Calvin or Louis XIV. Thucydides or Tacitus or Voltaire were not subjective or vague or fanciful in a sense in which Ranke or Savigny or Michelet were not. The new history was merely written from what is nowadays called a different 'angle'. The kinds of fact the new history was intended to record were different, the emphasis was different, a shift of interest had occurred in the questions asked and consequently in the methods used. The concepts and terminology reflect an altered view of what consti- tutes evidence and therefore, in the end, of what the 'facts' are. When the 'romances' of chroniclers were criticised by 'scientific' historians, at least part of the implied reproach lay in the alleged discrepancies in the work of the older writers from the findings of the most admired and trusted sciences of a later period; and these were in their turn due to the change in the prevalent conceptions of the patterns of human development – to the change in the models in terms of which the past was perceived, those artistic, theological, mechanical, biological or psychological models which were reflected in the fields of enquiry, in the new questions asked and the new types of technique used, to answer questions felt to be more interesting or important than those which had become outmoded.

The history of these changes of 'models' is to a large degree the history of human thought. The 'organic' or the Marxist methods of investigating history certainly owed part of their vogue to the prestige of the particular natural sciences, or the particular artistic techniques, upon whose model they were supposedly or genuinely constructed; the increased interest, for example, both in biology and in music, from which many basic metaphors and analogies derived, is relevant to the historical writing of the nineteenth century, as the new interest in physics and mathematics is to the philosophy and history of the eighteenth; and the deflationary methods and ironical temper of the historians who wrote after the war of 1914–18 were conspicuously influenced by – and accepted in terms of – the new psychological and sociological techniques which had gained public confidence during this period. The relative dominance of, say, social, economic and political concepts and presuppositions in a once admired historical work throws more light upon the general characteristics of its time and for this reason is a more reliable index to the standards adopted, the questions asked, the respective roles of 'facts' and 'interpretation', and, in effect, the entire social and political outlook of an age, than the putative distance of the work in question from some imaginary, fixed, unaltering ideal of absolute truth, metaphysical or scientific, empirical or a priori. It is in terms of such shifts in the methods of treating the past (or the present or the future), and in the idioms and catchwords, the doubts and hopes, fears and exhortations which they expressed, that the development of political ideas and the conceptual apparatus of society and of its most gifted and articulate representatives can best be judged. No doubt the concepts in terms of which people speak and think may be symptoms and effects of other processes – social, psychological, physical – the discovery of which is the task of this or that empirical science. But this does not detract from their importance and paramount interest for those who wish to know what constitutes the conscious experience of the most characteristic men of an age or a society, whatever its causes and whatever its fate. And we are, of course, for obvious reasons of perspective, in a better situation to determine this in the case of past societies than for our own. The historical approach is inescapable: the very sense of contrast and dissimilarity with which the past affects us provides the only relevant background against which the features peculiar to our own experience stand out in sufficient relief to be adequately discerned and described.

The student of the political ideas of, for example, the mid-nineteenth century must indeed be blind if he does not, sooner or later, become aware of the profound differences in ideas and terminology, in the general view of things – the ways in which the elements of experience are conceived to be related to one another – which divide that not very distant age from our own. He understands neither that time nor his own if he does not perceive the contrast between what was common to Comte and Mill, Mazzini and Michelet, Herzen and Marx, on the one hand, and to Max Weber and William James, Tawney and Beard, Lytton Strachey and Namier, on the other; the continuity of the European intellectual tradition without which no historical understanding at all would be possible is, at shorter range, a succession of specific discontinuities and dissimilarities. Consequently, the remarks which follow deliberately ignore the similarities in favour of the specific differences in political outlook which characterise our own time, and, to a large degree, solely our own.

II

The two great liberating political movements of the nineteenth century were, as every history book informs us, humanitarian individualism and romantic nationalism. Whatever their differences – and they were notoriously profound enough to lead to a sharp divergence and ultimate collision of these two ideals – they had this in common: they believed that the problems both of individuals and of societies could be solved if only the forces of intelligence and of virtue could be made to prevail over ignorance and wickedness. They believed, as against the pessimists and fatalists, both religious and secular, whose voices, audible indeed a good deal earlier, began to sound loudly only towards the end of the century, that all clearly understood questions could be solved by human beings with the moral and intellectual resources at their disposal. No doubt different schools of thought returned different answers to these varying problems; utilitarians said one thing, and neo-feudal romantics – Tory democrats, Christian Socialists, Pan-Germans, Slavophils – another. Liberals believed in the unlimited power of education and the power of rational morality to over-come economic misery and inequality. Socialists, on the contrary, believed that without radical alterations in the distribution and control of economic resources no amount of change of heart or mind on the part of individuals could be adequate; or, for that matter, occur at all. Conservatives and socialists believed in the power and influence of institutions and regarded them as a necessary safeguard against the chaos, injustice and cruelty caused by uncontrolled individualism; anarchists, radicals and liberals looked upon institutions as such with suspicion as being obstruc-tive to the realisation of that free (and, in the view of most such thinkers, rational) society which the will of man could both conceive and build, if it were not for the unliquidated residue of ancient abuses (or unreason) upon which the existing rulers of society – whether individuals or administrative machines – leaned too heavily, and of which so many of them indeed were typical expressions.

Arguments about the relative degree of the obligation of the individual to society, and vice versa, filled the air. It is scarcely necessary to rehearse these familiar questions, which to this day form the staple of discussion in the more conservative institutions of Western learning, to realise that however wide the disagreements about the proper answers to them, the questions themselves were common to liberals and conservatives alike. There were, of course, even at that time isolated irrationalists – Stirner, Kierkegaard, in certain moods Carlyle – but in the main all the parties to the great controversies, even Calvinists and ultramontane Catholics, accepted the notion of man as resembling in varying degrees one or the other of two idealised types. Either he is a creature free and naturally good, but hemmed in and frustrated[1] by obsolete or corrupt or sinister institutions masquerading as saviours, protectors and repositories of sacred traditions; or he is a being within limits, but never wholly, free, and to some degree, but never entirely, good, and consequently unable to save himself by his own wholly unaided efforts; and therefore rightly seeking salvation within the great frameworks – States, Churches, unions. For only these great edifices promote solidarity, security and sufficient strength to resist the shallow joys and dangerous, ultimately self-destructive, liberties peddled by those conscienceless or self-deceived individualists who, in the name of some bloodless intellectual dogma, or noble enthusiasm for an ideal unrelated to human lives, ignore or destroy the rich texture of social life, heavy with treasures from the past – blind leaders of the blind, robbing men of their most precious resources, exposing them again to the perils of a life that was 'solitary, poor, nasty, brutish and short'.[2] Yet there was at least one premiss common to all the disputants, namely the belief that the problems were real, that it took men of exceptional training and intelligence to formulate them properly, and men with exceptional grasp of the facts, will-power and capacity for effective thought to find and apply the correct solutions.

These two great currents finally ended in exaggerated and indeed distorted forms as Communism and Fascism – the first as the treacherous heir of the liberal internationalism of the previous century, the second as the culmination and bankruptcy of the mystical patriotism which animated the national movements of the

---

[1] According to some, for historically or metaphysically inevitable reasons or causes which, however, soon or late, will lose their potency.

[2] Thomas Hobbes, *Leviathan* (1651), part 1, chapter 13.

time. All movements have origins, forerunners, imperceptible beginnings: nor does the twentieth century seem divided from the nineteenth by so universal an explosion as the French Revolution, even in our day the greatest of all historical landmarks. Yet it is a fallacy to regard Fascism and Communism as being in the main only more uncompromising and violent manifestations of an earlier crisis, the culmination of a struggle fully discernible long before. The differences between the political movements of the twentieth century and the nineteenth are very sharp, and they spring from factors whose full force was not properly realised until our century was well under way. For there is a barrier which divides what is unmistakably past and done with from that which most characteristically belongs to our day. The familiarity of this barrier must not blind us to its relative novelty. One of the elements of the new outlook is the notion of unconscious and irrational influences which outweigh the forces of reason; another the notion that answers to problems exist not in rational solutions, but in the removal of the problems themselves by means other than thought and argument. The interplay between the old tradition, which saw history as the battleground between the easily identifiable forces of light and darkness, reason and obscurantism, progress and reaction; or alternatively between spiritualism and empiricism, intuition and scientific method, institutionalism and individualism – the conflict between this order and, on the other hand, the new factors violently opposed to the humanist psychology of bourgeois civilisation is to a large extent the history of political ideas in our time.

III

And yet to a casual observer of the politics and the thought of the twentieth century it might at first seem that every idea and movement typical of our time is best understood as a natural development of tendencies already prominent in the nineteenth century. In the case of the growth of international institutions, for instance, this seems a truism. What are the Hague Court, the old League of Nations and its modern successor, the numerous pre-war and post-war international agencies and conventions for political, economic, social and humanitarian purposes – what are they, if not the direct descendants of that liberal internationalism –

Tennyson's 'Parliament of man'[1] – which was the staple of all progressive thought and action in the nineteenth century, and indeed of much in the century before it? The language of the great founders of European liberalism – Condorcet, for example, or Helvétius – does not differ greatly in substance, or indeed in form, from the most characteristic moments in the speeches of Woodrow Wilson or Thomas Masaryk. European liberalism wears the appearance of a single coherent movement, little altered during almost three centuries, founded upon relatively simple intellectual foundations, laid by Locke or Grotius or even Spinoza; stretching back to Erasmus and Montaigne, the Italian Renaissance, Seneca and the Greeks. In this movement there is in principle a rational answer to every question. Man is, in principle at least, everywhere and in every condition able, if he wills it, to discover and apply rational solutions to his problems. And these solutions, because they are rational, cannot clash with one another, and will ultimately form a harmonious system in which the truth will prevail, and freedom, happiness and unlimited opportunity for untrammelled self-development will be open to all.

The consciousness of history which grew in the nineteenth century modified the severe and simple design of the classical theory as it was conceived in the eighteenth century. Human progress was presently seen to be conditioned by factors of greater complexity than had been conceived of in the springtime of liberal individualism: education, rationalist propaganda, even legislation were perhaps not always, or everywhere, quite enough. Such factors as the particular and special influences by which various societies were historically shaped – some due to physical conditions, others to socio-economic forces or to more elusive emotional and what were vaguely classified as 'cultural' factors – were presently allowed to have greater importance than they were accorded in the over-simple schemas of Condorcet or Bentham. Education, and all forms of social action, must, it was now thought, be fitted to take account of historical needs which made men and their institutions somewhat less easy to mould into the required pattern than had been too optimistically assumed in earlier and more naïve times.

Nevertheless, the original programme continued in its various forms to exercise an almost universal spell. This applied to the right

---

[1] 'Locksley Hall' (1842), line 128.

no less than to the left. Conservative thinkers, unless they were concerned solely with obstructing the liberals and their allies, believed and acted upon the belief that, provided no excessive violence was done to slow but certain processes of 'natural' development, all might yet be well; the faster must be restricted from pushing aside the slower, and in this way all would arrive in the end. This was the doctrine preached by Bonald early in the century, and it expressed the optimism of even the stoutest believers in original sin. Provided that traditional differences of outlook and social structure were protected from what conservatives were fond of describing as the 'unimaginative', 'artificial', 'mechanical' levelling processes favoured by the liberals; provided that the infinity of 'intangible' or 'historic' or 'natural' or 'providential' distinctions (which to them seemed to constitute the essence of fruitful forms of life) were preserved from being transformed into a uniform collection of homogeneous units moving at a pace dictated by some 'irrelevant' or 'extraneous' authority, contemptuous of prescriptive or traditional rights and habits; provided that adequate safeguards were instituted against too reckless a trampling upon the sacred past – with these guarantees, rational reforms and changes were allowed to be feasible and even desirable. Given these safeguards, conservatives no less than liberals were prepared to look upon the conscious direction of human affairs by qualified experts with a considerable degree of approval; and not merely by experts, but by a growing number of individuals and groups, drawn from, and representing, wider and wider sections of a society which was progressively becoming more and more enlightened.

This is a mood and attitude common to a wider section of opinion in the later nineteenth century in Europe, and not merely in the West but in the East too, than historians, affected by the political struggles of a later or earlier period, have allowed. One of the results of it – in so far as it was a causal factor and not merely a symptom of the process – was the wide development of political representation in the West, whereby in the end all classes of the population in the succeeding century began to attain to power, sooner or later, in one country or another. The nineteenth century was full of unrepresented groups engaged in the struggle for life, for self-expression, and later for control. Their members included the heroes and martyrs and men of moral and artistic power whom a genuine struggle of this kind brings forth. The twentieth century, by satisfying much of the social and political hunger of the Victorian period, did indeed witness a striking improvement in the material condition of the majority of the peoples of Western Europe, due in large measure to the energetic social legislation which transformed the social order.

But one of the least predicted results of this trend (although isolated thinkers like Tocqueville, Burckhardt, Herzen and, of course, Nietzsche had more than an inkling of it) was a decline in the quality of moral passion and force and of romantic, artistic rebelliousness which had marked the early struggles of the dissatisfied social groups during their heroic period, when, deeply divergent though they were, they fought together against tyrants, priests and militant philistines. Whatever the injustices and miseries of our time – and they are plainly no fewer than those of the immediate past – they are less likely to find expression in monuments of noble eloquence, because that kind of inspiration seems to spring only from the oppression or suppression of entire classes of society.[1] There arrives a brief moment when, as indeed Marx with much insight pointed out, the leaders of the most articulate, and socially and economically most developed, of these suppressed groups are lifted by the common mood and for a moment speak not for their own class or milieu alone, but in the name of all the oppressed; for a brief instant their utterance has a universal quality.

But a situation where all or nearly all the great sections of society have been, or are on the point of being, in at any rate the formal possession of power is unfavourable to that truly disinterested eloquence – disinterested partly at least because fulfilment is remote, because principles shine forth most clearly in the darkness and void, because the inner vision is still free from the confusions and obscurities, the compromises and blurred outlines of the external world inevitably forced upon it by the beginnings of practical action. No body of men which has tasted power, or is within a short distance of doing so, can avoid a certain degree of that cynicism which, like a chemical reaction, is generated by the sharp contact between the pure ideal, nurtured in the wilderness, and its realisation in some unpredicted form which seldom conforms to the hopes or fears of earlier times. It therefore takes an

---

[1] Hence, perhaps, the very different quality of the tone and substance of social protest, however legitimate, in the West in our time, as compared to that of Asian or African critics who speak for societies where large sections of the population are still crushed or submerged.

exceptional effort of the imagination to discard the context of later years, to cast ourselves back into the period when the views and movements which have since triumphed and lost their glamour long ago were still capable of stirring so much vehement idealistic feeling: when, for example, nationalism was not felt to be in principle incompatible with a growing degree of internationalism, or civil liberties with a rational organisation of society; when this was believed by some conservatives almost as much as their rivals, and the gap between the moderates of both sides was only that between the plea that reason must not be permitted to increase the pace of progress beyond the limits imposed by 'history' and the counterplea that *la raison a toujours raison*, that memories and shadows were less important than the direct perception of the real world in the clear light of day. This was a time when liberals in their turn themselves began to feel the impact of historicism, and to admit the need for a certain degree of adjustment and even control of social life, perhaps by the hated State itself, if only to mitigate the inhumanity of unbridled private enterprise, to protect the liberties of the weak, to safeguard those basic human rights without which there could be neither happiness nor justice nor freedom to pursue that which made life worth living.

The philosophical foundations of these liberal beliefs in the mid-nineteenth century were somewhat obscure. Rights described as 'natural' or 'inherent', absolute standards of truth and justice, were not compatible with tentative empiricism and utilitarianism; yet liberals believed in both. Nor was faith in full democracy strictly consistent with belief in the inviolable rights of minorities or dissident individuals. But so long as the right-wing opposition set itself against all these principles, the contradictions could, on the whole, be allowed to lie dormant, or to form the subject of peaceful academic disputes, not exacerbated by the urgent need for immediate practical application. Indeed, the very recognition of inconsistencies in doctrine or policy further enhanced the role of rational criticism, by which, in the end, all questions could and would one day be settled. Socialists for their part resembled the conservatives in believing in the existence of inexorable laws of history, and, like them, accused the liberals of legislating 'unhistorically' for timeless abstractions – an activity for which history would not neglect to take due revenge. But they also resembled the liberals in believing in the supreme value of rational analysis, in policies founded on theoretical considerations deduced from 'scientific' premisses, and with them accused the conservatives of misinterpreting 'the facts' to justify the miserable status quo, of condoning misery and injustice; not indeed, like the liberals, by ignoring history, but by misreading it in a manner consciously or unconsciously calculated to preserve their own power upon a specious moral basis. But genuinely revolutionary as some among them were, and a thoroughly new phenomenon in the Western world, the majority of them shared with the parties which they attacked the common assumption that men must be spoken and appealed to in terms of the needs and interests and ideals of which they were, or could be made to be, conscious.

Conservatives, liberals, radicals, socialists differed in their interpretation of historical change. They disagreed about what were the deepest needs, interests, ideals of human beings, about who held them, and how deeply or widely or for what length of time, about the method of their discovery, or their validity in this or that situation. They differed about the facts, they differed about ends and means, they seemed to themselves to agree on almost nothing. But what they had in common – too obviously to be fully aware of it themselves – was the belief that their age was ridden with social and political problems which could be solved only by the conscious application of truths upon which all men endowed with adequate mental powers could agree. The Marxists did indeed question this in theory, but not in practice: even they did not seriously attack the thesis that when ends were not yet attained and choice of means was limited, the proper way of setting about adapting the means to the ends was by the use of all the skill and energy and intellectual and moral insight available. And while some regarded these problems as akin to those of the natural sciences, some to those of ethics or religion, while others supposed that they were altogether *sui generis* and called for altogether unique solutions, they were agreed – it seemed too obvious to need stating – that the problems themselves were genuine and urgent and intelligible in more or less similar terms to all clear-headed men, that all answers were entitled to a hearing, and that nothing was gained by ignorance or the supposition that the problems did not exist.

This set of common assumptions – they are part of what the word 'Enlightenment' means – were, of course, deeply rationalistic. They were denied implicitly by the whole romantic movement, and explicitly by isolated thinkers – Carlyle, Dostoevsky, Baudelaire, Schopenhauer, Nietzsche. And there were obscurer prophets

– Büchner, Kierkegaard, Leontiev – who protested against the prevailing orthodoxy with a depth and originality which became clear only in our own time. Not that these thinkers represent any one single movement, or even an easily identifiable 'trend'; but in one relevant particular they display an affinity. They denied the importance of political action based on rational considerations, and to this extent they were rightly abhorred by the supporters of respectable conservatism. They said or implied that rationalism in any form was a fallacy derived from a false analysis of the character of human beings, because the springs of human action lay in regions unthought of by the sober thinkers whose views enjoyed prestige among the serious public. But their voices were few and discordant, and their eccentric views were ascribed to psychological aberrations. Liberals, however much they admired their artistic genius, were revolted by what they conceived as a perverted view of mankind, and either ignored it or rejected it violently. Conservatives looked upon them as allies against the exaggerated rationalism and infuriating optimism of both liberals and socialists, but treated them nervously as queer visionaries, a little unhinged, not to be imitated or approached too closely. The socialists looked on them as so many deranged reactionaries, scarcely worth their powder and shot. The main currents both on the right and on the left flowed round and over these immovable, isolated rocks with their absurd appearance of seeking to arrest or deflect the central current. What were they, after all, but survivals of a darker age, or interesting misfits, sad and at times fascinating casualties of the advance of history, worthy of sympathetic insight – men of talent or even genius born out of their time, gifted poets, remarkable artists, but surely not thinkers worthy of detailed attention on the part of serious students of social and political life?

There was (it is worth saying again) a somewhat sinister element dimly discernible from its very beginning in Marxism – in the main a highly rationalistic system – which seemed hostile to this entire outlook, denying the primacy of the individual's reason in the choice of ends and in effective government alike. But the worship of the natural sciences as the sole proper model for political theory and action which Marxism shared with its liberal antagonists was unpropitious to a clearer perception of its own full nature; and so this aspect of it lay largely unrecognised until Sorel brought it to life and combined it with the Bergsonian anti-rationalism by which his thought is very strongly coloured; and until Lenin, stemming from a different tradition, with his genius for organisation half instinctively recognised its superior insight into the irrational springs of human conduct, and translated it into effective practice. But Lenin did not, and his followers to this day do not, seem fully aware of the degree to which this essentially romantic element in Marxism influenced their actions. Or, if aware, they did not and do not admit it. This was so when the twentieth century opened.

IV

Chronological frontiers are seldom landmarks in the history of ideas, and the current of the old century, to all appearances irresistible, seemed to flow peacefully into the new. Presently the picture began to alter. Humanitarian liberalism encountered more and more obstacles to its reforming zeal from the conscious or unconscious opposition both of governments and other centres of social power, as well as the passive resistance of established institutions and habits. Militant reformers found themselves compelled to use increasingly radical means in organising the classes of the population on whose behalf they fought into something sufficiently powerful to work effectively against the old establishment.

The history of the transformation of gradualist and Fabian tactics into the militant formations of Communism and syndicalism, as well as the milder formations of social democracy and trade unionism, is a history not so much of principles as of their interplay with new material facts. In a sense Communism is doctrinaire humanitarianism driven to an extreme in the pursuit of effective offensive and defensive methods. No movement at first sight seems to differ more sharply from liberal reformism than does Marxism, yet the central doctrines – human perfectibility, the possibility of creating a harmonious society by a natural means, the belief in the compatibility (indeed the inseparability) of liberty and equality – are common to both. The historical transformation may occur continuously, or in sudden revolutionary leaps, but it must proceed in accordance with an intelligible, logically connected pattern, abandonment of which is always foolish, always Utopian. No one doubted that liberalism and socialism were bitterly opposed both on ends and in methods: yet at their edges they shaded off into one another.[1] Marxism is a doctrine which,

[1] The history and the logic of the transformation of liberalism in the

however strongly it may stress the class-conditioned nature of action and thought, nevertheless in theory sets out to appeal to reason, at least among the class destined by history to triumph – the proletariat alone can face the future without flinching, because it need not be driven into falsification of the facts by fear of what the future may bring. And, as a corollary, this applies also to those intellectuals who have liberated themselves from the prejudices and rationalisations – the 'ideological distortions' of their economic class – and have aligned themselves with the winning side in the social struggle. To them, since they are fully rational, the privileges of democracy and of free use of all their intellectual faculties may be accorded. They are to Marxists what the enlightened *philosophes* were to the Encyclopaedists: their task is to free men from 'false consciousness' and help to realise the means that will transform all those who are historically capable of it into their own liberated and rational likeness.

But in 1903 there occurred an event which marked the culmination of a process which has altered the history of our world. At the second congress of the Russian Social Democratic Party held in that year, which began in Brussels and ended in London, during the discussion of what seemed at first a purely technical question – how far centralisation and hierarchical discipline should govern the behaviour of the Party – a delegate whose name was Mandel'berg but who had adopted the *nom de guerre* of Posadovsky argued that the emphasis laid by the 'hard' socialists – Lenin and his friends – upon the need for the exercise of absolute authority by the revolutionary nucleus of the Party might prove incompatible with those fundamental liberties to whose realisation socialism, no less than liberalism, was officially dedicated. He insisted that the basic, minimum civil liberties – 'the sanctity of the person' – should be infringed and even violated if the party leaders so decided.[1] He

---

nineteenth century into socialism in the twentieth is a complex and fascinating subject of cardinal importance; but cannot, for reasons of space and relevance, even be touched upon in this short essay.

[1] According to the official account of the proceedings (I owe this information to Chimen Abramsky's expert knowledge), Posadovsky said:

> The statements made here for and against the amendments seem to me not mere differences about details, but to amount to a serious disagreement. There is no doubt that we do not agree about the following fundamental question: *Must we subordinate our future policies to this or that fundamental democratic principle or principles, recognising them as absolute values; or must all*

was supported by Plekhanov, one of the founders of Russian Marxism, and its most venerated figure, a cultivated, fastidious and morally sensitive scholar of wide outlook, who had for twenty years lived in Western Europe and was much respected by leaders of Western socialism, the very symbol of civilised 'scientific' thinking among Russian revolutionaries. Plekhanov, speaking solemnly, and with a splendid disregard for grammar, pronounced the words 'Salus revolutiae suprema lex.'[1] Certainly, if the revolution demanded it, everything – democracy, liberty, the rights of the individual – must be sacrificed to it. If the democratic assembly elected by the Russian people after the revolution proved amenable to Marxist tactics, it would be kept in being as a Long Parliament; if not, it would be disbanded as quickly as possible. A Marxist revolution could not be carried through by men obsessed by scrupulous regard for the principles of bourgeois liberals. Doubtless whatever was valuable in these principles, like everything else good and desirable, would ultimately be realised by the victorious working class; but during the revolutionary period preoccupation with such ideals was evidence of a lack of seriousness.

Plekhanov, who was brought up in a humane and liberal

> *democratic principles be subordinated exclusively to the objectives of our party?* I am quite definitely in favour of the latter. There are absolutely no democratic principles which we ought not to subordinate to the *objectives of our party*.' (Cries of 'And the sanctity of the person?') 'Yes, that too! As a revolutionary party, striving towards its final goal – *the social revolution* – we must be guided exclusively by considerations of what will help us to achieve this goal most rapidly. We must look on democratic principles solely from the point of view of the *objectives* of our party; if this or that claim does not suit us, we shall not allow it.
>
> Hence I am against the amendments that have been offered, because one day they may have the effect of curtailing our freedom of action.

Plekhanov merely dotted the 'i's and crossed the 't's of this unequivocal declaration, the first of its kind, so far as I know, in the history of European democracy. [Posadovsky's remarks appear on p. 169 in *Izveshchenie o vtorom ocherednom s'ezde Rossiiskoi Sotsial'demokraticheskoi Rabochei Partii* (Geneva, 1903), and on p. 181 in both *Protokoly s'ezdov i konferentsii Vsesoyuznoi Kommunisticheskoi Partii (B): vtoroi s'ezd RSDRP, iyul'–avgust 1903 g.*, ed. S. I. Gusev and P. N. Lepeshinsky (Moscow, 1932), and *Vtoroi s'ezd RSDRP, iyul'–avgust 1903 goda: protokoly* (Moscow, 1959).]

[1] 'The safety of the revolution is the highest law': ibid., p. 182. The erroneous 'revolutiae', which appears in Plekhanov's notes, and in the 1903 and 1932 volumes cited in the previous note, has been replaced by the correct 'revolutionis' in the 1959 edition: see 1932 ed., p. 182, note **. Ed.

tradition, did, of course, later retreat from this position himself. The mixture of Utopian faith and brutal disregard for civilised morality proved in the end too repulsive to a man who had spent the greater part of his civilised and productive life among Western workers and their leaders. Like the vast majority of Social Democrats, like Marx and Engels themselves, he was too European to try to realise a policy which, in the words of Shigalev in Dostoevsky's *The Devils*, 'starting from unlimited freedom [arrives] at unlimited despotism'.[1] But Lenin (like Posadovsky himself) accepted the premises, and, being logically driven to conclusions repulsive to most of his colleagues, accepted them easily and without apparent qualms. His assumptions were, perhaps, in some sense, still those of the optimistic rationalists of the eighteenth and nineteenth centuries: the coercion, violence, executions, the total suppression of individual differences, the rule of a small, virtually self-appointed minority were necessary only in the interim period, only so long as there was a powerful enemy to be destroyed. They were necessary only in order that the majority of mankind, once it was liberated from the exploitation of fools by knaves and of weak knaves by more powerful ones, could develop – trammelled no longer by ignorance or idleness or vice, free at last to realise to their fullest extent the infinitely rich potentialities of human nature. This dream may indeed have affinities with the dreams of Diderot or Saint-Simon or Kropotkin, but what marked it as something relatively novel was the assumption about the means required to translate it into reality. And the assumption, although apparently concerned solely with methods, and derived from Babeuf or Blanqui or Tkachev or the French Communards – or, as is quite likely, from Marx's own writings in 1847–51 – was very different from the practical programme set forth by the most 'activist' and least 'evolutionary' Western socialists towards the end of the nineteenth century. The difference was crucial and marked the birth of the new age.

What Lenin demanded was unlimited power for a small body of professional revolutionaries, trained exclusively for one purpose, and ceaselessly engaged in its pursuit by every means in their power. This was necessary because democratic methods, and the attempts to persuade and preach used by earlier reformers and rebels, were ineffective; and this in its turn was due to the fact that

[1] Dostoevsky, *The Devils*, part 2, chapter 7, section 2.

they rested on a false psychology, sociology and theory of history
– namely the assumption that men acted as they did because of
conscious beliefs which could be changed by argument. For if
Marx had done anything, he had surely shown that such beliefs and
ideals were mere 'reflections' of the condition of the socially and
economically determined classes of men, to some one of which
every individual must belong. A man's beliefs, if Marx and Engels
were right, flowed from the situation of his class, and could not
alter – so far, at least, as the mass of men was concerned – without a
change in that situation. The proper task of a revolutionary
therefore was to change the 'objective' situation, that is, to prepare
the class for its historical task in the overthrow of the hitherto
dominant class.

Lenin went further than this. He acted as if he believed not
merely that it was useless to talk and reason with persons
precluded by class interest from understanding and acting upon the
truths of Marxism, but that the mass of the proletarians themselves
were too benighted to grasp the role which history had called on
them to play. He saw the choice as being one between education,
the stimulation among the army of the dispossessed of a 'critical
spirit' (which would awaken them intellectually, but might lead to
a vast deal of discussion and controversy similar to that which
divided and enfeebled the intellectuals), and the turning of them
into an obedient force held together by a military discipline and a
set of perpetually ingeminated formulae (at least as powerful as the
patriotic patter used by the tsarist regime) to shut out independent
thought. If the choice had to be made, then it was mere irresponsibility to stress the former in the name of some abstract principle
such as democracy or enlightenment. The important thing was the
creation of a state of affairs in which human resources were
developed in accordance with a rational pattern. Men were moved
more often by irrational than by reasonable solutions. The masses
were too stupid and too blind to be allowed to proceed in the
direction of their own choosing. Tolstoy and the populists were
profoundly mistaken: the simple agricultural labourer had no deep
truths, no valuable way of life, to impart; he and the city worker
and the simple soldier were fellow serfs in a condition of abject
poverty and squalor, caught in a system which bred fratricidal
strife among themselves; they could be saved only by being
ruthlessly ordered by leaders who had acquired a capacity for

knowing how to organise the liberated slaves into a rational planned system.

Lenin himself was in certain respects oddly Utopian. He started with the egalitarian belief that with education, and a rational economic organisation, almost anyone could be brought in the end to perform almost any task efficiently. But his practice was strangely like that of those irrationalist reactionaries who believed that man was everywhere wild, bad, stupid and unruly, and must be held in check and provided with objects of uncritical worship. This must be done by a clear-sighted band of organisers, whose tactics – if not ideals – rested on the truths perceived by élitists – men like Nietzsche, Pareto or the French absolutist thinkers from Maistre to Maurras, and indeed Marx himself – men who had grasped the true nature of social development, and in the light of their discovery saw the liberal theory of human progress as something unreal, thin, pathetic and absurd. Whatever his crudities and errors, on the central issue Hobbes, not Locke, turned out to be right: men sought neither happiness nor liberty nor justice, but, above and before all, security. Aristotle, too, was right: a great number of men were slaves by nature, and when liberated from their chains did not possess the moral and intellectual resources with which to face the prospect of responsibility, of too wide a choice between alternatives; and therefore, having lost one set of chains, inevitably searched for another or forged new chains themselves. It follows that the wise revolutionary legislator, so far from seeking to emancipate human beings from the framework without which they feel lost and desperate, will seek rather to erect a framework of his own, corresponding to the new needs of the new age brought about by natural or technological change. The value of the framework will depend upon the unquestioning faith with which its main features are accepted; otherwise it no longer possesses sufficient strength to support and contain the wayward, potentially anarchical and self-destructive creatures who seek salvation in it. The framework is that system of political, social, economic and religious institutions, those 'myths', dogmas, ideals, categories of thought and language, modes of feeling, scales of values, 'socially approved' attitudes and habits (called by Marx 'superstructure') that represent 'rationalisations', 'sublimations' and symbolic representations, which cause men to function in an organised way, prevent chaos, fulfil the function of the Hobbesian State. This view, which inspires Jacobin tactics, though not, of course, either Jacobin or Communist doctrines, is not so very remote from Maistre's central and deliberately unprobed mystery – the supernatural authority whereby and in whose name rulers can rule and inhibit their subjects' unruly tendencies, above all the tendency to ask too many questions, to question too many established rules. Nothing can be permitted which might even a little weaken that sense of reliability and security which it is the business of the framework to provide. Only thus (in this view) can the founder of the new free society control whatever threatens to dissipate human energy or to slow down the relentless treadmill which alone prevents men from stopping to commit acts of suicidal folly, which alone protects them from too much freedom, from too little restraint, from the vacuum which mankind, no less than nature, abhors.

Henri Bergson had (following the German romantics) been speaking of something not too unlike this when he had contrasted the flow of life with the forces of critical reason which cannot create or unite, but only divide, arrest, make dead, disintegrate. Freud, too, contributed to this; not in his work of genius as the greatest healer and psychological theorist of our time, but as the originator, however innocent, of the misapplication of rational psychological and social methods by muddle-headed men of goodwill and quacks and false prophets of every hue. By giving currency to exaggerated versions of the view that the true reasons for men's beliefs were most often very different from what they themselves thought them to be, being frequently caused by events and processes of which they were neither aware nor in the least anxious to be aware, these eminent thinkers helped, however unwittingly, to discredit the rational foundations from which their own doctrines derived their logical force. For it was but a short step from this to the view that what made men most permanently contented was not – as they themselves supposed – the discovery of solutions to the questions which perplexed them, but rather some process, natural or artificial, whereby the problems were made to vanish altogether. They vanished because their psychological 'sources' had been diverted or dried up, leaving behind only those less exacting questions whose solutions did not demand resources beyond the patient's strength.

That this short way with the troubled and the perplexed, which underlay much traditionalist, anti-rationalist right-wing thought, should have influenced the left was new indeed. It is this change of attitude to the function and value of the intellect that is perhaps the best indication of the great gap which divided the twentieth century from the nineteenth.

V

The central point which I wish to make is this: during all the centuries of recorded history the course of intellectual endeavour, the purpose of education, the substance of controversies about the truth or value of ideas, presupposed the existence of certain crucial questions, the answers to which were of paramount importance. How valid, it was asked, were the various claims to provide the best methods of arriving at knowledge and truth made by such great and famous disciplines as metaphysics, ethics, theology and the sciences of nature and of man? What was the right life for men to lead, and how was it discovered? Did God exist, and could his purposes be known or even guessed at? Did the universe, and in particular human life, have a purpose? If so, whose purpose did it fulfil? How did one set about answering such questions? Were they, or were they not, analogous to the kind of questions to which the sciences or common sense provided satisfactory, generally accepted, replies? If not, did it make sense to ask them?

And as in metaphysics and ethics, so in politics too. The political problem was concerned, for example, with establishing why any individual or individuals should obey other individuals or associations of individuals. All the classical doctrines which deal with the familiar topics of liberty and authority, sovereignty and natural rights, the ends of the State and the ends of the individual, the General Will and the rights of minorities, secularism and theocracy, functionalism and centralisation – all these are various ways of attempting to formulate methods in terms of which this fundamental question can be answered in a manner compatible with the other beliefs and the general outlook of the enquirer and his generation. Great and sometimes mortal conflicts have arisen over the proper techniques for the answering of such questions. Some sought answers in sacred books, others in direct personal revelation, some in metaphysical insight, others in the pronouncements of infallible sages or in speculative systems or in laborious empirical investigations. The questions were of vital importance for the conduct of life. There were, of course, sceptics in every generation who suggested that there were, perhaps, no final answers, that solutions hitherto provided depended on highly variable factors such as the climate in which the theorist's life was lived, or his social or economic or political condition, or that of his fellows, or his or their emotional disposition, or the kinds of intellectual interests which absorbed him or them. But such sceptics were usually treated either as frivolous and therefore unimportant, or else as unduly disturbing and even dangerous; in times of instability they were liable to persecution. But even they – even Sextus Empiricus or Montaigne or Hume – did not actually doubt the importance of the questions themselves. What they doubted was the possibility of obtaining final and absolute solutions.

It was left to the twentieth century to do something more drastic than this. For the first time it was now conceived that the most effective way of dealing with questions, particularly those recurrent issues which had perplexed and often tormented original and honest minds in every generation, was not by employing the tools of reason, still less those of the most mysterious capacities called 'insight' and 'intuition', but by obliterating the questions them-selves. And this method consists not in removing them by rational means – by proving, for example, that they are founded on intellectual error or verbal muddles or ignorance of the facts – for to prove this would in its turn presuppose the need for rational methods of philosophical or psychological argument. Rather it consists in so treating the questioner that problems which appeared at once overwhelmingly important and utterly insoluble vanish from the questioner's consciousness like evil dreams and trouble him no more. It consists, not in developing the logical implications and elucidating the meaning, the context or the relevance and origin of a specific problem – in seeing what it 'amounts to' – but in altering the outlook which gave rise to it in the first place. Questions for whose solution no ready-made technique could easily be produced are all too easily classified as obsessions from which the patient must be cured. Thus, if a man is haunted by the suspicion that, for example, full individual liberty is not compatible with coercion by the majority in a democratic State, and yet continues to hanker after both democracy and individual liberty, it may be possible by appropriate treatment to rid him of his *idée fixe*, so that it will disappear, to return no more. The worried questioner of political institutions is thereby relieved of his burden and freed to pursue socially useful tasks, unhampered by disturbing and distracting reflections which have been eliminated by the eradication of their cause.

The method has the bold simplicity of genius: it secures agreement on matters of political principle by removing the psychological possibility of alternatives, which itself depends, or is held to depend, on the older form of social organisation, rendered obsolete by the revolution and the new social order. And this is how Communist and Fascist States – and all other quasi- and semi-totalitarian societies and secular and religious creeds – have in fact proceeded in the task of imposing political and ideological conformity.

For this the works of Karl Marx are certainly no more responsible than the other tendencies of our time. Marx was a typical nineteenth-century social theorist, in the same sense as Mill or Comte or Buckle. A policy of deliberate psychological conditioning was as alien to him as to them. He believed that many of the questions of his predecessors were quite genuine, and thought that he had solved them. He supported his solutions with arguments which he certainly supposed to conform to the best scientific and philosophical canons of his time. Whether his outlook was in fact as scientific as he claimed, or his solutions are plausible, is another question. What matters is that he recognised the genuineness of the questions he was attempting to answer and offered a theory with a claim to being scientific in the accepted sense of the term; and thereby poured much light (and some darkness) on many vexed problems, and led to much fruitful (and sterile) revaluation and reinterpretation.

But the practice of Communist States and, more logically, of Fascist States (since they openly deny and denounce the value of the rational question-and-answer method) has not been the training of the critical, or solution-finding, powers of their citizens, nor yet the development in them of any capacity for special insights or intuitions regarded as likely to reveal the truth. It consists in something which any nineteenth-century thinker with respect for the sciences would have regarded with genuine horror – the training of individuals incapable of being troubled by questions which, when raised and discussed, endanger the stability of the system; the building and elaboration of a strong framework of institutions, 'myths', habits of life and thought intended to preserve it from sudden shocks or slow decay. This is the intellectual outlook which attends the rise of totalitarian ideologies – the substance of the hair-raising satires of George Orwell and Aldous Huxley – the state of mind in which troublesome questions appear as a form of mental perturbation, noxious to the mental health of individuals and, when too widely discussed, to the health of societies. This is an attitude, far removed from Marx or Freud, which looks on all inner conflict as an evil, or at best as a form of futile self-frustration; which considers the kind of friction, the moral or emotional or intellectual collisions, the particular kind of acute mental discomfort which rises to a condition of agony from which great works of the human intellect and imagination have sprung, as being no better than purely destructive diseases – neuroses, psychoses, mental derangements, genuinely requiring psychiatric aid; above all as being dangerous deviations from that line to which individuals and societies must adhere if they are to march towards a state of well-ordered, painless, contented, self-perpetuating equilibrium.

This is a truly far-reaching conception, and something more powerful than the pessimism or cynicism of thinkers like Plato or Maistre, Swift or Carlyle, who looked on the majority of mankind as unalterably stupid or incurably vicious, and therefore concerned themselves with how the world might be made safe for the exceptional, enlightened or otherwise superior minority or individual. For their view did at least concede the reality of the painful problems, and merely denied the capacity of the majority to solve them; whereas the more radical attitude looks upon intellectual perplexity as being caused either by a technical problem to be settled in terms of practical policy, or else as a neurosis to be cured, that is, made to disappear; if possible without a trace. This leads to a novel conception of the truth and of disinterested ideals in general, which would hardly have been intelligible to previous centuries. To adopt it is to hold that outside the purely technical sphere (where one asks only what are the most efficient means towards this or that practical end) words like 'true', or 'right', or 'free', and the concepts which they denote, are to be re-defined in terms of the only activity recognised as valuable, namely the organisation of society as a smoothly working machine providing for the needs of such of its members as are permitted to survive. The words and ideas in such a society will reflect the outlook of the citizens, being so adjusted as to involve as little friction as possible between, and within, individuals, leaving them free to make the 'optimum' use of the resources available to them.

This is indeed Dostoevsky's utilitarian nightmare. In the course of their pursuit of social welfare, humanitarian liberals, deeply outraged by cruelty, injustice and inefficiency, discover that the only sound method of preventing these evils is not by providing the widest opportunities for free intellectual or emotional development – for who can tell where this might not lead? – but by eliminating the motives for the pursuit of these perilous ends, by suppressing any tendencies likely to lead to criticism, dissatisfaction, disorderly forms of life. I shall not attempt here to trace historically how this came to pass. No doubt the story must at some stage include the fact that mere disparity in tempo and extent between technical development and social change, together with the fact that the two could not be guaranteed to harmonise – despite the optimistic hopes of Adam Smith – and indeed clashed more and more often, led to increasingly destructive and apparently unavertable economic crises. These were accompanied by social, political and moral disasters which the general framework – the patterns of behaviour, habits, outlook, language, that is, the 'ideological superstructure' of the victims – could not sustain. The result was a loss of faith in existing political activities and ideals, and a desperate desire to live in a universe which, however dull and flat, was at any rate secure against the repetition of such catastrophes. An element in this was a growing sense of the greater or lesser meaninglessness of such ancient battle-cries as liberty or equality or civilisation or truth, since the application to the surrounding scene was no longer as intelligible as it had been in the nineteenth century.

Together with this development, in the majority of cases, there went a reluctance to face it. But the once hallowed phrases were not abandoned. They were used – robbed of their original value – to cover the different and sometimes diametrically opposed notions of the new morality, which, in terms of the old system of values, seemed both unscrupulous and brutal. The Fascists alone did not take the trouble to pretend to retain the old symbols, and while political diehards and the representatives of the more unbridled forms of modern big business clung half cynically, half hopefully, to such terms as 'freedom' or 'democracy', the Fascists rejected them outright with theatrical gestures of disdain and loathing, and poured scorn upon them as the outworn husks of ideals which had long ago rotted away. But despite the differences of policy concerning the use of specific symbols there is a substantial similarity between all the variants of the new political attitude.

Observers in the twenty-first century will doubtless see these similarities of pattern more easily than we who are involved can possibly do today.[1] They will distinguish them as naturally and clearly from their immediate past – that *hortus inclusus* of the nineteenth century in which so many writers both of history and of journalism and of political addresses today still seem to be living – as we distinguish the growth of romantic nationalism or of naïve positivism from that of enlightened despotism or of patrician republics. Still, even we who live in them can discern something novel in our own times. Even we perceive the growth of new characteristics common to widely different spheres. On the one hand, we can see the progressive and conscious subordination of political to social and economic interests. The most vivid symptoms of this subordination are the open self-identification and conscious solidarity of men as capitalists or workers; these cut across, though they seldom even weaken, national and religious loyalties. On the other, we meet with the conviction that political liberty is useless without the economic strength to use it, and consequently implied or open denial of the rival proposition that economic opportunity is of use only to politically free men. This in its turn carries with it a tacit acceptance of the proposition that the responsibilities of the State to its citizens must and will grow and not diminish, a theorem which is today taken for granted by masters and men alike, in Europe perhaps more unquestioningly than in the United States, but accepted even there to a degree which seemed Utopian only thirty, let alone fifty, years ago. This great transformation, with its genuine material gains, and no less genuine growth in social equality in the least liberal societies, is accompanied by something which forms the obverse side of the medal – the elimination, or, at the very best, strong disapproval, of those propensities for free enquiry and creation which cannot, without losing their nature, remain as conformist and law-abiding as the twentieth century demands. A century ago Auguste Comte asked why, if there was rightly no demand for freedom to disagree in mathematics, it should be allowed and even encouraged in ethics or

[1] 1950.

the social sciences.[1] And indeed, if the creation of certain 'optimum' patterns of behaviour (and of thought and feeling) in individuals or entire societies is the main goal of social and individual action, Comte's case is unanswerable. Yet it is the extent of this very right to disregard the forces of order and convention, even the publicly accepted 'optimum' goals of action, that forms the glory of that bourgeois culture which reached its zenith in the nineteenth century and of which we have only now begun to witness the beginning of the end.

VI

The new attitude, resting as it does upon the policy of diminishing strife and misery by the atrophy of the faculties capable of causing them, is naturally hostile to, or at least suspicious of, disinterested curiosity (which might end anywhere), and looks upon the practice of all arts not obviously useful to society as being at best forms of social frivolity. Such occupations, when they are not a positive menace, are, in this view, an irritating and wasteful irrelevance, a trivial fiddling, a dissipation or diversion of energy which is in any case difficult enough to accumulate and should therefore be directed wholeheartedly and unceasingly to the task of building and maintaining the well-adjusted – sometimes called the 'integrated' – social whole. In this state of mind it is only natural that such terms as 'truth' or 'honour' or 'obligation' or 'beauty' become transformed into purely offensive or defensive weapons, used by a State or a party in the struggle to create a community impervious to influences beyond its own direct control. This result can be achieved either by rigid censorship and insulation from the rest of the world – a world which remains free at least in the sense that many of its inhabitants continue to say what they wish, in which words are relatively unorganised, with all the unpredictable and consequently 'dangerous' consequences that flow from this; or else it can be achieved by extending the area of strict control until it stretches over all possible sources of anarchy, that is, the whole of

---

[1] See *Plan des travaux scientifiques nécessaires pour réorganiser la société* (1822): p. 53 in Auguste Comte, *Appendice général du système de politique positive* (Paris, 1854), published as part of vol. 4 of *Système de politique positive* (Paris, 1851–4). [Mill quotes this passage in *Auguste Comte and Positivism*: vol. 10, pp. 301–2, in *Collected Works of John Stuart Mill*, ed. J. M. Robson and others (Toronto/London, 1963–91).]

mankind. Only by one of these two expedients can a state of affairs be achieved in which human behaviour can be manipulated with relative ease by technically qualified specialists – adjusters of conflicts and promoters of peace both of body and of mind, engineers and other scientific experts in the service of the ruling group, psychologists, sociologists, economic and social planners and so on. Clearly this is not an intellectual climate which favours originality of judgement, moral independence or uncommon powers of insight. The entire trend of such an order is to reduce all issues to technical problems of lesser or greater complexity, in particular the problem of how to survive, get rid of maladjustments, achieve a condition in which the individual's psychological or economic capacities are harnessed to producing the maximum of unclouded social contentment compatible with opposition to all experiment outside the bounds of the system; and this in its turn depends upon the suppression of whatever in the individual might raise doubt or assert itself against the single all-embracing, all-clarifying, all-satisfying plan.

This tendency, present in all stable societies – perhaps in all societies as such – has, owing to the repression of all rival influences, assumed a particularly acute form in, for example, the Soviet Union. There, subordination to the central plan, and the elimination of disturbing forces, whether by education or repression, has been enacted with that capacity for believing in the literal inspiration of ideologies – in the ability and duty of human beings to translate ideas into practice fully, rigorously and immediately – to which Russian thinkers of all schools seem singularly addicted. The Soviet pattern is clear, simple and deduced from 'scientifically demonstrated' premisses. The task of realising it must be entrusted to technically trained believers who look on the human beings at their disposal as material which is infinitely malleable within the confines revealed by the sciences. Stalin's remark that creative artists are 'engineers of human souls'[1] is a very precise expression

[1] Stalin used the phrase 'engineers of human souls' in a speech on the role of Soviet writers made at Maxim Gorky's house on 26 October 1932, recorded in an unpublished manuscript in the Gorky archive – K. L. Zelinsky, 'Vstrecha pisatelei s I. V. Stalinym' ('A meeting of writers with I. V. Stalin') – and published for the first time, in English, in A. Kemp-Welch, Stalin and the Literary Intelligentsia, 1928–39 (Basingstoke and London, 1991), pp. 128–31: for this phrase see p. 131 (and, for the Russian original, 'inzhenery chelovecheskikh dush', I. V. Stalin, Sochineniya (Moscow, 1946–67), vol. 13, p. 410). Ed.

of this spirit. The presence of something analogous in various Fascist societies, with intuition or instinct substituted for science, and cynicism for hypocrisy, are equally clear for all to see. In Western Europe this tendency has taken the milder form of a shift of emphasis away from disagreement about political principles (and from party struggles which at least in part sprang from genuine differences of outlook) towards disagreements, ultimately technical, about methods – about the best ways of achieving that degree of minimum economic or social stability without which arguments concerned with fundamental principles and the ends of life are felt to be 'abstract', 'academic' and unrelated to the urgent needs of the hour. It leads to that noticeably growing lack of interest in long-term political issues – as opposed to current day-to-day economic or social problems – on the part of the populations of the Western European continent which is occasionally deplored by shocked American and British observers, who mistakenly ascribe it to the growth of cynicism and disenchantment with ideals.

No doubt all abandonment of old values for new may appear to the surviving adherents of the former as conscienceless disregard for morality as such. If so, it is a great delusion. There is all too little disbelief, whether conscienceless or apathetic, in the new values. On the contrary, they are clung to with unreasoning faith and that blind intolerance towards scepticism which springs, as often as not, from an inner bankruptcy or terror, the hope against hope that here at least is a safe haven, narrow, dark, cut off, but secure. Growing numbers of human beings are prepared to purchase this sense of security even at the cost of allowing vast tracts of life to be controlled by persons who, whether consciously or not, act systematically to narrow the horizon of human activity to manageable proportions, to train human beings into more easily combinable parts – interchangeable, almost prefabricated – of a total pattern. In the face of such a strong desire to stabilise, if need be, at the lowest level – upon the floor from which you cannot fall, which cannot betray you, let you down – all the ancient political principles begin to vanish, feeble symbols of creeds no longer relevant to the new realities.

This process does not move at a uniform pace everywhere. In the United States, perhaps, for obvious economic reasons, the nineteenth century survives more powerfully than anywhere else. The political issues and conflicts, the topics of discussion and the idealised personalities of democratic leaders are more reminiscent

of Victorian Europe than anything to be found on the Continent
now.

Woodrow Wilson was a nineteenth-century liberal in a very full
and unqualified sense. The New Deal and the personality of
President Roosevelt excited political passions far more like those of
the battles which raged round Gladstone or Lloyd George, or the
anti-clerical governments at the turn of the century in France, than
anything actually contemporary with it in Europe; and this great
liberal enterprise, certainly the most constructive compromise
between individual liberty and economic security which our own
time has witnessed, corresponds more closely to the political and
economic ideals of John Stuart Mill in his last, humanitarian-
socialist phase than to left-wing thought in Europe in the 1930s.
The controversy about international organisation, about the
United Nations and its subsidiaries, as well as the other post-war
international institutions, like the controversies which in the years
after 1918 surrounded the League of Nations, are fully intelligible
in terms of nineteenth-century political ideals, and therefore
occupied far more attention and meant much more in America than
in Europe. The United States may have disavowed President
Wilson, but it continued to live in a moral atmosphere not very
different from that of Wilson's time – the easily recognisable black-
and-white moral world of the Victorian values. The events of 1918
preyed on the American conscience for twenty-five years, whereas
in Europe the *exalté* atmosphere of 1918–19 was soon dissipated –
a brief moment of illumination which in retrospect seems more
American than European, the last manifestation in Europe of a
great but dying tradition in a world already living, and fully
conscious of living, in a new medium, too well aware of its
differences from, and resentful of, its past. The break was not
sudden and total, a dramatic *coup de théâtre*. Many of the seeds
planted in the eighteenth or nineteenth century have flowered only
in the twentieth: the political and ethical climate in which trade
unions flourished, for instance, in Germany, or England, or
France, contained as elements the old, familiar doctrines of human
rights and duties which were the common property, avowed or
not, of almost all parties and views in the liberal, humanitarian,
expansionist hundred years of peace and technological progress.

The main current of the nineteenth century does, of course,
survive into the present and especially in America, Scandinavia and
the British Commonwealth; but it is not what is most characteristic

of our time. For in the past there were conflicts of ideas; whereas what characterises our time is less the struggle of one set of ideas against another than the mounting wave of hostility to all ideas as such. Since ideas are considered the source of too much disquiet, there is a tendency to suppress the conflict between liberal claims to individual political rights and the patent economic injustice which can result from their satisfaction (which forms the substance of socialist criticism) by the submersion of both in an authoritarian regime which removes the free area within which such conflict can occur. What is genuinely typical of our time is a new concept of society, the values of which are analysable not in terms of the desires or the moral sense which inspire the view of its ultimate ends held by a group or an individual, but from some factual hypothesis or metaphysical dogma about history, or race, or national character, in terms of which the answers to the question what is good, right, required, desirable, fitting can be 'scientifically' deduced, or intuited, or expressed in this or that kind of behaviour. There is one and only one direction in which a given aggregate of individuals is conceived to be travelling, driven thither by quasi-occult impersonal forces, such as their class structure, or their collective unconscious, or their racial origin, or the 'real' social or physical roots of this or that 'popular' or 'group' 'mythology'. The direction is alterable, but only by tampering with the hidden cause of behaviour – those who wish to tamper being, according to this view, free to a limited degree to determine their own direction and that of others not by the increase of rationality and by argument addressed to it, but by having a superior understanding of the machinery of social behaviour and skill in manipulating it.

   In this sinister fashion has Saint-Simon's prophecy about (in Engels's paraphrase) 'replacing the government of persons by the administration of things'[1] finally come true – a prophecy which once seemed so brave and optimistic. The cosmic forces are conceived as omnipotent and indestructible. Hopes, fears, prayers cannot wish them out of existence; but the élite of experts can canalise them and control them to some extent. The task of these experts is to adjust human beings to these forces and to develop in them an unshakeable faith in the new order, and unquestioning

---

[1] Engels in *Anti-Duhring* (1877–8): Karl Marx, Friedrich Engels, *Werke* (Berlin, 1956–83), vol. 19, p. 195. Cf. 'Lettres de Henri Saint-Simon à un américain', eighth letter, in *L'Industrie* (1817), vol. 1: pp. 182–91 in *Oeuvres de Saint-Simon et d'Enfantin* (Paris, 1865–78), vol. 18.

loyalty to it, which will anchor it securely and for ever. Consequently the technical disciplines which direct natural forces and adjust men to the new order must take primacy over humane pursuits – philosophical, historical, artistic. Such pursuits, at most, will serve only to prop up and embellish the new establishment. Turgenev's naïve materialist, the hero of his novel *Fathers and Children*, the 'nihilistic' scientist Bazarov, has finally come into his own, as Saint-Simon and his more pedestrian follower Comte always felt sure that he would, but for reasons very different from those which seemed plausible a century ago. Bazarov's faith rested on the claim that the dissection of frogs was more important than poetry because it led to the truth, whereas the poetry of Pushkin did not.

The motive at work today is more devastating: anatomy is superior to art because it generates no independent ends of life, provides no experiences which act as independent criteria of good or evil, truth or falsehood, and are therefore liable to clash with the orthodoxy which we have created as the only bulwark strong enough to preserve us from doubts and despairs and all the horrors of maladjustment. To be borne this way and that emotionally or intellectually is a form of *malaise*. Against it nothing will work but the elimination of alternatives so nearly in equal balance that choice between them is – or at least appears to be – possible.

This is, of course, the position of the Grand Inquisitor in Dostoevsky's *The Brothers Karamazov*: he said that what men dreaded most was freedom of choice, to be left alone to grope their way in the dark; and the Church, by lifting the responsibility from their shoulders, made them willing, grateful and happy slaves. The Grand Inquisitor stood for the dogmatic organisation of the life of the spirit: Bazarov for its theoretical opposite – free scientific enquiry, the facing of the 'hard' facts, the acceptance of the truth however brutal or upsetting. By an irony of history (not unforeseen by Dostoevsky) they have formed a pact, they are allies, and today are often indistinguishable. Buridan's ass, we are told, unable to choose between two equidistant bundles of hay, starved to death. Against this fate the only remedy is blind obedience and faith. Whether the refuge is a dogmatic religious faith or a dogmatic faith in social or natural science matters relatively little: for without such obedience and faith there is no confidence and no hope, no optimistic, 'constructive', 'positive' form of life. That the disciples of those who first exposed the idolatry of ideas frozen into oppressive institutions – Fourier, Feuerbach and Marx – should be the most ferocious supporters of the new forms of 'reification' and 'dehumanisation' is indeed an irony of history.

VII

One of the most fascinating and disquieting symptoms of this trend is to be found in the policy of the great philanthropic foundations of the West. The criticism of these institutions most frequently made by both European and American observers is that their aims are too crudely utilitarian: that instead of seeking to support the pursuit of truth or creative activity as such (basic research, for example, or artistic activity) they are dedicated to the most direct and immediate improvement of human life conceived in crudely material terms – physical well-being, solutions to short-term social and economic problems, the manufacture of prophy-lactics against politically 'undesirable' views, and so on. But these charges seem to me misconceived. The efforts of the celebrated and munificent bodies engaged in this type of activity rest, I am convinced, on a genuine and disinterested desire to serve the deepest interests of mankind, and not merely its material needs. But these interests are all conceived almost entirely in therapeutic terms: tensions (within or between individuals or groups or nations) that need to be released, wounds, conflicts, fixations, 'phobias' and fears, psychical and psychophysical abnormalities of all sorts which require the aid of specialised healers – doctors, economists, social workers, teams of diagnosticians or engineers or other masters of the craft of helping the sick and the perplexed – individual and collective sources of practical wisdom of every kind.

To the degree to which such suffering exists and can be treated by the applied sciences – genuine physical or mental sickness, poverty, social and economic inequality, squalor, misery, oppres-sion, which men and money, experts and equipment can cure or alleviate – such policies are, of course, entirely beneficent and their organised support is a great moral asset to an age and a country. But the reverse of this coin is the tendency – difficult to avoid, but disastrous – to assimilate all men's primary needs to those that are capable of being met by these methods: the reduction of all questions and aspirations to dislocations which the expert can set right. Some believe in coercion, others in gentler methods; but the conception of human needs in their entirety as those of the inmates of a prison or a reformatory or a school or a hospital, however sincerely it may be held, is a gloomy, false and ultimately degraded view, resting on denial of the rational and productive nature of all, or even the majority of, men. The resistance to it, whether in the form of attacks on American 'materialism' (when it springs from a genuine, if naïve, and often crude form of altruistic idealism) or on Communist or nationalist fanaticism (when it is, more often than not, a misconceived, over-pragmatic search for human emancipation), derives from an obscure realisation that both these tendencies – which spring from a common root – are hostile to the development of men as creative and self-directing beings. If men are indeed such beings, even this tendency, overwhelming as it seems to be at present, will not, in the end, prove fatal to human progress. This circular argument, which is, in essence, that of all critical rationalists – of Marx (at any rate in his youth) and Freud as well as Spinoza and Kant, Mill and Tocqueville – if it is valid, offers some ground for a cautious and highly qualified optimism about the moral and intellectual future of the human race.

VIII

At this point it might be said that the situation I have described is not altogether new. Has not every authoritarian institution, every irrationalist movement been engaged upon something of this kind – the artificial stilling of doubts, the attempt either to discredit uncomfortable questions or to educate men not to ask them? Was this not the practice of the great organised Churches, indeed of every institution from the national State to small sectarian establishments? Was this not the attitude of the enemies of reason from the earliest mystery cults to the romanticism, anarchistic nihilism, surrealism, neo-Oriental cults of the last century and a half? Why should our age be specially accused of addiction to the particular tendency which formed a central theme of social doctrines which go back to Plato, or the sect of the medieval Assassins, or much Eastern thought and mysticism?

But there are two great differences which separate the political characteristics of our age from their origins in the past. In the first place, the reactionaries or romantics of previous periods, however much they might have advocated the superior wisdom of institutional authority or the revealed word over that of individual reason, did not in their moments of wildest unreason minimise the importance of the questions to be answered. On the contrary, they maintained that so crucial was it to obtain the correct answer that only hallowed institutions, or inspired leaders, or mystical revelation, or divine grace, could vouchsafe a solution of sufficient depth and universality. No doubt an order of importance of questions underlies any established social system – a hierarchical order the authority of which is itself not open to question. Moreover, the obscurity of some among the answers offered has in every age concealed their lack of truth or their irrelevance to the questions which they purported to solve. And perhaps much hypocrisy has traditionally been necessary to secure their success. But hypocrisy is very different from cynicism or blindness. Even the censors of opinion and the enemies of the truth felt compelled to pay formal homage to the vital importance of obtaining true answers to the great problems by the best available means. If their practice belied this, at least there was something to be belied: traitors and heretics often keep alive the memory – and the authority – of the beliefs which they are intent on betraying.

The second difference consists in the fact that in the past such attempts to obscure the nature of the issues were mostly associated with the avowed enemies of reason and individual freedom. The alignment of forces has been clear at any rate since the Renaissance; progress and reaction, however much these words have been abused, are not empty concepts. On one side stood the supporters of authority, unreasoning faith, suspicious of, or openly opposed to, the uncontrolled pursuit of truth or the free realisation of individual ideals. On the other, whatever their differences, were those supporters of free enquiry and self-expression who looked upon Voltaire and Lessing, Mill and Darwin, even Ibsen as their prophets. Their common quality – perhaps their only common quality – was some degree of devotion to the ideals of the Renaissance and a hatred of all that was associated, whether justly or not, with the Middle Ages – darkness, suppression, the stifling of all heterodoxy, the hatred of the flesh and of gaiety, of freedom of thought and expression, and of the love of natural beauty. There were of course many who cannot be classified so simply or so crudely; but until our own day the lines were drawn sharply enough to determine clearly the position of the men who most deeply influenced their age. A combination of devotion to scientific principles with 'obscurantist' social theory seemed altogether unthinkable. Today the tendency to circumscribe and confine and limit, to determine the range of what may be asked and what may not, what may be believed and what may not, is no longer a distinguishing mark of the old 'reactionaries'. On the contrary, it comes as powerfully from the heirs of the radicals, rationalists, 'progressives' of the nineteenth century as from the descendants of their enemies. There is a persecution not only of science, but by science or at least in its name; and this is a nightmare scarcely foreseen by the most Cassandra-like prophets of either camp.

We are often told that the present is an age of cynicism and despair, of crumbling values and the dissolution of the fixed standards and landmarks of Western civilisation. But this is neither true nor even plausible. So far from showing the loose texture of a collapsing order, the world is today stiff with rigid rules and codes and ardent, irrational religions. So far from evincing the toleration which springs from cynical disregard of the ancient sanctions, it treats heterodoxy as the supreme danger.

Whether in the East or West, the danger has not been greater since the ages of faith. Conformities are called for much more eagerly today than yesterday; loyalties are tested far more severely; sceptics, liberals, individuals with a taste for private life and their own inner standards of behaviour, if they do not take care to identify themselves with an organised movement, are objects of fear or derision and targets of persecution for either side, execrated or despised by all the embattled parties in the great ideological wars of our time. And although this is less acute in societies traditionally averse to extremes – Great Britain, say, or Denmark or Switzerland – this makes little difference to the general pattern. In the world today individual stupidity and wickedness are forgiven more easily than failure to be identified with a recognised party or attitude, to achieve an approved political or economic or intellectual status. In earlier periods, when more than one authority rules human life, a man might escape the pressure of the State by taking refuge in the fortress of the opposition – of an organised Church or dissident feudal establishment. The mere fact of conflict between authorities allowed room for a narrow and shifting, but still never entirely non-existent, no man's land, where private lives might still precariously be lived, because neither side dared to go too far for fear of too greatly strengthening the other. Today the very virtues of even the best-intentioned paternalistic State, its genuine anxiety to reduce destitution and disease and inequality, to penetrate all the neglected nooks and crannies of life which may stand in need of its justice and its bounty – its very success in those beneficent activities – have narrowed the area within which the individual may commit blunders, and curtailed his liberties in the interest (the very real interest) of his welfare or of his sanity, his health, his security, his freedom from want and fear. His area of choice has grown smaller not in the name of some opposing principle – as in the Dark Ages or during the rise of the nationalities – but in order to create a situation in which the very possibility of opposed principles, with all their unlimited capacity to cause mental stress and danger and destructive collisions, is eliminated in favour of a simpler and better regulated life, a robust faith in an efficiently working order, untroubled by agonising moral conflict.

Yet this is not a gratuitous development: the social and economic situation in which we are placed, the failure to harmonise the effects of technical progress with the forces of political and economic organisation inherited from an earlier phase, do call for a measure of social control to prevent chaos and destitution, which can be no less fatal to the development of human faculties than blind conformity. It is neither realistic nor morally conceivable that we should give up our social gains and meditate for an instant the possibility of a return to ancient injustice and inequality and hopeless misery. The progress of technological skill makes it rational and indeed imperative to plan, and anxiety for the success of a particular planned society naturally inclines the planners to seek insulation from dangerous, because incalculable, forces which may jeopardise the plan. And this is a powerful incentive to 'autarky' and 'socialism in one country', whether imposed by conservatives, or New Dealers, or isolationists, or social democrats, or, indeed, imperialists. And this in its turn generates artificial barriers and increasingly restricts the planners' own resources. In extreme cases this policy leads to repression of the discontented and a perpetual tightening of discipline, until it absorbs more and more of the time and ingenuity of those who originally conceived it only as a means to a minimum of efficiency. Presently it grows to be a hideous end in itself, since its realisation leads to a vicious circle of repression in order to survive and of survival mainly to repress. So the remedy grows to be worse than the disease, and takes the form of those orthodoxies which rest on the simple puritanical faith of individuals who never knew or have forgotten what *douceur de vivre*, free self-expression, the infinite variety of persons and of the relationships between them, and the right of free choice, difficult to endure but more intolerable to surrender, can ever have been like.

The dilemma is logically insoluble: we cannot sacrifice either freedom or the organisation needed for its defence, or a minimum standard of welfare. The way out must therefore lie in some logically untidy, flexible and even ambiguous compromise. Every situation calls for its own specific policy, since 'out of the crooked timber of humanity', as Kant once remarked, 'no straight thing was ever made'.[1] What the age calls for is not (as we are so often told) more faith, or stronger leadership, or more scientific organisation. Rather is it the opposite – less Messianic ardour, more enlightened scepticism, more toleration of idiosyncrasies, more frequent *ad hoc* measures to achieve aims in a foreseeable future, more room for the attainment of their personal ends by individuals and by minorities whose tastes and beliefs find (whether rightly or wrongly must not matter) little response among the majority. What is required is a less mechanical, less fanatical application of general principles, however rational or righteous, a more cautious and less arrogantly self-confident application of accepted, scientifically tested, general solutions to unexamined individual cases. The wicked Talleyrand's 'Surtout, Messieurs, point de zèle'[2] can be more humane than the demand for uniformity of the virtuous Robespierre, and a salutary brake upon too much control of men's lives in an age of social planning and technology. We must submit to authority not because it is infallible, but only for strictly and openly utilitarian reasons, as a necessary expedient.

Since no solution can be guaranteed against error, no disposition is final. And therefore a loose texture and toleration of a minimum of inefficiency, even a degree of indulgence in idle talk, idle curiosity, aimless pursuit of this or that without authorisation – 'conspicuous waste' itself – allow more spontaneous, individual variation (for which the individual must in the end assume full

[1] op. cit. (p. 7 above, note 2), vol. 8, p. 23, line 22.
[2] 'Above all, gentlemen, no zeal whatsoever.' This maxim of Talleyrand's appears in various forms. The earliest I have found is 'N'ayez pas de zèle' ('Don't be zealous'), in C.-A. Sainte-Beuve, 'Madame de Staël' (1835): vol. 2, p. 1104, in Sainte-Beuve, *Oeuvres*, ed. Maxime Leroy ([Paris], 1949–51). The version in the text appears in Philarète Chasles, *Voyages d'un critique à travers la vie et les livres* (1865–8), vol. 2, *Italie et Espagne*, p. 204. In this latter version 'point' is often replaced by 'pas trop' ('not too much'), as on p. 304 below, but I have found no nineteenth-century authority for this wording. Ed.

responsibility), and will always be worth more than the neatest and most delicately fashioned imposed pattern. Above all, it must be realised that the kinds of problems which this or that method of education or system of scientific or religious or social organisation is guaranteed to solve are not *eo facto* the only central questions of human life. Injustice, poverty, slavery, ignorance – these may be cured by reform or revolution. But men do not live only by fighting evils. They live by positive goals, individual and collective, a vast variety of them, seldom predictable, at times incompatible. It is from intense preoccupation with these ends, ultimate, incommensurable, guaranteed neither to change nor to stand still – it is through the absorbed individual or collective pursuit of these, unplanned and at times without wholly adequate technical equipment, more often than not without conscious hope of success, still less of the approbation of the official auditor, that the best moments come in the lives of individuals and peoples.

HISTORICAL INEVITABILITY

... those vast impersonal forces ...

T. S. Eliot[1]

I

WRITING some ten years ago[2] in his place of refuge during the German occupation of northern Italy, Bernard Berenson set down his thoughts on what he called the 'Accidental View of History': they 'led me', he declared, 'far from the doctrine, lapped up in my youth, about the inevitability of events and the Moloch still devouring us today, "historical inevitability". I believe less and less in these more than doubtful and certainly dangerous dogmas, which tend to make us accept whatever happens as irresistible and foolhardy to oppose.'[3] The famous critic's words are particularly timely at a moment when there is, at any rate among philosophers of history, if not among historians, a tendency to return to the ancient view that all that is, is ('objectively viewed') best; that to explain is ('in the last resort') to justify; or that to know all is to forgive all; ringing fallacies (charitably described as half-truths) which have led to special pleading and, indeed, obfuscation of the issue on a heroic scale.

This is the theme on which I should like to speak; but before doing so I must express my gratitude for the honour done me by the invitation to deliver this, the first of the Auguste Comte Memorial Lectures. For, indeed, Comte is worthy of commemoration and praise. He was in his own day a very celebrated thinker, and if his works are today seldom mentioned, at any rate in this country, that is partly due to the fact that he has

[1] *Notes towards the Definition of Culture* (London, 1948), p. 88.
[2] This was written in 1953.
[3] Bernard Berenson, *Rumour and Reflection: 1941:1944* (London, 1952), p. 116 (entry dated 11 January 1943).

done his work too well. For Comte's views have affected the categories of our thought more deeply than is commonly supposed. Our view of the natural sciences, of the material basis of cultural evolution, of all that we call progressive, rational, enlightened, Western; our view of the relationships of institutions and of public symbolism and ceremonial to the emotional life of individuals and societies, and consequently our view of history itself, owes a good deal to his teaching and his influence. His grotesque pedantry, the unreadable dullness of much of his writing, his vanity, his eccentricity, his solemnity, the pathos of his private life, his dogmatism, his authoritarianism, his philosophical fallacies, all that is bizarre and Utopian in his character and writings, need not blind us to his merits. The father of sociology is by no means the ludicrous figure he is too often represented as being. He understood the role of natural science and the true reasons for its prestige better than most contemporary thinkers. He saw no depth in mere darkness; he demanded evidence; he exposed shams; he denounced intellectual impressionism; he fought many metaphysical and theological mythologies, some of which, but for the blows he struck, might have been with us still; he provided weapons in the war against the enemies of reason, many of which are far from obsolete today. Above all he grasped the central issue of all philosophy – the distinction between words (or thoughts) that are about words, and words (or thoughts) that are about things, and thereby helped to lay the foundation of what is best and most illuminating in modern empiricism; and, of course, he made a great mark on historical thinking. He believed in the application of scientific, that is, naturalistic, canons of explanation in all fields: and saw no reason why they should not apply to relations of human beings as well as relations of things.

This doctrine was not original, and by his time growing somewhat out of date; the writings of Vico had been rediscovered; Herder had transformed the concepts of nation, society and culture; Ranke and Michelet were changing both the art and the science of history. The notion that human history could be turned into a natural science by the extension to human beings of a kind of sociological zoology, analogous to the study of bees and beavers, which Condorcet had so ardently advocated and so confidently prophesied – this simple behaviourism had provoked a reaction against itself. It was seen to be a distortion of the facts, a denial of the evidence of direct experience, a deliberate suppression of much of what we knew about ourselves, our motives, purposes, choices, perpetrated in order to achieve by hook or by crook a single, unitary method in all knowledge. Comte did not commit the enormities of a La Mettrie or a Büchner. He did not say that history was, or was reducible to, a kind of physics; but his conception of sociology pointed in that direction – of one complete and all-embracing pyramid of scientific knowledge; one method; one truth; one scale of rational, 'scientific' values. This naïve craving for unity and symmetry at the expense of experience is with us still.

II

The notion that one can discover large patterns or regularities in the procession of historical events is naturally attractive to those who are impressed by the success of the natural sciences in classifying, correlating, and above all predicting. They consequently seek to extend historical knowledge to fill gaps in the past (and, at times, to build into the limitless gap of the future) by applying 'scientific' method: by setting forth, armed with a metaphysical or empirical system, from such islands of certain, or virtually certain, knowledge of the facts as they claim to possess. And no doubt a great deal has been done, and will be done, in historical as in other fields by arguing from the known to the unknown, or from the little known to the even less known.[1] But

---

[1] I do not wish here to enter into the question of what such procedures are, for example, what is meant by speaking of history as a science – whether the methods of historical discovery are inductive, or 'deductive-hypothetical', or analogical, or to what degree they are or should be similar to the methods of the natural sciences, and to which of these methods, and in which of the natural sciences; for there plainly exists a greater variety of methods and procedures than is usually provided for in textbooks on logic or scientific method. It may be that the methods of historical research are, in at least some respects, unique, and some of them are more unlike than like those of the natural sciences; while others resemble given scientific techniques, particularly when they approach such ancillary enquiries as archaeology or palaeography or physical anthropology. Or again they may depend upon the kind of historical research pursued – and may not be the same in demography as in history, in political history as in the history of art, in the history of technology as in the history of religion. The 'logic' of various human studies has been insufficiently examined, and convincing accounts of its varieties with an adequate range of concrete examples drawn from actual practice are much to be desired.

whatever value the perception of patterns or uniformities may have in stimulating or verifying specific hypotheses about the past or the future, it has played, and is increasingly playing, another and more dubious role in determining the outlook of our time. It has affected not merely ways of observing and describing the activities and characters of human beings, but moral and political and religious attitudes towards them. For among the questions which are bound to arise in any consideration of how and why human beings act and live as they do are questions of human motive and responsibility.

In describing human behaviour it has always been artificial and over-austere to omit questions of the character, purposes and motives of individuals. And in considering these one automatically evaluates not merely the degree and kind of influence of this or that motive or character upon what happens, but also its moral or political quality in terms of whatever scale of values one consciously or semi-consciously accepts in one's thought or action. How did this or that situation arise? Who or what was or is (or will be, or could be) responsible for a war, a revolution, an economic collapse, a renaissance of arts and letters, a discovery or an invention or a spiritual transformation altering the lives of men? It is by now a familiar story that there exist personal and impersonal theories of history. On the one hand, there are theories according to which the lives of entire peoples and societies have been decisively influenced by exceptional individuals[1] – or, alternatively, doctrines according to which what happens occurs as a result not of the wishes and purposes of identifiable individuals, but of those of large numbers of unspecified persons, with the qualification that these collective wishes and goals are not solely or even largely determined by impersonal factors, and are therefore not wholly or even largely deducible from knowledge of natural forces alone, such as environment, or climate, or physical, physiological and psychological processes. On either view, it becomes the

[1] Indeed, the very notion of great men, however carefully qualified, however sophisticated, embodies this belief; for this concept, even in its most attenuated form, would be empty unless it were thought that some men played a more decisive role in the course of history than others. The notion of greatness, unlike those of goodness or wickedness or talent or beauty, is not a mere characteristic of individuals in a more or less private context, but is, as we ordinarily use it, directly connected with social effectiveness, the capacity of individuals to alter things radically on a large scale.

business of historians to investigate who wanted what, and when, and where, in what way; how many men avoided or pursued this or that goal, and with what intensity; and, further, to ask under what circumstances such wants or fears have proved effective, and to what extent, and with what consequences.

Against this kind of interpretation, in terms of the purposes and characters of individuals, there is a cluster of views (to which the progress of the natural sciences has given a great and growing prestige) according to which all explanations in terms of human intentions stem from a mixture of vanity and stubborn ignorance. These views rest on the assumption that belief in the importance of the motives is delusive; that the behaviour of men is in fact made what it is by causes largely beyond the control of individuals; for instance by the influence of physical factors or of environment or of custom; or by the 'natural' growth of some larger unit – a race, a nation, a class, a biological species; or (according to some writers) by some entity conceived in even less empirical terms – a 'spiritual organism', a religion, a civilisation, a Hegelian (or Buddhist) World Spirit; entities whose careers or manifestations on earth are the object either of empirical or of metaphysical enquiries, depending on the cosmological outlook of particular thinkers.

Those who incline to this kind of impersonal interpretation of historical change, whether because they believe that it possesses greater scientific value (that is, enables them to predict the future or 'retrodict' the past more successfully or precisely), or because they believe that it embodies some crucial insight into the nature of the universe, are committed by it to tracing the ultimate responsibility for what happens to the acts or behaviour of impersonal or 'trans-personal' or 'super-personal' entities or 'forces' whose evolution is identified with human history. It is true that the more cautious and clear-headed among such theorists try to meet the objections of empirically minded critics by adding, in a footnote or as an afterthought, that, whatever their terminology, they are on no account to be taken to believe that there literally exist such creatures as civilisations or races or spirits of nations living side by side with the individuals who compose them; and they add that they fully realise that all institutions 'in the last analysis' consist of individual men and women, and are not themselves personalities but only convenient devices – idealised models, or types, or labels, or metaphors – different ways of classifying, grouping, explaining or predicting the properties or behaviour of individual human beings in terms of their more important (that is, historically effective) empirical characteristics. Nevertheless these protestations too often turn out to be mere lip-service to principles which those who profess them do not really believe. Such writers seldom write or think as if they took these deflationary caveats over-seriously; and the more candid or naïve among them do not even pretend to subscribe to them. Thus nations or cultures or civilisations, for Schelling or Hegel (and Spengler; and one is inclined, though somewhat hesitantly, to add Toynbee), are certainly not merely convenient collective terms for individuals possessing certain characteristics in common; but seem more 'real' and more 'concrete' than the individuals who compose them. Individuals remain 'abstract' precisely because they are mere 'elements' or 'aspects', 'moments' artificially abstracted for *ad hoc* purposes, and literally without reality (or, at any rate, 'historical' or 'philosophical' or 'real' being) apart from the wholes of which they form a part, much as the colour of a thing, or its shape, or its value are 'elements' or 'attributes' or 'modes' or 'aspects' of concrete objects – isolated for convenience, and thought of as existing independently, on their own, only because of some weakness or confusion in the analysing intellect.

Marx and Marxists are more ambiguous. We cannot be quite sure what to make of such a category as a social 'class' whose emergence and struggles, victories and defeats, condition the lives of individuals, sometimes against, and most often independently of, such individuals' conscious or expressed purposes. Classes are never proclaimed to be literally independent entities: they are constituted by individuals in their (mainly economic) interaction. Yet to seek to explain, or put a moral or political value on, the actions of individuals by examining such individuals one by one, even to the limited extent to which such examination is possible, is considered by Marxists to be not merely impracticable and time-wasting (as indeed it may be), but absurd in a more fundamental sense – because the 'true' (or 'deeper') causes of human behaviour lie not in the specific circumstances of an individual life or in the individual's thoughts or volitions (as a psychologist or biographer or novelist might describe them), but in a pervasive interrelationship between a vast variety of such lives with their natural and man-made environment. Men do as they do, and think as they think, largely as a 'function of' the inevitable evolution of the 'class' as a whole – from which it follows that the history and

development of classes can be studied independently of the
biographies of their component individuals. It is the 'structure' and
the 'evolution' of the class alone that (causally) matters in the end.
This is, *mutatis mutandis*, similar to the belief in the primacy of
collective patterns held by those who attribute active properties to
race or culture, whether they be benevolent internationalists like
Herder who thought that different peoples can and should admire,
love and assist one another as individuals can and do, because
peoples are in some sense individuals (or super-individuals); or by
the ferocious champions of national or racial self-assertion and
war, like Gobineau or Houston Stewart Chamberlain or Hitler.
And the same note, sometimes mild and civilised, sometimes
harshly aggressive, is heard in the voices of all those upholders of
collectivist mystiques who appeal from individual to tradition, or
to the collective consciousness (or 'Unconscious') of a race or a
nation or a culture, or, like Carlyle, feel that abstract nouns deserve
capital letters, and tell us that Tradition or History (or 'the past', or
the species, or 'the masses') is wiser than we, or that the great
society of the quick and the dead, of our ancestors and of
generations yet unborn, has larger purposes than any single
creature, purposes of which our lives are but a puny fragment, and
that we belong to this larger unity with the 'deepest' and perhaps
least conscious parts of ourselves.[1] There are many versions of

[1] We are further told that we belong to such wholes and are 'organically' one
with them, whether we know it or not; and that we have such significance as we
do only to the degree to which we are sensitive to, and identify ourselves with,
these unanalysable, imponderable, scarcely explicable relationships; for it is only
in so far as we belong to an entity greater than ourselves, and are thereby carriers
of 'its' values, instruments of 'its' purposes, living 'its' life, suffering and dying for
'its' richer self-realisation, that we are, or are worth, anything at all. This familiar
line of thought should be distinguished from the no less familiar but less ethically
charged supposition that men's outlooks and behaviour are largely conditioned by
the habits of other past and present members of their society; that the hold of
prejudice and tradition is very strong; that there may be inherited characteristics
both mental and physical; and that any effort to influence human beings and to
judge their conduct must take such non-rational factors into account. For whereas
the former view is metaphysical and normative (what Karl Popper calls 'essentia-
list'), the latter is empirical and descriptive; and while the former is largely found
as an element in the kind of ethical or political anti-individualism held by
romantic nationalists, Hegelians and other transcendentalists, the latter is a
sociological and psychological hypothesis which doubtless carries its own ethical
and political implications, but rests its claim on observation of empirical facts, and
can be confirmed or refuted or rendered less or more plausible by it. In their

this belief, with varying proportions of empiricism and mysticism, 'tender'- and 'tough'-mindedness, optimism and pessimism, collectivism and individualism; but what all such views have in common is the fundamental distinction on which they rest, between, on the one hand, 'real' and 'objective', and, on the other, 'subjective' or 'arbitrary' judgements, based respectively on acceptance or rejection of this ultimately mystical act of self-identification with a reality which transcends empirical experience.

For Bossuet, for Hegel, for Marx,[1] for Spengler (and for almost all thinkers for whom history is 'more' than past events, namely a theodicy) this reality takes on the form of an objective 'march of history'. The process may be thought of as being in time and space or beyond them; as being cyclical or spiral or rectilinear, or as occurring in the form of a peculiar zigzag movement, sometimes called dialectical; as continuous and uniform, or irregular, broken by sudden leaps to 'new levels'; as due to the changing forms of one single 'force', or to conflicting elements locked (as in some ancient myth) in an eternal Pyrrhic struggle; as the history of one deity or 'force' or 'principle', or of several; as being destined to end well or badly; as holding out to human beings the prospect of eternal beatitude, or eternal damnation, or both in turn, or neither. But whatever version of the story is accepted – and it is never a scientific, that is, empirically testable theory, stated in quantitative terms, still less a description of what our eyes see and our ears hear[2] – the moral of it is always one and the same: that we must learn to distinguish the 'real' course of things from the dreams and fancies and 'rationalisations' which we construct unconsciously for our solace or amusement; for these may comfort us for a while, but will betray us cruelly in the end. There is, we are told, a nature of things, and it has a pattern in time: 'Things and actions are what

---

extreme forms these views contradict each other; in their softer and less consistent forms they tend to overlap, and even coalesce.

[1] Or, some prefer to say, Engels.

[2] No one has demonstrated this with more devastating lucidity than Karl Popper. While he seems to me somewhat to underestimate the differences between the methods of natural science and those of history or common sense (Hayek's *The Counter-Revolution of Science* seems, despite some exaggerations, to be more convincing on this topic), he has, in his *The Open Society and its Enemies* and *The Poverty of Historicism*, exposed some of the fallacies of metaphysical 'historicism' with such force and precision, and made so clear its incompatibility with any kind of scientific empiricism, that there is no further excuse for confounding the two.

they are,' said a sober English philosopher over two centuries ago,
'and the consequences of them will be what they will be: why then
should we desire to be deceived?'[1]

What, then, must we do to avoid deception? At the very least – if
we cannot swallow the notion of super-personal 'spirits' or 'forces'
– we must admit that all events occur in discoverable, uniform,
unaltering patterns; for if some did not, how could we find the
laws of such occurrences? And without universal order – a system
of true laws – how could history be 'intelligible'? How could it
'make sense', 'have meaning', be more than a picaresque account of
a succession of random episodes, a mere collection (as Descartes,
for this very reason, seems to have thought) of old wives' tales?
Our values – what we think good and bad, important and trivial,
right and wrong, noble and contemptible – all these are conditioned by the place we occupy in the pattern, on the moving stair.
We praise and blame, worship and condemn whatever fits or does
not fit the interests and needs and ideals that we seek to satisfy –
the ends that (being made as we are) we cannot help pursuing –
according to our lights, that is, our own perception of our
condition, our place in 'Nature'. Such attitudes are held to be
'rational' and 'objective' to the degree to which we perceive this
condition accurately, that is, understand where we are in terms of
the great world plan, the movement whose regularities we discern
as well as our historical sense and knowledge permit. To each
condition and generation its own perspectives on the past and
future, depending upon where it has arrived, what it has left
behind, and whither it is moving; its values depend on this same
awareness. To condemn the Greeks or the Romans or the Assyr-
ians or the Aztecs for this or that folly or vice may be not more
than to say that what they did or wished or thought conflicts with
our own view of life, which may be the true or 'objective' view for
the stage which we have reached, and which is perceived less or
more clearly according to the depth and accuracy of our understanding of what this stage is, and of the manner in which it is
developing. If the Romans and the Aztecs judged differently from
us, they may have judged no less well and truly and 'objectively',
to the degree to which they understood their own condition and
their own very different stage of development. For us to condemn

---

[1] Joseph Butler, *Fifteen Sermons Preached at the Rolls Chapel* (London, 1726),
sermon 7, p. 136 [§ 16].

their scale of values is valid enough for our condition, which is the sole frame of reference we have. And if they had known us they might have condemned us as harshly and, because their circumstances and values were what they inevitably were, with equal validity.

According to this view there is nothing, no point of rest outside the general movement, where we or they can take up a stand, no static absolute standards in terms of which things and persons can be finally evaluated. Hence the only attitudes correctly described, and rightly condemned, as relative, subjective and irrational are forms of failure to relate our judgement to our own truest interests, that is, to what will fulfil our natures most fully – to all that the next step in our inevitable development necessarily holds in store. Some thinkers of this school view subjective aberrations with compassion and condone them as temporary attitudes from which the enlightenment of the future will henceforward preserve mankind. Others gloat exultantly or ironically over the inevitable doom of those who misinterpret, and therefore fall foul of, the inexorable march of events. But whether the tone is charitable or sardonic, whether one condemns the errors of foolish individuals or the blind mob, or applauds their inevitable annihilation, this attitude rests on the belief that everything is caused to occur as it does by the machinery of history itself – by the impersonal forces of class, race, culture, History, Reason, the Life-Force, Progress, the Spirit of the Age. Given this organisation of our lives, which we did not create, and cannot alter, it, and it alone, is ultimately responsible for everything. To blame or praise individuals or groups of individuals for acting rightly or wrongly, so far as this entails a suggestion that they are in some sense genuinely free to choose between alternatives, and may therefore be justly and reasonably blamed or praised for choosing as they did and do, is a vast blunder, a return to some primitive or naïve conception of human beings as being able somehow to evade total determination of their lives by forces natural or supernatural, a relapse into a childish animism which the study of the relevant scientific or metaphysical system should swiftly dispel. For if such choices were real, the determined world structure which alone, on this view, makes complete explanation, whether scientific or metaphysical, possible could not exist. And this is ruled out as unthinkable, 'reason rejects it', it is confused, delusive, superficial, a piece of puerile megalomania, pre-scientific, unworthy of civilised men.

The notion that history obeys laws, whether natural or supernatural, that every event of human life is an element in a necessary
pattern, has deep metaphysical origins: infatuation with the natural
sciences feeds this stream, but is not its sole or, indeed, its principal
source. In the first place there is the teleological outlook whose
roots reach back to the beginnings of human thought. It occurs in
many versions, but what is common to them all is the belief that
men, and all living creatures and perhaps inanimate things as well,
not merely are as they are, but have functions and pursue purposes.
These purposes are either imposed upon them by a creator who has
made every person and thing to serve each a specific goal; or else
these purposes are not, indeed, imposed by a creator but are, as it
were, internal to their possessors, so that every entity has a 'nature'
and pursues a specific goal which is 'natural' to it, and the measure
of its perfection consists in the degree to which it fulfils it. Evil,
vice, imperfection, all the various forms of chaos and error, are, on
this view, forms of frustration, impeded efforts to reach such goals,
failures due either to misfortune, which puts obstacles in the path
of self-fulfilment, or to misdirected attempts to fulfil some goal not
'natural' to the entity in question.

In this cosmology the world of men (and, in some versions, the
entire universe) is a single all-inclusive hierarchy; so that to explain
why each ingredient of it is as, and where, and when it is, and does
what it does, is *eo ipso* to say what its goal is, how far it successfully
fulfils it, and what are the relations of co-ordination and subordination between the goals of the various goal-pursuing entities in
the harmonious pyramid which they collectively form. If this is a
true picture of reality, then historical explanation, like every other
form of explanation, must consist, above all, in the attribution to
individuals, groups, nations, species of their proper place in the
universal pattern. To know the 'cosmic' place of a thing or a person
is to say what it is and does, and at the same time why it should be
and do as it is and does. Hence to be and to have value, to exist and
to have a function (and to fulfil it less or more successfully) are one
and the same. The pattern, and it alone, brings into being, and
causes to pass away, and confers purpose, that is to say, value and
meaning, on all there is. To understand is to perceive patterns. To
offer historical explanations is not merely to describe a succession
of events, but to make it intelligible; to make intelligible is to reveal
the basic pattern – not one of several possible patterns, but the one
unique plan which, by being as it is, fulfils only one particular

purpose, and consequently is revealed as fitting in a specifiable fashion within the single 'cosmic' overall schema which is the goal of the universe, the goal in virtue of which alone it is a universe at all, and not a chaos of unrelated bits and pieces. The more thoroughly the nature of this purpose is understood, and with it the pattern it entails in the various forms of human activity, the more explanatory or illuminating – the 'deeper' – the activity of the historian will be. Unless an event, or the character of an individual, or the activity of this or that institution or group or historical personage, is explained as a necessary consequence of its place in the pattern (and the larger, that is, the more comprehensive the schema, the more likely it is to be the true one), no explanation – and therefore no historical account – is being provided. The more inevitable an event or an action or a character can be exhibited as being, the better it has been understood, the profounder the researcher's insight, the nearer we are to the one embracing, ultimate truth.

This attitude is profoundly anti-empirical. We attribute purposes to all things and persons not because we have evidence for this hypothesis; for if there were a question of evidence for it, there could in principle be evidence against it; and then some things and events might turn out to have no purpose and therefore, in the sense used above, be incapable of being fitted into the pattern, that is, of being explained at all; but this cannot be, and is rejected in advance, a priori. We are plainly dealing not with an empirical theory but with a metaphysical attitude which takes for granted that to explain a thing – to describe it as it 'truly' is, even to define it more than verbally, that is, superficially – is to discover its purpose. Everything is in principle explicable, for everything has a purpose, although our minds may be too feeble or too distraught to discover in any given case what this purpose is. On such a view to say of things or persons that they exist is to say that they pursue goals; to say that they exist or are real, yet literally lack a purpose, whether imposed from outside or 'inherent' or 'innate', is to say something not false, but literally self-contradictory and therefore meaningless. Teleology is not a theory, or a hypothesis, but a category or a framework in terms of which everything is, or should be, conceived and described.

The influence of this attitude on the writing of history from the epic of Gilgamesh to those enjoyable games of patience which Arnold Toynbee plays with the past and future of mankind – and plays with exhilarating skill and imagination – is too familiar to need emphasis. It enters, however unconsciously, into the thought and language of those who speak of the 'rise' and 'fall' of States or movements or classes or individuals as if they obeyed some irresistible rhythm, a rising or falling wave of some cosmic river, a tidal ebb or flow in human affairs, subject to natural or supernatural laws; as if discoverable regularities had been imposed on individuals or 'super-individuals' by a Manifest Destiny, as if the notion of life as a play were more than a vivid metaphor.[1] To those who use this figure history is a piece – or succession of pieces – comical or tragical, a libretto whose heroes and villains, winners and losers, speak their lines and suffer their fate in accordance with the text conceived in terms of them but not by them; for otherwise nothing could be rightly conceived as tragical or comical; no pattern – no rules – no explanation. Historians, journalists, ordinary men speak in these terms; they have become part and parcel of ordinary speech. Yet to take such metaphors and turns of phrase literally; to believe that such patterns are not invented but intuitively discovered or discerned, that they are not only some among many possible tunes which the same sounds can be made to yield to the musical ear, but are in some sense unique; to think that there

[1] I do not, of course, wish to imply that metaphors and figures of speech can be dispensed with in ordinary utterance, still less in the sciences; only that the danger of illicit 'reification' – the mistaking of words for things, metaphors for realities – is even greater in this sphere than is usually supposed. The most notorious cases are, of course, those of the State or the Nation, the quasi-personification of which has rightly made philosophers and even plain men uneasy or indignant for over a century. But many other words and usages offer similar dangers. Historical movements exist, and we must be allowed to call them such. Collective acts do occur; societies do rise, flourish, decay, die. Patterns, 'atmospheres', complex interrelationships of men or cultures are what they are, and cannot be analysed away into atomic constituents. Nevertheless, to take such expressions so literally that it becomes natural and normal to attribute to them causal properties, active powers, transcendent properties, demands for human sacrifice, is to be fatally deceived by myths. 'Rhythms' in history occur, but it is a sinister symptom of one's condition to speak of them as 'inexorable'. Cultures possess patterns, and ages spirits; but to explain human actions as their 'inevitable' consequences or expressions is to be a victim of misuse of words. There is no formula which guarantees a successful escape from either the Scylla of populating the world with imaginary powers and dominions, or the Charybdis of reducing everything to the verifiable behaviour of identifiable men and women in precisely denotable places and times. One can do no more than point to the existence of these perils; one must navigate between them as best one can.

exists the pattern, the basic rhythm of history – something which both creates and justifies all that there is – that is to take the game too seriously, to see in it a key to reality. Certainly it is to commit oneself to the view that the notion of individual responsibility is, 'in the end', an illusion. No effort, however ingenious, to re-interpret that much-tormented expression will, within a teleological system, restore its normal meaning to the notion of free choice. The puppets may be conscious and identify themselves happily with the inevitable process in which they play their parts; but it remains inevitable, and they remain marionettes.

Teleology is not, of course, the only metaphysics of history; side by side with it there has persisted a distinction of appearance and reality even more celebrated but of a somewhat different kind. For the teleological thinker all apparent disorder, inexplicable disaster, gratuitous suffering, unintelligible concatenations of random events are due not to the nature of things but to our failure to discover their purpose. Everything that seems useless, discordant, mean, ugly, vicious, distorted is needed, if we but knew it, for the harmony of the whole which only the Creator of the world, or the world itself (if it could become wholly aware of itself and its goals), can know. Total failure is excluded a priori, for at a 'deeper' level all processes will always be seen to culminate in success; and since there must always exist a level 'deeper' than that of any given insight, there is in principle no empirical test of what constitutes 'ultimate' success or failure. Teleology is a form of faith capable of neither confirmation nor refutation by any kind of experience; the notions of evidence, proof, probability and so on are wholly inapplicable to it.

But there is a second, no less time-honoured view according to which it is not goals, less or more dimly discerned, which explain and justify whatever happens, but a timeless, permanent, transcend-ent reality, 'above', or 'outside', or 'beyond'; which is as it is for ever, in perfect, inevitable, self-explaining harmony. Each element of it is necessitated to be what it is by its relations to the other elements and to the whole. If the world does not appear to manifest this, if we do not see actual events and persons as connected with each other by those relations of logical necessity which would make it inconceivable that anything could be other than it is, that is due solely to the failure of our own vision. We are blinded by ignorance, stupidity, passion, and the task of explana-tion in science or in history is the attempt to show the chaos of appearances as an imperfect reflection of the perfect order of reality, so that once more everything falls into its proper place. Explanation is the discovery of the 'underlying' pattern. The ideal is now not a distant prospect beckoning all things and persons towards self-realisation, but a self-consistent, eternal, ultimate 'structure of reality', compresent 'timelessly', as it were, with the confused world of the senses which it casts as a distorted image or a feeble shadow, and of which it is at once the origin, the cause, the explanation and the justification. The relation of this reality to the world of appearances forms the subject-matter of all the departments of true philosophy – of ethics, aesthetics, logic, of the philosophy of history and of law and of politics, according to the 'aspect' of the basic relation that is selected for attention. But under all its various names – form and matter, the one and the many, ends and means, subject and object, order and chaos, change and rest, the perfect and the imperfect, the natural and the artificial, nature and mind – the central issue, that of Reality and Appearance, remains one and the same. To understand truly is to understand it and it alone. It plays the part which the notion of function and purpose plays in teleology. It alone at once explains and justifies.

Finally there is the influence of the natural sciences. At first this seems a paradox: scientific method is surely the very negation of metaphysical speculation. But historically the one is closely interwoven with the other, and, in the field of which I speak, shows important affinities with it, namely, the notion that all that exists is necessarily an object in material nature, and therefore susceptible to explanation by scientific laws. If Newton was able in principle to explain every movement of every particular constituent of physical nature in terms of a small number of laws of great generality, is it not reasonable to suppose that psychological events, which constitute the conscious and unconscious lives of individuals, as well as social facts – the internal relationships and activities and 'experiences' of societies – could be explained by the use of similar methods? It is true that we seem to know a good deal less about the subject-matter of psychology and sociology than about the facts dealt with by physics or chemistry; but is there any objection in principle to the view that a sufficiently scrupulous and imaginative investigation of human beings might, one day, reveal laws capable of yielding predictions as powerful and as precise as those which are now possible in the natural sciences? If psychology and sociology ever attain to their proper stature – and why should they not? – we shall have laws enabling us, at least in theory (for it might still be difficult in practice), to predict (or reconstruct) every detail in the lives of every single human being in the future, present and past. If this is (as surely it is) the theoretical ideal of such sciences as psychology, sociology and anthropology, historical explanations will, if they are successful, simply consist in the application of the laws – the established hypotheses – of these sciences to specific individual situations. There will perhaps be 'pure' psychology, sociology, history, that is, the principles themselves; and there will be their 'application': there will come into being social mathematics, social physics, social engineering, the 'physiology' of every feeling and attitude and inclination, as precise and powerful and useful as their originals in the natural sciences. And indeed this is the very phraseology and ideal of eighteenth-century rationalists like Holbach and d'Alembert and Condorcet. The metaphysicians are victims of a delusion; nothing in nature is transcendent, nothing purposive; everything is measurable; the day will dawn when, in answer to all the painful problems now besetting us, we shall be able to say with Leibniz, 'calculemus',[1] and return the answers clearly, exactly and conclusively.

What all these concepts – metaphysical and scientific alike – have in common (despite their even vaster differences) is the notion that to explain is to subsume under general formulae, to represent as examples of laws which cover an infinite number of instances; so that with knowledge of all the relevant laws, and of a sufficient range of relevant facts, it will be possible to tell not merely what happens, but also why; for, if the laws have been correctly established, to describe something is, in effect, to assert that it cannot happen otherwise. The question 'Why?' for teleologists means 'In pursuit of what unalterable goal?'; for the non-teleological metaphysical 'realists' it means 'Determined unalterably by what ultimate pattern?'; and for the upholders of the Comtean ideals of social statics and dynamics it means 'Resulting from what causes?' – actual causes which are as they are, whether they might have been otherwise or not. The inevitability of historical processes, of trends, of 'rises' and 'falls', is merely *de facto* for those who believe that the universe obeys only 'natural laws' which make it

---

[1] 'Let us calculate': e.g. *Die philosophischen Schriften von Gottfried Wilhelm Leibniz*, ed. C. I. Gerhardt (Berlin, 1875–90), vol. 7, p. 200. Condorcet, in particular, had the same attitude.

what it is; it is *de jure* as well – the justification as well as the explanation – for those who see such uniformity as not merely something given, brute fact, something unchangeable and unquestionable, but as patterns, plans, purposes, ideals, as thoughts in the mind of a rational Deity or Universal Reason, as goals, as aesthetic, self-fulfilling wholes, as metaphysical rationales, theological other-worldly justifications, as theodicies, which satisfy the craving to know not merely why the world exists, but why it is worthy of existence; and why it is this particular world that exists, rather than some other, or no world at all; the solution being provided in terms of values which are either somehow 'embedded' in the facts themselves or 'determine' them from some 'transcendent' height or depth. All these theories are, in one sense or another, forms of determinism, whether they be teleological, metaphysical, mechanistic, religious, aesthetic or scientific. And one common characteristic of all such outlooks is the implication that the individual's freedom of choice (at any rate here, below) is ultimately an illusion, that the notion that human beings could have chosen otherwise than they did usually rests upon ignorance of facts; with the consequence that any assertion that they should have acted thus or thus, might have avoided this or that, and deserve (and not merely elicit or respond to) praise or blame, approval or condemnation, rests upon the presupposition that some area, at any rate, of their lives is not totally determined by laws, whether metaphysical or theological or expressing the generalised probabilities of the sciences. And this assumption, it is then maintained, is patently false. The advance of knowledge constantly brings new areas of experience under the sway of laws which make systematic inference and prediction possible. Hence we can, if we seek to be rational, praise and condemn, warn and encourage, advocate justice or self-interest, forgive, condone, make resolutions, issue orders, feel justified remorse, only to the degree to which we remain ignorant of the true nature of the world. The more we know, the farther the area of human freedom, and consequently of responsibility, is narrowed. For the omniscient being, who sees why nothing can be otherwise than as it is, the notions of responsibility or guilt, of right and wrong, are necessarily empty; they are a mere measure of ignorance, of adolescent illusion; and the perception of this is the first sign of moral and intellectual maturity.

This doctrine has taken several forms. There are those who believe that moral judgements are groundless because we know too much, and there are those who believe that they are unjustified because we know too little. And again, among the former there are those whose determinism is optimistic and benevolent, and those whose determinism is pessimistic, or else confident of a happy ending yet at the same time indignantly or sardonically malevolent. Some look to history for salvation; others for justice; for vengeance; for annihilation. Among the optimistic are the confident rationalists, in particular the heralds and prophets (from Bacon to modern social theorists) of the natural sciences and of material progress, who maintain that vice and suffering are in the end always the product of ignorance. The foundation of their faith is the conviction that it is possible to find out what all men at all times truly want; and also what they can do and what is for ever beyond their power; and, in the light of this, to invent, discover and adapt means to realisable ends. Weakness and misery, folly and vice, moral and intellectual defects are due to maladjustment. To understand the nature of things is (at the very least) to know what you (and others who, if they are human, will be like you) truly want, and how to get it. All that is bad is due to ignorance of ends or of means; to attain to knowledge of both is the purpose and function of the sciences. The sciences will advance; true ends as well as efficient means will be discovered; knowledge will increase, men will know more, and therefore be wiser and better and happier. Condorcet, whose *Esquisse* is the simplest and most moving statement of this belief, has no doubt that happiness, scientific knowledge, virtue and liberty are bound as 'by an indissoluble chain',[1] while stupidity, vice, injustice and unhappiness are forms of a disease which the advance of science will eliminate for ever; for we are made what we are by natural causes; and when we understand them, this alone will suffice to bring us into harmony with 'Nature'.

Praise and blame are functions of ignorance; we are what we are, like stones and trees, like bees and beavers, and if it is irrational to blame or demand justice from things or animals, climates or soils or wild beasts, when they cause us pain, it is no less irrational to blame the no less determined characters or acts of men. We can regret – and deplore and expose – the depth of human cruelty, injustice and stupidity, and comfort ourselves with the certainty

---

[1] *Esquisse d'un tableau historique des progres de l'esprit humain*, ed. O. H. Prior and Yvon Belaval (Paris, 1970), p. 228.

that with the rapid progress of our new empirical knowledge this will soon pass away like an evil dream; for progress and education, if not inevitable, are at any rate highly probable. The belief in the possibility (or probability) of happiness as the product of rational organisation unites all the benevolent sages of modern times, from the metaphysicians of the Italian Renaissance to the evolutionary thinkers of the German *Aufklärung*, from the radicals and utilitarians of pre-revolutionary France to the science-worshipping visionaries of the nineteenth and twentieth centuries. It is the heart of all the Utopias from Bacon and Campanella to Lessing and Condorcet, Saint-Simon and Cabet, Fourier and Owen, culminating in the bureaucratic fantasies of Auguste Comte, with his fanatically tidy world of human beings joyfully engaged in fulfilling their functions, each within his own rigorously defined province, in the rationally ordered, totally unalterable hierarchy of the perfect society. These are the benevolent humanitarian prophets – our own age has known not a few of them, from Jules Verne and H. G. Wells and Anatole France and Bernard Shaw to their unnumbered American disciples – generously disposed towards all mankind, genuinely seeking to rescue every living being from its burden of ignorance, sorrow, poverty and humiliating dependence on others.

The other variant of this attitude is a good deal less amiable in tone and in feeling. When Hegel, and after him Marx, describe historical processes, they too assume that human beings and their societies are part and parcel of a wider nature, which Hegel regards as spiritual, and Marx as material, in character. Great social forces are at work of which only the acutest and most gifted individuals are ever aware; the ordinary run of men are blind in varying degrees to that which truly shapes their lives, they worship fetishes and invent childish mythologies, which they dignify with the title of views or theories in order to explain the world in which they live. From time to time the real forces – impersonal and irresistible – which truly govern the world develop to a point where a new historical advance is 'due'. Then (as both Hegel and Marx notoriously believed) the crucial moments of advance are reached; these take the form of violent, cataclysmic leaps, destructive revolutions which, often with fire and sword, establish a new order upon the ruins of the old. Inevitably the foolish, obsolete, purblind, home-made philosophies of the denizens of the old establishment are knocked over and swept away together with their possessors.

For Hegel, and for a good many others, though by no means all, among the philosophers and poets of the romantic movement, history is a perpetual struggle of vast spiritual forces embodied now in institutions – Churches, races, civilisations, empires, national States – now in individuals of more than human stature – 'world-historical figures' – of bold and ruthless genius, towering over, and contemptuous of, their puny contemporaries. For Marx, the struggle is a fight between socially conditioned, organised groups – classes shaped by the struggle for subsistence and survival and consequently for the control of power. There is a sardonic note (inaudible only to their most benevolent and single-hearted followers) in the words of both these thinkers as they contemplate the discomfiture and destruction of the philistines, the ordinary men and women caught in one of the decisive moments of history. Both Hegel and Marx conjure up an image of peaceful and foolish human beings, largely unaware of the part they play in history, building their homes, with touching hope and simplicity, upon the green slopes of what seems to them a peaceful mountainside, trusting in the permanence of their particular way of life, their own economic, social and political order, treating their own values as if they were eternal standards, living, working, fighting without any awareness of the cosmic processes of which their lives are but a passing stage. But the mountain is no ordinary mountain; it is a volcano; and when (as the philosopher always knew that it would) the inevitable eruption comes, their homes and their elaborately tended institutions and their ideals and their ways of life and values will be blown out of existence in the cataclysm which marks the leap from the 'lower' to a 'higher' stage. When this point is reached, the two great prophets of destruction are in their element; they enter into their inheritance; they survey the conflagration with a defiant, almost Byronic, irony and disdain. To be wise is to understand the direction in which the world is inexorably moving, to identify oneself with the rising power which ushers in the new world. Marx – and it is part of his attraction to those of a similar emotional cast – identifies himself exultantly, in his way no less passionately than Nietzsche or Bakunin, with the great force which in its very destructiveness is creative, and is greeted with bewilderment and horror only by those whose values are hopelessly subjective, who listen to their consciences, their feelings, or to what their nurses or teachers tell them, without realising the glories of life in a world which moves from explosion to explosion to fulfil the great cosmic design. When history takes her revenge – and every *enragé* prophet in the nineteenth century looks to her to avenge him against those he hates most – the mean, pathetic, ludicrous, stifling human anthills will be justly pulverised; justly, because what is just and unjust, good and bad, is determined by the goal towards which all creation is tending. Whatever is on the side of victorious reason is just and wise; whatever is on the other side, on the side of the world that is doomed to destruction by the working of the forces of reason, is rightly called foolish, ignorant, subjective, arbitrary, blind; and, if it goes so far as to try to resist the forces that are destined to supplant it, then it – that is to say, the fools and knaves and mediocrities who constitute it – is rightly called retrograde, wicked, obscurantist, perversely hostile to the deepest interests of mankind.

Different though the tone of these forms of determinism may be – whether scientific, humanitarian and optimistic or furious, apocalyptic and exultant – they agree in this: that the world has a direction and is governed by laws, and that the direction and the laws can in some degree be discovered by employing the proper techniques of investigation; and moreover that the working of these laws can only be grasped by those who realise that the lives, characters and acts of individuals, both mental and physical, are governed by the larger 'wholes' to which they belong, and that it is the independent evolution of these 'wholes' that constitutes the so-called 'forces' in terms of whose direction truly 'scientific' (or 'philosophic') history must be formulated. To find the explanation of why given individuals, or groups of them, act or think or feel in one way rather than another, one must first seek to understand the structure, the state of development and the direction of such 'wholes', for example, the social, economic, political, religious institutions to which such individuals belong; once that is known, the behaviour of the individuals (or the most characteristic among them) should become almost logically deducible, and does not constitute a separate problem. Ideas about the identity of these large entities or forces, and their functions, differ from theorist to theorist. Race, colour, Church, nation, class; climate, irrigation, technology, geopolitical situation; civilisation, social structure, the Human Spirit, the Collective Unconscious, to take some of these concepts at random, have all played their parts in theologico-historical systems as the protagonists upon the stage of history. They are represented as the real forces of which individuals are ingredients, at once constitutive, and the most articulate expressions, of this or that phase of them. Those who are more clearly and deeply aware than others of the part which they play, whether willingly or not, to that degree play it more boldly and effectively; these are the natural leaders. Others, led by their own petty personal concerns into ignoring or forgetting that they are parts of a continuous or convulsive pattern of change, are deluded into assuming that (or, at any rate, into acting as if) they and their fellows are stabilised at some fixed level for ever.

What the variants of either of these attitudes entail, like all forms of genuine determinism, is the elimination of the notion of individual responsibility. It is, after all, natural enough for men, whether for practical reasons or because they are given to reflection, to ask who or what is responsible for this or that state of affairs which they view with satisfaction or anxiety, enthusiasm or horror. If the history of the world is due to the operation of identifiable forces other than, and little affected by, free human wills and free choices (whether these occur or not), then the proper explanation of what happens must be given in terms of the evolution of such forces. And there is then a tendency to say that not individuals, but these larger entities, are ultimately 'responsible'. I live at a particular moment of time in the spiritual and social and economic circumstances into which I have been cast: how then can I help choosing and acting as I do? The values in terms of which I conduct my life are the values of my class, or race, or Church, or civilisation, or are part and parcel of my 'station' – my position in the 'social structure'. Nobody denies that it would be stupid as well as cruel to blame me for not being taller than I am, or to regard the colour of my hair or the qualities of my intellect or heart as being due principally to my own free choice; these attributes are as they are through no decision of mine. If I extend this category without limit, then whatever is, is necessary and inevitable. This unlimited extension of necessity, on any of the views described above, becomes intrinsic to the explanation of everything. To blame and praise, consider possible alternative courses of action, accuse or defend historical figures for acting as they do or did, becomes an absurd activity. Admiration and contempt for this or that individual may indeed continue, but it becomes akin to aesthetic judgement. We can eulogise or deplore, feel love or hatred, satisfaction or shame, but we can neither blame nor justify. Alexander, Caesar, Attila, Muhammad, Cromwell,

Hitler are like floods and earthquakes, sunsets, oceans, mountains; we may admire or fear them, welcome or curse them, but to denounce or extol their acts is (ultimately) as sensible as addressing sermons to a tree (as Frederick the Great pointed out with his customary pungency in the course of his attack on Holbach's *System of Nature*).[1]

[1] Determinism is, of course, not identical with fatalism, which is only one, and not the most plausible, species of the vast determinist genus. The majority of determinists seem to maintain that such distinctions as those between voluntary behaviour, or between acts and mechanical movements or states, or what a man is and what he is not accountable for, and therefore the very notion of a moral agent, depend on what is or could be affected by individual choice, effort or decision. They hold that I normally praise or blame a man only if, and because, I think that what occurred was (or might at any rate in part be) caused by his choice or the absence of it; and should not praise or blame him if his choices, efforts etc. were conspicuously unable to affect the result that I applaud or deplore; and that this is compatible with the most rigorous determinism, since choice, effort etc. are themselves causally inevitable consequences of identifiable spatio-temporal antecedents. This (in substance the classical 'dissolution' of the problem of free will by the British empiricists – Hobbes, Locke, Hume and their modern followers Russell, Schlick, Ayer, Nowell-Smith, Hampshire etc.) does not seem to me to solve the problem, but merely to push it a step further back. It may be that for legal or other purposes I may define responsibility, moral accountability etc. on some such lines as these. But if I were convinced that although acts of choice, dispositional characteristics etc. did affect what occurred, yet they were themselves wholly determined by factors not within the individual's control (including his own motives and springs of action), I should certainly not regard him as morally praiseworthy or blameworthy. In such circumstances the concept of worth and desert, as these terms are now used, would become empty for me.

The same kind of objection seems to me to apply to the connected doctrine that free will is tantamount to capacity for being (causally) affected by praise, blame, persuasion, education etc. Whether the causes that are held completely to determine human action are physical or psychical or of some other kind, and in whatever pattern or proportion they are deemed to occur, if they are truly causes – if their outcomes are thought to be as unalterable as, say, the effects of physical or physiological causes – this of itself seems to me to make the notion of a free choice between alternatives inapplicable. On this view 'I could have acted otherwise' is made to mean 'I could have acted otherwise if I had chosen', i.e. if there were no insuperable obstacle to hinder me (with the rider that my choice may well be affected by praise, social disapproval etc.); but if my choice is itself the result of antecedent causes, I am, in the relevant sense, not free. Freedom to act depends not on absence of only this or that set of fatal obstacles to action – physical or biological, let us say – while other obstacles, e.g. psychological ones – character, habits, 'compulsive' motives etc. – are present; it requires a situation in which no sum total of such causal factors wholly determines the result – in which there remains some area, however narrow, within which choice is not completely

To assess degrees of their responsibility, to attribute this or that consequence to their free decision, to set them up as examples or deterrents, to seek to derive lessons from their lives, becomes senseless. We can feel ashamed of our acts or of our states of mind, or of theirs, as a hunchback may be ashamed of his hump; but we cannot feel remorse: for that entails the belief that we not only could have acted otherwise, but also could have freely chosen to do so. These men were what they were; and so are we. They acted as they acted; and so do we. Their behaviour can be explained in terms of whatever fundamental category is to be used, whereby history is reducible to a natural science or a metaphysical or theological schema. So much we can do for them, and, to a more limited degree, for ourselves and our contemporaries. This is all that can be done.

Yet we are adjured, oddly enough, by tough-minded determinists, in the very name of the scientific status of the subject, to avoid bias; regular appeals are made to historians to refrain from sitting in judgement, to remain objective, not to read the values of the present into the past, or of the West into the East; not to admire or condemn ancient Romans for being like or unlike modern Americans; not to denounce the Middle Ages because they failed to practise toleration as it was conceived by Voltaire, nor applaud the Gracchi because we are shocked by the social injustices of our time, or criticise Cicero because of our own experience of lawyers in politics. What are we to make of such exhortations, or of the

---

determined. This is the minimal sense of 'can' in this context. Kant's argument that where there is no freedom there is no obligation, where there is no independence of causes there is no responsibility and therefore no desert, and consequently no occasion for praise or reproach, carries conviction. If I can correctly say 'I cannot help choosing thus or thus', I am not free. To say that among the factors which determine the situation are my own character, habits, decisions, choices etc. – which is, of course, conspicuously true – does not alter the case, or render me, in the only relevant sense, free. The feeling of those who have recognised free will as a genuine issue, and are not deceived by the latest efforts to interpret it away, turns out, as so often in the case of major problems which have plagued thoughtful men in every generation, to be sound as against philosophers armed with some all-conquering simple method of sweeping troublesome questions out of sight. Dr Johnson, as in other matters affecting common-sense notions, here, too, seems to have been guided by a sound linguistic sense. It does not, of course, follow that any of the analyses so far provided of the relevant senses of 'can', 'freedom', 'uncaused' etc. is satisfactory. To cut the knot, as Dr Johnson did, is not to untie it.

perpetual pleas to use our imagination or our powers of sympathy or of understanding in order to avoid the injustice that springs from an insufficient grasp of the aims and codes and customs of cultures distant from us in time or space? What meaning has this, save on the assumption that to give moral praise and blame, to seek to be just, is not totally irrational, that human beings deserve justice as stocks or stones do not, and that therefore we must seek to be fair, and not praise and blame arbitrarily, or mistakenly, through ignorance, or prejudice, or lack of imagination? Yet once we transfer responsibility for what happens from the backs of individuals to the casual or teleological operation of institutions or cultures or psychical or physical factors, what can be meant by calling upon our sympathy or sense of history, or sighing after the ideal of total impartiality, which may not indeed be fully attainable, but to which some come nearer than others? Few are accused of biased accounts of geological changes or lack of intuitive sympathy in describing the effect of the Italian climate upon the agriculture of ancient Rome.

To this it may be answered that even if history, like natural science, is satisfaction of curiosity about unalterable processes – merely disfigured by the intrusion of moral judgements – we shall attain a less adequate grasp of even the bare facts unless we have some degree of imaginative insight into ways of life alien, or little known, to us. This is doubtless true; but it does not penetrate to the heart of the objection brought against historians who are accused of prejudice or of colouring their accounts too strongly. It may be (and has doubtless often been said) that Gibbon or Macaulay or Treitschke or Belloc fail to reproduce the facts as we suspect them to have been. To say this is, of course, to accuse the writers of serious inadequacy as historians; but that is not the main gravamen of the charge. It is rather that they are in some sense not merely inaccurate or superficial or incomplete, but that they are unjust; that they are seeking to secure our approval for one side, and, in order to achieve this, unfairly denigrate the other; that in dealing with one side they cite evidence and use methods of inference or presentation which, for no good reason, they deny to the other; and that their motive for doing this derives from their conviction of how men should be, and what they should do; and sometimes also that these convictions spring from views which (judged in terms of the ordinary standards and scales of value which prevail in the societies to which they and we belong) are too narrow; or irrational or inapplicable to the historical period in question; and that because of this they have suppressed or distorted the true facts, as true facts are conceived by the educated society of their, or our, time. We complain, that is to say, not merely of suppression or distortion, but of propagandist aims to which we think this may be due; and to speak of propaganda at all, let alone assume that it can be dangerously effective, is to imply that the notion of injustice is not inoperative, that marks for conduct are, and can properly be, awarded; it is in effect to say that I must either seek not to praise or blame at all, or, if I cannot avoid doing so because I am a human being and my views are inevitably shot through with moral assessments, I should seek to do so justly, with detachment, on the evidence, not blaming men for failing to do the impossible, and not praising them for it either. And this, in its turn, entails belief in individual responsibility – at any rate some degree of it. How great a degree – how wide the realm of possibility, of alternatives freely choosable – will depend on one's reading of nature and history; but it will never be nothing at all.

And yet it is this, it seems to me, that is virtually denied by those historians and sociologists, steeped in metaphysical or scientific determinism, who think it right to say that in (what they are fond of calling) 'the last analysis', everything – or so much of it as makes no difference – boils down to the effects of class, or race, or civilisation, or social structure. Such thinkers seem to me committed to the belief that although we may not be able to plot the exact curve of each individual life with the data at our disposal and the laws we claim to have discovered, yet, in principle, if we were omniscient, we could do so, at any rate in the case of others, as precisely as the techniques of scientific prediction will allow; and that consequently even that minimum residue of value judgement which no amount of conscious self-discipline and self-effacement can wholly eliminate, which colours and is a part of our very choice of historical material, of our emphasis, however tentative, upon some events and persons as being more important or interesting or unusual than others, must be either the result of our own 'ineluctable' conditioning, or else the fruit of our own incurable vanity and ignorance; and in either case remains in practice unavoidable – the price of our human status, part of the imperfection of man; and must be accepted only because it literally cannot be rejected, because men and their outlooks are what they are, and men judge as they do; because they are finite, and forget, or cannot face, the fact that they are so.

This stern conclusion is not, of course, actually accepted by any working historian, or any human being in his non-theoretical moments; even though, paradoxically enough, the arguments by which we are led to such untenable conclusions, by stressing how much narrower is the area of human freedom, and therefore of responsibility, than it was believed to be during the ages of scientific ignorance, have taught many admirable lessons in restraint and humility. But to maintain that, since men are 'determined', history, by which I mean the activity of historians, cannot, strictly speaking, ever be just or unjust but only true or false, wise or stupid, is to expound a noble fallacy, and one that can seldom, if ever, have been acted upon. For its theoretical acceptance, however half-hearted, has led to the drawing of exceedingly civilised consequences, and checked much traditional cruelty and injustice.

III

The proposition that everything that we do and suffer is part of a fixed pattern – that Laplace's observer (supplied with adequate knowledge of facts and laws) could at any moment of historical time describe correctly every past and future event, including those of the 'inner' life, that is, human thoughts, feelings, acts – has often been entertained, and very different implications have been drawn from it; belief in its truth has dismayed some and inspired others. But whether or not determinism is true or even coherent, it seems clear that acceptance of it does not in fact colour the ordinary thoughts of the majority of human beings, including historians, nor even those of natural scientists outside the laboratory. For if it did, the language of the believers would reflect this fact, and be different from that of the rest of us.

There is a class of expressions which we constantly use (and can scarcely do without), like 'You should not [or need not] have done this'; 'Need you have made this terrible mistake?'; 'I could do it, but I would rather not'; 'Why did the King of Ruritania abdicate? Because, unlike the King of Abyssinia, he lacked the strength of will to resist'; '*Must* the Commander-in-Chief be quite so stupid?' Expressions of this type plainly involve the notion of more than the merely logical possibility of the realisation of alternatives other than those which were in fact realised, namely of differences between situations in which individuals can be reasonably regarded as being responsible for their acts, and those in which they can not. For no one will wish to deny that we do often argue about the best among the possible courses of action open to human beings in the present and past and future, in fiction and in dreams; that historians (and detectives and judges and juries) do attempt to establish, as well as they are able, what these possibilities are; that the ways in which these lines are drawn mark the frontiers between reliable and unreliable history; that what is called realism (as opposed to fancy or ignorance of life or Utopian dreams) consists precisely in the placing of what occurred (or might occur) in the context of what could have happened (or could happen) and in the demarcation of this from what could not; that this is what (as I think L. B. Namier once suggested) the sense of history, in the end, comes to; that upon this capacity historical (as well as legal) justice depends; that it alone makes it possible to speak of criticism, or praise and blame, as just or deserved or absurd or unfair; or that this is the sole and obvious reason why accidents, *force majeure* – being unavoidable – are necessarily outside the category of responsibility and consequently beyond the bounds of criticism, of the attribution of praise and blame. The difference between the expected and the exceptional, the difficult and the easy, the normal and the perverse, rests upon the drawing of these same lines.

All this seems too self-evident to argue. It seems superfluous to add that all the discussions of historians about whether a given policy could or could not have been prevented, and what view should therefore be taken of the acts and characters of the actors, are intelligible only on the assumption of the reality of human choices. If determinism were a valid theory of human behaviour, these distinctions would be as inappropriate as the attribution of moral responsibility to the planetary system or the tissues of a living cell. These categories permeate all that we think and feel so pervasively and universally that to think them away, and conceive what and how we should be thinking, feeling and talking without them, or in the framework of their opposites, psychologically greatly strains our capacity – is nearly, if not quite, as impracticable as, let us say, to pretend that we live in a world in which space, time or number in the normal sense no longer exist. We may indeed always argue about specific situations, about whether a given occurrence is best explained as the inevitable effect of antecedent events beyond human control, or on the contrary as due to free human choice; free in the sense not merely that the case would have been altered if we had chosen – tried to act – differently; but that nothing prevented us from so choosing.

It may well be that the growth of science and historical knowledge does in fact tend to show – make probable – that much of what was hitherto attributed to the acts of the unfettered wills of individuals can be satisfactorily explained only by the working of other, 'natural', impersonal factors; that we have, in our ignorance or vanity, extended the realm of human freedom much too far. Yet the very meaning of such terms as 'cause' and 'inevitable' depends on the possibility of contrasting them with at least their imaginary opposites. These alternatives may be improbable; but they must at least be conceivable, if only for the purpose of contrasting them with causal necessities and law-observing uniformities; unless we attach some meaning to the notion of free acts, that is, acts not wholly determined by antecedent events or by the nature and 'dispositional characteristics' of either persons or things, it is difficult to see why we come to distinguish acts to which responsibility is attached from mere segments in a physical, psychical or psychophysical causal chain of events – a distinction signified (even if all particular applications of it are mistaken) by the cluster of expressions which deal with open alternatives and free choices. Yet it is this distinction that underlies our normal attribution of values, in particular the notion that praise and blame can ever be justly (not merely usefully or effectively) bestowed. If the determinist hypothesis were true, and adequately accounted for the actual world, there is a clear sense in which, despite all the extraordinary casuistry which has been brought to bear to avoid this conclusion, the notion of human responsibility, as ordinarily understood, would no longer apply to any actual, but only to imaginary or conceivable, states of affairs.

I do not here wish to say that determinism is necessarily false, only that we neither speak nor think as if it could be true, and that it is difficult, and perhaps beyond our normal powers, to conceive what our picture of the world would be if we seriously believed it; so that to speak, as some theorists of history (and scientists with a philosophical bent) tend to do, as if one might (in life and not only in the study) accept the determinist hypothesis, and yet continue to think and speak much as we do at present, is to breed intellectual confusion. If the belief in freedom – which rests on the assumption

that human beings do occasionally choose, and that their choices
are not wholly accounted for by the kind of causal explanations
which are accepted in, say, physics or biology – if this is a
necessary illusion, it is so deep and so pervasive that it is not felt as
such.[1] No doubt we can try to convince ourselves that we are
systematically deluded;[2] but unless we attempt to think out the
implications of this possibility, and alter our modes of thought and
speech to allow for it accordingly, this hypothesis remains hollow;
that is, we find it impracticable even to entertain it seriously, if our
behaviour is to be taken as evidence of what we can and what we
cannot bring ourselves to believe or suppose not merely in theory,
but in practice.

My submission is that to make a serious attempt to adapt our
thoughts and words to the hypothesis of determinism is a fearful
task, as things are now, and have been within recorded history. The
changes involved are very radical; our moral and psychological
categories are, in the end, more flexible than our physical ones, but
not much more so; it is not much easier to begin to think out in
real terms, to which behaviour and speech would correspond, what
the universe of the genuine determinist would be like, than to think
out, with the minimum of indispensable concrete detail (that is,
begin to imagine) what it would be like to be in a timeless world,
or one with a seventeen-dimensional space. Let those who doubt
this try for themselves; the symbols with which we think will
hardly lend themselves to the experiment; they, in their turn, are
too deeply involved in our normal view of the world, allowing for
every difference of period and clime and culture, to be capable of
so violent a break. We can, of course, work out the logical

---

[1] What can and what cannot be done by particular agents in specific
circumstances is an empirical question, properly settled, like all such questions, by
an appeal to experience. If all acts were causally determined by antecedent
conditions which were themselves similarly determined, and so on ad infinitum,
such investigations would rest on an illusion. As rational beings we should, in that
case, make an effort to disillusion ourselves – to cast off the spell of appearances;
but we should surely fail. The delusion, if it is one, belongs to the order of what
Kant called 'empirically real' and 'transcendentally ideal'. To try to place
ourselves outside the categories which govern our empirical ('real') experience is
what he regarded as an unintelligible plan of action. This thesis is surely valid, and
can be stated without the paraphernalia of the Kantian system.

[2] This desperate effort to remain at once within and without the engulfing
dream, to say the unsayable, is irresistible to German metaphysicians of a certain
type: e.g. Schopenhauer and Vaihinger.

implications of any set of internally consistent premisses – logic
and mathematics will do any work that is required of them – but
this is a very different thing from knowing how the result would
look 'in practice', what the concrete innovations are; and, since
history is not a deductive science (and even sociology becomes
progressively less intelligible as it loses touch with its empirical
foundations), such hypotheses, being abstract models, pure and
unapplied, will be of little use to students of human life. Hence the
ancient controversy between free will and determinism, while it
remains a genuine problem for theologians and philosophers, need
not trouble the thoughts of those whose concern is with empirical
matters – the actual lives of human beings in the space and time of
normal experience. For practising historians determinism is not,
and need not be, a serious issue.

Yet, inapplicable as it may be as a theory of human action,
specific forms of the deterministic hypothesis have played an
arresting, if limited, role in altering our views of human responsibility. The irrelevance of the general hypothesis to historical
studies must not blind us to its importance, touched on above, as a
specific corrective to ignorance, prejudice, dogmatism and fantasy
on the part of those who judge the behaviour of others. For it is
plainly a good thing that we should be reminded by social
scientists that the scope of human choice is a good deal more
limited than we used to suppose; that the evidence at our disposal
shows that many of the acts too often assumed to be within the
individual's control are not so – that man is an object in (scientifically predictable) nature to a larger degree than has at times been
supposed, that human beings more often than not act as they do
because of characteristics due to heredity or physical or social
environment or education, or biological or physical characteristics,
or the interplay of these factors with each other and with the
obscurer factors loosely called psychical characteristics; and that
the resultant habits of thought, feeling and expression are, at least
in principle, as capable of being classified and made subject to
hypotheses and systematic laws as the behaviour of material
objects. And this certainly alters our ideas about the limits of
freedom and responsibility. If we are told that a given case of
stealing is due to kleptomania, we protest that the appropriate
treatment is not punishment but a remedy for a disease; and,
similarly, if a destructive act or a vicious character is ascribed to a

specific psychological or social cause, we decide, if we are convinced that the explanation is valid, that the agent is not responsible
for his acts, and consequently deserves therapeutic rather than
penal treatment. It is salutary to be reminded of the narrowness of
the field within which we can begin to claim to be free; and some
would claim that such knowledge is still increasing, and the field
still contracting.

Where the frontier between freedom and causal laws is to be
determined is a crucial practical issue; knowledge of it is a powerful
and indispensable antidote to ignorance and irrationality, and
offers us new types of explanation – historical, psychological,
sociological, biological – which previous generations have lacked.
What we cannot alter, or cannot alter as much as we had supposed,
cannot be used as evidence for or against us as free moral agents; it
can cause us to feel pride, shame, regret, interest, but not remorse;
it can be admired, envied, deplored, enjoyed, feared, wondered at,
but not (save in some quasi-aesthetic sense) praised or condemned;
our tendency to indignation is curbed, we desist from passing
judgement. 'Je ne propose rien, je ne suppose rien, je n'impose rien
... j'expose,' said a French writer proudly, and such exposition
meant for him the treatment of all events as causal or statistical
phenomena, as scientific material, to the exclusion of moral
judgement.

Historians of this persuasion, anxious to avoid all personal,
above all, all moral, judgements, tend to emphasise the immense
predominance of impersonal factors in history, of the physical
media in which life is lived, the power of geographical, psychological, social factors which are not, at any rate consciously, man-made,
and are often beyond human control. This does tend to check our
arrogance, to induce humility by forcing us to admit that our own
outlook and scales of value are neither permanent nor universally
accepted, that the over-confident, too complacent, moral classifications of past historians and of their societies sprang all too
obviously from specific historical conditions, specific forms of
ignorance or vainglory, or from particular temperamental traits in
the historian (or moralist), or from other causes and circumstances
which, from our vantage-point, we perceive to belong to their own
place and time, and to have given rise to interpretations which later
seem idiosyncratic, smug, shallow, unjust and often grotesque in
the light of our own standards of accuracy or objectivity. And,
what is even more important, such a line of approach throws doubt

upon all attempts to establish a definitive boundary between the individual's free choice and his natural or social necessitation, and does this by bringing to light the egregious blunders of some of those who tried to solve this or that problem in the past, and made mistakes of fact which now, all too plainly, seem due to their (unalterable) milieu, or character, or interests. And this tends to make us ask whether the same might not be equally true of us and our own historical judgements; and so, by suggesting that every generation is 'subjectively' conditioned by its own cultural and psychological peculiarities, leads us to wonder whether it might not be best to avoid all moral judgement, all ascription of responsibility, might not be safest to confine ourselves to impersonal terms, and leave whatever cannot be said in such terms altogether unsaid. Have we learned nothing from the intolerable moral dogmatism and the mechanical classifications of those historians and moralists and politicians whose views are now so dated, so obsolete, and so justly discredited? And, indeed, who are we to make such a parade of our personal opinions, to give such importance to what are no more than symptoms of our own ephemeral outlook? And what right, in any case, have we to sit in judgement on our fellows, whose moral codes are the products of their specific historical environments, as our own are of ours? Is it not better to analyse, to describe, to present the events, and then withdraw and let them 'speak for themselves', refraining from the intolerable presumption of awarding marks, meting out justice, dividing the sheep from the goats according to our own personal criteria, as if these were eternal and not, as in fact they are, neither more nor less valid than those of others with other interests, in other conditions?

Such advice to us (in itself salutary enough) to retain a certain scepticism about our own powers of judgement, especially to beware of ascribing too much authority to our own moral views, comes to us, as I have said, from at least two quarters; from those who think that we know too much, and from those who think that we know too little. We know now, say the former, that we are as we are, and our moral and intellectual criteria are what they are, in virtue of the evolving historical situation. Let me once more mention their varieties. Some among them, who feel sure that the natural sciences will in the end account for everything, explain our behaviour in terms of natural causes. Others, who accept a more metaphysical interpretation of the world, explain it by speaking of invisible powers and dominions, nations, races, cultures; the Spirit of the Age, the 'workings', overt and occult, of 'the Classical Spirit', 'the Renaissance', 'the Medieval Mind', 'the French Revolution', 'the Twentieth Century', conceived as impersonal entities, at once patterns and realities, in terms of whose 'structure' or 'purpose' their elements and expressions – men and institutions – must behave as they do. Still others speak in terms of some teleological procession, or hierarchy, whereby all individuals, countries, institutions, cultures, ages, fulfil their several parts in some cosmic drama, and are what they are in virtue of the part cast for them, but not by them, by the divine Dramatist himself. From this it is not far to the views of those who say that History is wiser than we, that its purposes are unfathomable to us, that we, or some amongst us, are but the means, the instruments, the manifestations, worthy or unworthy, of some vast all-embracing schema of eternal human progress, or of the German Spirit, or of the Proletariat, or of post-Christian civilisation, or of Faustian man, or of Manifest Destiny, or of the American Century, or of some other myth or mystery or abstraction. To know all is to understand all; it is to know why things are and must be as they are; therefore the more we know the more absurd we must think those who suppose that things could have been otherwise, and so fall into the irrational temptation to praise or blame. *Tout comprendre, c'est tout pardonner* is transformed into a mere truism. Any form of moral censure – the accusing finger of historians or publicists or politicians, and indeed the agonies of the private conscience, too – tends, so far as possible, to be explained away as one or other sophisticated version of primitive taboos or psychical tensions or conflicts, now appearing as moral consciousness, now as some other sanction, growing out of, and battening upon, that ignorance which alone generates fallacious beliefs in free will and uncaused choice, doomed to disappear in the growing light of scientific or metaphysical truth.

Or, again, we find that the adherents of a sociological or historical or anthropological metaphysics tend to interpret the sense of mission and dedication, the voice of duty, all forms of inner compulsion of this type, as being an expression within each individual's conscious life of the 'vast impersonal forces' which control it, and which speak 'in us', 'through us', 'to us', for their own inscrutable purposes. To hear is then literally to obey – to be drawn towards the true goal of our 'real' self, or its 'natural' or 'rational' development – that to which we are called in virtue of belonging to this or that class, or nation, or race, or Church, or station in society, or tradition, or age, or culture. The explanation, and in some sense the weight of responsibility, for all human action is (at times with ill-concealed relief) transferred to the broad backs of these vast impersonal forces – institutions or historic trends – better made to bear such burdens than a feeble thinking reed like man, a creature that, with a megalomania scarcely appropriate to his physical and moral frailty, claims, as he too often does, to be responsible for the workings of Nature or of the Spirit; and, flown with his importance, praises and blames, worships and tortures, murders and immortalises other creatures like himself for conceiving, willing or executing policies for which neither he nor they can be remotely responsible; as if flies were to sit in solemn judgement upon each other for causing the revolutions of the sun or the changes of the seasons which affect their lives. But no sooner do we acquire adequate insight into the 'inexorable' and 'inevitable' parts played by all things animate and inanimate in the cosmic process than we are freed from the sense of personal endeavour. Our sense of guilt and of sin, our pangs of remorse and self-condemnation, are automatically dissolved; the tension, the fear of failure and frustration, disappear as we become aware of the elements of a larger 'organic whole' of which we are variously described as limbs or members, or reflections, or emanations, or finite expressions; our sense of freedom and independence, our belief in an area, however circumscribed, in which we can choose to act as we please, falls from us; in its place we are provided with a sense of membership in an ordered system, each with a unique position sacred to himself alone. We are soldiers in an army, and no longer suffer the pains and penalties of solitude; the army is on the march, or goals are set for us, not chosen by us; doubts are stilled by authority. The growth of knowledge brings with it relief from moral burdens, for if powers beyond and above us are at work, it is wild presumption to claim responsibility for their activity or blame ourselves for failing in it. Original sin is thus transferred to an impersonal plane, and acts hitherto regarded as wicked or unjustifiable are seen in a more 'objective' fashion – in a larger context – as part of the process of history which, being responsible for providing us with our scale of values, must not therefore itself be judged in terms of it; and viewed in this new light they turn out no longer wicked but right and good because necessitated by the whole.

This is a doctrine which lies at the heart equally of scientific attempts to explain moral sentiments as psychological or sociological 'residues' or the like, and of the metaphysical vision for which whatever is – 'truly' is – is good. To understand all is to see that nothing could be otherwise than as it is; that all blame, indignation, protest is mere complaint about what seems discordant, about elements which do not seem to fit, about the absence of an intellectually or spiritually satisfying pattern. But this is always evidence only of failure on the part of the observer, of his blindness and ignorance; it can never be an objective assessment of reality, for in reality everything necessarily fits, nothing is superfluous, nothing amiss, every ingredient is 'justified' in being where it is by the demands of the transcendent whole; and all sense of guilt, injustice, ugliness, all resistance or condemnation, is mere proof of (at times unavoidable) lack of vision, misunderstanding, subjective aberration. Vice, pain, folly, maladjustment, all come from failure to understand, from failure, in E. M. Forster's celebrated phrase, to 'connect'.[1]

This is the sermon preached to us by great and noble thinkers of very different outlooks, by Spinoza and Godwin, by Tolstoy and Comte, by mystics and rationalists, theologians and scientific materialists, metaphysicians and dogmatic empiricists, American sociologists, Russian Marxists and German historicists alike. Thus Godwin (and he speaks for many humane and civilised persons) tells us that to understand a human act we must always avoid applying general principles and examine each case in its full individual detail. When we scrupulously examine the texture and pattern of this or that life, we shall not, in our haste and blindness, seek to condemn or to punish; for we shall see why this or that man was caused to act in this or that manner by ignorance or poverty or some other moral or intellectual or physical defect – as (Godwin optimistically supposes) we can always see, if we arm ourselves with sufficient patience, knowledge and sympathy – and we shall then blame him no more than we should an object in nature; and since it is axiomatic that we cannot both act upon our knowledge, and yet regret the result, we can and shall in the end succeed in making men good, just, happy and wise. So, too, Condorcet and Henri de Saint-Simon, and their disciple, Auguste Comte, starting from the opposite conviction – namely that men are not unique or in need, each one of them, of individual

[1] E. M. Forster, *Howards End* (London, 1910), chapter 22, pp. 183–4.

treatment, but, no less than inhabitants of the animal, vegetable and mineral kingdoms, belong to types and obey general laws – maintain no less stoutly that once these laws have been discovered (and therefore applied) this will by itself lead to universal felicity. And this conviction has since been echoed by many idealistic liberals and rationalists, technocrats, positivists and believers in the scientific organisation of society; and in very different keys by theocrats, neo-medieval romantics, authoritarians and political mystics of various kinds. This, too, is in substance the morality preached, if not by Marx, then by most of the disciples of Engels and Plekhanov, by Prussian nationalist historians, by Spengler, and by many another thinker who believes that there is a pattern which he has seen but others have not seen, or at least not so clearly seen, and that by this vision men may be saved.

Know and you will not be lost. What it is that we must know differs from thinker to thinker, differs as views of the nature of the world differ. Know the laws of the universe, animate and inanimate, or the principles of growth, or of evolution, or of the rise and fall of civilisations, or the goals towards which all creation tends, or the stages of the Idea, or something less tangible still. Know, in the sense of identifying yourself with it, realising your oneness with it, for, do what you may, you cannot escape from the laws to which you are subject, of whatever kind they may be, 'mechanistic', 'vitalistic', causal, purposive, imposed, transcendent, immanent, or the myriad impalpable strands which bind you to the past – to your land and to the dead, as Barrès declared; to the milieu, the race and the moment, as Taine asserted; to Burke's great society of the dead and living, who have made you what you are; so that the truth in which you believe, the values in terms of which you judge, from the profoundest principles to the most trivial whims, are part and parcel of the historical continuum to which you belong. Tradition or blood or class or human nature or progress or humanity; the *Zeitgeist* or the social structure or the laws of history or the true ends of life; know these – be true to them – and you will be free. From Zeno to Spinoza, from the Gnostics to Leibniz, from Thomas Hobbes to Lenin and Freud, the battle-cry has been essentially the same; the object of knowledge and the methods of discovery have often been violently opposed, but that reality is knowable, and that knowledge and only knowledge liberates, and absolute knowledge liberates absolutely – that is common to many doctrines which are so large and valuable a part of Western civilisation.

To understand is to explain and to explain is to justify. The notion of individual freedom is a delusion. The further we are from omniscience, the wider our notion of our freedom and responsibility and guilt, products of ignorance and fear which populate the unknown with terrifying fictions. Personal freedom is a noble delusion and has had its social value; society might have crumbled without it; it is a necessary instrument – one of the greatest devices of the 'cunning' of Reason or of History, or of whatever other cosmic force we may be invited to worship. But a delusion, however noble, useful, metaphysically justified, historically indispensable, is still a delusion. And so individual responsibility and the perception of the difference between right and wrong choices, between avoidable evil and misfortune, are mere symptoms, evidences of vanity, of our imperfect adjustment, of human inability to face the truth. The more we know, the greater the relief from the burden of choice; we forgive others for what they cannot avoid being, and by the same token we forgive ourselves. In ages in which the choices seem peculiarly agonising, when strongly held ideals cannot be reconciled and collisions cannot be averted, such doctrines seem peculiarly comforting. We escape moral dilemmas by denying their reality; and, by directing our gaze towards the greater wholes, we make them responsible in our place. All we lose is an illusion, and with it the painful and superfluous emotions of guilt and remorse. Freedom notoriously involves responsibility, and it is for many spirits a source of welcome relief to lose the burden of both, not by some ignoble act of surrender, but by daring to contemplate in a calm spirit things as they must be; for this is to be truly philosophical. Thereby we reduce history to a kind of physics; as well blame the galaxy or gamma-rays as Genghis Khan or Hitler. 'To know all is to forgive all' turns out to be, in A. J. Ayer's striking phrase (used in another context), nothing but a dramatised tautology.

IV

We have spoken thus far of the view that we cannot praise or blame because we know – or may one day know, or at any rate could know – too much for that. By a queer paradox the same position is reached by some of those who hold what seems at first the diametrical opposite of this position, that we cannot praise or blame not because we know too much, but because we know too little. Historians imbued with a sense of humility before the scope and difficulties of their task, viewing the magnitude of human claims and the smallness of human knowledge and judgement, warn us sternly against setting up our parochial values as universally valid and applying what may, at most, hold for a small portion of humanity for a brief span in some insignificant corner of the universe to all beings in all places and at all times. Tough-minded realists influenced by Marxism and Christian apologists differ profoundly in outlook, in method, in conclusions, but they are at one in this. The former[1] tell us that the social or economic principles which, for example, Victorian Englishmen accepted as basic and eternal were but the interests of one particular island community at one particular moment of its social and commercial development, and the truths which they so dogmatically bound upon themselves and upon others, and in the name of which they felt justified in acting as they did, were but their own passing economic or political needs and claims masquerading as universal truths, and rang progressively more hollow in the ears of other nations with increasingly opposed interests, as they found themselves frequently the losers in a game where the rules had been invented by the stronger side. Then the day began to dawn when they in their turn acquired sufficient power, and turned the tables, and transformed international morality, albeit unconsciously, to suit themselves. Nothing is absolute, moral rules vary directly as the distribution of power: the prevalent morality is always that of the victors; we cannot pretend to hold the scales of justice even between them and their victims, for we ourselves belong to one side or the other; *ex hypothesi* we cannot see the world from more than one vantage-point at a time. If we insist on judging others in terms of our transient standards we must not protest too much if they, in their turn, judge us in terms of theirs, which sanctimonious persons among us are too swift to denounce for no better reason than that they are not ours.

And some among their Christian opponents, starting from very different assumptions, see men as feeble creatures groping in darkness, knowing but little of how things come about, or what in

---

[1] See, for example, the impressive and influential writings of E. H. Carr on the history of our time.

history inexorably causes what, and how things might have turned out but for this or that scarcely perceptible, all but untraceable, fact or situation. Men, they argue, often seek to do what is right according to their lights, but these lights are dim, and such faint illumination as they give reveals very different aspects of life to different observers. Thus the English follow their own traditions; the Germans fight for the development of theirs; the Russians to break with their own and those of other nations; and the result is often bloodshed, widespread suffering, the destruction of what is most highly valued in the various cultures which come into violent conflict. Man proposes, but it is cruel and absurd to lay upon him – a fragile creature, born to sorrows – responsibility for many of the disasters that occur. For these are entailed by what, to take a Christian historian of distinction, Herbert Butterfield calls the 'human predicament' itself – wherein we often seem to ourselves virtuous enough, but, being imperfect, and doomed to stay so by Man's original sin, being ignorant, hasty, vainglorious, self-centred, lose our way, do unwitting harm, destroy what we seek to save and strengthen what we seek to destroy. If we understood more, perhaps we could do better, but our intellect is limited. For Butterfield, if I understand him correctly, the 'human predicament' is a product of the complex interaction of innumerable factors, few among them known, fewer still controllable, the greater number scarcely recognised at all. The least that we can do, therefore, is to acknowledge our condition with due humility, and since we are involved in a common darkness, and few of us stumble in it to much greater purpose than others (at least in the perspective of the whole of human history), we should practise understanding and charity. The least we can do as historians, scrupulous to say no more than we are entitled to say, is to suspend judgement; neither praise nor condemn; for the evidence is always insufficient, and the alleged culprits are like swimmers for ever caught in cross-currents and whirlpools beyond their control.

   A not dissimilar philosophy is, it seems to me, to be found in the writings of Tolstoy and other pessimists and quietists, both religious and irreligious. For these, particularly the most conservative among them, life is a stream moving in a given direction, or perhaps a tideless ocean stirred by occasional breezes. The number of factors which cause it to be as it is, is very great, but we know only very few of them. To seek to alter things radically in terms of our knowledge is therefore unrealistic, often to the point of absurdity. We cannot resist the central currents, for they are much stronger than we, we can only tack, only trim to the winds and avoid collisions with the great fixed institutions of our world, its physical and biological laws, and the great human establishments with their roots deep in the past – the empires, the Churches, the settled beliefs and habits of mankind. For if we resist these, our small craft will be sunk, and we shall lose our lives to no purpose. Wisdom lies in avoiding situations where we may capsize, in using the winds that blow as skilfully as we can, so that we may last at any rate our own time, preserve the heritage of the past, and not hurry towards a future which will come soon enough, and may be darker even than the gloomy present. On this view it is the human predicament – the disproportion between our vast designs and our feeble means – that is responsible for much of the suffering and injustice of the world. Without help, without divine grace, or one or other form of divine intervention, we shall not, in any case, succeed. Let us then be tolerant and charitable and understanding, and avoid the folly of accusation and counter-accusation which will expose us to the laughter or pity of later generations. Let us seek to discern what we can – some dim outline of a pattern – in the shadows of the past, for even so much is surely difficult enough.

In one important sense, of course, the hard-boiled realists and the Christian pessimists are right. Censoriousness, recrimination, moral or emotional blindness to the ways of life and outlooks and complex predicaments of others, intellectual or ethical fanaticism are vices in the writing of history as in life. No doubt Gibbon and Michelet, Macaulay and Carlyle, Taine and Trotsky (to mention only the eminent dead) do try the patience of those who do not accept their opinions. Nevertheless this corrective to dogmatic partiality, like its opposite, the doctrine of inevitable bias, by shifting responsibility on to human weakness and ignorance, and identifying the human predicament itself as the ultimate central factor in human history, in the end leads us by a different road to the very same position as the doctrine that to know all is to forgive all; only for the latter it substitutes the formula that the less we know, the fewer reasons we can have for just condemnation; for knowledge can lead only to a clearer realisation of how small a part men's wishes or even their unconscious desires play in the life of the universe, and thereby reveals the absurdity of placing any serious responsibility upon the shoulders of individuals, or, for that matter, of classes, or States, or nations.[1]

Two separate strands of thought are involved in the modern plea for a greater effort at understanding, and the fashionable warnings against censoriousness, moralising, and partisan history. There is, in the first place, the view that individuals and groups always, or at any rate more often than not, aim at what seems to them desirable; but, owing to ignorance, or weakness, or the complexities of the world, which mere human insight and skill cannot adequately understand or control, they feel and act in such a manner that the result is too often disastrous both for themselves and for others, caught in the common human predicament. Yet it is not men's purposes – only the human predicament itself, man's imperfection – that is largely to blame for this. There is, in the second place, the further thesis that in attempting to explain historical situations and to analyse them, to unwind their origins and trace their consequences, and, in the course of this, to fix the responsibility for this or that element in the situation, the historian, however detached, clear-headed, scrupulous, dispassionate he may be, however skilled at imagining himself in other men's shoes, is nevertheless faced with a network of facts so minute, connected by links so many and complex, that his ignorance must always far outweigh his knowledge. Consequently his judgement, particularly his evaluative judgement, must always be founded on insufficient data; and if he succeeds in casting even a little light upon some small corner of the vast and intricate pattern of the past, he has done as well as any human being can ever hope to do. The difficulties of disentangling even a minute portion of the truth are so great that he must, if he is an honest and serious practitioner, soon realise how far he is from being in a position to moralise; consequently to praise and blame, as historians and publicists do so easily and glibly, is presumptuous, foolish, irresponsible, unjust.

This prima facie very humane and convincing thesis[2] is,

---

[1] I do not, of course, mean to imply that the great Western moralists, e.g. the philosophers of the medieval Church (and in particular Thomas Aquinas) or those of the Enlightenment, denied moral responsibility; nor that Tolstoy was not agonised by problems raised by it. My thesis is that their determinism committed these thinkers to a dilemma which some among them did not face, and none escaped.

[2] Held, unless I have gravely misunderstood his writings, by Herbert Butterfield.

however, not one but two. It is one thing to say that man proposes, but the consequences are too often beyond his control or powers of prediction or prevention; that since human motives have so seldom had any decisive influence on the actual course of events, they should not play any great part in the accounts of the historian; and that since the historian's business is to discover and describe what occurred, and how and why, if he allows his moral opinions of men's characters and motives – those least effective of all historical factors – to colour his interpretations, he thereby exaggerates their importance for purely subjective or psychological reasons. For to treat what may be morally significant as *eo ipso* historically influential is to distort the facts. That is one perfectly clear position. Quite distinct from it is the other thesis, namely, that our knowledge is never sufficient to justify us in fixing responsibility, if there is any, where it truly belongs. An omniscient being (if that is a tenable notion) could do so, but we are not omniscient, and our attributions are therefore absurdly presumptuous; to realise this and feel an appropriate degree of humility is the beginning of historical wisdom.

It may well be that both these theses are true. And it may further be that they both spring from the same kind of pessimistic conviction of human weakness, blindness and ineffectiveness both in thought and in action. Nevertheless, these melancholy views are two, not one: the first is an argument from ineffectiveness, the second from ignorance; and either might be true and the other false. Moreover, neither seems to accord with common belief, nor with the common practice either of ordinary men or of ordinary historians; each seems plausible and unplausible in its own way, and each deserves its own defence or refutation. There is, however, at least one implication common to them: in both these doctrines individual responsibility is made to melt away. We may neither applaud nor condemn individuals or groups either because they cannot help themselves (and all knowledge is a growing understanding of precisely this), or conversely because we know too little to know either this or its opposite. But then – this surely follows – neither may we bring charges of moralism or bias against those historians who are prone to praise and blame, for we are all in the same boat together, and no one standard can be called objectively superior to any other. For what, on this view, could 'objective' mean? What standard can we use to measure its degree? It is plain that there can exist no 'super-standard' for the comparison of entire scales of value, which itself derives from no specific set of beliefs, no one specific culture. All such tests must be internal, like the laws of a State that apply only to its own citizens. The case against the notion of historical objectivity is like the case against international law or international morality: that it does not exist. More than this: that the very notion has no meaning, because ultimate standards are what we measure things by, and cannot by definition themselves be measured in terms of anything else.

This is indeed to be hoist by one's own petard. Because all standards are pronounced relative, to condemn bias or moralism in history, and to defend them, turn out themselves to express attitudes which, in the absence of a super-standard, cannot be rationally defended or condemned. All attitudes turn out to be morally neutral; but even this cannot be said, for the contradictory of this proposition cannot be refuted. Hence nothing on this topic can be said at all. This is surely a *reductio ad absurdum* of the entire position. A fatal fallacy must be lurking somewhere in the argument of the anti-moralistic school.[1]

[1] The paradox arising out of general scepticism about historical objectivity may perhaps be put in another fashion. One of the principal reasons for complaining about the moralistic attitude of this or that historian is that his scale of values is thought to distort his judgements, to cause him to pervert the truth. But if we start from the assumption that historians, like other human beings, are wholly conditioned to think as they do by specific material (or immaterial) factors, however incalculable or impalpable, then their so-called bias is, like everything else about their thought, the inevitable consequence of their 'predicament', and so equally are our objections to it – our own ideals of impartiality, our own standards of objective truth in terms of which we condemn, say, nationalistic or woodenly Marxist historians, or other forms of animus or *parti pris*. For what is sauce for the subjective goose must be sauce for the objective gander; if we look at the matter from the vantage-point of a Communist or a chauvinist, our 'objective' attitude is an equal offence against their standards, which are in their own eyes no less self-evident, absolute, valid etc. In this relativistic view the very notion of an absolute standard, presupposing as it does the rejection of all specific vantage-points as such, must, of course, be an absurdity. All complaints about partiality and bias, about moral (or political) propaganda, seem, on this view, beside the point. Whatever does not agree with our views we call misleading, but if this fault is to be called subjectivism, so must the condemnation of it; it ought to follow that no point of view is superior to any other, save in so far as it proceeds from wider knowledge (given that there is a commonly agreed standard for measuring such width). We are what we are, and when and where we are; and when we are historians, we select and emphasise, interpret and evaluate, reconstruct and present facts as we do, each in his own way. Each nation and culture and class does this in its own way – and on this view all that we are doing

Let us consider the normal thoughts of ordinary men on this topic. In ordinary circumstances we do not feel that we are saying something peculiarly hazardous or questionable if we attempt to assess the value of Cromwell's statesmanship, or if we describe Pasteur as a benefactor of mankind or condemn Hitler's actions. Nor do we feel that we are saying something strange if we maintain that, let us say, Belloc or Macaulay do not seem to apply the same standards of objective truth, or apply them as impartially, as did, let us say, Ranke, or Creighton, or Élie Halévy. In saying this, what are we doing? Are we merely expressing our private approval or disapproval of Cromwell's or Pasteur's or Hitler's character or activities? Are we merely saying that we agree with Ranke's conclusions or Halévy's general tone, that they are more to our taste, please us better (because of our own outlook and temperament) than the tone and conclusions of Macaulay or Belloc? If there is an unmistakable tinge of reproach in our assessment of, say, Cromwell's policies or of Belloc's account of those policies, is that no more than an indication that we are not favourably disposed towards one or other of them, that our moral or intellectual ideals differ from what we take to be theirs, with no indication that we think that they could, and moreover should, have acted differently? And if we do imply that their behaviour might, or should, have been different, is that merely a symptom of our psychological inability to realise that they could not (for no one can) have acted differently, or of an ignorance too deep to entitle us to tell how they could, let alone should, have acted? With the further implication that it would be more civilised not to say such things, but to remember that we may all be equally, or almost equally, deluded, and remember, too, that moral responsibility is a pre-scientific fiction, that with the increase of knowledge and a more scrupulous and appropriate use of language such 'value-charged' expressions, and the false notions of human freedom on which they rest, will, it is to be hoped, finally disappear from the

when we reject this or that historian as a conscious or unconscious propagandist is solely to indicate our own moral or intellectual or historical distance from him; nothing more: we are merely underlining our personal position. And this seems to be a fatal internal contradiction in the views of those who believe in the historical conditioning of historians and yet protest against moralising by them, whether they do so contemptuously like E. H. Carr, or sorrowfully like Herbert Butterfield.

vocabulary of enlightened men, at least in their public utterances? For this seems to me to follow directly from the doctrines outlined above. Determinism, whether benevolent or malevolent, no less than the view that our moral judgements are rendered absurd either because we know too much or because we know too little, seems to point to this. It is a view that in its various forms has been held by many civilised and sensitive thinkers, particularly in the present day. Nevertheless it rests on beliefs about the world and about human beings which are too difficult to accept; which are unplausible because they render illegitimate certain basic distinctions which we all draw – distinctions which are inevitably reflected in our everyday use of words. If such beliefs were true, too much that we accept without question would turn out to be sensationally false. Yet these paradoxes are urged upon us, although there is no strong factual evidence or logical argument to force us to embrace them.

It is part of the same tendency to maintain that, even if total freedom from moralising is not to be looked for in this world (for all human beings inevitably live and think by their own varying moral or aesthetic or religious standards), yet in the writing of history an effort must be made to repress such tendencies. As historians it is our duty only to describe and explain, not to pronounce verdicts. The historian is, we are told, not a judge but a detective; he provides the evidence, and the reader, who has none of the professional responsibilities of the expert, can form what moral conclusions he likes. As a general warning against moralising history this is, particularly in times of acute partisan emotion, timely enough. But it must not be interpreted literally. For it depends upon a false analogy with some among the more exact of the natural sciences. In these last, objectivity has a specific meaning. It means that methods and criteria of a less or more precisely defined kind are being used with scrupulous care; and that evidence, arguments, conclusions are formulated in the special terminology invented or employed for the specific purpose of each science, and that there is no intrusion (or almost none) of irrelevant considerations or concepts or categories, that is, those specifically excluded by the canons of the science in question.

I am not sure whether history can usefully be called a science at all, but certainly it is not a science in this sense. For it employs few, if any, concepts or categories peculiar to itself. Attempts to construct special sets of concepts and special techniques for history[1] have proved sterile, for they either misdescribed – over-schematised – our experience, or they were felt not to provide answers to our questions. We can accuse historians of bias, or inaccuracy, or stupidity, or dishonesty, as we can accuse one another of these vices in our ordinary daily intercourse; and we can praise them for the corresponding virtues; and usually with the same degree of justice and reason. But just as our ordinary speech would become fantastically distorted by a conscious effort to eliminate from it some basic ingredient – say, everything remotely liable to convey value judgements, our normal, scarcely noticed, moral or psychological attitudes – and just as this is not regarded as indispensable for the preservation of what we should look upon as a normal modicum of objectivity, impartiality and accuracy, so, for the same reason, no such radical remedy is needed for the preservation of a reasonable modicum of these qualities in the writing of history. There is a sense in which a physicist can, to a large degree, speak with different voices as a physicist and as a human being; although even there the line between the two vocabularies is anything but clear or absolute. It is possible that this may in some measure be true of economists or psychologists; it grows progressively less true as we leave mathematical methods behind us, for example, in palaeography, or the history of science or that of the woollen trade; and it comes perilously near an absurdity when demanded of social or political historians, however skilled in the appropriate techniques, however professional, how-ever rigorous. History is not identical with imaginative literature, but it is certainly not free from what, in a natural science, would be rightly condemned as unwarrantably subjective and even, in an empirical sense of the term, intuitive. Except on the assumption that history must deal with human beings purely as material objects in space – must, in short, be behaviourist – its method can scarcely be assimilated to the standards of an exact natural science.[2] The invocation to historians to suppress even that

[1] As opposed to making profitable use of other disciplines, e.g. sociology or economics or psychology.

[2] That history is in this sense different from physical description is a truth discovered long ago by Vico, and most imaginatively and vividly presented by Herder and his followers, and, despite the exaggerations and extravagances to which it led some nineteenth-century philosophers of history, still remains the greatest contribution of the romantic movement to our knowledge. What was then shown, albeit often in a very misleading and confused fashion, was that to

minimal degree of moral or psychological insight and evaluation which is necessarily involved in viewing human beings as creatures with purposes and motives (and not merely as causal factors in the procession of events) seems to me to spring from a confusion of the aims and methods of the humane studies with those of natural science. Purely descriptive, wholly depersonalised history remains, what it has always been, a figment of abstract theory, a violently exaggerated reaction to the cant and vanity of earlier generations.

V

All judgements, certainly all judgements dealing with facts, rest on – embody – generalisations, whether of fact or value or of both, and would make no sense save in terms of such generalisations. This truism, while it does not seem startling in itself, can nevertheless lead to formidable fallacies. Thus some of the heirs of Descartes who assume that whatever is true must be capable of being (at any rate in principle) stated in the form of scientific (that is, at least quasi-mathematical or mathematically clear) generalisations conclude, as Comte and his disciples did, that the generalisations unavoidable in historical judgements must, to be worth anything, be capable of being so formulated, that is, as demonstrable sociological laws; while valuations, if they cannot be stated in such terms, must be relegated to some 'subjective' lumber-room, as 'psychological' odds and ends, expressions of purely personal attitudes, unscientific superfluities, in principle capable of being eliminated altogether, and must certainly be kept out so far as possible from the objective realm in which they have no place. Every science (we are invited to believe) must sooner or later shake itself free of what are at best irrelevances, at worst serious impediments, to clear vision.

This view springs from a very understandable fascination with the morally 'neutral' attitude of natural scientists, and a desire to

reduce history to a natural science was deliberately to leave out of account what we know to be true, to suppress great portions of our most familiar introspective knowledge, on the altar of a false analogy with the sciences and their mathematical and scientific disciplines. This exhortation to the students of humanity to practise austerities, and commit deliberate acts of self-laceration, that, like Origen, they might escape all temptation to sin (involved in any lapse from 'neutral' protocols of the data of observation), is to render the writing of history (and, it may be added, of sociology) gratuitously sterile.

emulate them in other fields. But it rests on a false analogy. For the generalisations of the historians differ from those of the scientists in that the valuations which they embody, whether moral, political, aesthetic or (as they often suppose) purely historical, are intrinsic, and not, as in the sciences, external, to the subject-matter. If I am a historian and wish to explain the causes of the great French Revolution, I naturally assume or take for granted certain general propositions. Thus I assume that all the ordinarily accepted physical laws of the external world apply. I also assume that all or most men need and consciously seek food, clothing, shelter, some degree of protection for their persons, and facilities for getting their grievances listened to or redressed. Perhaps I assume something more specific, namely, that persons who have acquired a certain degree of wealth or economic power will not be indefinitely content to lack political rights or social status; or that human beings are prey to various passions – greed, envy, lust for power; or that some men are more ambitious, ruthless, cunning or fanatical than others; and so forth. These are the assumptions of common experience; some of them are probably false; some are exaggerated, some confused, or inapplicable to given situations. Few among them are capable of being formulated in the form of hypotheses of natural science; still fewer are testable by crucial experiment, because they are not often sufficiently clear and sharp and precisely defined to be capable of being organised in a formal structure which allows of systematic mutual entailments or exclusions, and consequently of strictly logical or mathematical treatment. More than this: if they do prove capable of such formulation they will lose some of their usefulness; the idealised models of economics (not to speak of those of physics or physiology) will be of limited use in historical research or description. These inexact disciplines depend on a certain measure of concreteness, vagueness, ambiguity, suggestiveness, vividness and so on, embodied in the properties of the language of common sense and of literature and the humanities. Degrees and kinds of precision doubtless depend on the context, the field, the subject-matter; and the rules and methods of algebra lead to absurdities if applied to the art of, say, the novel, which has its own appallingly exacting standards. The precise disciplines of Racine or Proust require as great a degree of genius, and are as creditable to the intellect (as well as to the imagination) of the human race, as those of Newton or Darwin or Hilbert, but these kinds of method (and there is no theoretical limit to their number) are not interchangeable. They may have much or little to learn from each other; Stendhal may have learnt something from the Sensationalists of the eighteenth century, or the *Idéologues* of his own time, or from the *Code Napoléon*. But when Zola seriously contemplated the possibility of a literally 'experimental novel', founded directly on, and controlled by, the results of scientific method and conclusions, the idea remained largely stillborn, as, for similar reasons, the collective novel of the early Russian communist theorists still remains: and that not because we do not (as yet) know a sufficient number of facts (or laws), but because the concepts involved in the worlds described by novelists (or historians) are not the artificially refined concepts of scientific models – the idealised entities in terms of which natural laws are formulated – but a great deal richer in content and less logically simple or streamlined in structure.

Some interplay there is, of course, between a given scientific 'world-picture' and views of life in the normal meaning of this word; the former can give very sharp impulsions to the latter. Writers like H. G. Wells or Aldous Huxley would not have described (or so egregiously misunderstood) both social and individual life as at times they did, had they not been influenced by the natural sciences of their day to an excessive degree. But even such writers as these do not actually deduce anything from scientific generalisations; do not in their writings use any semblance of truly scientific methods; for this cannot be done outside its proper field without total absurdity. The relation of the sciences to historical writing is complex and close: but it is certainly not one of identity or even similarity. Scientific method is indispensable in, say, such disciplines as palaeography, or epigraphy, or archaeology, or economics, or in other activities which are propaedeutic to history, and supply it with evidence, and help to solve specific problems. But what they establish can never suffice to constitute a historical narrative. We select certain events or persons because we believe them to have had a special degree of 'influence' or 'power' or 'importance'. These attributes are not, as a rule, quantitatively measurable, or capable of being symbolised in the terminology of an exact, or even semi-exact, science. Yet they can no more be subtracted or abstracted from the facts – from events or persons – than physical or chronological characteristics; they enter even the driest, barest chronicles of events: it is a truism to say this. And is it so very clear that the most obviously moral categories, the notions of good and bad, right and wrong, so far as they enter into our assessments of societies, individuals, characters, political action, states of mind, are in principle utterly different from such indispensable 'non-moral' categories of value as 'important', 'trivial', 'significant' and so forth? It might perhaps be maintained that views of what is generally regarded as 'important' – the conquests of Alexander or Genghis Khan, or the fall of the Roman Empire, or the French Revolution, or the rise and fall of Hitler – embody relatively more stable assessments than more obviously 'ethical' valuations, or that there would be more general agreement about the fact that the French or Russian Revolutions are 'major' events (in the sense in which the tune which I hummed yesterday afternoon is not) than about whether Robespierre was a good man or a bad one, or whether it was right or wrong to execute the leaders of the National Socialist regime in Germany. And no doubt some concepts and categories are in this sense more universal or more 'stable' than others.[1] But they are not therefore 'objective' in some absolutely clear sense in which ethical notions are not. For our historical language, the words and thoughts with which we attempt to reflect about or describe past events and persons, embody moral concepts and categories – standards both permanent and transient – just as deeply as other notions of value. Our notions of Napoleon or Robespierre as historically important, as worthy of our attention in the sense in which their minor followers are not (as well as the very meaning of terms like 'major' and

---

[1] Such 'stability' is a matter of degree. All our categories are, in theory, subject to change. The physical categories – e.g. the three dimensions and infinite extent of ordinary perceptual space, the irreversibility of temporal processes, the multiplicity and countability of material objects – are perhaps the most fixed. Yet even a shift in these most general characteristics is in principle conceivable. After these come orders and relations of sensible qualities – colours, shapes, tastes etc.; then the uniformities on which the sciences are based – these can be quite easily thought away in fairy tales or scientific romances. The categories of value are more fluid than these; and within them tastes fluctuate more than rules of etiquette, and these more than moral standards. Within each category some concepts seem more liable to change than others. When such differences of degree become so marked as to constitute what are called differences of kind, we tend to speak of the wider and more stable distinctions as 'objective', of the narrower and less stable as the opposite. Nevertheless there is no sharp break, no frontier. The concepts form a continuous series from the 'permanent' standards to fleeting momentary reactions, from 'objective' truths and rules to 'subjective' attitudes, and they criss-cross each other in many dimensions, sometimes at unexpected angles, to perceive, discriminate and describe which can be a mark of genius.

'minor'), derive from the fact that the part of the former in forwarding or retarding the interests or the ideals of a great many of their contemporaries (with which our own are bound up) was very considerable; but then so do our 'moral' judgements about them. Where to draw the line – where to exclude judgements as being too subjective to be admitted into an account which we desire to make as 'objective' as possible, that is, as well supported by publicly discoverable, inspectable, comparable facts as we can make it – that is a question for ordinary judgement, that is to say, for what passes as such in our society, in our own time and place, among the people to whom we are addressing ourselves, with all the assumptions which are taken for granted, more or less, in normal communication.

Because there is no hard and fast line between 'subjective' and 'objective', it does not follow that there is no line at all; and because judgements of 'importance', normally held to be 'objective', differ in some respects from moral judgements, which are so often suspected of being merely 'subjective', it does not follow that 'moral' is tantamount to 'subjective': that there is some mysterious property in virtue of which those quasi-aesthetic or political judgements which distinguish essential from inessential, or crucial from trivial, are somehow intrinsic to our historical thinking and description. It does not follow that the ethical implications, concerned with responsibility and moral worth, can somehow be sloughed off as if they constituted an external adjunct, a set of subjective emotional attitudes towards a body of commonly accepted, 'hard', publicly inspectable facts; as if these 'facts' were not themselves shot through with such valuations, as if a hard and fast distinction could be made, by historians or anyone else, between what is truly factual and what is a valuation of the facts, in the sense in which such a valuation truly would be an irrelevant and avoidable intrusion in, say, such fields as physics or chemistry (and doubtfully so in economics or sociology), where 'facts' can and should, according to the rules of these sciences, be described, as far as possible, with no moral overtones.

VI

When everything has been said in favour of attributing responsibility for character and action to natural and institutional causes; when everything possible has been done to correct blind or over-simple interpretations of conduct which fix too much responsibility on individuals and their free acts; when in fact there is strong evidence to show that it was difficult or impossible for men to do otherwise than as they did, given their material environment or education or the influence upon them of various 'social pressures'; when every relevant psychological and sociological consideration has been taken into account, every impersonal factor given due weight; after 'hegemonist', nationalist, and other historical heresies have been exposed and refuted; after every effort has been made to induce history to aspire, so far as it can without open absurdity, after the pure, *wertfrei* condition of a science; after all these severities, we continue to praise and to blame. We blame others as we blame ourselves; and the more we know, the more, it may be, are we disposed to blame. Certainly it will surprise us to be told that the better we understand our own actions – our own motives and the circumstances surrounding them – the freer from self-blame we shall inevitably feel. The contrary is surely often true. The more deeply we investigate the course of our own conduct, the more blameworthy our behaviour may seem to us to be, the more remorse we may be disposed to feel; and if this holds for ourselves, it is not reasonable to expect us necessarily, and in all cases, to withhold it from others. Our situations may differ from theirs, but not always so widely as to make all comparisons unfair. We ourselves may be accused unjustly, and so become acutely sensitive to the dangers of unjustly blaming others. But because blame can be unjust and the temptation to utter it too strong, it does not follow that it is never just; and because judgements can be based on ignorance, can spring from violent, or perverse, or silly, or shallow, or unfair notions, it does not follow that the opposites of these qualities do not exist at all; that we are mysteriously doomed to a degree of relativism and subjectivism in history, from which we are no less mysteriously free, or at any rate more free, in our normal daily thought and transactions with one another.

Indeed, the major fallacy of this position must by now be too obvious to need pointing out. We are told that we are creatures of nature or environment, or of history, and that this colours our temperament, our judgements, our principles. Every judgement is relative, every evaluation subjective, made what and as it is by the interplay of the factors of its own time and place, individual or collective. But relative to what? Subjective in contrast with what? Made to conform as it does to some ephemeral pattern as opposed to what conceivable timeless independence of such distorting factors? Relative terms (especially pejoratives) need correlatives, or else they turn out to be without meaning themselves, mere gibes, propagandist phrases designed to throw discredit, and not to describe or analyse. We know what we mean by disparaging a judgement or a method as subjective or biased – we mean that proper methods of weighing evidence have been too far ignored; or that what are normally called facts have been overlooked or suppressed or perverted; or that evidence normally accepted as sufficient to account for the acts of one individual or society is, for no good reason, ignored in some other case similar in all relevant respects; or that canons of interpretation are arbitrarily altered from case to case, that is, without consistency or principle; or that we have reasons for thinking that the historian in question wished to establish certain conclusions for reasons other than those constituted by the evidence, according to canons of valid inference accepted as normal in his day or in ours, and that this has blinded him to the criteria and methods normal in his field for verifying facts and proving conclusions; or all, or any, of these together; or other considerations like them. These are the kinds of ways in which superficiality is, in practice, distinguished from depth, bias from objectivity, perversion of facts from honesty, stupidity from perspicacity, passion and confusion from detachment and lucidity. And if we grasp these rules correctly, we are fully justified in denouncing breaches of them on the part of anyone; why should we not?

But, it may be objected, what of the words such as those we have used so liberally above – 'valid', 'normal', 'proper', 'relevant', 'perverted', 'suppression of facts', 'interpretation' – what do they signify? Is the meaning and use of these crucial terms so very fixed and unambiguous? May not that which is thought relevant or convincing in one generation be regarded as irrelevant in the next? What are unquestioned facts to one historian may, often enough, seem merely a suspicious piece of theorising to another. This is indeed so. Rules for the weighing of evidence do change. The accepted data of one age seem to its remote successors shot through with metaphysical presuppositions so queer as to be scarcely intelligible. All objectivity, we shall again be told, is subjective, is what it is relatively to its own time and place; all veracity, reliability, all the insights and gifts of an intellectually fertile period are such only relatively to their own 'climate of opinion'; nothing is eternal, everything flows.

Yet, frequently as this kind of thing has been said, and plausible as it may seem, it remains in this context mere rhetoric. We do distinguish facts, not indeed sharply from the valuations which enter into their very texture, but from interpretations of them; the borderline may not be distinct, but if I say that Stalin is dead and General Franco still alive, my statement may be accurate or mistaken, but nobody in his senses could, as words are used, take me to be advancing a theory or an interpretation. But if I say that Stalin exterminated a great many peasant proprietors because in his infancy he had been swaddled by his nurse, and that this made him aggressive, while General Franco did not do so because he did not go through this kind of experience, no one but a very naïve student of the social sciences would take me to be claiming to assert a fact, no matter how many times I begin my sentences with the words 'It is a fact that . . . '. And I shall not readily believe you if you tell me that for Thucydides (or even for some Sumerian scribe) no fundamental distinction existed between relatively 'hard' facts and relatively 'disputable' interpretations. The borderline has, no doubt, always been wide and vague; it may be a shifting frontier; it is affected by the level of generality of the propositions involved; but unless we know where, within certain limits, it lies, we fail to understand descriptive language altogether. The modes of thought of cultures remote from our own are comprehensible to us only to the degree to which we share some, at any rate, of their basic categories; and the distinction between fact and theory is among these. I may dispute whether a given historian is profound or shallow, objective and impartial in his judgements, or borne on the wings of some obsessive hypothesis or overpowering emotion: but what I mean by these contrasted terms will not be utterly different for those who disagree with me, else there would be no argument; and will not, if I can claim to decipher texts at all correctly, be so widely different in different cultures and times and places as to make all communication systematically misleading and delusive. 'Objective', 'true', 'fair' are words of large content, their uses are many, their edges often blurred. Ambiguities and confusions are always possible and often dangerous. Nevertheless such terms do possess meanings, which may, indeed, be fluid, but stay within limits recognised by normal usage, and refer to standards commonly accepted by those who work in relevant fields; and that not merely within one generation or society, but across large stretches of time and space. The mere claim that these crucial terms, these concepts or categories or standards, change in meaning or application, is to assume that such changes can to some degree be traced by methods which themselves are, *pro tanto*, not held liable to such traceable change; for if these change in their turn, then, *ex hypothesi*, they do so in a way scarcely discoverable by us.[1] And if not discoverable, then not discountable, and therefore of no use as a stick with which to beat us for our alleged subjectiveness or relativity, our delusions of grandeur and permanence, of the absoluteness of our standards in a world of ceaseless change.

Such charges resemble suggestions, sometimes casually advanced, that life is a dream. We protest that 'everything' cannot be a dream, for then, with nothing to contrast with dreams, the notion of a 'dream' loses all specific reference. We may be told that we shall have an awakening: that is, have an experience in relation to which the recollection of our present lives will be somewhat as remembered dreams now are, when compared to our normal waking experience at present. That may be true; but, as things are, we can have little or no empirical evidence for or against this hypothesis. We are offered an analogy one term of which is hidden from our view; and if we are invited, on the strength of it, to discount the reality of our normal waking life, in terms of another form of experience which is literally not describable and not utterable in terms of our daily experience and normal language – an experience of whose criteria for discriminating between realities and dreams we cannot in principle have any inkling – we may reasonably reply that we do not understand what we are asked to do; that the proposal is quite literally meaningless. Indeed, we may advance the old, but nevertheless sound, platitude that one cannot cast doubt on everything at once, for then nothing is more dubious than anything else, so that there are no standards of comparison and nothing is altered. So too, and for the same reason, we may reject as empty those general warnings which beg us to remember that all norms and criteria, factual, logical, ethical, political, aesthetic, are hopelessly infected by historical or social or some other

---

[1] Unless indeed we embark on the extravagant path of formulating and testing the reliability of such methods by methods of methods (at times called the study of methodology), and these by methods of methods of methods; but we shall have to stop somewhere before we lose count of what we are doing: and accept that stage, willy-nilly, as absolute, the home of 'permanent standards'.

kind of conditioning; that all are but temporary makeshifts, none are stable or reliable; for time and chance will bear them all away. But if all judgements are thus infected, there is nothing whereby we can discriminate between various degrees of infection, and if everything is relative, subjective, accidental, biased, nothing can be judged to be more so than anything else. If words like 'subjective' and 'relative', 'prejudiced' and 'biased', are terms not of comparison and contrast – if they do not imply the possibility of their own opposites, of 'objective' (or at least 'less subjective') or 'unbiased' (or at least 'less biased') – what meaning have they for us? To use them in order to refer to everything whatever, to use them as absolute terms, and not as correlatives, is a rhetorical perversion of their normal sense, a kind of general *memento mori*, an invocation to all of us to remember how weak and ignorant and trivial we are, a stern and virtuous maxim, and merited perhaps, but not a serious doctrine concerned with the question of the attribution of responsibility in history, relevant to any particular group of moralists or statesmen or human beings.

It may, at this stage, be salutary to be reminded once again of the occasions which stimulated respected thinkers to such views. If, moved to indignation by the crudity and lack of scruple of those 'ideological' schools of history which, ignoring all that we know about human beings, paint individuals or classes or societies as heroes and villains, wholly white or unimaginably black, other, more sensitive and honest, historians or philosophers of history protest against this, and warn us about the dangers of moralising, of applying dogmatic standards, we applaud, we subscribe to the protest, yet we must be on our guard lest we protest too much, and, on the plea of curbing excesses, use means which promote some of the diseases of which they purport to be the cure. To blame is always to fail in understanding, say the advocates of toleration; to speak of human responsibility, guilt, crime, wickedness is only a way of saving oneself the effort, the long, patient, subtle or tedious labour, of unravelling the tangled skein of human affairs. It is always open to us, we shall be told, by a feat of imaginative sympathy to place ourselves in the circumstances of an individual or a society; if only we take the trouble to 'reconstruct' the conditions, the intellectual and social and religious 'climate', of another time or place, we shall thereby obtain insight into, or at least a glimpse of, motives and attitudes in terms of which the act we are judging may seem no longer either gratuitous, stupid, wicked or, above all, unintelligible.

These are proper sentiments. It follows that we must, if we are to judge fairly, have adequate evidence before us; possess sufficient imagination, sufficient sense of how institutions develop, how human beings act and think, to enable us to achieve understanding of times and places and characters and predicaments very unlike our own; not let ourselves be blinded by prejudice and passion; make every effort to construct cases for those whom we condemn – better cases, as Acton said, than they made or could have made for themselves; not look at the past solely through the eyes of the victors; not lean over too far towards the vanquished, as if truth and justice were the monopoly of the martyrs and the minorities; and strive to remain fair even to the big battalions.

All this cannot be gainsaid: it is true, just, relevant, but perhaps hardly startling. And we can add as a corollary: other times, other standards; nothing is absolute or unchanging; time and chance alter all things; and that too would be a set of truisms. Surely it is not necessary to dramatise these simple truths, which are by now, if anything, too familiar, in order to remember that the purposes, the ultimate ends of life, pursued by men are many, even within one culture and generation; that some of these come into conflict, and lead to clashes between societies, parties, individuals, and not least within individuals themselves; and furthermore that the ends of one age and country differ widely from those of other times and other outlooks. And if we understand how conflicts between ends equally ultimate and sacred, but irreconcilable within the breast of even a single human being, or between different men or groups, can lead to tragic and unavoidable collisions, we shall not distort the moral facts by artificially ordering them in terms of some one absolute criterion; recognising that (*pace* the moralists of the eighteenth century) not all good things are necessarily compatible with one another; and shall seek to comprehend the changing ideas of cultures, peoples, classes and individual human beings, without asking which are right, which wrong, at any rate not in terms of some simple home-made dogma. We shall not condemn the Middle Ages simply because they fell short of the moral or intellectual standard of the *révolté* intelligentsia of Paris in the eighteenth century, or denounce these latter because in their turn they earned the disapprobation of moral bigots in England in the nineteenth or in America in the twentieth century. Or, if we do condemn societies or individuals, we shall do so only after taking into account their social and material conditions, their aspirations, codes of value, degrees of progress and reaction, measured in terms of their own situation and outlook; and judge them, when we do (and why in the world should we not?), as we judge anyone or anything: in terms partly of what we like, approve, believe in and think right ourselves, partly of the views of the societies and individuals in question, and of what we think about such views, and of how far we, being what we are, think it natural or desirable to have a wide variety of views; and of what we think of the importance of motives as against that of consequences, or of the value of consequences as against the quality of motives, and so on. We judge as we judge, we take the risks which this entails, we accept correction wherever this seems valid, we go too far, and under pressure we retract. We make hasty generalisations, we prove mistaken, and, if we are honest, we withdraw. We seek to be understanding and just, or we seek to derive practical lessons, or to be amused, and we expose ourselves to praise and blame and criticism and correction and misunderstanding. But in so far as we claim to understand the standards of others, whether members of our own societies or those of distant countries and ages, to grasp what we are told by spokesmen of many different traditions and attitudes, to understand why they think as they think and say what they say, then, so long as these claims are not absurdly false, the 'relativism' and 'subjectivism' of other civilisations do not preclude us from sharing common assumptions, sufficient for some communication with them, for some degree of understanding and being understood.

This common ground is what is correctly called objective – that which enables us to identify other men and other civilisations as human and civilised at all. When this breaks down we do cease to understand, and, *ex hypothesi*, we misjudge; but since by the same hypothesis we cannot be sure how far communication has broken down, how far we are being deluded by historical mirages, we cannot always take steps to avert this or discount its consequences. We seek to understand by putting together as much as we can out of the fragments of the past, make out the best, most plausible cases for persons and ages remote from or unsympathetic or for some reason inaccessible to us; we do our utmost to extend the frontiers of knowledge and imagination; as to what happens beyond all possible frontiers, we cannot tell and consequently cannot care; for it is nothing to us. What we can discern we seek to describe as accurately and fully as possible; as for the darkness which surrounds the field of our vision, it is opaque to us, concerning it our judgements are neither subjective nor objective; what is beyond the horizon of vision cannot disturb us in what we are able to see or seek to know; what we can never know cannot make us doubt or reject that which we do. Some of our judgements are, no doubt, relative and subjective, but others are not; for if none were so, if objectivity were in principle inconceivable, the terms 'subjective' and 'objective', no longer contrasted, would mean nothing; for all correlatives stand and fall together. So much for the secular argument that we must not judge, lest – all standards being relative – we be judged, with the equally fallacious corollary that no individual in history can rightly be pronounced innocent or guilty, for the values in terms of which he is so described are subjective, spring from self-interest or class interest or a passing phase of a culture or from some other such cause; and the verdict has therefore no 'objective' status and no real authority.

And what of the other argument – the *tout comprendre* maxim? It appeals to the world order. If the world follows a fixed design and every element in it is determined by every other, then to understand a fact, a person, a civilisation is to grasp its relationship to the cosmic design, in which it plays a unique part; and to grasp its meaning is to grasp, as we have shown before, its value, its justification, too. To understand the cosmic symphony wholly is to understand the necessity for every note of it; to protest, condemn, complain is merely to show that one has not understood. In its metaphysical form this theory claims to perceive the 'real' design, so that the outer disorder is but a distorted reflection of the universal order – at once the ground and the purpose of all there is – 'within' or 'beyond' or 'beneath'. This is the *philosophia perennis* of Platonists and Aristotelians, Scholastics and Hegelians, Eastern philosophers and contemporary metaphysicians, who distinguish between the harmonious reality which is invisible and the visible chaos of appearances. To understand, to justify, to explain are identical processes.

The empirical versions of this view take the form of belief in some kind of universal sociological causation. Some are optimistic like the theories of Turgot and Comte, emergent evolutionists, scientific Utopians and other convinced believers in the inevitable increase in the quality and variety of human happiness. Alternatively, as in Schopenhauer's version, they may be pessimistic, and hold out the prospect of perpetual suffering which all human efforts to prevent it will only serve to increase. Or they may take a neutral attitude and seek only to establish that there exists an inexorable sequence of cause and effect; that everything, both mental and physical, is subject to discoverable laws; that to understand them is not necessarily to approve, but at least makes it pointless to blame men for not having done better; for there was no other alternative which such men could – causally could – have chosen; so that their historical alibi is unbreakable. We can still, of course, complain in a purely aesthetic fashion. We can complain of ugliness, although we know we cannot alter it; and in the same way we can complain of stupidity, cruelty, cowardice, injustice, and feel anger or shame or despair, while remembering that we cannot put an end to their objects; and in the process of convincing ourselves that we cannot change behaviour, we shall duly cease to speak of cruelty or injustice, but merely of painful or annoying events; and to escape from them we should re-educate ourselves (assuming, inconsistently enough, like many a Greek sage and eighteenth-century radical, that we are free in matters of education, although rigidly conditioned in almost every other respect) to adjust ourselves into conformity with the universe; and, distinguishing what is relatively permanent from what is transient, seek so to form our tastes and views and activities as to fit in with the pattern of things. For if we are unhappy, because we cannot have something we want, we must seek happiness by teaching ourselves to want only what we cannot anyhow avoid. That is the lesson of the Stoics, as it is, less obviously, that of some modern sociologists. Determinism is held to be 'demonstrated' by scientific observation; responsibility is a delusion; praise and blame are subjective attitudes put to flight by the advance of knowledge. To explain is to justify; one cannot complain of what cannot be otherwise; and natural morality – the life of reason – is the morality and the life whose values are identified with the actual march of events, whether it be metaphysically deduced from some intuitive insight into the nature of reality and its ultimate purpose, or established by scientific methods.

But does any ordinary human being, does any practising historian, begin to believe one word of this strange tale?

VII

Two powerful doctrines are at large in contemporary thought, relativism and determinism. The first of these, for all that it is represented as being an antidote to overweening self-confidence, or arrogant dogmatism, or moral self-satisfaction, is nevertheless founded on a fallacious interpretation of experience; the second, for all that its chains are decked with flowers, and despite its parade of noble stoicism and the splendour and vastness of its cosmic design, nevertheless represents the universe as a prison. Relativism opposes to individual protest and belief in moral principles the resignation or the irony of those who have seen many worlds crumble, many ideals turned tawdry or ridiculous by time. Determinism claims to bring us to our senses by showing where the true, the impersonal and unalterable, machinery of life and thought is to be found. The first, when it ceases to be a maxim, or merely a salutary reminder to us of our limitations or of the complexity of the issue, and claims our attention as a serious *Weltanschauung*, rests on the misuse of words, a confusion of ideas, and relies upon a logical fallacy. The second, when it goes beyond indicating specific obstacles to free choice where examinable evidence for this can be adduced, turns out to rest either on a mythology or on a metaphysical dogma. Both have, at times, succeeded in reasoning or frightening men out of their most human moral or political convictions in the name of a deeper and more devastating insight into the nature of things. Yet, perhaps, this is no more than a sign of neurosis and confusion: for neither view seems to be supported by human experience. Why then should either doctrine (but especially determinism) have bound its spell so powerfully on so many otherwise clear and honest minds?

One of the deepest of human desires is to find a unitary pattern in which the whole of experience, past, present and future, actual, possible and unfulfilled, is symmetrically ordered. It is often expressed by saying that once upon a time there was a harmonious unity – 'the unmediated whole of feeling and thought', 'the unity of the knower and the known', of 'the outer and the inner', of subject and object, form and matter, self and not-self; that this was somehow broken; and that the whole of human experience has consisted in an endless effort to reassemble the fragments, to restore the unity, and so to escape or 'transcend' categories – ways of thinking – which split and isolate and 'kill' the living reality, and 'dirempt' us from it. We are told of an endless quest to find an answer to the puzzle, to return to the seamless whole, to the paradise whence we were expelled, or to inherit one which we have still not done enough to earn.

This central conception, whatever its origin or value, is surely at the heart of much metaphysical speculation, of much striving for the unification of the sciences, and of a large proportion of aesthetic and logical, social and historical thought. But whether or not the discovery of a single pattern of experience offers that satisfaction of our reason to which many metaphysicians aspire, and in the name of which they reject empirical science as a mere *de facto* collocation of 'brute' facts – descriptions of events or persons or things not connected by those 'rational' links which alone reason is held to be able to accept – whether or not this lies at the back of so much metaphysics and religion, it does not alter the order of the actual appearances – the empirical scene – with which alone history can properly claim to deal. From the days of Bossuet to those of Hegel and increasingly thereafter, claims have been made, widely varying in degree of generality and confidence, to be able to trace a structure of history (usually a priori, for all protests to the contrary), to discover the one and only true pattern into which alone all facts will be found to fit. But this is not, and can never be, accepted by any serious historian who wishes to establish the truth as it is understood by the best critics of his time, working by standards accepted as realistic by his most scrupulous and enlightened fellow workers. For he does not perceive one unique schema as the truth – the only real framework in which alone the facts truly lie; he does not distinguish the one real, cosmic pattern from false ones, as he certainly seeks to distinguish real facts from fiction. The same facts can be arranged in more than one single pattern, seen from several perspectives, displayed in many lights, all of them valid, although some will be more suggestive or fertile in one field than in another, or unify many fields in some illuminating fashion, or, alternatively, bring out disparities and open chasms. Some of these patterns will lie closer than others to the meta-physical or religious outlook of this or that historian or historical thinker. Yet through it all the facts themselves will remain relatively 'hard'. Relatively, but, of course, not absolutely; and, whenever obsession by a given pattern causes a given writer to interpret the facts too artificially, to fill the gaps in his knowledge too smoothly, without sufficient regard to the empirical evidence, other historians will instinctively perceive that some kind of violence is being done to the facts, that the relation between evidence and interpretation is in some way abnormal; and that this is so not because there is doubt about the facts, but because there is an obsessive pattern at work.[1] Freedom from such *idées fixes* – the degree of such freedom – distinguishes true history from the mythology of a given period; for there is no historical thought, properly speaking, save where facts can be distinguished not merely from fiction, but from theory and interpretation, not, it may be, absolutely, but to a lesser or greater degree.

We shall be reminded that there is no sharp break between history and mythology; or history and metaphysics; and that in the same sense there is no sharp line between 'facts' and theories: that no absolute touchstone can in principle be produced; and this is true enough, but from it nothing startling follows. That such differences exist only metaphysicians have disputed; yet history as an independent discipline did, nevertheless, emerge; and that is tantamount to saying that the frontier between facts and cosmic patterns, empirical or metaphysical or theological, indistinct and shifting as it may be, is a genuine concept for all those who take the problems of history seriously. So long as we remain historians the two levels must be kept distinct. The attempt, therefore, to shuffle off responsibility, which, at an empirical level, seems to rest upon this or that historical individual or society, or on a set of opinions held or propagated by one of these, on to some metaphysical machinery which, because it is impersonal, excludes the very idea of moral responsibility, must always be invalid; and the desire to do so may, as often as not, be written down to the wish to escape from an untidy, cruel and above all seemingly purposeless world, into a realm where all is harmonious, clear, intelligible, mounting towards some perfect culmination which satisfies the demands of 'reason', or an aesthetic feeling, or a metaphysical impulse or religious craving; above all, where nothing can be the object of criticism or complaint or condemnation or despair.

The matter is more serious when empirical arguments are advanced for a historical determinism which excludes the notion of personal responsibility. We are here no longer dealing with the

[1] Criteria of what is a fact or what constitutes empirical evidence are seldom in grave dispute within a given culture or profession.

metaphysics of history – the theodicies, say, of Schelling or Toynbee – as obvious substitutes for theology. We have before us the great sociological theories of history – the materialistic or scientific interpretations which began with Montesquieu and the *philosophes*, and led to the great schools of the nineteenth century, from the Saint-Simonians and Hegelians to the followers of Comte, Marx, Darwin and the liberal economists; from Freud, Pareto and Sorel to the ideologists of Fascism. Of these Marxism is much the boldest and the most intelligent, but its practitioners, much as they have added to our understanding, have not succeeded in their gallant and powerful attempt to turn history into a science. Arising out of this great movement we have the vast proliferation of anthropological and sociological studies of civilised societies, with their tendency to trace all character and behaviour to the same kind of relatively irrational and unconscious causes as those which are held to have so successfully explained the behaviour of primitive societies; we have witnessed the rebirth of the notion of the 'sociology of knowledge', which suggests that not only our methods but our conclusions and our reasons for believing them, in the entire realm of knowledge, can be shown to be wholly or largely determined by the stage reached in the development of our class or group, or nation or culture, or whatever other unit may be chosen; followed, in due course, by the fusion of these at times unconvincing, but, usually, at least quasi-scientific, doctrines with such non-empirical figments – at times all but personified powers both good and bad – as 'the collectivist spirit', or 'the Myth of the Twentieth Century', or 'the contemporary collapse of values' (sometimes called 'the crisis of faith'), or 'modern man', or 'the last stage of capitalism'.

All these modes of speech have peopled the air with supernatural entities of great power, Neoplatonic and Gnostic spirits, angels and demons who play with us as they will, or, at any rate, make demands on us which, we are told, we ignore at our peril. There has grown up in our modern time a pseudo-sociological mythology which, in the guise of scientific concepts, has developed into a new animism – certainly a more primitive and naïve religion than the traditional European faiths which it seeks to replace.[1] This

---

[1] I need hardly add that responsibility (if I may still venture to use this term) for this cannot be placed at the door of the great thinkers who founded modern sociology – Marx, Durkheim, Weber – nor of the rational and scrupulous

new cult leads troubled persons to ask such questions as 'Is war inevitable?' or 'Must collectivism triumph?', or 'Is civilisation doomed?' These questions, and the tone in which they are posed, and the way in which they are discussed, imply a belief in the occult presence of vast impersonal entities – wars, collectivism, doom – agencies and forces at large in the world which we have but little power to control or deflect. Sometimes these are said to 'embody themselves' in great men, titanic figures who, because they are at one with their age, achieve superhuman results – Napoleon, Bismarck, Lenin; sometimes in the actions of classes – the great capitalist combines, which work for ends that their members scarcely understand themselves, ends towards which their economic and social position 'inevitably' drives them; sometimes in huge inchoate entities called 'the masses', which do the work of history, little knowing of what mighty forces they are the 'creative vehicles'. Wars, revolutions, dictatorships, military and economic transformations are apt to be conceived like the genii of some oriental demonology, djinns which, once set free from the jars in which they have been confined for centuries, become uncontrollable, and capriciously play with the lives of men and nations. It is perhaps not to be wondered at that, with so luxurious a growth of similes and metaphors, many innocent persons nowadays tend to believe that their lives are dominated not merely by relatively stable, easily identifiable, material factors – physical nature and the laws dealt with by the natural sciences; but by even more powerful and sinister, and far less intelligible, factors – the impersonal struggles of classes which members of these classes may not intend, the collision of social forces, the incidences of slumps and booms which, like tides and harvests, can scarcely be controlled by those whose lives depend upon them – above all, by inexorable 'societal' and 'behavioural' patterns, to quote but a few sacred words from the barbarous vocabulary of the new mythologies.

Cowed and humbled by the panoply of the new divinities, men are eager, and seek anxiously, for knowledge and comfort in the sacred books and in the new orders of priesthood which affect to tell them about the attributes and habits of their new masters. And the books and their expositors do speak words of comfort: demand creates supply. Their message is simple and very ancient. In a world

followers and critics whose work they have inspired.

where such monsters clash, individual human beings can have but little responsibility for what they do; the discovery of the new, terrifying, impersonal forces may render life infinitely more dangerous, yet if they serve no other purpose, they do, at any rate, divest their victims of all responsibility – from all those moral burdens which men in less enlightened days used to carry with such labour and anguish. So that what we have lost on the swings we make up on the roundabouts: if we lose freedom of choice, at any rate we can no longer blame or be blamed for a world largely out of our control. The terminology of praise and condemnation turns out to be *eo ipso* uncivilised and obscurantist. To record what occurs and why, in impersonal chronicles, as was done by detached and studious monks in other times of violence and strife, is represented as more honourable and more dignified, and more in keeping with the noble humility and integrity of a scholar who in a time of doubt and crisis will at least preserve his soul if he abstains from the easy path of self-indulgence in moral sentiments. Agonising doubts about the conduct of individuals caught in historical crises, and the feeling of hope and despair, guilt, pride and remorse which accompanies such reflections, are taken from us; like soldiers in an army driven by forces too great to resist, we lose those neuroses which spring from the fear of having to choose among alternatives. Where there is no choice there is no anxiety; and a happy release from responsibility. Some human beings have always preferred the peace of imprisonment, a contented security, a sense of having at last found one's proper place in the cosmos, to the painful conflicts and perplexities of the disordered freedom of the world beyond the walls.

Yet this is odd. For the assumptions upon which this kind of determinism has been erected are, when examined, exceedingly unplausible. What are these forces and these inexorable historical laws? What historiographer, what sociologist, can claim as yet to have produced empirical generalisations comparable to the great uniformities of the natural sciences? It is a commonplace to say that sociology still awaits its Newton, but even this seems much too audacious a claim; it has yet to find its Euclid and its Archimedes, before it can begin to dream of a Copernicus. On one side a patient and useful accumulation of facts and analyses, taxonomy, useful comparative studies, cautious and limited hypotheses, still hamstrung by too many exceptions to have any appreciable predictive power;[1] on the other, imposing, sometimes ingenious, theoretical constructions, obscured by picturesque metaphors and a bold mythology, often stimulating to workers in other fields; and between these a vast gap, such as has not existed in historical times between the theories and the factual evidence of the natural sciences. It is idle for sociology to plead that she is still young and has a glorious future. The eponymous hero to honour whose memory these words are being uttered, Auguste Comte, founded it a full hundred years ago, and its great nomothetic conquests are still to come.[2] It has affected other disciplines most fruitfully, notably history, to which it has added a dimension;[3] but it has as yet succeeded in discovering so few laws, or wide generalisations supported by adequate evidence, that its plea to be treated as a natural science can scarcely be entertained, nor are these few poor laws sufficiently revolutionary to make it seem an urgent matter to test their truth. In the great and fertile field of sociology (unlike her more speculative but far more effective younger sister, psychology) the loose generalisations of historically trained minds still, at times, seem more fruitful than their 'scientific' equivalents.

Social determinism is, at least historically, closely bound up with the 'nomothetic' ideals of sociology. And it may, indeed, be a true doctrine. But if it is true, and if we begin to take it seriously, then, indeed, the changes in the whole of our language, our moral terminology, our attitudes toward one another, our views of history, of society and of everything else will be too profound to be even adumbrated. The concepts of praise and blame, innocence and guilt and individual responsibility from which we started are but a small element in the structure which would collapse or disappear. If social and psychological determinism were established as an accepted truth, our world would be transformed more radically than was the teleological world of the classical and medieval ages by the triumphs of mechanistic principles or those of natural selection. Our words – our modes of speech and thought –

[1] And a collection of isolated insights and *aperçus*, like the dubious 'All power either corrupts or intoxicates', or 'Man is a political animal', or 'Der Mensch ist was er ißt' ('Man is what he eats').

[2] I do not mean to imply that other 'sciences' – e.g. 'political science' or social anthropology – have fared much better in establishing laws; but their claims are more modest.

[3] As well as new methods for testing the validity of old conclusions.

would be transformed in literally unimaginable ways; the notions of choice, of responsibility, of freedom are so deeply embedded in our outlook that our new life, as creatures in a world genuinely lacking in these concepts, can, I should maintain, be conceived by us only with the greatest difficulty.

But there is, as yet, no need to alarm ourselves unduly. We are speaking only of pseudo-scientific ideals; the reality is not in sight. The evidence for a thoroughgoing determinism is not to hand; and if there is a persistent tendency to believe in it in some theoretical fashion, that is surely due far more to the lure of a 'scientistic' or metaphysical ideal or to a tendency on the part of those who desire to change society to believe that the stars in their courses are fighting for them. Or it may be due to a longing to lay down moral burdens, or minimise individual responsibility and transfer it to impersonal forces which can be accused of causing all our discontents, rather than to any increase in our powers of critical reflection or improvement in our scientific techniques. Belief in historical determinism of this type is, of course, very widespread, particularly in what I should like to call its 'historiosophical' form, by which I mean metaphysico-theological theories of history, which attract many who have lost their faith in older religious orthodoxies. Yet perhaps this attitude, so prevalent recently, is ebbing; and a contrary trend is discernible today. Our best historians use empirical tests in sifting facts, make microscopic examinations of the evidence, deduce no patterns, and show no false fear in attributing responsibility to individuals. Their specific attributions and analyses may be mistaken, but both they and their readers would rightly reject the notion that their very activity had been superseded and stultified by the advances of sociology, or by some deeper metaphysical insight, like that of oriental star-gazers by the discoveries of the disciples of Kepler.

In their own queer way, some modern existentialists, too, proclaim the crucial importance of individual acts of choice. The condemnation by some among them of all philosophical systems, and of all moral (as of other) doctrines, as equally hollow, simply because they are systems and doctrines, may be invalid; but the more serious of them are no less insistent than Kant upon the reality of human autonomy, that is, upon the reality of free self-commitment to an act or a form of life for what it is in itself. Whether recognition of freedom in this last sense does or does not entitle one logically to preach to others, or judge the past, is another matter; at any rate, it shows a commendable strength of intellect to have seen through the pretensions of those all-explanatory, all-justifying theodicies which promised to assimilate the human sciences to the natural in the quest for a unified schema of all there is.

It needs more than infatuation with a programme to overthrow some of the most deeply rooted moral and intellectual habits of human beings, whether they be plumbers or historians. We are told that it is foolish to judge Charlemagne or Napoleon or Genghis Khan or Hitler or Stalin for their massacres, that it is at most a comment upon ourselves and not upon 'the facts'. Likewise we are told that we should not describe as benefactors of humanity those whom the followers of Comte so faithfully celebrated; or at least that to do so is not our business as historians: because as historians our categories are 'neutral' and differ from the categories we use as ordinary human beings, as those of chemists undeniably do. We are also told that as historians it is our task to describe, let us say, the great revolutions of our own time without so much as hinting that certain individuals involved in them not merely caused, but were responsible for, great misery and destruction – using such words according to the standards not merely of the twentieth century, which is soon over, or of our declining capitalist society, but of the human race at all the times and in all the places in which we have known it; and told that we should practise such austerities out of respect for some imaginary scientific canon which distinguishes between facts and values very sharply, so sharply that it enables us to regard the former as being objective, 'inexorable' and therefore self-justifying, and the latter as merely a subjective gloss upon events – due to the moment, the milieu, the individual temperament – and consequently unworthy of serious scholarship.

To this we can only answer that to accept this doctrine is to do violence to the basic notions of our morality, to misrepresent our sense of our past, and to ignore some among the most general concepts and categories of normal thought. Those who are concerned with human affairs are committed to the use of the moral categories and concepts which normal language incorporates and expresses. Chemists, philologists, logicians, even sociologists with a strong quantitative bias, by using morally neutral technical terms, can avoid these concepts. But historians can scarcely do so. They need not – they are certainly not obliged to – moralise: but neither can they avoid the use of normal language with all its associations and 'built in' moral categories. To seek to avoid this is to adopt another moral outlook, not none at all. The time will come when men will wonder how this strange view, which combines a misunderstanding of the relation of value to fact with cynicism disguised as stern impartiality, can ever have achieved such remarkable fame and influence and respectability. For it is not scientific; nor can its reputation be due entirely to a commendable fear of undue arrogance or philistinism or of too bland and uncritical an imposition of our own dogmas and standards upon others. In part it is due to a genuine misunderstanding of the philosophical implications of the natural sciences, the great prestige of which has been misappropriated by many a fool and impostor since their earliest triumphs. But principally it seems to me to spring from a desire to resign our responsibility, to cease from judging, provided we ourselves are not judged and, above all, are not compelled to judge ourselves; from a desire to flee for refuge to some vast amoral, impersonal, monolithic whole – nature, or history,[1] or class, or race, or the 'harsh realities of our time', or the irresistible evolution of the social structure[2] – that will absorb and integrate us into its limitless, indifferent, neutral texture, which it is senseless to evaluate or criticise, and against which we fight to our certain doom.

This is an image which has often appeared in the history of mankind, always at moments of confusion and inner weakness. It is one of the great alibis, pleaded by those who cannot or do not wish to face the fact of human responsibility, the existence of a limited but nevertheless real area of human freedom, either because they have been too deeply wounded or frightened to wish to return to the traffic of normal life, or because they are filled with moral indignation against the false values and the, to them, repellent moral codes of their own society, or class, or profession, and take up arms against all ethical codes as such, as a dignified means of casting off a morality which is to them, perhaps justifiably, repulsive. Nevertheless, such views, although they may spring from a natural reaction against too much moral rhetoric, are a desperate remedy; those who hold them use history as a method of

[1] 'History has seized us by the throat', Mussolini is reported to have cried on learning of the Allied landing in Sicily. Men could be fought; but once 'History' herself took up arms against one, resistance was vain.

[2] 'The irresistible', Justice Louis Brandeis is said to have remarked, 'is often only that which is not resisted.'

escape from a world which has, for some reason, grown odious to them, into a fantasy where impersonal entities avenge their grievances and set everything right, to the greater or lesser discomfiture of their persecutors, real and imaginary. And in the course of this they describe the normal lives lived by men in terms which fail to mark the most important psychological and moral distinctions known to us. This they do in the service of an imaginary science; and, like the astrologers and soothsayers whom they have succeeded, cast up their eyes to the clouds, and speak in immense, unsubstantiated images and similes, in deeply misleading metaphors and allegories, and make use of hypnotic formulae with little regard for experience, or rational argument, or tests of proven reliability. Thereby they throw dust in their own eyes as well as in ours, obstruct our vision of the real world, and further confuse an already sufficiently bewildered public about the relations of morality to politics, and about the nature and methods of the natural sciences and historical studies alike.

TWO CONCEPTS OF LIBERTY

IF MEN never disagreed about the ends of life, if our ancestors had remained undisturbed in the Garden of Eden, the studies to which the Chichele Chair of Social and Political Theory is dedicated could scarcely have been conceived.[1] For these studies spring from, and thrive on, discord. Someone may question this on the ground that even in a society of saintly anarchists, where no conflicts about ultimate purposes can take place, political problems, for example constitutional or legislative issues, might still arise. But this objection rests on a mistake. Where ends are agreed, the only questions left are those of means, and these are not political but technical, that is to say, capable of being settled by experts or machines, like arguments between engineers or doctors. That is why those who put their faith in some immense, world-transforming phenomenon, like the final triumph of reason or the proletarian revolution, must believe that all political and moral problems can thereby be turned into technological ones. That is the meaning of Engels' famous phrase (paraphrasing Saint-Simon) about 'replacing the government of persons by the administration of things',[2] and the Marxist prophecies about the withering away of the State and the beginning of the true history of humanity. This outlook is called Utopian by those for whom speculation about this condition of perfect social harmony is the play of idle fancy. Nevertheless, a visitor from Mars to any British – or American – university today might perhaps be forgiven if he sustained the impression that its members lived in something very like this innocent and idyllic state, for all the serious attention that is paid to

[1] This essay is based on an Inaugural Lecture delivered in 1958. Berlin succeeded G. D. H. Cole in this Chair in 1957.

[2] loc. cit. (p. 83 above, note 1).

fundamental problems of politics by professional philosophers.

Yet this is both surprising and dangerous. Surprising because there has, perhaps, been no time in modern history when so large a number of human beings, in both the East and the West, have had their notions, and indeed their lives, so deeply altered, and in some cases violently upset, by fanatically held social and political doctrines. Dangerous, because when ideas are neglected by those who ought to attend to them – that is to say, those who have been trained to think critically about ideas – they sometimes acquire an unchecked momentum and an irresistible power over multitudes of men that may grow too violent to be affected by rational criticism. Over a hundred years ago, the German poet Heine warned the French not to underestimate the power of ideas: philosophical concepts nurtured in the stillness of a professor's study could destroy a civilisation. He spoke of Kant's *Critique of Pure Reason* as the sword with which German deism had been decapitated, and described the works of Rousseau as the blood-stained weapon which, in the hands of Robespierre, had destroyed the old regime; and prophesied that the romantic faith of Fichte and Schelling would one day be turned, with terrible effect, by their fanatical German followers, against the liberal culture of the West. The facts have not wholly belied this prediction; but if professors can truly wield this fatal power, may it not be that only other professors, or, at least, other thinkers (and not governments or congressional committees), can alone disarm them?

Our philosophers seem oddly unaware of these devastating effects of their activities. It may be that, intoxicated by their magnificent achievements in more abstract realms, the best among them look with disdain upon a field in which radical discoveries are less likely to be made, and talent for minute analysis is less likely to be rewarded. Yet, despite every effort to separate them, conducted by a blind scholastic pedantry, politics has remained indissolubly intertwined with every other form of philosophical enquiry. To neglect the field of political thought, because its unstable subject-matter, with its blurred edges, is not to be caught by the fixed concepts, abstract models and fine instruments suitable to logic or to linguistic analysis – to demand a unity of method in philosophy, and reject whatever the method cannot successfully manage – is merely to allow oneself to remain at the mercy of primitive and uncriticised political beliefs. It is only a very vulgar historical materialism that denies the power of ideas, and says that ideals are mere material interests in disguise. It may be that, without the pressure of social forces, political ideas are stillborn: what is certain is that these forces, unless they clothe themselves in ideas, remain blind and undirected.

Political theory is a branch of moral philosophy, which starts from the discovery, or application, of moral notions in the sphere of political relations. I do not mean, as I think some Idealist philosophers may have believed, that all historical movements or conflicts between human beings are reducible to movements or conflicts of ideas or spiritual forces, nor even that they are effects (or aspects) of them. But I do mean that to understand such movements or conflicts is, above all, to understand the ideas or attitudes to life involved in them, which alone make such movements a part of human history, and not mere natural events. Political words and notions and acts are not intelligible save in the context of the issues that divide the men who use them. Consequently our own attitudes and activities are likely to remain obscure to us, unless we understand the dominant issues of our own world. The greatest of these is the open war that is being fought between two systems of ideas which return different and conflicting answers to what has long been the central question of politics – the question of obedience and coercion. 'Why should I (or anyone) obey anyone else?' 'Why should I not live as I like?' 'Must I obey?' 'If I disobey, may I be coerced?' 'By whom, and to what degree, and in the name of what, and for the sake of what?'

Upon the answers to the question of the permissible limits of coercion opposed views are held in the world today, each claiming the allegiance of very large numbers of men. It seems to me, therefore, that any aspect of this issue is worthy of examination.

I

To coerce a man is to deprive him of freedom – freedom from what? Almost every moralist in human history has praised freedom. Like happiness and goodness, like nature and reality, it is a term whose meaning is so porous that there is little interpretation that it seems able to resist. I do not propose to discuss either the history of this protean word or the more than two hundred senses of it recorded by historians of ideas. I propose to examine no more than two of these senses – but they are central ones, with a great deal of human history behind them, and, I dare say, still to come. The first of these political senses of freedom or liberty (I shall use both words to mean the same), which (following much precedent) I shall call the 'negative' sense, is involved in the answer to the question 'What is the area within which the subject – a person or group of persons – is or should be left to do or be what he is able to do or be, without interference by other persons?' The second, which I shall call the 'positive' sense, is involved in the answer to the question 'What, or who, is the source of control or interference that can determine someone to do, or be, this rather than that?' The two questions are clearly different, even though the answers to them may overlap.

The notion of negative freedom

I am normally said to be free to the degree to which no man or body of men interferes with my activity. Political liberty in this sense is simply the area within which a man can act unobstructed by others. If I am prevented by others from doing what I could otherwise do, I am to that degree unfree; and if this area is contracted by other men beyond a certain minimum, I can be described as being coerced, or, it may be, enslaved. Coercion is not, however, a term that covers every form of inability. If I say that I am unable to jump more than ten feet in the air, or cannot read because I am blind, or cannot understand the darker pages of Hegel, it would be eccentric to say that I am to that degree enslaved or coerced. Coercion implies the deliberate interference of other human beings within the area in which I could otherwise act. You lack political liberty or freedom only if you are prevented from attaining a goal by human beings.[1] Mere incapacity to attain a goal is not lack of political freedom.[2] This is brought out by the use of such modern expressions as 'economic freedom' and its counterpart, 'economic slavery'. It is argued, very plausibly, that if a man is too poor to afford something on which there is no legal ban – a loaf of bread, a journey round the world, recourse to the law courts – he is as little free to have it as he would be if it were

[1] I do not, of course, mean to imply the truth of the converse.

[2] Helvétius made this point very clearly: 'The free man is the man who is not in irons, not imprisoned in a gaol, nor terrorised like a slave by the fear of punishment.' It is not lack of freedom not to fly like an eagle or swim like a whale. De l'esprit, first discourse, chapter 4.

forbidden him by law. If my poverty were a kind of disease which prevented me from buying bread, or paying for the journey round the world or getting my case heard, as lameness prevents me from running, this inability would not naturally be described as a lack of freedom, least of all political freedom. It is only because I believe that my inability to get a given thing is due to the fact that other human beings have made arrangements whereby I am, whereas others are not, prevented from having enough money with which to pay for it, that I think myself a victim of coercion or slavery. In other words, this use of the term depends on a particular social and economic theory about the causes of my poverty or weakness. If my lack of material means is due to my lack of mental or physical capacity, then I begin to speak of being deprived of freedom (and not simply about poverty) only if I accept the theory.[1] If, in addition, I believe that I am being kept in want by a specific arrangement which I consider unjust or unfair, I speak of economic slavery or oppression. The nature of things does not madden us, only ill will does, said Rousseau.[2] The criterion of oppression is the part that I believe to be played by other human beings, directly or indirectly, with or without the intention of doing so, in frustrating my wishes. By being free in this sense I mean not being interfered with by others. The wider the area of non-interference the wider my freedom.

This is what the classical English political philosophers meant when they used this word.[3] They disagreed about how wide the area could or should be. They supposed that it could not, as things were, be unlimited, because if it were, it would entail a state in which all men could boundlessly interfere with all other men; and this kind of 'natural' freedom would lead to social chaos in which men's minimum needs would not be satisfied; or else the liberties of the weak would be suppressed by the strong. Because they

[1] The Marxist conception of social laws is, of course, the best-known version of this theory, but it forms a large element in some Christian and utilitarian, and all socialist, doctrines.

[2] *Émile*, book 2: vol. 4, p. 320, in *Oeuvres complètes*, ed. Bernard Gagnebin and others (Paris, 1959–95).

[3] 'A free man', said Hobbes, 'is he that . . . is not hindered to do what he has a will to.' *Leviathan*, chapter 21: p. 146 in Richard Tuck's edition (Cambridge, 1991). Law is always a fetter, even if it protects you from being bound in chains that are heavier than those of the law, say some more repressive law or custom, or arbitrary despotism or chaos. Bentham says much the same.

perceived that human purposes and activities do not automatically harmonise with one another, and because (whatever their official doctrines) they put high value on other goals, such as justice, or happiness, or culture, or security, or varying degrees of equality, they were prepared to curtail freedom in the interests of other values and, indeed, of freedom itself. For, without this, it was impossible to create the kind of association that they thought desirable. Consequently, it is assumed by these thinkers that the area of men's free action must be limited by law. But equally it is assumed, especially by such libertarians as Locke and Mill in England, and Constant and Tocqueville in France, that there ought to exist a certain minimum area of personal freedom which must on no account be violated; for if it is overstepped, the individual will find himself in an area too narrow for even that minimum development of his natural faculties which alone makes it possible to pursue, and even to conceive, the various ends which men hold good or right or sacred. It follows that a frontier must be drawn between the area of private life and that of public authority. Where it is to be drawn is a matter of argument, indeed of haggling. Men are largely interdependent, and no man's activity is so completely private as never to obstruct the lives of others in any way. 'Freedom for the pike is death for the minnows';[1] the liberty of some must depend on the restraint of others. Freedom for an Oxford don, others have been known to add, is a very different thing from freedom for an Egyptian peasant.

This proposition derives its force from something that is both true and important, but the phrase itself remains a piece of political claptrap. It is true that to offer political rights, or safeguards against intervention by the State, to men who are half-naked, illiterate, underfed and diseased is to mock their condition; they need medical help or education before they can understand, or make use of, an increase in their freedom. What is freedom to those who cannot make use of it? Without adequate conditions for the use of freedom, what is the value of freedom? First things come first: there are situations in which – to use a saying satirically attributed to the nihilists by Dostoevsky – boots are superior to Pushkin; individual freedom is not everyone's primary need. For freedom is not the mere absence of frustration of whatever kind; this would

---

[1] R. H. Tawney, *Equality* (1931), 3rd ed. (London, 1938), chapter 5, section 2, 'Equality and Liberty', p. 208 (not in previous editions).

inflate the meaning of the word until it meant too much or too little. The Egyptian peasant needs clothes or medicine before, and more than, personal liberty, but the minimum freedom that he needs today, and the greater degree of freedom that he may need tomorrow, is not some species of freedom peculiar to him, but identical with that of professors, artists and millionaires.

What troubles the consciences of Western liberals is, I think, the belief, not that the freedom that men seek differs according to their social or economic conditions, but that the minority who possess it have gained it by exploiting, or, at least, averting their gaze from, the vast majority who do not. They believe, with good reason, that if individual liberty is an ultimate end for human beings, none should be deprived of it by others; least of all that some should enjoy it at the expense of others. Equality of liberty; not to treat others as I should not wish them to treat me; repayment of my debt to those who alone have made possible my liberty or prosperity or enlightenment; justice, in its simplest and most universal sense – these are the foundations of liberal morality. Liberty is not the only goal of men. I can, like the Russian critic Belinsky, say that if others are to be deprived of it – if my brothers are to remain in poverty, squalor and chains – then I do not want it for myself, I reject it with both hands and infinitely prefer to share their fate. But nothing is gained by a confusion of terms. To avoid glaring inequality or widespread misery I am ready to sacrifice some, or all, of my freedom: I may do so willingly and freely; but it is freedom that I am giving up for the sake of justice or equality or the love of my fellow men. I should be guilt-stricken, and rightly so, if I were not, in some circumstances, ready to make this sacrifice. But a sacrifice is not an increase in what is being sacrificed, namely freedom, however great the moral need or the compensation for it. Everything is what it is: liberty is liberty, not equality or fairness or justice or culture, or human happiness or a quiet conscience. If the liberty of myself or my class or nation depends on the misery of a number of other human beings, the system which promotes this is unjust and immoral. But if I curtail or lose my freedom in order to lessen the shame of such inequality, and do not thereby materially increase the individual liberty of others, an absolute loss of liberty occurs. This may be compensated for by a gain in justice or in happiness or in peace, but the loss remains, and it is a confusion of values to say that although my 'liberal', individual freedom may go by the board, some other kind of freedom – 'social' or 'economic' – is increased. Yet it remains true that the freedom of some must at times be curtailed to secure the freedom of others. Upon what principle should this be done? If freedom is a sacred, untouchable value, there can be no such principle. One or other of these conflicting rules or principles must, at any rate in practice, yield: not always for reasons which can be clearly stated, let alone generalised into rules or universal maxims. Still, a practical compromise has to be found.

Philosophers with an optimistic view of human nature and a belief in the possibility of harmonising human interests, such as Locke or Adam Smith or, in some moods, Mill, believed that social harmony and progress were compatible with reserving a large area for private life over which neither the State nor any other authority must be allowed to trespass. Hobbes, and those who agreed with him, especially conservative or reactionary thinkers, argued that if men were to be prevented from destroying one another and making social life a jungle or a wilderness, greater safeguards must be instituted to keep them in their places; he wished correspondingly to increase the area of centralised control and decrease that of the individual. But both sides agreed that some portion of human existence must remain independent of the sphere of social control. To invade that preserve, however small, would be despotism. The most eloquent of all defenders of freedom and privacy, Benjamin Constant, who had not forgotten the Jacobin dictatorship, declared that at the very least the liberty of religion, opinion, expression, property must be guaranteed against arbitrary invasion. Jefferson, Burke, Paine, Mill compiled different catalogues of individual liberties, but the argument for keeping authority at bay is always substantially the same. We must preserve a minimum area of personal freedom if we are not to 'degrade or deny our nature'.[1] We cannot remain absolutely free, and must give up some of our liberty to preserve the rest. But total self-surrender is self-defeating. What then must the minimum be? That which a man cannot give up without offending against the essence of his human nature. What is this essence? What are the standards which it entails? This has been, and perhaps always will be, a matter of infinite debate. But whatever the principle in terms of which the area of non-interference is to be drawn, whether it is that of natural law or

---

[1] Constant, *Principes de politique*, chapter 1: p. 318 in op. cit. (p. 3 above, note 1).

natural rights, or of utility, or the pronouncements of a categorical imperative, or the sanctity of the social contract, or any other concept with which men have sought to clarify and justify their convictions, liberty in this sense means liberty *from*; absence of interference beyond the shifting, but always recognisable, frontier. 'The only freedom which deserves the name, is that of pursuing our own good in our own way,' said the most celebrated of its champions.[1] If this is so, is compulsion ever justified? Mill had no doubt that it was. Since justice demands that all individuals be entitled to a minimum of freedom, all other individuals were of necessity to be restrained, if need be by force, from depriving anyone of it. Indeed, the whole function of law was the prevention of just such collisions: the State was reduced to what Lassalle contemptuously described as the functions of a night-watchman or traffic policeman.

What made the protection of individual liberty so sacred to Mill? In his famous essay he declares that, unless the individual is left to live as he wishes in 'the part [of his conduct] which merely concerns himself',[2] civilisation cannot advance; the truth will not, for lack of a free market in ideas, come to light; there will be no scope for spontaneity, originality, genius, for mental energy, for moral courage. Society will be crushed by the weight of 'collective mediocrity'.[3] Whatever is rich and diversified will be crushed by the weight of custom, by men's constant tendency to conformity, which breeds only 'withered' capacities, 'pinched and hidebound', 'cramped and dwarfed' human beings. 'Pagan self-assertion' is as worthy as 'Christian self-denial'.[4] 'All errors which [a man] is likely to commit against advice and warning, are far outweighed by the evil of allowing others to constrain him to what they deem his good.'[5] The defence of liberty consists in the 'negative' goal of warding off interference. To threaten a man with persecution unless he submits to a life in which he exercises no choices of his goals; to block before him every door but one, no matter how noble the prospect upon which it opens, or how benevolent the motives of those who arrange this, is to sin against the truth that he

---

[1] J. S. Mill, *On Liberty*, chapter 1: vol. 18, p. 226, in op. cit. (p. 81 above, note 1).

[2] ibid., p. 224.   [3] ibid., chapter 3, p. 268.

[4] ibid., pp. 265–6. The last two phrases are from John Sterling's essay on Simonides: vol 1, p. 190, in his *Essays and Tales*, ed. Julius Charles Hare (London, 1848).

[5] ibid., chapter 4, p. 277.

is a man, a being with a life of his own to live. This is liberty as it has been conceived by liberals in the modern world from the days of Erasmus (some would say of Occam) to our own. Every plea for civil liberties and individual rights, every protest against exploitation and humiliation, against the encroachment of public authority, or the mass hypnosis of custom or organised propaganda, springs from this individualistic, and much disputed, conception of man.

Three facts about this position may be noted. In the first place Mill confuses two distinct notions. One is that all coercion is, in so far as it frustrates human desires, bad as such, although it may have to be applied to prevent other, greater evils; while non-interference, which is the opposite of coercion, is good as such, although it is not the only good. This is the 'negative' conception of liberty in its classical form. The other is that men should seek to discover the truth, or to develop a certain type of character of which Mill approved – critical, original, imaginative, independent, non-conforming to the point of eccentricity, and so on – and that truth can be found, and such character can be bred, only in conditions of freedom. Both these are liberal views, but they are not identical, and the connection between them is, at best, empirical. No one would argue that truth or freedom of self-expression could flourish where dogma crushes all thought. But the evidence of history tends to show (as, indeed, was argued by James Stephen in his formidable attack on Mill in his *Liberty, Equality, Fraternity*) that integrity, love of truth and fiery individualism grow at least as often in severely disciplined communities, among, for example, the puritan Calvinists of Scotland or New England, or under military discipline, as in more tolerant or indifferent societies; and if this is so, Mill's argument for liberty as a necessary condition for the growth of human genius falls to the ground. If his two goals proved incompatible, Mill would be faced with a cruel dilemma, quite apart from the further difficulties created by the inconsistency of his doctrines with strict utilitarianism, even in his own humane version of it.[1]

---

[1] This is but another illustration of the natural tendency of all but a very few thinkers to believe that all the things they hold good must be intimately connected, or at least compatible, with one another. The history of thought, like the history of nations, is strewn with examples of inconsistent, or at least disparate, elements artificially yoked together in a despotic system, or held together by the danger of some common enemy. In due course the danger passes, and conflicts between the allies arise, which often disrupt the system, sometimes to the great benefit of mankind.

In the second place, the doctrine is comparatively modern. There seems to be scarcely any discussion of individual liberty as a conscious political ideal (as opposed to its actual existence) in the ancient world. Condorcet had already remarked that the notion of individual rights was absent from the legal conceptions of the Romans and Greeks; this seems to hold equally of the Jewish, Chinese and all other ancient civilisations that have since come to light.[1] The domination of this ideal has been the exception rather than the rule, even in the recent history of the West. Nor has liberty in this sense often formed a rallying cry for the great masses of mankind. The desire not to be impinged upon, to be left to oneself, has been a mark of high civilisation on the part of both individuals and communities. The sense of privacy itself, of the area of personal relationships as something sacred in its own right, derives from a conception of freedom which, for all its religious roots, is scarcely older, in its developed state, than the Renaissance or the Reformation.[2] Yet its decline would mark the death of a civilisation, of an entire moral outlook.

The third characteristic of this notion of liberty is of greater importance. It is that liberty in this sense is not incompatible with some kinds of autocracy, or at any rate with the absence of self-government. Liberty in this sense is principally concerned with the area of control, not with its source. Just as a democracy may, in fact, deprive the individual citizen of a great many liberties which he might have in some other form of society, so it is perfectly conceivable that a liberal-minded despot would allow his subjects a large measure of personal freedom. The despot who leaves his subjects a wide area of liberty may be unjust, or encourage the wildest inequalities, care little for order, or virtue, or knowledge; but provided he does not curb their liberty, or at least curbs it less than many other regimes, he meets with Mill's specification.[3]

[1] See the valuable discussion of this in Michel Villey, *Leçons d'histoire de la philosophie du droit* (Paris, 1957), chapter 14, which traces the embryo of the notion of subjective rights to Occam (see p. 272).

[2] Christian (and Jewish or Muslim) belief in the absolute authority of divine or natural laws, or in the equality of all men in the sight of God, is very different from belief in freedom to live as one prefers.

[3] Indeed, it is arguable that in the Prussia of Frederick the Great or in the Austria of Joseph II men of imagination, originality and creative genius, and, indeed, minorities of all kinds, were less persecuted and felt the pressure, both of institutions and custom, less heavy upon them than in many an earlier or later democracy.

Freedom in this sense is not, at any rate logically, connected with democracy or self-government. Self-government may, on the whole, provide a better guarantee of the preservation of civil liberties than other regimes, and has been defended as such by libertarians. But there is no necessary connection between individual liberty and democratic rule. The answer to the question 'Who governs me?' is logically distinct from the question 'How far does government interfere with me?' It is in this difference that the great contrast between the two concepts of negative and positive liberty, in the end, consists.[1] For the 'positive' sense of liberty comes to light if we try to answer the question, not 'What am I free to do or be?', but 'By whom am I ruled?' or 'Who is to say what I

---

[1] 'Negative liberty' is something the extent of which, in a given case, it is difficult to estimate. It might, prima facie, seem to depend simply on the power to choose between at any rate two alternatives. Nevertheless, not all choices are equally free, or free at all. If in a totalitarian State I betray my friend under threat of torture, perhaps even if I act from fear of losing my job, I can reasonably say that I did not act freely. Nevertheless, I did, of course, make a choice, and could, at any rate in theory, have chosen to be killed or tortured or imprisoned. The mere existence of alternatives is not, therefore, enough to make my action free (although it may be voluntary) in the normal sense of the word. The extent of my freedom seems to depend on (a) how many possibilities are open to me (although the method of counting these can never be more than impressionistic; possibilities of action are not discrete entities like apples, which can be exhaustively enumerated); (b) how easy or difficult each of these possibilities is to actualise; (c) how important in my plan of life, given my character and circumstances, these possibilities are when compared with each other; (d) how far they are closed and opened by deliberate human acts; (e) what value not merely the agent, but the general sentiment of the society in which he lives, puts on the various possibilities. All these magnitudes must be 'integrated', and a conclusion, necessarily never precise, or indisputable, drawn from this process. It may well be that there are many incommensurable kinds and degrees of freedom, and that they cannot be drawn up on any single scale of magnitude. Moreover, in the case of societies, we are faced by such (logically absurd) questions as 'Would arrangement X increase the liberty of Mr A more than it would that of Messrs B, C and D between them, added together?' The same difficulties arise in applying utilitarian criteria. Nevertheless, provided we do not demand precise measurement, we can give valid reasons for saying that the average subject of the King of Sweden is, on the whole, a good deal freer today [1958] than the average citizen of Spain or Albania. Total patterns of life must be compared directly as wholes, although the method by which we make the comparison, and the truth of the conclusions, are difficult or impossible to demonstrate. But the vagueness of the concepts, and the multiplicity of the criteria involved, are attributes of the subject-matter itself, not of our imperfect methods of measurement, or of incapacity for precise thought.

am, and what I am not, to be or do?' The connection between democracy and individual liberty is a good deal more tenuous than it seemed to many advocates of both. The desire to be governed by myself, or at any rate to participate in the process by which my life is to be controlled, may be as deep a wish as that for a free area for action, and perhaps historically older. But it is not a desire for the same thing. So different is it, indeed, as to have led in the end to the great clash of ideologies that dominates our world. For it is this, the 'positive' conception of liberty, not freedom from, but freedom to – to lead one prescribed form of life – which the adherents of the 'negative' notion represent as being, at times, no better than a specious disguise for brutal tyranny.

II

The notion of positive freedom

The 'positive' sense of the word 'liberty' derives from the wish on the part of the individual to be his own master. I wish my life and decisions to depend on myself, not on external forces of whatever kind. I wish to be the instrument of my own, not of other men's, acts of will. I wish to be a subject, not an object; to be moved by reasons, by conscious purposes, which are my own, not by causes which affect me, as it were, from outside. I wish to be somebody, not nobody; a doer – deciding, not being decided for, self-directed and not acted upon by external nature or by other men as if I were a thing, or an animal, or a slave incapable of playing a human role, that is, of conceiving goals and policies of my own and realising them. This is at least part of what I mean when I say that I am rational, and that it is my reason that distinguishes me as a human being from the rest of the world. I wish, above all, to be conscious of myself as a thinking, willing, active being, bearing responsibility for my choices and able to explain them by reference to my own ideas and purposes. I feel free to the degree that I believe this to be true, and enslaved to the degree that I am made to realise that it is not.

The freedom which consists in being one's own master, and the freedom which consists in not being prevented from choosing as I do by other men, may, on the face of it, seem concepts at no great logical distance from each other – no more than negative and positive ways of saying much the same thing. Yet the 'positive' and 'negative' notions of freedom historically developed in divergent directions, not always by logically reputable steps, until, in the end, they came into direct conflict with each other.

One way of making this clear is in terms of the independent momentum which the, initially perhaps quite harmless, metaphor of self-mastery acquired. 'I am my own master'; 'I am slave to no man'; but may I not (as Platonists or Hegelians tend to say) be a slave to nature? Or to my own 'unbridled' passions? Are these not so many species of the identical genus 'slave' – some political or legal, others moral or spiritual? Have not men had the experience of liberating themselves from spiritual slavery, or slavery to nature, and do they not in the course of it become aware, on the one hand, of a self which dominates, and, on the other, of something in them which is brought to heel? This dominant self is then variously identified with reason, with my 'higher nature', with the self which calculates and aims at what will satisfy it in the long run, with my 'real', or 'ideal', or 'autonomous' self, or with my self 'at its best'; which is then contrasted with irrational impulse, uncontrolled desires, my 'lower' nature, the pursuit of immediate pleasures, my 'empirical' or 'heteronomous' self, swept by every gust of desire and passion, needing to be rigidly disciplined if it is ever to rise to the full height of its 'real' nature. Presently the two selves may be represented as divided by an even larger gap; the real self may be conceived as something wider than the individual (as the term is normally understood), as a social 'whole' of which the individual is an element or aspect: a tribe, a race, a Church, a State, the great society of the living and the dead and the yet unborn. This entity is then identified as being the 'true' self which, by imposing its collective, or 'organic', single will upon its recalcitrant 'members', achieves its own, and therefore their, 'higher' freedom. The perils of using organic metaphors to justify the coercion of some men by others in order to raise them to a 'higher' level of freedom have often been pointed out. But what gives such plausibility as it has to this kind of language is that we recognise that it is possible, and at times justifiable, to coerce men in the name of some goal (let us say, justice or public health) which they would, if they were more enlightened, themselves pursue, but do not, because they are blind or ignorant or corrupt. This renders it easy for me to conceive of myself as coercing others for their own sake, in their, not my, interest. I am then claiming that I know what they truly need better than they know it themselves. What, at most, this entails is that they would not resist me if they were rational and as wise as I and understood their interests as I do. But I may go on to claim a good deal more than this. I may declare that they are actually aiming at what in their benighted state they consciously resist, because there exists within them an occult entity – their latent rational will, or their 'true' purpose – and that this entity, although it is belied by all that they overtly feel and do and say, is their 'real' self, of which the poor empirical self in space and time may know nothing or little; and that this inner spirit is the only self that deserves to have its wishes taken into account.[1] Once I take this view, I am in a position to ignore the actual wishes of men or societies, to bully, oppress, torture them in the name, and on behalf, of their 'real' selves, in the secure knowledge that whatever is the true goal of man (happiness, performance of duty, wisdom, a just society, self-fulfilment) must be identical with his freedom – the free choice of his 'true', albeit often submerged and inarticulate, self.

This paradox has been often exposed. It is one thing to say that I know what is good for X, while he himself does not; and even to ignore his wishes for its – and his – sake; and a very different one to say that he has eo ipso chosen it, not indeed consciously, not as he seems in everyday life, but in his role as a rational self which his empirical self may not know – the 'real' self which discerns the good, and cannot help choosing it once it is revealed. This monstrous impersonation, which consists in equating what X would choose if he were something he is not, or at least not yet, with what X actually seeks and chooses, is at the heart of all political theories of self-realisation. It is one thing to say that I may be coerced for my own good, which I am too blind to see: this may, on occasion, be for my benefit; indeed it may enlarge the scope of my liberty. It is another to say that if it is my good, then I am not being coerced, for I have willed it, whether I know this or not, and am free (or 'truly' free) even while my poor earthly body and foolish mind bitterly reject it, and struggle with the greatest

---

[1] '[T]he ideal of true freedom is the maximum of power for all members of human society alike to make the best of themselves', said T. H. Green in 1881: op. cit. (p. 41 above, note 1), p. 200. Apart from the confusion of freedom with equality, this entails that if a man chose some immediate pleasure – which (in whose view?) would not enable him to make the best of himself (what self?) – what he was exercising was not 'true' freedom: and if deprived of it, he would not lose anything that mattered. Green was a genuine liberal: but many a tyrant could use this formula to justify his worst acts of oppression.

desperation against those who seek, however benevolently, to impose it.

This magical transformation, or sleight of hand (for which William James so justly mocked the Hegelians), can no doubt be perpetrated just as easily with the 'negative' concept of freedom, where the self that should not be interfered with is no longer the individual with his actual wishes and needs as they are normally conceived, but the 'real' man within, identified with the pursuit of some ideal purpose not dreamed of by his empirical self. And, as in the case of the 'positively' free self, this entity may be inflated into some super-personal entity – a State, a class, a nation, or the march of history itself, regarded as a more 'real' subject of attributes than the empirical self. But the 'positive' conception of freedom as self-mastery, with its suggestion of a man divided against himself, has in fact, and as a matter of history, of doctrine and of practice, lent itself more easily to this splitting of personality into two: the transcendent, dominant controller, and the empirical bundle of desires and passions to be disciplined and brought to heel. It is this historical fact that has been influential. This demonstrates (if demonstration of so obvious a truth is needed) that conceptions of freedom directly derive from views of what constitutes a self, a person, a man. Enough manipulation of the definition of man, and freedom can be made to mean whatever the manipulator wishes. Recent history has made it only too clear that the issue is not merely academic.

The consequences of distinguishing between two selves will become even clearer if one considers the two major forms which the desire to be self-directed – directed by one's 'true' self – has historically taken: the first, that of self-abnegation in order to attain independence; the second, that of self-realisation, or total self-identification with a specific principle or ideal in order to attain the selfsame end.

III

The retreat to the inner citadel

I am the possessor of reason and will; I conceive ends and I desire to pursue them; but if I am prevented from attaining them I no longer feel master of the situation. I may be prevented by the laws of nature, or by accidents, or the activities of men, or the effect, often undesigned, of human institutions. These forces may be too much for me. What am I to do to avoid being crushed by them? I must liberate myself from desires that I know I cannot realise. I wish to be master of my kingdom, but my frontiers are long and insecure, therefore I contract them in order to reduce or eliminate the vulnerable area. I begin by desiring happiness, or power, or knowledge, or the attainment of some specific object. But I cannot command them. I choose to avoid defeat and waste, and therefore decide to strive for nothing that I cannot be sure to obtain. I determine myself not to desire what is unattainable. The tyrant threatens me with the destruction of my property, with imprisonment, with the exile or death of those I love. But if I no longer feel attached to property, no longer care whether or not I am in prison, if I have killed within myself my natural affections, then he cannot bend me to his will, for all that is left of myself is no longer subject to empirical fears or desires. It is as if I had performed a strategic retreat into an inner citadel – my reason, my soul, my 'noumenal' self – which, do what they may, neither external blind force, nor human malice, can touch. I have withdrawn into myself; there, and there alone, I am secure. It is as if I were to say: 'I have a wound in my leg. There are two methods of freeing myself from pain. One is to heal the wound. But if the cure is too difficult or uncertain, there is another method. I can get rid of the wound by cutting off my leg. If I train myself to want nothing to which the possession of my leg is indispensable, I shall not feel the lack of it.' This is the traditional self-emancipation of ascetics and quietists, of stoics or Buddhist sages, men of various religions or of none, who have fled the world, and escaped the yoke of society or public opinion, by some process of deliberate self-transformation that enables them to care no longer for any of its values, to remain, isolated and independent, on its edges, no longer vulnerable to its weapons.[1] All political isolationism, all economic autarky, every form of autonomy, has in it some element of this attitude. I eliminate the obstacles in my path by abandoning the path; I retreat into my own sect, my own planned economy, my own deliberately insulated territory, where no voices from outside need be listened to,

---

[1] 'A wise man, though he be a slave, is at liberty, and from this it follows that though a fool rule, he is in slavery,' said St Ambrose. It might equally well have been said by Epictetus or Kant. *Corpus scriptorum ecclesiasticorum latinorum*, vol. 82, part 1, ed. Otto Faller (Vienna, 1968), letter 7, §24 (p. 55).

and no external forces can have effect. This is a form of the search for security; but it has also been called the search for personal or national freedom or independence.

From this doctrine, as it applies to individuals, it is no very great distance to the conceptions of those who, like Kant, identify freedom not indeed with the elimination of desires, but with resistance to them, and control over them. I identify myself with the controller and escape the slavery of the controlled. I am free because, and in so far as, I am autonomous. I obey laws, but I have imposed them on, or found them in, my own uncoerced self. Freedom is obedience, but, in Rousseau's words, 'obedience to a law which we prescribe to ourselves',[1] and no man can enslave himself. Heteronomy is dependence on outside factors, liability to be a plaything of the external world that I cannot myself fully control, and which *pro tanto* controls and 'enslaves' me. I am free only to the degree to which my person is 'fettered' by nothing that obeys forces over which I have no control; I cannot control the laws of nature; my free activity must therefore, *ex hypothesi*, be lifted above the empirical world of causality. This is not the place in which to discuss the validity of this ancient and famous doctrine; I only wish to remark that the related notions of freedom as resistance to (or escape from) unrealisable desire, and as independence of the sphere of causality, have played a central role in politics no less than in ethics.

For if the essence of men is that they are autonomous beings – authors of values, of ends in themselves, the ultimate authority of which consists precisely in the fact that they are willed freely – then nothing is worse than to treat them as if they were not autonomous, but natural objects, played on by causal influences, creatures at the mercy of external stimuli, whose choices can be manipulated by their rulers, whether by threats of force or offers of rewards. To treat men in this way is to treat them as if they were not self-determined. 'Nobody may compel me to be happy in his own way,' said Kant. Paternalism is 'the greatest despotism imaginable'.[2] This is so because it is to treat men as if they were not free, but human material for me, the benevolent reformer, to mould in accordance with my own, not their, freely adopted purpose. This

---

[1] *Social Contract*, book 1, chapter 8: vol. 3, p. 365 in *Oeuvres complètes* (op. cit., p. 170 above, note 2).

[2] op. cit. (p. 7 above, note 2), vol. 8, p. 290, line 27, and p. 291, line 3.

is, of course, precisely the policy that the early utilitarians recommended. Helvétius (and Bentham) believed not in resisting, but in using, men's tendency to be slaves to their passions; they wished to dangle rewards and punishments before men – the acutest possible form of heteronomy -- if by this means the 'slaves' might be made happier.[1] But to manipulate men, to propel them towards goals which you – the social reformer – see, but they may not, is to deny their human essence, to treat them as objects without wills of their own, and therefore to degrade them. That is why to lie to men, or to deceive them, that is, to use them as means for my, not their own, independently conceived ends, even if it is for their own benefit, is, in effect, to treat them as subhuman, to behave as if their ends are less ultimate and sacred than my own. In the name of what can I ever be justified in forcing men to do what they have not willed or consented to? Only in the name of some value higher than themselves. But if, as Kant held, all values are made so by the free acts of men, and called values only so far as they are this, there is no value higher than the individual. Therefore to do this is to coerce men in the name of something less ultimate than themselves – to bend them to my will, or to someone else's particular craving for (his or their) happiness or expediency or security or convenience. I am aiming at something desired (from whatever motive, no matter how noble) by me or my group, to which I am using other men as means. But this is a contradiction of what I know men to be, namely ends in themselves. All forms of tampering with human beings, getting at them, shaping them against their will to your own pattern, all thought-control and conditioning,[2] is, therefore, a denial of that in men which makes them men and their values ultimate.

Kant's free individual is a transcendent being, beyond the realm of natural causality. But in its empirical form – in which the notion

[1] 'Proletarian coercion, in all its forms, from executions to forced labour, is, paradoxical as it may sound, the method of moulding communist humanity out of the human material of the capitalist period.' These lines by the Bolshevik leader Nikolay Bukharin, especially the term 'human material', vividly convey this attitude. Nikolay Bukharin, *Ekonomika perekhodnogo perioda* ['Economics in the Transitional Period'] (Moscow, 1920), chapter 10, p. 146.

[2] Kant's psychology, and that of the Stoics and Christians too, assumed that some element in man – the 'inner fastness of his mind' – could be made secure against conditioning. The development of the techniques of hypnosis, 'brainwashing', subliminal suggestion and the like has made this a priori assumption, at least as an empirical hypothesis, less plausible.

of man is that of ordinary life – this doctrine was the heart of liberal humanism, both moral and political, that was deeply influenced both by Kant and by Rousseau in the eighteenth century. In its a priori version it is a form of secularised Protestant individualism, in which the place of God is taken by the conception of the rational life, and the place of the individual soul which strains towards union with him is replaced by the conception of the individual, endowed with reason, straining to be governed by reason and reason alone, and to depend upon nothing that might deflect or delude him by engaging his irrational nature. Autonomy, not heteronomy: to act and not to be acted upon. The notion of slavery to the passions is – for those who think in these terms – more than a metaphor. To rid myself of fear, or love, or the desire to conform is to liberate myself from the despotism of something which I cannot control. Sophocles, whom Plato reports as saying that old age alone has liberated him from the passion of love – the yoke of a cruel master – is reporting an experience as real as that of liberation from a human tyrant or slave owner. The psychological experience of observing myself yielding to some 'lower' impulse, acting from a motive that I dislike, or of doing something which at the very moment of doing I may detest, and reflecting later that I was 'not myself', or 'not in control of myself', when I did it, belongs to this way of thinking and speaking. I identify myself with my critical and rational moments. The consequences of my acts cannot matter, for they are not in my control; only my motives are. This is the creed of the solitary thinker who has defied the world and emancipated himself from the chains of men and things. In this form the doctrine may seem primarily an ethical creed, and scarcely political at all; nevertheless its political implications are clear, and it enters into the tradition of liberal individualism at least as deeply as the 'negative' concept of freedom.

It is perhaps worth remarking that in its individualistic form the concept of the rational sage who has escaped into the inner fortress of his true self seems to arise when the external world has proved exceptionally arid, cruel or unjust. 'He is truly free', said Rousseau, 'who desires what he can perform, and does what he desires.'[1] In a world where a man seeking happiness or justice or freedom (in whatever sense) can do little, because he finds too many avenues of

---

[1] op. cit. (p. 170 above, note 2), p. 309.

action blocked to him, the temptation to withdraw into himself may become irresistible. It may have been so in Greece, where the Stoic ideal cannot be wholly unconnected with the fall of the independent democracies before centralised Macedonian autocracy. It was so in Rome, for analogous reasons, after the end of the Republic.[1] It arose in Germany in the seventeenth century, during the period of the deepest national degradation of the German States that followed the Thirty Years War, when the character of public life, particularly in the small principalities, forced those who prized the dignity of human life, not for the first or last time, into a kind of inner emigration. The doctrine that maintains that what I cannot have I must teach myself not to desire, that a desire eliminated, or successfully resisted, is as good as a desire satisfied, is a sublime, but, it seems to me, unmistakable, form of the doctrine of sour grapes: what I cannot be sure of, I cannot truly want.

This makes it clear why the definition of negative liberty as the ability to do what one wishes – which is, in effect, the definition adopted by Mill – will not do. If I find that I am able to do little or nothing of what I wish, I need only contract or extinguish my wishes, and I am made free. If the tyrant (or 'hidden persuader') manages to condition his subjects (or customers) into losing their original wishes and embracing ('internalising') the form of life he has invented for them, he will, on this definition, have succeeded in liberating them. He will, no doubt, have made them *feel* free – as Epictetus feels freer than his master (and the proverbial good man is said to feel happy on the rack). But what he has created is the very antithesis of political freedom.

Ascetic self-denial may be a source of integrity or serenity and spiritual strength, but it is difficult to see how it can be called an enlargement of liberty. If I save myself from an adversary by retreating indoors and locking every entrance and exit, I may remain freer than if I had been captured by him, but am I freer than if I had defeated or captured him? If I go too far, contract myself into too small a space, I shall suffocate and die. The logical culmination of the process of destroying everything through which I can possibly be wounded is suicide. While I exist in the natural

---

[1] It is not perhaps far-fetched to assume that the quietism of the Eastern sages was, similarly, a response to the despotism of the great autocracies, and flourished at periods when individuals were apt to be humiliated, or at any rate ignored or ruthlessly managed, by those possessed of the instruments of physical coercion.

world, I can never be wholly secure. Total liberation in this sense (as Schopenhauer correctly perceived) is conferred only by death.[1]

I find myself in a world in which I meet with obstacles to my will. Those who are wedded to the 'negative' concept of freedom may perhaps be forgiven if they think that self-abnegation is not the only method of overcoming obstacles; that it is also possible to do so by removing them: in the case of non-human objects, by physical action; in the case of human resistance, by force or persuasion, as when I induce somebody to make room for me in his carriage, or conquer a country which threatens the interests of my own. Such acts may be unjust, they may involve violence, cruelty, the enslavement of others, but it can scarcely be denied that thereby the agent is able in the most literal sense to increase his own freedom. It is an irony of history that this truth is repudiated by some of those who practise it most forcibly, men who, even while they conquer power and freedom of action, reject the 'negative' concept of it in favour of its 'positive' counterpart. Their view rules over half our world; let us see upon what metaphysical foundation it rests.

IV

Self-realisation

The only true method of attaining freedom, we are told, is by the use of critical reason, the understanding of what is necessary and what is contingent. If I am a schoolboy, all but the simplest truths of mathematics obtrude themselves as obstacles to the free functioning of my mind, as theorems whose necessity I do not understand; they are pronounced to be true by some external authority, and present themselves to me as foreign bodies which I am expected mechanically to absorb into my system. But when I

---

[1] It is worth remarking that those who demanded – and fought for – liberty for the individual or for the nation in France during this period of German quietism did not fall into this attitude. Might this not be precisely because, despite the despotism of the French monarchy and the arrogance and arbitrary behaviour of privileged groups in the French State, France was a proud and powerful nation, where the reality of political power was not beyond the grasp of men of talent, so that withdrawal from battle into some untroubled heaven above it, whence it could be surveyed dispassionately by the self-sufficient philosopher, was not the only way out? The same holds for England in the nineteenth century and well after it, and for the United States today.

understand the functions of the symbols, the axioms, the formation
and transformation rules – the logic whereby the conclusions are
obtained – and grasp that these things cannot be otherwise, because
they appear to follow from the laws that govern the processes of
my own reason,[1] then mathematical truths no longer obtrude
themselves as external entities forced upon me which I must receive
whether I want to or not, but as something which I now freely will
in the course of the natural functioning of my own rational
activity. For the mathematician, the proof of these theorems is part
of the free exercise of his natural reasoning capacity. For the
musician, after he has assimilated the pattern of the composer's
score, and has made the composer's ends his own, the playing of
the music is not obedience to external laws, a compulsion and a
barrier to liberty, but a free, unimpeded exercise. The player is not
bound to the score as an ox to the plough, or a factory worker to
the machine. He has absorbed the score into his own system, has,
by understanding it, identified it with himself, has changed it from
an impediment to free activity into an element in that activity itself.

What applies to music or mathematics must, we are told, in
principle apply to all other obstacles which present themselves as
so many lumps of external stuff blocking free self-development.
That is the programme of enlightened rationalism from Spinoza to
the latest (at times unconscious) disciples of Hegel. *Sapere aude.*
What you know, that of which you understand the necessity – the
rational necessity – you cannot, while remaining rational, want to
be otherwise. For to want something to be other than what it must
be is, given the premisses – the necessities that govern the world –
to be *pro tanto* either ignorant or irrational. Passions, prejudices,
fears, neuroses spring from ignorance, and take the form of myths
and illusions. To be ruled by myths, whether they spring from the
vivid imaginations of unscrupulous charlatans who deceive us in
order to exploit us, or from psychological or sociological causes, is
a form of heteronomy, of being dominated by outside factors in a
direction not necessarily willed by the agent. The scientific determinists of the eighteenth century supposed that the study of the
sciences of nature, and the creation of sciences of society on the
same model, would make the operation of such causes transparently clear, and thus enable individuals to recognise their own part

[1] Or, as some modern theorists maintain, because I have, or could have,
invented them for myself, since the rules are man-made.

in the working of a rational world, frustrating only when misunderstood. Knowledge liberates, as Epicurus taught long ago, by automatically eliminating irrational fears and desires.

Herder, Hegel and Marx substituted their own vitalistic models of social life for the older, mechanical, ones, but believed, no less than their opponents, that to understand the world is to be freed. They merely differed from them in stressing the part played by change and growth in what made human beings human. Social life could not be understood by an analogy drawn from mathematics or physics. One must also understand history, that is, the peculiar laws of continuous growth, whether by 'dialectical' conflict or otherwise, that govern individuals and groups in their interplay with each other and with nature. Not to grasp this is, according to these thinkers, to fall into a particular kind of error, namely the belief that human nature is static, that its essential properties are the same everywhere and at all times, that it is governed by unvarying natural laws, whether they are conceived in theological or materialistic terms, which entails the fallacious corollary that a wise lawgiver can, in principle, create a perfectly harmonious society at any time by appropriate education and legislation, because rational men, in all ages and countries, must always demand the same unaltering satisfactions of the same unaltering basic needs. Hegel believed that his contemporaries (and indeed all his predecessors) misunderstood the nature of institutions because they did not understand the laws – the rationally intelligible laws, since they spring from the operation of reason – that create and alter institutions and transform human character and human action. Marx and his disciples maintained that the path of human beings was obstructed not only by natural forces, or the imperfections of their own characters, but, even more, by the workings of their own social institutions, which they had originally created (not always consciously) for certain purposes, but whose functioning they systematically came to misconceive, in practice even more than in theory, and which thereupon became obstacles to their creators' progress. Marx offered social and economic hypotheses to account for the inevitability of such misunderstanding, in particular of the illusion that such man-made arrangements were independent forces, as inescapable as the laws of nature. As instances of such pseudo-objective forces, he pointed to the laws of supply and demand, or the institution of property, or the eternal division of society into rich and poor, or owners and workers, as so many unaltering human categories. Not until we had reached a stage at which the spells of these illusions could be broken, that is, until enough men reached a social stage that alone enabled them to understand that these laws and institutions were themselves the work of human minds and hands, historically needed in their day, and later mistaken for inexorable, objective powers, could the old world be destroyed, and more adequate and liberating social machinery substituted.

We are enslaved by despots – institutions or beliefs or neuroses – which can be removed only by being analysed and understood. We are imprisoned by evil spirits which we have ourselves – albeit not consciously – created, and can exorcise them only by becoming conscious and acting appropriately: indeed, for Marx understanding is appropriate action. I am free if, and only if, I plan my life in accordance with my own will; plans entail rules; a rule does not oppress me or enslave me if I impose it on myself consciously, or accept it freely, having understood it, whether it was invented by me or by others, provided that it is rational, that is to say, conforms to the necessities of things. To understand why things must be as they must be is to will them to be so. Knowledge liberates not by offering us more open possibilities amongst which we can make our choice, but by preserving us from the frustration of attempting the impossible. To want necessary laws to be other than they are is to be prey to an irrational desire – a desire that what must be X should also be not-X. To go further, and believe these laws to be other than what they necessarily are, is to be insane. That is the metaphysical heart of rationalism. The notion of liberty contained in it is not the 'negative' conception of a field (ideally) without obstacles, a vacuum in which nothing obstructs me, but the notion of self-direction or self-control. I can do what I will with my own. I am a rational being; whatever I can demonstrate to myself as being necessary, as incapable of being otherwise in a rational society – that is, in a society directed by rational minds, towards goals such as a rational being would have – I cannot, being rational, wish to sweep out of my way. I assimilate it into my substance as I do the laws of logic, of mathematics, of physics, the rules of art, the principles that govern everything of which I understand, and therefore will, the rational purpose, by which I can never be thwarted, since I cannot want it to be other than it is.

This is the positive doctrine of liberation by reason. Socialised forms of it, widely disparate and opposed to each other as they are, are at the heart of many of the nationalist, Communist, authoritarian, and totalitarian creeds of our day. It may, in the course of its evolution, have wandered far from its rationalist moorings. Nevertheless, it is this freedom that, in democracies and in dictatorships, is argued about, and fought for, in many parts of the earth today. Without attempting to trace the historical evolution of this idea, I should like to comment on some of its vicissitudes.

v

The Temple of Sarastro

Those who believed in freedom as rational self-direction were bound, sooner or later, to consider how this was to be applied not merely to a man's inner life, but to his relations with other members of his society. Even the most individualistic among them – and Rousseau, Kant and Fichte certainly began as individualists – came at some point to ask themselves whether a rational life not only for the individual, but also for society, was possible, and if so, how it was to be achieved. I wish to be free to live as my rational will (my 'real self') commands, but so must others be. How am I to avoid collisions with their wills? Where is the frontier that lies between my (rationally determined) rights and the identical rights of others? For if I am rational, I cannot deny that what is right for me must, for the same reasons, be right for others who are rational like me. A rational (or free) State would be a State governed by such laws as all rational men would freely accept; that is to say, such laws as they would themselves have enacted had they been asked what, as rational beings, they demanded; hence the frontiers would be such as all rational men would consider to be the right frontiers for rational beings.

But who, in fact, was to determine what these frontiers were? Thinkers of this type argued that if moral and political problems were genuine – as surely they were – they must in principle be soluble; that is to say, there must exist one and only one true solution to any problem. All truths could in principle be discovered by any rational thinker, and demonstrated so clearly that all other rational men could not but accept them; indeed, this was already to a large extent the case in the new natural sciences. On this assumption the problem of political liberty was soluble by

establishing a just order that would give to each man all the
freedom to which a rational being was entitled. My claim to
unfettered freedom can prima facie at times not be reconciled with
your equally unqualified claim; but the rational solution of one
problem cannot collide with the equally true solution of another,
for two truths cannot logically be incompatible; therefore a just
order must in principle be discoverable – an order of which the
rules make possible correct solutions to all possible problems that
could arise in it. This ideal, harmonious state of affairs was
sometimes imagined as a Garden of Eden before the Fall of Man,
an Eden from which we were expelled, but for which we were still
filled with longing; or as a golden age still before us, in which men,
having become rational, will no longer be 'other-directed', nor
'alienate' or frustrate one another. In existing societies justice and
equality are ideals which still call for some measure of coercion,
because the premature lifting of social controls might lead to the
oppression of the weaker and the stupider by the stronger or abler
or more energetic and unscrupulous. But it is only irrationality on
the part of men (according to this doctrine) that leads them to wish
to oppress or exploit or humiliate one another. Rational men will
respect the principle of reason in each other, and lack all desire to
fight or dominate one another. The desire to dominate is itself a
symptom of irrationality, and can be explained and cured by
rational methods. Spinoza offers one kind of explanation and
remedy, Hegel another, Marx a third. Some of these theories may
perhaps, to some degree, supplement each other, others are not
combinable. But they all assume that in a society of perfectly
rational beings the lust for domination over men will be absent or
ineffective. The existence of, or cravings for, oppression will be the
first symptom that the true solution to the problems of social life
has not been reached.

   This can be put in another way. Freedom is self-mastery, the
elimination of obstacles to my will, whatever these obstacles may
be – the resistance of nature, of my ungoverned passions, of
irrational institutions, of the opposing wills or behaviour of others.
Nature I can, at least in principle, always mould by technical
means, and shape to my will. But how am I to treat recalcitrant
human beings? I must, if I can, impose my will on them too,
'mould' them to my pattern, cast parts for them in my play. But
will this not mean that I alone am free, while they are slaves? They
will be so if my plan has nothing to do with their wishes or values,

only with my own. But if my plan is fully rational, it will allow for
the full development of their 'true' natures, the realisation of their
capacities for rational decisions, for 'making the best of themselves'
– as a part of the realisation of my own 'true' self. All true solutions
to all genuine problems must be compatible: more than this, they
must fit into a single whole; for this is what is meant by calling
them all rational and the universe harmonious. Each man has his
specific character, abilities, aspirations, ends. If I grasp both what
these ends and natures are, and how they all relate to one another, I
can, at least in principle, if I have the knowledge and the strength,
satisfy them all, so long as the nature and the purposes in question
are rational. Rationality is knowing things and people for what
they are: I must not use stones to make violins, nor try to make
born violin-players play flutes. If the universe is governed by
reason, then there will be no need for coercion; a correctly planned
life for all will coincide with full freedom – the freedom of rational
self-direction – for all. This will be so if, and only if, the plan is the
true plan – the one unique pattern which alone fulfils the claims of
reason. Its laws will be the rules which reason prescribes: they will
only seem irksome to those whose reason is dormant, who do not
understand the true 'needs' of their own 'real' selves. So long as
each player recognises and plays the part set him by reason – the
faculty that understands his true nature and discerns his true ends –
there can be no conflict. Each man will be a liberated, self-directed
actor in the cosmic drama. Thus Spinoza tells us that children,
although they are coerced, are not slaves, because they obey orders
given in their own interests, and that the subject of a true
commonwealth is no slave, because the common interests must
include his own.[1] Similarly, Locke says 'Where there is no law
there is no freedom', because rational law is a direction to a man's
'proper interests' or 'general good'; and adds that since law of this
kind is what 'hedges us in only from bogs and precipices' it 'ill
deserves the name of confinement',[2] and speaks of desires to
escape from it as being irrational, forms of 'licence', as 'brutish',[3]
and so on. Montesquieu, forgetting his liberal moments, speaks of
political liberty as being not permission to do what we want, or
even what the law allows, but only 'the power of doing what we

---

[1] *Tractatus Theologico-Politicus*, chapter 16: p. 137 in Benedict de Spinoza,
The Political Works, ed. A. G. Wernham (Oxford, 1958).
[2] *Two Treatises of Government*, second treatise, § 57.
[3] ibid., §§ 6, 163.

ought to will',[1] which Kant virtually repeats. Burke proclaims the individual's 'right' to be restrained in his own interest, because 'the presumed consent of every rational creature is in unison with the predisposed order of things'.[2]

The common assumption of these thinkers (and of many a schoolman before them and Jacobin and Communist after them) is that the rational ends of our 'true' natures must coincide, or be made to coincide, however violently our poor, ignorant, desire-ridden, passionate, empirical selves may cry out against this process. Freedom is not freedom to do what is irrational, or stupid, or wrong. To force empirical selves into the right pattern is no tyranny, but liberation.[3] Rousseau tells me that if I freely surrender all the parts of my life to society, I create an entity which, because it has been built by an equality of sacrifice of all its members, cannot wish to hurt any one of them; in such a society, we are informed, it can be in nobody's interest to damage anyone else. 'In giving myself to all, I give myself to none',[4] and get back as much as I lose, with enough new force to preserve my new gains. Kant tells us that when 'the individual has entirely abandoned his wild, lawless freedom, to find it again, unimpaired, in a state of dependence according to law', that alone is true freedom, 'for this dependence is the work of my own will acting as a lawgiver'.[5] Liberty, so far from being incompatible with authority, becomes virtually identical with it. This is the thought and language of all the declarations of the rights of man in the

---

[1] *De l'esprit des lois*, book 11, chapter 3: p. 205 in *Oeuvres complètes de Montesquieu*, ed. A. Masson (Paris, 1950–5), vol. 1 A.

[2] *Appeal from the Old to the New Whigs* (1791): pp. 93–4 in *The Works of the Right Honourable Edmund Burke* (World's Classics edition), vol. 5 (London, 1907).

[3] On this Bentham seems to me to have said the last word: 'The liberty of doing evil, is it not liberty? If it is not liberty, what is it then? . . . Do we not say that liberty should be taken away from fools, and wicked persons, because they abuse it?' *The Works of Jeremy Bentham*, ed. John Bowring (Edinburgh, 1843), vol. 1, p. 301. Compare with this the view of the Jacobins in the same period, discussed by Crane Brinton in 'Political Ideas in the Jacobin Clubs', *Political Science Quarterly* 43 (1928), 249–64, esp. 257: 'no man is free in doing evil. To prevent him is to free him.' This view is echoed in almost identical terms by British Idealists at the end of the following century.

[4] *Social Contract*, book 1, chapter 6: vol 3, p. 361, in *Oeuvres complètes* (op. cit., p. 170 above, note 2).

[5] op. cit. (p. 7 above, note 2), vol. 6, p. 316, line 2.

eighteenth century, and of all those who look upon society as a design constructed according to the rational laws of the wise lawgiver, or of nature, or of history, or of the Supreme Being. Bentham, almost alone, doggedly went on repeating that the business of laws was not to liberate but to restrain: every law is an infraction of liberty[1] – even if such infraction leads to an increase of the sum of liberty.

If the underlying assumptions had been correct – if the method of solving social problems resembled the way in which solutions to the problems of the natural sciences are found, and if reason were what rationalists said that it was – all this would perhaps follow. In the ideal case, liberty coincides with law: autonomy with authority. A law which forbids me to do what I could not, as a sane being, conceivably wish to do is not a restraint of my freedom. In the ideal society, composed of wholly responsible beings, rules, because I should scarcely be conscious of them, would gradually wither away. Only one social movement was bold enough to render this assumption quite explicit and accept its consequences – that of the Anarchists. But all forms of liberalism founded on a rationalist metaphysics are less or more watered-down versions of this creed.

In due course, the thinkers who bent their energies to the solution of the problem on these lines came to be faced with the question of how in practice men were to be made rational in this way. Clearly they must be educated. For the uneducated are irrational, heteronomous, and need to be coerced, if only to make life tolerable for the rational if they are to live in the same society and not be compelled to withdraw to a desert or some Olympian height. But the uneducated cannot be expected to understand or co-operate with the purposes of their educators. Education, says Fichte, must inevitably work in such a way that 'you will later recognise the reasons for what I am doing now'.[2] Children cannot be expected to understand why they are compelled to go to school, nor the ignorant – that is, for the moment, the majority of mankind – why they are made to obey the laws that will presently make them rational. 'Compulsion is also a kind of education.'[3] You learn the great virtue of obedience to superior persons. If you

---

[1] op. cit. (p. 194 above, note 3), ibid.: 'every law is contrary to liberty'.

[2] *Johann Gottlieb Fichte's sämmtliche Werke*, ed. I. H. Fichte (Berlin, 1845–6), vol. 7, p. 576.

[3] ibid., p. 574.

cannot understand your own interests as a rational being, I cannot be expected to consult you, or abide by your wishes, in the course of making you rational. I must, in the end, force you to be protected against smallpox, even though you may not wish it. Even Mill is prepared to say that I may forcibly prevent a man from crossing a bridge if there is not time to warn him that it is about to collapse, for I know, or am justified in assuming, that he cannot wish to fall into the water. Fichte knows what the uneducated German of his time wishes to be or do better than he can possibly know this for himself. The sage knows you better than you know yourself, for you are the victim of your passions, a slave living a heteronomous life, purblind, unable to understand your true goals. You want to be a human being. It is the aim of the State to satisfy your wish. 'Compulsion is justified by education for future insight.'[1] The reason within me, if it is to triumph, must eliminate and suppress my 'lower' instincts, my passions and desires, which render me a slave; similarly (the fatal transition from individual to social concepts is almost imperceptible) the higher elements in society – the better educated, the more rational, those who 'possess the highest insight of their time and people'[2] – may exercise compulsion to rationalise the irrational section of society. For – so Hegel, Bradley, Bosanquet have often assured us – by obeying the rational man we obey ourselves: not indeed as we are, sunk in our ignorance and our passions, weak creatures afflicted by diseases that need a healer, wards who require a guardian, but as we could be if we were rational; as we could be even now, if only we would listen to the rational element which is, *ex hypothesi*, within every human being who deserves the name.

The philosophers of 'Objective Reason', from the tough, rigidly centralised, 'organic' State of Fichte, to the mild and humane liberalism of T. H. Green, certainly supposed themselves to be fulfilling, and not resisting, the rational demands which, however inchoate, were to be found in the breast of every sentient being.

But I may reject such democratic optimism, and turning away from the teleological determinism of the Hegelians towards some more voluntarist philosophy, conceive the idea of imposing on my society – for its own betterment – a plan of my own, which in my rational wisdom I have elaborated; and which, unless I act on my own, perhaps against the permanent wishes of the vast majority

[1] ibid., p. 578.   [2] ibid., p. 576.

of my fellow citizens, may never come to fruition at all. Or, abandoning the concept of reason altogether, I may conceive myself as an inspired artist, who moulds men into patterns in the light of his unique vision, as painters combine colours or composers sounds; humanity is the raw material upon which I impose my creative will; even though men suffer and die in the process, they are lifted by it to a height to which they could never have risen without my coercive – but creative – violation of their lives. This is the argument used by every dictator, inquisitor and bully who seeks some moral, or even aesthetic, justification for his conduct. I must do for men (or with them) what they cannot do for themselves, and I cannot ask their permission or consent, because they are in no condition to know what is best for them; indeed, what they will permit and accept may mean a life of contemptible mediocrity, or perhaps even their ruin and suicide. Let me quote from the true progenitor of the heroic doctrine, Fichte, once again: 'No one has ... rights against reason.' 'Man is afraid of subordinating his subjectivity to the laws of reason. He prefers tradition or arbitrariness.'[1] Nevertheless, subordinated he must be.[2] Fichte puts forward the claims of what he called reason; Napoleon, or Carlyle, or romantic authoritarians may worship other values, and see in their establishment by force the only path to 'true' freedom.

The same attitude was pointedly expressed by August Comte, who asked why, if we do not allow free thinking in chemistry or biology, we should allow it in morals or politics.[3] Why indeed? If it makes sense to speak of political truths – assertions of social ends which all men, because they are men, must, once they are discovered, agree to be such; and if, as Comte believed, scientific method will in due course reveal them; then what case is there for freedom of opinion or action – at least as an end in itself, and not merely as a stimulating intellectual climate – either for individuals or for groups? Why should any conduct be tolerated that is not authorised by appropriate experts? Comte put bluntly what had been implicit in the rationalist theory of politics from its ancient Greek beginnings. There can, in principle, be only one correct way of life; the wise lead it spontaneously, that is why they are called

---

[1] ibid., pp. 578, 580.

[2] 'To compel men to adopt the right form of government, to impose Right on them by force, is not only the right, but the sacred duty of every man who has both the insight and the power to do so.' ibid., vol. 4, p. 436.

[3] loc. cit. (p. 81 above, note 1).

wise. The unwise must be dragged towards it by all the social means in the power of the wise; for why should demonstrable error be suffered to survive and breed? The immature and untutored must be made to say to themselves: 'Only the truth liberates, and the only way in which I can learn the truth is by doing blindly today what you, who know it, order me, or coerce me, to do, in the certain knowledge that only thus will I arrive at your clear vision, and be free like you.'

We have wandered indeed from our liberal beginnings. This argument, employed by Fichte in his latest phase, and after him by other defenders of authority, from Victorian schoolmasters and colonial administrators to the latest nationalist or Communist dictator, is precisely what the Stoic and Kantian morality protests against most bitterly in the name of the reason of the free individual following his own inner light. In this way the rationalist argument, with its assumption of the single true solution, has led by steps which, if not logically valid, are historically and psychologically intelligible from an ethical doctrine of individual responsibility and individual self-perfection to an authoritarian State obedient to the directives of an élite of Platonic guardians.

What can have led to so strange a reversal – the transformation of Kant's severe individualism into something close to a pure totalitarian doctrine on the part of thinkers some of whom claimed to be his disciples? This question is not of merely historical interest, for not a few contemporary liberals have gone through the same peculiar evolution. It is true that Kant insisted, following Rousseau, that a capacity for rational self-direction belonged to all men; that there could be no experts in moral matters, since morality was a matter not of specialised knowledge (as the Utilitarians and *philosophes* had maintained), but of the correct use of a universal human faculty; and consequently that what made men free was not acting in certain self-improving ways, which they could be coerced to do, but knowing why they ought to do so, which nobody could do for, or on behalf of, anyone else. But even Kant, when he came to deal with political issues, conceded that no law, provided that it was such that I should, if I were asked, approve it as a rational being, could possibly deprive me of any portion of my rational freedom. With this the door was opened wide to the rule of experts. I cannot consult all men about all enactments all the time. The government cannot be a continuous plebiscite. Moreover, some men are not as well attuned to the voice of their own reason as others: some seem singularly deaf. If I am a legislator or a ruler, I must assume that if the law I impose is rational (and I can consult only my own reason) it will automatically be approved by all the members of my society so far as they are rational beings. For if they disapprove, they must, *pro tanto*, be irrational; then they will need to be repressed by reason: whether their own or mine cannot matter, for the pronouncements of reason must be the same in all minds. I issue my orders and, if you resist, take it upon myself to repress the irrational element in you which opposes reason. My task would be easier if you repressed it in yourself; I try to educate you to do so. But I am responsible for public welfare, I cannot wait until all men are wholly rational. Kant may protest that the essence of the subject's freedom is that he, and he alone, has given himself the order to obey. But this is a counsel of perfection. If you fail to discipline yourself, I must do so for you; and you cannot complain of lack of freedom, for the fact that Kant's rational judge has sent you to prison is evidence that you have not listened to your own inner reason, that, like a child, a savage, an idiot, you are either not ripe for self-direction, or permanently incapable of it.[1]

[1] Kant came nearest to asserting the 'negative' ideal of liberty when (in one of his political treatises) he declared that 'The greatest problem of the human race, to the solution of which it is compelled by nature, is the establishment of a civil society universally administering right according to law. It is only in a society which possesses the greatest liberty . . . – and also the most exact determination and guarantee of the limits of [the] liberty [of each individual] in order that it may co-exist with the liberty of others – that the highest purpose of nature, which is the development of all her capacities, can be attained in the case of mankind.' 'Idee zu einer allgemeinen Geschichte in weltburgerlicher Absicht' (1784), in op. cit. (p. 7 above, note 2), vol. 8, p. 22, line 6. Apart from the teleological implications, this formulation does not at first appear very different from orthodox liberalism. The crucial point, however, is how to determine the criterion for the 'exact determination and guarantee of the limits' of individual liberty. Most modern liberals, at their most consistent, want a situation in which as many individuals as possible can realise as many of their ends as possible, without assessment of the value of these ends as such, save in so far as they may frustrate the purposes of others. They wish the frontiers between individuals or groups of men to be drawn solely with a view to preventing collisions between human purposes, all of which must be considered to be equally ultimate, uncriticisable ends in themselves. Kant, and the rationalists of his type, do not regard all ends as of equal value. For them the limits of liberty are determined by applying the rules of 'reason', which is much more than the mere generality of rules as such, and is a faculty that creates or reveals a purpose identical in, and for, all men. In the name of reason anything

If this leads to despotism, albeit by the best or the wisest – to Sarastro's temple in *The Magic Flute* – but still despotism, which turns out to be identical with freedom, can it be that there is something amiss in the premisses of the argument? That the basic assumptions are themselves somewhere at fault? Let me state them once more: first, that all men have one true purpose, and one only, that of rational self-direction; second, that the ends of all rational beings must of necessity fit into a single universal, harmonious pattern, which some men may be able to discern more clearly than others; third, that all conflict, and consequently all tragedy, is due solely to the clash of reason with the irrational or the insufficiently rational – the immature and undeveloped elements in life, whether individual or communal – and that such clashes are, in principle, avoidable, and for wholly rational beings impossible; finally, that when all men have been made rational, they will obey the rational laws of their own natures, which are one and the same in them all, and so be at once wholly law-abiding and wholly free. Can it be that Socrates and the creators of the central Western tradition in ethics and politics who followed him have been mistaken, for more than two millennia, that virtue is not knowledge, nor freedom identical with either? That despite the fact that it rules the lives of more men than ever before in its long history, not one of the basic assumptions of this famous view is demonstrable, or, perhaps, even true?

VI

The search for status

There is yet another historically important approach to this topic, which, by confounding liberty with her sisters, equality and

---

that is non-rational may be condemned, so that the various personal aims which their individual imaginations and idiosyncrasies lead men to pursue – for example, aesthetic and other non-rational kinds of self-fulfilment – may, at least in theory, be ruthlessly suppressed to make way for the demands of reason. The authority of reason and of the duties it lays upon men is identified with individual freedom, on the assumption that only rational ends can be the 'true' objects of a 'free' man's 'real' nature.

I have never, I must own, understood what 'reason' means in this context; and here merely wish to point out that the a priori assumptions of this philosophical psychology are not compatible with empiricism: that is to say, with any doctrine founded on knowledge derived from experience of what men are and seek.

fraternity, leads to similarly illiberal conclusions. Ever since the issue was raised towards the end of the eighteenth century, the question of what is meant by 'an individual' has been asked persistently, and with increasing effect. In so far as I live in society, everything that I do inevitably affects, and is affected by, what others do. Even Mill's strenuous effort to mark the distinction between the spheres of private and social life breaks down under examination. Virtually all Mill's critics have pointed out that everything that I do may have results which will harm other human beings. Moreover, I am a social being in a deeper sense than that of interaction with others. For am I not what I am, to some degree, in virtue of what others think and feel me to be? When I ask myself what I am, and answer: an Englishman, a Chinese, a merchant, a man of no importance, a millionaire, a convict – I find upon analysis that to possess these attributes entails being recognised as belonging to a particular group or class by other persons in my society, and that this recognition is part of the meaning of most of the terms that denote some of my most personal and permanent characteristics. I am not disembodied reason. Nor am I Robinson Crusoe, alone upon his island. It is not only that my material life depends upon interaction with other men, or that I am what I am as a result of social forces, but that some, perhaps all, of my ideas about myself, in particular my sense of my own moral and social identity, are intelligible only in terms of the social network in which I am (the metaphor must not be pressed too far) an element.

The lack of freedom about which men or groups complain amounts, as often as not, to the lack of proper recognition. I may be seeking not for what Mill would wish me to seek, namely security from coercion, arbitrary arrest, tyranny, deprivation of certain opportunities of action, or for room within which I am legally accountable to no one for my movements. Equally, I may not be seeking for a rational plan of social life, or the self-perfection of a dispassionate sage. What I may seek to avoid is simply being ignored, or patronised, or despised, or being taken too much for granted – in short, not being treated as an individual, having my uniqueness insufficiently recognised, being classed as a member of some featureless amalgam, a statistical unit without identifiable, specifically human features and purposes of my own. This is the degradation that I am fighting against – I am not seeking equality of legal rights, nor liberty to do as I wish (although I may want these too), but a condition in which I can feel that I am, because I am taken to be, a responsible agent, whose will is taken into consideration because I am entitled to it, even if I am attacked and persecuted for being what I am or choosing as I do.

This is a hankering after status and recognition: 'The poorest he that is in England hath a life to live as the greatest he.'[1] I desire to be understood and recognised, even if this means to be unpopular and disliked. And the only persons who can so recognise me, and thereby give me the sense of being someone, are the members of the society to which, historically, morally, economically, and perhaps ethnically, I feel that I belong.[2] My individual self is not something which I can detach from my relationship with others, or from those attributes of myself which consist in their attitude towards me. Consequently, when I demand to be liberated from, let us say, the status of political or social dependence, what I demand is an alteration of the attitude towards me of those whose opinions and behaviour help to determine my own image of myself.

And what is true of the individual is true of groups, social, political, economic, religious, that is, of men conscious of needs and purposes which they have as members of such groups. What oppressed classes or nationalities, as a rule, demand is neither simply unhampered liberty of action for their members, nor, above everything, equality of social or economic opportunity, still less assignment of a place in a frictionless, organic State devised by the rational lawgiver. What they want, as often as not, is simply recognition (of their class or nation, or colour or race) as an

---

[1] Thomas Rainborow, speaking at Putney in 1647: p. 301 in *The Clarke Papers: Selections from the Papers of William Clarke*, ed. C. H. Firth, vol. 1 ([London], 1891).

[2] This has an obvious affinity with Kant's doctrine of human freedom; but it is a socialised and empirical version of it, and therefore almost its opposite. Kant's free man needs no public recognition for his inner freedom. If he is treated as a means to some external purpose, that is a wrong action on the part of his exploiters, but his own 'noumenal' status is untouched, and he is fully free, and fully a man, however he may be treated. The need spoken of here is bound up wholly with the relation that I have with others; I am nothing if I am unrecognised. I cannot ignore the attitude of others with Byronic disdain, fully conscious of my own intrinsic worth and vocation, or escape into my inner life, for I am in my own eyes as others see me. I identify myself with the point of view of my milieu: I feel myself to be somebody or nobody in terms of my position and function in the social whole; this is the most 'heteronomous' condition imaginable.

independent source of human activity, as an entity with a will of its own, intending to act in accordance with it (whether it is good or legitimate, or not), and not to be ruled, educated, guided, with however light a hand, as being not quite fully human, and therefore not quite fully free.

This gives a far wider than a purely rationalist sense to Kant's remark that paternalism is 'the greatest despotism imaginable'.[1] Paternalism is despotic, not because it is more oppressive than naked, brutal, unenlightened tyranny, nor merely because it ignores the transcendental reason embodied in me, but because it is an insult to my conception of myself as a human being, determined to make my own life in accordance with my own (not necessarily rational or benevolent) purposes, and, above all, entitled to be recognised as such by others. For if I am not so recognised, then I may fail to recognise, I may doubt, my own claim to be a fully independent human being. For what I am is, in large part, determined by what I feel and think; and what I feel and think is determined by the feeling and thought prevailing in the society to which I belong, of which, in Burke's sense, I form not an isolable atom, but an ingredient (to use a perilous but indispensable metaphor) in a social pattern. I may feel unfree in the sense of not being recognised as a self-governing individual human being; but I may feel it also as a member of an unrecognised or insufficiently respected group: then I wish for the emancipation of my entire class, or community, or nation, or race, or profession. So much can I desire this, that I may, in my bitter longing for status, prefer to be bullied and misgoverned by some member of my own race or social class, by whom I am, nevertheless, recognised as a man and a rival – that is, as an equal – to being well and tolerantly treated by someone from some higher and remoter group, someone who does not recognise me for what I wish to feel myself to be.

This is the heart of the great cry for recognition on the part of both individuals and groups, and, in our own day, of professions and classes, nations and races. Although I may not get 'negative' liberty at the hands of the members of my own society, yet they are members of my own group; they understand me, as I understand them; and this understanding creates within me the sense of being somebody in the world. It is this desire for reciprocal recognition that leads the most authoritarian democracies to be, at times, consciously preferred by their members to the most enlightened oligarchies, or sometimes causes a member of some

[1] loc. cit. (p. 183 above, note 2).

newly liberated Asian or African State to complain less today, when he is rudely treated by members of his own race or nation, than when he was governed by some cautious, just, gentle, well-meaning administrator from outside. Unless this phenomenon is grasped, the ideals and behaviour of entire peoples who, in Mill's sense of the word, suffer deprivation of elementary human rights, and who, with every appearance of sincerity, speak of enjoying more freedom than when they possessed a wider measure of these rights, become an unintelligible paradox.

Yet it is not with individual liberty, in either the 'negative' or the 'positive' sense of the word, that this desire for status and recognition can easily be identified. It is something no less profoundly needed and passionately fought for by human beings – it is something akin to, but not itself, freedom; although it entails negative freedom for the entire group, it is more closely related to solidarity, fraternity, mutual understanding, need for association on equal terms, all of which are sometimes – but misleadingly – called social freedom. Social and political terms are necessarily vague. The attempt to make the vocabulary of politics too precise may render it useless. But it is no service to the truth to loosen usage beyond necessity. The essence of the notion of liberty, in both the 'positive' and the 'negative' senses, is the holding off of something or someone – of others who trespass on my field or assert their authority over me, or of obsessions, fears, neuroses, irrational forces – intruders and despots of one kind or another. The desire for recognition is a desire for something different: for union, closer understanding, integration of interests, a life of common dependence and common sacrifice. It is only the confusion of desire for liberty with this profound and universal craving for status and understanding, further confounded by being identified with the notion of social self-direction, where the self to be liberated is no longer the individual but the 'social whole', that makes it possible for men, while submitting to the authority of oligarchs or dictators, to claim that this in some sense liberates them.

Much has been written on the fallacy of regarding social groups as being literally persons or selves, whose control and discipline of their members is no more than self-discipline, voluntary self-control which leaves the individual agent free. But even on the 'organic' view, would it be natural or desirable to call the demand for recognition and status a demand for liberty in some third sense? It is true that the group from which recognition is sought must itself have a sufficient measure of 'negative' freedom – from control by any outside authority – otherwise recognition by it will not give the claimant the status he seeks. But is the struggle for higher status, the wish to escape from an inferior position, to be called a struggle for liberty? Is it mere pedantry to confine this word to the main senses discussed above, or are we, as I suspect, in danger of calling any improvement of his social situation favoured by a human being an increase of his liberty, and will this not render this term so vague and distended as to make it virtually useless? And yet we cannot simply dismiss this case as a mere confusion of the notion of freedom with that of status, or solidarity, or fraternity, or equality, or some combination of these. For the craving for status is, in certain respects, very close to the desire to be an independent agent.

We may refuse this goal the title of liberty; yet it would be a shallow view that assumed that analogies between individuals and groups, or organic metaphors, or several senses of the word 'liberty', are mere fallacies, due either to assertions of likeness between entities in respects in which they are unlike, or simple semantic confusion. What is wanted by those who are prepared to barter their own and others' liberty of individual action for the status of their group, and their own status within the group, is not simply a surrender of liberty for the sake of security, of some assured place in a harmonious hierarchy in which all men and all classes know their place, and are prepared to exchange the painful privilege of choosing – 'the burden of freedom' – for the peace and comfort and relative mindlessness of an authoritarian or totalitarian structure. No doubt there are such men and such desires, and no doubt such surrenders of individual liberty can occur, and, indeed, have often occurred. But it is a profound misunderstanding of the temper of our times to assume that this is what makes nationalism or Marxism attractive to nations which have been ruled by alien masters, or to classes whose lives were directed by other classes in a semi-feudal, or some other hierarchically organised, regime. What they seek is more akin to what Mill called 'Pagan self-assertion',[1] but in a collective, socialised form. Indeed, much of what he says about his own reasons for desiring liberty – the value that he puts on boldness and non-conformity, on the assertion of the individual's own values in the face of the prevailing opinion, on strong and self-reliant personalities free from the leading-strings of the official

---

[1] Following Sterling: loc. cit. (p. 174 above, note 4), at p. 266.

lawgivers and instructors of society – has little enough to do with his conception of freedom as non-interference, but a great deal with the desire of men not to have their personalities set at too low a value, assumed to be incapable of autonomous, original, 'authentic' behaviour, even if such behaviour is to be met with opprobrium, or social restrictions, or inhibitive legislation.

This wish to assert the 'personality' of my class, or group or nation, is connected both with the answer to the question 'What is to be the area of authority?' (for the group must not be interfered with by outside masters), and, even more closely, with the answer to the question 'Who is to govern us?' – govern well or badly, liberally or oppressively, but above all 'Who?' And such answers as 'Representatives elected by my own and others' untrammelled choice', or 'All of us gathered together in regular assemblies', or 'The best', or 'The wisest', or 'The nation as embodied in these or those persons or institutions', or 'The divine leader' are answers that are logically, and at times also politically and socially, independent of what extent of 'negative' liberty I demand for my own or my group's activities. Provided the answer to 'Who shall govern me?' is somebody or something which I can represent as 'my own', as something which belongs to me, or to whom I belong, I can, by using words which convey fraternity and solidarity, as well as some part of the connotation of the 'positive' sense of the word 'freedom' (which it is difficult to specify more precisely), describe it as a hybrid form of freedom; at any rate as an ideal which is perhaps more prominent than any other in the world today, yet one which no existing term seems precisely to fit. Those who purchase it at the price of their 'negative', Millian freedom certainly claim to be 'liberated' by this means, in this confused, but ardently felt, sense. 'Whose service is perfect freedom' can in this way be secularised, and the State, or the nation, or the race, or an assembly, or a dictator, or my family or milieu, or I myself, can be substituted for the Deity, without thereby rendering the word 'freedom' wholly meaningless.[1]

---

[1] This argument should be distinguished from the traditional approach of some of the disciples of Burke or Hegel, who say that, since I am made what I am by society or history, to escape from them is impossible and to attempt it irrational. No doubt I cannot leap out of my skin, or breathe outside my proper element; it is a mere tautology to say that I am what I am, and cannot want to be liberated from my essential characteristics, some of which are social. But it does not follow that all my attributes are intrinsic and inalienable, and that I cannot

No doubt every interpretation of the word 'liberty', however unusual, must include a minimum of what I have called 'negative' liberty. There must be an area within which I am not frustrated. No society literally suppresses all the liberties of its members; a being who is prevented by others from doing anything at all on his own is not a moral agent at all, and could not either legally or morally be regarded as a human being, even if a physiologist or a biologist, or even a psychologist, felt inclined to classify him as a man. But the fathers of liberalism – Mill and Constant – want more than this minimum: they demand a maximum degree of non-interference compatible with the minimum demands of social life. It seems unlikely that this extreme demand for liberty has ever been made by any but a small minority of highly civilised and self-conscious human beings. The bulk of humanity has certainly at most times been prepared to sacrifice this to other goals: security, status, prosperity, power, virtue, rewards in the next world; or justice, equality, fraternity, and many other values which appear wholly, or in part, incompatible with the attainment of the greatest degree of individual liberty, and certainly do not need it as a precondition for their own realisation. It is not a demand for *Lebensraum* for each individual that has stimulated the rebellions and wars of liberation for which men have been ready to die in the past, or, indeed, in the present. Men who have fought for freedom have commonly fought for the right to be governed by themselves or their representatives – sternly governed, if need be, like the Spartans, with little individual liberty, but in a manner which allowed them to participate, or at any rate to believe that they were participating, in the legislation and administration of their collective lives. And men who have made revolutions have, as often as not, meant by liberty no more than the conquest of power and authority by a given sect of believers in a doctrine, or by a class, or by some other social group, old or new. Their victories certainly frustrated those whom they ousted, and sometimes repressed, enslaved or exterminated vast numbers of human beings. Yet such revolutionaries have usually felt it necessary to argue that, despite this, they represented the party of liberty, or 'true' liberty, by

seek to alter my status within the 'social network', or 'cosmic web', which determines my nature; if this were the case, no meaning could be attached to such words as 'choice' or 'decision' or 'activity'. If they are to mean anything, attempts to protect myself against authority, or even to escape from my 'station and its duties', cannot be excluded as automatically irrational or suicidal.

claiming universality for their ideal, which the 'real selves' of even those who resisted them were also alleged to be seeking, although they were held to have lost the way to the goal, or to have mistaken the goal itself owing to some moral or spiritual blindness. All this has little to do with Mill's notion of liberty as limited only by the danger of doing harm to others. It is the non-recognition of this psychological and political fact (which lurks behind the apparent ambiguity of the term 'liberty') that has, perhaps, blinded some contemporary liberals to the world in which they live. Their plea is clear, their cause is just. But they do not allow for the variety of basic human needs. Nor yet for the ingenuity with which men can prove to their own satisfaction that the road to one ideal also leads to its contrary.

VII

Liberty and sovereignty

The French Revolution, like all great revolutions, was, at least in its Jacobin form, just such an eruption of the desire for 'positive' freedom of collective self-direction on the part of a large body of Frenchmen who felt liberated as a nation, even though the result was, for a good many of them, a severe restriction of individual freedoms. Rousseau had spoken exultantly of the fact that the laws of liberty might prove to be more austere than the yoke of tyranny. Tyranny is service to human masters. The law cannot be a tyrant. Rousseau does not mean by liberty the 'negative' freedom of the individual not to be interfered with within a defined area, but the possession by all, and not merely by some, of the fully qualified members of a society of a share in the public power which is entitled to interfere with every aspect of every citizen's life. The liberals of the first half of the nineteenth century correctly foresaw that liberty in this 'positive' sense could easily destroy too many of the 'negative' liberties that they held sacred. They pointed out that the sovereignty of the people could easily destroy that of individuals. Mill explained, patiently and unanswerably, that government by the people was not, in his sense, necessarily freedom at all. For those who govern are not necessarily the same 'people' as those who are governed, and democratic self-government is not the government 'of each by himself', but, at best, 'of each by all the

rest'.[1] Mill and his disciples spoke of 'the tyranny of the majority'
and of the tyranny of 'the prevailing opinion and feeling',[2] and
saw no great difference between that and any other kind of tyranny
which encroaches upon men's activities beyond the sacred frontiers
of private life.

No one saw the conflict between the two types of liberty better,
or expressed it more clearly, than Benjamin Constant. He pointed
out that the transference by a successful rising of unlimited
authority, commonly called sovereignty, from one set of hands to
another does not increase liberty, but merely shifts the burden of
slavery. He reasonably asked why a man should deeply care
whether he is crushed by a popular government or by a monarch,
or even by a set of oppressive laws. He saw that the main problem
for those who desire 'negative', individual freedom is not who
wields this authority, but how much authority should be placed in
any set of hands. For unlimited authority in anybody's grasp was
bound, he believed, sooner or later, to destroy somebody. He
maintained that usually men protested against this or that set of
governors as oppressive, when the real cause of oppression lay in
the mere fact of the accumulation of power itself, wherever it might
happen to be, since liberty was endangered by the mere existence
of absolute authority as such. 'It is not against the arm that one
must rail,' he wrote, 'but against the weapon. Some weights are too
heavy for the human hand.'[3] Democracy may disarm a given
oligarchy, a given privileged individual or set of individuals, but it
can still crush individuals as mercilessly as any previous ruler. An
equal right to oppress – or interfere – is not equivalent to liberty.
Nor does universal consent to loss of liberty somehow miracu-
lously preserve it merely by being universal, or by being consent. If
I consent to be oppressed, or acquiesce in my condition with
detachment or irony, am I the less oppressed? If I sell myself into
slavery, am I the less a slave? If I commit suicide, am I the less dead
because I have taken my own life freely? 'Popular government is
merely a spasmodic tyranny, monarchy a more centralised despotism.'[4] Constant saw in Rousseau the most dangerous enemy of
individual liberty, because he had declared that 'In giving myself to

[1] op. cit. (p. 174 above, note 1), p. 219.   [2] ibid., pp. 219–20.
[3] op. cit. (p. 3 above, note 1), p. 312.   [4] ibid., p. 316.

all, I give myself to none.'[1] Constant could not see why, even
though the sovereign is 'everybody', it should not oppress one of
the 'members' of its indivisible self, if it so decided. I may, of
course, prefer to be deprived of my liberties by an assembly, or a
family, or a class in which I am a minority. It may give me an
opportunity one day of persuading the others to do for me that to
which I feel I am entitled. But to be deprived of my liberty at the
hands of my family or friends or fellow citizens is to be deprived of
it just as effectively. Hobbes was at any rate more candid: he did
not pretend that a sovereign does not enslave; he justified this
slavery, but at least did not have the effrontery to call it freedom.

Throughout the nineteenth century liberal thinkers maintained
that if liberty involved a limit upon the powers of any man to force
me to do what I did not, or might not, wish to do, then, whatever
the ideal in the name of which I was coerced, I was not free; that
the doctrine of absolute sovereignty was a tyrannical doctrine in
itself. If I wish to preserve my liberty, it is not enough to say that it
must not be violated unless someone or other – the absolute ruler,
or the popular assembly, or the King in Parliament, or the judges,
or some combination of authorities, or the laws themselves (for the
laws may be oppressive) – authorises its violation. I must establish
a society in which there must be some frontiers of freedom which
nobody should be permitted to cross. Different names or natures
may be given to the rules that determine these frontiers: they may
be called natural rights, or the word of God, or natural law, or the
demands of utility or of the 'permanent interests of man';[2] I may
believe them to be valid a priori, or assert them to be my own
ultimate ends, or the ends of my society or culture. What these
rules or commandments will have in common is that they are
accepted so widely, and are grounded so deeply in the actual nature
of men as they have developed through history, as to be, by now,
an essential part of what we mean by being a normal human being.
Genuine belief in the inviolability of a minimum extent of
individual liberty entails some such absolute stand. For it is clear
that it has little to hope for from the rule of majorities; democracy
as such is logically uncommitted to it, and historically has at times
failed to protect it, while remaining faithful to its own principles.
Few governments, it has been observed, have found much diffi-

---

[1] loc. cit. (p. 194 above, note 4); cf. Constant, ibid., p. 313.
[2] Mill, op. cit. (p. 174 above, note 1), p. 224.

culty in causing their subjects to generate any will that the government wanted. The triumph of despotism is to force the slaves to declare themselves free. It may need no force; the slaves may proclaim their freedom quite sincerely: but they are none the less slaves. Perhaps the chief value for liberals of political – 'positive' – rights, of participating in the government, is as a means for protecting what they hold to be an ultimate value, namely individual – 'negative' – liberty.

But if democracies can, without ceasing to be democratic, suppress freedom, at least as liberals have used the word, what would make a society truly free? For Constant, Mill, Tocqueville, and the liberal tradition to which they belong, no society is free unless it is governed by at any rate two interrelated principles: first, that no power, but only rights, can be regarded as absolute, so that all men, whatever power governs them, have an absolute right to refuse to behave inhumanly; and, second, that there are frontiers, not artificially drawn, within which men should be inviolable, these frontiers being defined in terms of rules so long and widely accepted that their observance has entered into the very conception of what it is to be a normal human being, and, therefore, also of what it is to act inhumanly or insanely; rules of which it would be absurd to say, for example, that they could be abrogated by some formal procedure on the part of some court or sovereign body. When I speak of a man as being normal, a part of what I mean is that he could not break these rules easily, without a qualm of revulsion. It is such rules as these that are broken when a man is declared guilty without trial, or punished under a retroactive law; when children are ordered to denounce their parents, friends to betray one another, soldiers to use methods of barbarism; when men are tortured or murdered, or minorities are massacred because they irritate a majority or a tyrant. Such acts, even if they are made legal by the sovereign, cause horror even in these days, and this springs from the recognition of the moral validity – irrespective of the laws – of some absolute barriers to the imposition of one man's will on another. The freedom of a society, or a class or a group, in this sense of freedom, is measured by the strength of these barriers, and the number and importance of the paths which they keep open for their members – if not for all, for at any rate a great number of them.[1]

[1] In Great Britain such legal power is, of course, constitutionally vested in the

This is almost at the opposite pole from the purposes of those who believe in liberty in the 'positive' – self-directive – sense. The former want to curb authority as such. The latter want it placed in their own hands. That is a cardinal issue. These are not two different interpretations of a single concept, but two profoundly divergent and irreconcilable attitudes to the ends of life. It is as well to recognise this, even if in practice it is often necessary to strike a compromise between them. For each of them makes absolute claims. These claims cannot both be fully satisfied. But it is a profound lack of social and moral understanding not to recognise that the satisfaction that each of them seeks is an ultimate value which, both historically and morally, has an equal right to be classed among the deepest interests of mankind.

VIII

The One and the Many

One belief, more than any other, is responsible for the slaughter of individuals on the altars of the great historical ideals – justice or progress or the happiness of future generations, or the sacred mission or emancipation of a nation or race or class, or even liberty itself, which demands the sacrifice of individuals for the freedom of society. This is the belief that somewhere, in the past or in the future, in divine revelation or in the mind of an individual thinker, in the pronouncements of history or science, or in the simple heart of an uncorrupted good man, there is a final solution. This ancient faith rests on the conviction that all the positive values in which men have believed must, in the end, be compatible, and perhaps even entail one another. 'Nature binds truth, happiness and virtue together by an indissoluble chain,' said one of the best men who ever lived, and spoke in similar terms of liberty, equality and justice.[1]

---

absolute sovereign – the Monarch in Parliament. What makes this country comparatively free, therefore, is the fact that this theoretically omnipotent entity is restrained by custom or opinion from behaving as such. It is clear that what matters is not the form of these restraints on power – whether they are legal, or moral, or constitutional – but their effectiveness.

[1] Condorcet, from whose *Esquisse* these words are quoted (loc. cit.: see p. 111 above, note 1), declares that the task of social science is to show 'by what bonds nature has united the progress of enlightenment with that of liberty, virtue and respect for the natural rights of man; how these ideals, which alone are truly good,

But is this true? It is a commonplace that neither political equality nor efficient organisation nor social justice is compatible with more than a modicum of individual liberty, and certainly not with unrestricted *laissez-faire*; that justice and generosity, public and private loyalties, the demands of genius and the claims of society can conflict violently with each other. And it is no great way from that to the generalisation that not all good things are compatible, still less all the ideals of mankind. But somewhere, we shall be told, and in some way, it must be possible for all these values to live together, for unless this is so, the universe is not a cosmos, not a harmony; unless this is so, conflicts of values may be an intrinsic, irremovable element in human life. To admit that the fulfilment of some of our ideals may in principle make the fulfilment of others impossible is to say that the notion of total human fulfilment is a formal contradiction, a metaphysical chimera. For every rationalist metaphysician, from Plato to the last disciples of Hegel or Marx, this abandonment of the notion of a final harmony in which all riddles are solved, all contradictions reconciled, is a piece of crude empiricism, abdication before brute facts, intolerable bankruptcy of reason before things as they are, failure to explain and to justify, to reduce everything to a system, which 'reason' indignantly rejects.

But if we are not armed with an a priori guarantee of the proposition that a total harmony of true values is somewhere to be found – perhaps in some ideal realm the characteristics of which we can, in our finite state, not so much as conceive – we must fall back on the ordinary resources of empirical observation and ordinary human knowledge. And these certainly give us no warrant for supposing (or even understanding what would be meant by saying) that all good things, or all bad things for that matter, are reconcilable with each other. The world that we encounter in ordinary experience is one in which we are faced with choices between ends equally ultimate, and claims equally absolute, the

yet so often separated from each other that they are even believed to be incompatible, should, on the contrary, become inseparable, as soon as enlightenment has reached a certain level simultaneously among a large number of nations'. He goes on to say that 'Men still preserve the errors of their childhood, of their country and of their age long after having recognised all the truths needed for destroying them.' ibid., pp. 9, 10. Ironically enough, his belief in the need for and possibility of uniting all good things may well be precisely the kind of error he himself so well described.

realisation of some of which must inevitably involve the sacrifice of others. Indeed, it is because this is their situation that men place such immense value upon the freedom to choose; for if they had assurance that in some perfect state, realisable by men on earth, no ends pursued by them would ever be in conflict, the necessity and agony of choice would disappear, and with it the central import- ance of the freedom to choose. Any method of bringing this final state nearer would then seem fully justified, no matter how much freedom were sacrificed to forward its advance.

It is, I have no doubt, some such dogmatic certainty that has been responsible for the deep, serene, unshakeable conviction in the minds of some of the most merciless tyrants and persecutors in history that what they did was fully justified by its purpose. I do not say that the ideal of self-perfection – whether for individuals or nations or Churches or classes – is to be condemned in itself, or that the language which was used in its defence was in all cases the result of a confused or fraudulent use of words, or of moral or intellectual perversity. Indeed, I have tried to show that it is the notion of freedom in its 'positive' sense that is at the heart of the demands for national or social self-direction which animate the most powerful and morally just public movements of our time, and that not to recognise this is to misunderstand the most vital facts and ideas of our age. But equally it seems to me that the belief that some single formula can in principle be found whereby all the diverse ends of men can be harmoniously realised is demonstrably false. If, as I believe, the ends of men are many, and not all of them are in principle compatible with each other, then the possibility of conflict – and of tragedy – can never wholly be eliminated from human life, either personal or social. The necessity of choosing between absolute claims is then an inescapable characteristic of the human condition. This gives its value to freedom as Acton conceived of it – as an end in itself, and not as a temporary need, arising out of our confused notions and irrational and disordered lives, a predicament which a panacea could one day put right.

I do not wish to say that individual freedom is, even in the most liberal societies, the sole, or even the dominant, criterion of social action. We compel children to be educated, and we forbid public executions. These are certainly curbs to freedom. We justify them on the ground that ignorance, or a barbarian upbringing, or cruel pleasures and excitements are worse for us than the amount of restraint needed to repress them. This judgement in turn depends on how we determine good and evil, that is to say, on our moral, religious, intellectual, economic and aesthetic values; which are, in their turn, bound up with our conception of man, and of the basic demands of his nature. In other words, our solution of such problems is based on our vision, by which we are consciously or unconsciously guided, of what constitutes a fulfilled human life, as contrasted with Mill's 'cramped and dwarfed', 'pinched and hidebound' natures.[1] To protest against the laws governing censorship or personal morals as intolerable infringements of personal liberty presupposes a belief that the activities which such laws forbid are fundamental needs of men as men, in a good (or, indeed, any) society. To defend such laws is to hold that these needs are not essential, or that they cannot be satisfied without sacrificing other values which come higher – satisfy deeper needs – than individual freedom, determined by some standard that is not merely subjective, a standard for which some objective status – empirical or a priori – is claimed.

The extent of a man's, or a people's, liberty to choose to live as he or they desire must be weighed against the claims of many other values, of which equality, or justice, or happiness, or security, or public order are perhaps the most obvious examples. For this reason, it cannot be unlimited. We are rightly reminded by R. H. Tawney that the liberty of the strong, whether their strength is physical or economic, must be restrained. This maxim claims respect, not as a consequence of some a priori rule, whereby the respect for the liberty of one man logically entails respect for the liberty of others like him; but simply because respect for the principles of justice, or shame at gross inequality of treatment, is as basic in men as the desire for liberty. That we cannot have everything is a necessary, not a contingent, truth. Burke's plea for the constant need to compensate, to reconcile, to balance; Mill's plea for novel 'experiments in living'[2] with their permanent possibility of error – the knowledge that it is not merely in practice but in principle impossible to reach clear-cut and certain answers, even in an ideal world of wholly good and rational men and wholly clear ideas – may madden those who seek for final solutions and single, all-embracing systems, guaranteed to be eternal. Nevertheless, it is a conclusion that cannot be escaped by those who, with

[1] loc. cit. (p. 174 above, note 4).   [2] loc. cit. (p. 225 below, note 2).

Kant, have learnt the truth that 'Out of the crooked timber of humanity no straight thing was ever made.'[1]

There is little need to stress the fact that monism, and faith in a single criterion, has always proved a deep source of satisfaction both to the intellect and to the emotions. Whether the standard of judgement derives from the vision of some future perfection, as in the minds of the *philosophes* in the eighteenth century and their technocratic successors in our own day, or is rooted in the past – *la terre et les morts* – as maintained by German historicists or French theocrats, or neo-Conservatives in English-speaking countries, it is bound, provided it is inflexible enough, to encounter some unforeseen and unforeseeable human development, which it will not fit; and will then be used to justify the a priori barbarities of Procrustes – the vivisection of actual human societies into some fixed pattern dictated by our fallible understanding of a largely imaginary past or a wholly imaginary future. To preserve our absolute categories or ideals at the expense of human lives offends equally against the principles of science and of history; it is an attitude found in equal measure on the right and left wings in our days, and is not reconcilable with the principles accepted by those who respect the facts.

Pluralism, with the measure of 'negative' liberty that it entails, seems to me a truer and more humane ideal than the goals of those who seek in the great disciplined, authoritarian structures the ideal of 'positive' self-mastery by classes, or peoples, or the whole of mankind. It is truer, because it does, at least, recognise the fact that human goals are many, not all of them commensurable, and in perpetual rivalry with one another. To assume that all values can be graded on one scale, so that it is a mere matter of inspection to determine the highest, seems to me to falsify our knowledge that men are free agents, to represent moral decision as an operation which a slide-rule could, in principle, perform. To say that in some ultimate, all-reconciling yet realisable synthesis duty is interest, or individual freedom is pure democracy or an authoritarian State, is to throw a metaphysical blanket over either self-deceit or deliberate hypocrisy. It is more humane because it does not (as the system-builders do) deprive men, in the name of some remote, or incoherent, ideal, of much that they have found to be indispensable

---

[1] loc. cit. (p. 92 above, note 1).

to their life as unpredictably self-transforming human beings.[1] In the end, men choose between ultimate values; they choose as they do because their life and thought are determined by fundamental moral categories and concepts that are, at any rate over large stretches of time and space, and whatever their ultimate origins, a part of their being and thought and sense of their own identity; part of what makes them human.

It may be that the ideal of freedom to choose ends without claiming eternal validity for them, and the pluralism of values connected with this, is only the late fruit of our declining capitalist civilisation: an ideal which remote ages and primitive societies have not recognised, and one which posterity will regard with curiosity, even sympathy, but little comprehension. This may be so; but no sceptical conclusions seem to me to follow. Principles are not less sacred because their duration cannot be guaranteed. Indeed, the very desire for guarantees that our values are eternal and secure in some objective heaven is perhaps only a craving for the certainties of childhood or the absolute values of our primitive past. 'To realise the relative validity of one's convictions', said an admirable writer of our time, 'and yet stand for them unflinchingly is what distinguishes a civilised man from a barbarian.'[2] To demand more than this is perhaps a deep and incurable metaphysical need; but to allow such a need to determine one's practice is a symptom of an equally deep, and more dangerous, moral and political immaturity.

[1] On this also Bentham seems to me to have spoken well: 'Individual interests are the only real interests . . . Can it be conceived that there are men so absurd as to . . . prefer the man who is not, to him who is; to torment the living, under pretence of promoting the happiness of those who are not born, and who may never be born?' op. cit. (p. 194 above, note 3), p. 321. This is one of the infrequent occasions when Burke agrees with Bentham; for this passage is at the heart of the empirical, as against the metaphysical, view of politics.

[2] Joseph A. Schumpeter, *Capitalism, Socialism, and Democracy* (London, 1943), p. 243.

JOHN STUART MILL
AND THE ENDS OF LIFE

... the importance, to man and society ... of giving full freedom to
human nature to expand itself in innumerable and conflicting directions.

J. S. Mill, *Autobiography*[1]

IN A WORLD in which human rights were never trampled on, and
men did not persecute each other for what they believed or what
they were, the cause of toleration would not need to be defended.
This, however, is not our world. We are a good deal remoter from
this desirable condition than some of our more civilised ancestors,
and, in this respect, unfortunately conform only too well to the
common pattern of human experience. The periods and societies in
which civil liberties were respected, and variety of opinion and
faith tolerated, have been very few and far between – oases in the
desert of human uniformity, intolerance and oppression. Among
the great Victorian preachers, Carlyle and Marx have turned out to
be better prophets than Macaulay and the Whigs, but not necessarily better friends to mankind; sceptical, to put it at its lowest, of the
principles on which toleration rests. Their greatest champion, the
man who formulated these principles most clearly and thereby
founded modern liberalism, was, as everyone knows, the author of
the essay *On Liberty*, John Stuart Mill. This book – this 'great
short book', as R. W. Livingstone has justly called it[2] – was
published one hundred years ago.[3]

[1] Chapter 7: vol. 1, p. 259, in *Collected Works of John Stuart Mill*, ed. J. M.
Robson and others (Toronto/London, 1963–91). Subsequent references to Mill's
writings are followed by a reference to this edition by volume and page in the
form CW i 259, except that references to *On Liberty* are given by chapter and a
page reference to vol. 18 of this edition, thus: L 4/281.
[2] Sir Richard Livingstone, *Tolerance in Theory and in Practice*, First Robert
Waley Cohen Memorial Lecture [1954] (London, 1954), p. 8.
[3] This was written in 1959.

The subject was then in the forefront of discussion. The year 1859 saw the death of the two best-known champions of individual liberty in Europe, Macaulay and Tocqueville. It marked the centenary of the birth of Friedrich Schiller, who was acclaimed as the poet of the free and creative personality fighting against great odds. The individual was seen by some as the victim of, by others as rising to his apotheosis in, the new and triumphant forces of nationalism and industrialism which exalted the power and the glory of great disciplined human masses that were transforming the world in factories or battlefields or political assemblies. The predicament of the individual versus the State or the nation or the industrial organisation or the social or political group was becoming an acute personal and public problem. In the same year there appeared Darwin's *The Origin of Species*, probably the most influential work of science of its century, which at once did much to destroy the ancient accumulation of dogma and prejudice, and, in its misapplication to psychology, ethics and politics, was used to justify violent imperialism and naked competition. Almost simultaneously with it there appeared an essay, written by an obscure economist expounding a doctrine which has had a decisive influence on mankind. The author was Karl Marx, the book was *A Contribution to the Critique of Political Economy*, the preface to which contained the clearest statement of the materialist interpretation of history – the heart of all that goes under the name of Marxism today. But the impact made upon political thought by Mill's treatise was more immediate, and perhaps no less permanent. It superseded earlier formulations of the case for individualism and toleration, from Milton and Locke to Montesquieu and Voltaire, and, despite its outdated psychology and lack of logical cogency, it remains the classic statement of the case for individual liberty. We are sometimes told that a man's behaviour is a more genuine expression of his beliefs than his words. In Mill's case there is no conflict. His life embodied his beliefs. His single-minded devotion to the cause of toleration and reason was unique even among the dedicated lives of the nineteenth century.

I

Everyone knows the story of John Stuart Mill's extraordinary education. His father, James Mill, was the last of the great *raisonneurs* of the eighteenth century, and remained completely unaffected by the new romantic currents of the time in which he lived. Like his teacher Bentham and the French philosophical materialists, he saw man as a natural object and considered that a systematic study of the human species – conducted on lines similar to those of zoology or botany or physics – could and should be established on firm empirical foundations. He believed himself to have grasped the principles of the new science of man, and was firmly convinced that any man educated in the light of it, brought up as a rational being by other rational beings, would thereby be preserved from ignorance and weakness, the two great sources of unreason in thought and action, which was alone responsible for the miseries and vices of mankind. He brought up his son, John Stuart, in isolation from other – less rationally educated – children; his own brothers and sisters were virtually his only companions. The boy knew Greek by the age of five, algebra and Latin by the age of nine. He was fed on a carefully distilled intellectual diet, prepared by his father, compounded by natural science and the classical literatures. No religion, no metaphysics, little poetry – nothing that Bentham had stigmatised as the accumulation of human idiocy and error – were permitted to reach him. Music, perhaps because it was supposed that it could not easily misrepresent the real world, was the only art in which he could indulge himself freely. The experiment was, in a sense, an appalling success. John Mill, by the time he reached the age of twelve, possessed the learning of an exceptionally erudite man of thirty. In his own sober, clear, literal-minded, painfully honest account of himself, he says that his emotions were starved while his mind was violently overdeveloped. His father had no doubt of the value of his experiment. He had succeeded in producing an excellently informed and perfectly rational being. The truth of Bentham's views on education had been thoroughly vindicated.

The results of such treatment will astonish no one in our psychologically less naïve age. In his early manhood John Mill went through his first agonising crisis. He felt lack of purpose, a paralysis of the will, and terrible despair. With his well-trained and, indeed, ineradicable habit of reducing emotional dissatisfaction to a clearly formulated problem, he asked himself a simple question: supposing that the noble Benthamite ideal of universal happiness which he had been taught to believe, and to the best of his ability did believe, were realised, would this, in fact, fulfil all his desires? He admitted to himself, to his horror, that it would not. What, then, was the true end of life? He saw no purpose in existence: everything in his world now seemed dry and bleak. He tried to analyse his condition. Was he perhaps totally devoid of feeling – was he a monster with a large part of normal human nature atrophied? He felt that he had no motives for continuing to live, and wished for death.

One day, as he was reading a pathetic story in the memoirs of the now almost forgotten French writer Marmontel, he was suddenly moved to tears. This convinced him that he was capable of emotion, and with this his recovery began. It took the form of a revolt, slow, concealed, reluctant, but profound and irresistible, against the view of life inculcated by his father and the Benthamites. He read the poetry of Wordsworth, he read and met Coleridge; his view of the nature of man, his history and his destiny, was transformed. John Mill was not by temperament rebellious. He loved and deeply admired his father, and was convinced of the validity of his main philosophical tenets. He stood with Bentham against dogmatism, transcendentalism, obscurantism, all that resisted the march of reason, analysis and empirical science. To these beliefs he held firmly all his life. Nevertheless his conception of man, and therefore of much else, suffered a great change. He became not so much an open heretic from the original Utilitarian movement, as a disciple who quietly left the fold, preserving what he thought true or valuable, but feeling bound by none of the rules and principles of the movement. He continued to profess that happiness was the sole end of human existence, but his conception of what contributed to it changed into something very different from that of his mentors, for what he came to value most was neither rationality nor contentment, but diversity, versatility, fullness of life – the unaccountable leap of individual genius, the spontaneity and uniqueness of a man, a group, a civilisation. What he hated and feared was narrowness, uniformity, the crippling effect of persecution, the crushing of individuals by the weight of authority or of custom or of public opinion; he set himself against the worship of order or tidiness, or even peace, if they were bought at the price of obliterating the variety and colour of untamed human beings with unextinguished passions and untrammelled imaginations. This was, perhaps, a natural enough compensation for his own drilled, emotionally shrivelled, warped childhood and adolescence.

By the time he was seventeen he was mentally fully formed. John

Mill's intellectual equipment was probably unique in that or any other age. He was clear-headed, candid, highly articulate, intensely serious, and without any trace of fear, vanity or humour. During the next ten years he wrote articles and reviews, with all the weight of the official heir presumptive of the whole Utilitarian movement upon his shoulders; and although his articles made him a great name, and he grew to be a formidable publicist and a source of pride to his mentors and allies, yet the note of his writings is not theirs. He praised what his father had praised – rationality, empirical method, democracy, equality – and he attacked what the Utilitarians attacked – religion, belief in intuitive and undemonstrable truths and their dogmatic consequences, which, in their view and in his, led to the abandonment of reason, hierarchical societies, vested interests, intolerance of free criticism, prejudice, reaction, injustice, despotism, misery. Yet the emphasis had shifted. James Mill and Bentham had wanted literally nothing but pleasure, obtained by whatever means were the most effective. If someone had offered them a medicine which could scientifically be shown to put those who took it into a state of permanent contentment, their premisses would have bound them to accept this as the panacea for all that they thought evil. Provided that the largest number of men receive lasting happiness, or even freedom from pain, it should not matter how this is achieved. Bentham and James Mill believed in education and legislation as the roads to happiness. But if a shorter way had been discovered, in the form of pills to swallow, techniques of subliminal suggestion or other means of conditioning human beings, in which our century has made such strides, then, being men of fanatical consistency, they might well have accepted this as a better, because more effective and perhaps less costly, alternative than the means that they had advocated. John Stuart Mill, as he made plain both by his life and by his writings, would have rejected with both hands any such solution. He would have condemned it as degrading the nature of man. For him man differs from animals primarily neither as the possessor of reason, nor as an inventor of tools and methods, but as a being capable of choice, one who is most himself in choosing and not being chosen for; the rider and not the horse; the seeker of ends, and not merely of means, ends that he pursues, each in his own fashion: with the corollary that the more various these fashions, the richer the lives of men become; the larger the field of interplay between individuals, the greater the opportunities of the new and the unexpected; the more numerous the possibilities for altering his own character in some fresh or unexplored direction, the more paths will open before each individual, and the wider will be his freedom of action and thought.

In the last analysis, all appearances to the contrary, this is what Mill seems to me to have cared about most of all. He is officially committed to the exclusive pursuit of happiness. He believes deeply in justice, but his voice is most his own when he describes the glories of individual freedom, or denounces whatever seeks to curtail or extinguish it. Bentham, too, unlike his French predecessors who trusted in moral and scientific experts, had laid it down that each man is the best judge of his own happiness. Nevertheless, his principle would remain valid for Bentham even after every living man had swallowed the happiness-inducing pill and society was thereby lifted or reduced to a condition of unbroken and uniform bliss. For Bentham individualism is a psychological datum; for Mill it is an ideal. Mill likes dissent, independence, solitary thinkers, those who defy the establishment. In an article published when he was eighteen years old (demanding toleration for a now almost forgotten atheist named Richard Carlile), he strikes a note which sounds and resounds in his writings through the rest of his life: 'Christians, whose reformers perished in the dungeon or at the stake as heretics, apostates and blasphemers; Christians, whose religion breathes charity, liberty, and mercy in every line; that *they* having gained the power to which so long they were victims, should employ it in the self-same way ... [in] vindictive persecution, is most monstrous.'[1] He remained the champion of heretics, apostates, the blasphemers, of liberty and mercy, for the rest of his life.

[1] This passage occurs in a review of two pamphlets on the Carlile prosecutions in *Westminster Review* 2 (July–October 1824) No 3 (July), 1–27, at 26. Since Alexander Bain – see *John Stuart Mill: A Criticism* (London, 1882), p. 33 – confidently ascribes this article to Mill, even though it does not appear in Mill's own list of his work, Berlin too, not unnaturally, took it as Mill's. The review is also reprinted in *Prefaces to Liberty: Selected Writings of John Stuart Mill*, ed. Bernard Wishy (Boston, 1959; repr. Lanham, Md, etc., 1983), where the quoted passage appears on p. 99. However, a letter from Joseph Parkes to John Bowring (then co-editor of the *Review*) of 1 March 1824 (HM 30805, The Huntington Library, San Marino, CA) suggests that the review may in fact be by William Johnson Fox (1768–1864), though Parkes refers to 'Persecution papers'. But even if the words are not Mill's, the sentiments are certainly Millian. Ed.

His acts were in harmony with his professions. The public policies with which Mill's name was associated as a journalist, a reformer and a politician, were seldom connected with the typically Utilitarian projects advocated by Bentham and successfully realised by many of his disciples: great industrial, financial, educational schemes, reforms of public health or the organisation of labour or leisure. The issues to which Mill was dedicated, whether in his published views or his actions, were concerned with something different: the extension of individual freedom, especially freedom of speech: seldom with anything else. When Mill declared that war was better than oppression, or that a revolution that would kill all men with an income of more than £500 per annum might improve things greatly, or that the Emperor Napoleon III of France was the vilest man alive; when he expressed delight at Palmerston's fall over the Bill that sought to make conspiracy against foreign despots a criminal offence in England; when he denounced the Southern States in the American Civil War, or made himself violently unpopular by speaking in the House of Commons in defence of Fenian assassins (and thereby probably saving their lives), or for the rights of women, or of workers, or of colonial peoples, and thereby made himself the most passionate and best-known champion in England of the insulted and the oppressed, it is difficult to suppose that it was not liberty and justice (at whatever cost) but utility (which counts the cost) that were uppermost in his mind. His articles and his political support saved Durham and his Report, when both were in danger of being defeated by the combination of right- and left-wing adversaries, and thereby did much to ensure self-government in the British Commonwealth. He helped to destroy the reputation of Governor Eyre, who had perpetrated brutalities in Jamaica. He saved the right of public meeting and of free speech in Hyde Park, against a Government that wished to destroy it. He wrote and spoke for proportional representation because this alone, in his view, would allow minorities (not necessarily virtuous or rational ones) to make their voices heard. When, to the surprise of radicals, he opposed the dissolution of the East India Company, for which he, like his father before him, had worked so devotedly, he did this because he feared the dead hand of the Government more than the paternalist and not inhumane rule of the Company's officials. On the other hand he did not oppose State intervention as such; he welcomed it in education or labour legislation because he thought that without it the weakest would be enslaved and crushed; and because it would increase the range of choices for the great majority of men, even if it restrained some. What is common to all these causes is not any direct connection they might have with the 'greatest happiness' principle[1] but the fact that they turn on the issue of human rights – that is to say, of liberty and toleration.

I do not, of course, mean to suggest that there was no such connection in Mill's own mind. He often seems to advocate freedom on the ground that without it the truth cannot be discovered – we cannot perform those experiments either in thought or 'in living'[2] which alone reveal to us new, unthought-of ways of maximising pleasure and minimising pain – the only ultimate source of value. Freedom, then, is valuable as a means, not as an end. But when we ask what Mill meant either by pleasure or by happiness, the answer is far from clear. Whatever happiness may be, it is, according to Mill, not what Bentham took it to be: for his conception of human nature is pronounced too narrow and altogether inadequate; he has no imaginative grasp of history or society or individual psychology; he does not understand either what holds, or what should hold, society together – common ideals, loyalties, national character; he is not aware of honour, dignity, self-culture, or the love of beauty, order, power, action; he understands only the 'business' aspects of life.[3] Are these goals, which Mill rightly regards as central, so many means to a single universal goal – happiness? Or are they species of it? Mill never clearly tells us. He says that happiness – or utility – is of no use as a criterion of conduct – destroying at one blow the proudest claim, and indeed the central doctrine, of the Benthamite system. 'We think', he says in his essay on Bentham (published only after his

---

[1] '[I]t is the greatest happiness of the greatest number that is the measure of right and wrong.' From the Preface to Bentham's A Fragment of Government (1776): p. 393 in A Comment on the Commentaries and A Fragment of Government, ed. J. H. Burns and H. L. A. Hart (London, 1977). Cf. 'the greatest happiness of the greatest number is the foundation of morals and legislation', from Bentham's commonplace book (1781–5): see vol. 10, p. 142, in op. cit. (p. 194 above, note 3). Bentham later dropped the reference to the greatest number. The career of this idea before Bentham, and in Bentham's hands, is complex, but distilled with great clarity by Robert Shackleton in 'The Greatest Happiness of the Greatest Number: The History of Bentham's Phrase', Studies on Voltaire and the Eighteenth Century 90 (1972), 1461–82. Ed.

[2] L 4/281; cf. L 3/261, where Mill speaks of 'experiments of living'.

[3] 'Bentham': CW x 99–100.

father's death), 'utility, or happiness, much too complex or indefin-
nite an end to be sought except through the medium of various
secondary ends, concerning which there may be, and often is,
agreement among persons who differ in their ultimate standard.'[1]
This is simple and definite enough in Bentham; but Mill rejects his
formula because it rests on a false view of human nature. It is
'complex' and 'indefinite' in Mill because he packs into it the many
diverse (and, perhaps, not always compatible) ends which men in
fact pursue for their own sake, and which Bentham had either
ignored or falsely classified under the head of pleasure: love,
hatred, desire for justice, for action, for freedom, for power, for
beauty, for knowledge, for self-sacrifice. In J. S. Mill's writings
'happiness' comes to mean something very like 'realisation of one's
wishes', whatever they may be. This stretches its meaning to the
point of vacuity. The letter remains; but the spirit – the old, tough-
minded Benthamite view for which happiness, if it was not a clear
and concrete criterion of action, was nothing at all, as worthless as
the 'transcendental' intuitionist moonshine it was meant to replace
– the true Utilitarian spirit – has fled. Mill does indeed add that
'when two or more of the secondary principles conflict . . . a direct
appeal to some first principle becomes necessary'.[2] This principle
is utility; but he gives no indication how this notion, drained of its
old, materialistic but intelligible, content, is to be applied.

It is this tendency of Mill's to escape into what Bentham called
'vague generalities'[3] that leads one to ask what, in fact, was Mill's
real scale of values as shown in his writings and action. If his life
and the causes he advocated are any evidence, then it seems clear
that in public life the highest values for him – whether or not he
calls them 'secondary ends'[4] – were individual liberty, variety and
justice. If challenged about variety Mill would have defended it on
the ground that without a sufficient degree of it many, at present
wholly unforeseeable, forms of human happiness (or satisfaction,
or fulfilment, or higher levels of life – however the degrees of these
were to be determined and compared) would be left unknown,
untried, unrealised; among them happier lives than any yet experienced. This is his thesis and he chooses to call it Utilitarianism. But

---

[1] ibid. 110.   [2] ibid. 111.

[3] Bentham used this phrase frequently: for examples see his 'Legislator of the
World': Writings on Codification, Law, and Education, ed. Philip Schofield and
Jonathan Harris (Oxford: 1998), pp. 46, 282 (note). Ed.

[4] As he does in 'Bentham': CW x 110.

if anyone were to argue that a given, actual or attainable, social arrangement yielded enough happiness – that given the virtually impassable limitations of the nature of men and their environment (for example, the very high improbability of men's becoming immortal or growing as tall as Everest), it was better to concentrate on the best that we have, since change would, in all empirical likelihood, lead to lowering of general happiness, and should therefore be avoided, we may be sure that Mill would have rejected this argument out of hand. He was committed to the answer that we can never tell (until we have tried) where greater truth or happiness (or any other form of experience) may lie. Finality is therefore in principle impossible: all solutions must be tentative and provisional. This is the voice of a disciple of both Saint-Simon and Constant or Humboldt. It runs directly counter to traditional – that is, eighteenth-century – Utilitarianism, which rested on the view that there exists an unalterable nature of things, and that answers to social, as to other, problems, can, at least in principle, be scientifically discovered once and for all. It is this, perhaps, that, despite his fear of ignorant and irrational democracy and consequent craving for government by the enlightened and the expert (and insistence, early and late in his life, on the importance of objects of common, even uncritical, worship) checked his Saint-Simonism, turned him against Comte, and preserved him from the élitist tendency of his Fabian disciples.

There was a spontaneous and uncalculating idealism in his mind and his actions that was wholly alien to the dispassionate and penetrating irony of Bentham, or the vain and stubborn rationalism of James Mill. He tells us that his father's educational methods had turned him into a desiccated calculating machine, not too far removed from the popular image of the inhuman Utilitarian philosopher; his very awareness of this makes one wonder whether it can ever have been wholly true. Despite the solemn bald head, the black clothes, the grave expression, the measured phrases, the total lack of humour, Mill's life is an unceasing revolt against his father's outlook and ideals, the greater for being subterranean and unacknowledged.

Mill had scarcely any prophetic gift. Unlike his contemporaries Marx, Burckhardt, Tocqueville he had no vision of what the twentieth century would bring, neither of the political and social consequences of industrialisation, nor of the discovery of the strength of irrational and unconscious factors in human behaviour, nor of the terrifying techniques to which this knowledge has led and is leading. The transformation of society which has resulted – the rise of dominant secular ideologies and the wars between them, the awakening of Africa and Asia, the peculiar combination of nationalism and socialism in our day – these were outside Mill's horizon. But if he was not sensitive to the contours of the future, he was acutely aware of the destructive factors at work in his own world. He detested and feared standardisation. He perceived that in the name of philanthropy, democracy and equality a society was being created in which human objectives were artificially made narrower and smaller and the majority of men were being converted, to use his admired friend Tocqueville's image, into mere industrious sheep,[1] in which, in his own words, 'collective mediocrity'[2] was gradually strangling originality and individual gifts. He was against what have been called 'organisation men', a class of persons to whom Bentham could have had in principle no rational objection. He knew, feared and hated timidity, mildness, natural conformity, lack of interest in human issues. This was common ground between him and his friend, his suspicious and disloyal friend, Thomas Carlyle. Above all he was on his guard against those who, for the sake of being left in peace to cultivate their gardens, were ready to sell their fundamental human right to self-government in the public spheres of life. These characteristics of our lives today he would have recognised with horror. He took human solidarity for granted, perhaps altogether too much for granted. He did not fear the isolation of individuals or groups, the factors that make for the alienation and disintegration of individuals and societies. He was preoccupied with the opposite evils of socialisation and uniformity.[3] He longed for the widest variety

[1] *Democracy in America*, part 2 (1840), book 4, chapter 6, 'What Sort of Despotism Democratic Nations Have to Fear': vol. 2, p. 319, in the edition by Phillips Bradley of the translation by Henry Reeve and Francis Bowen (New York, 1945).

[2] L 3/268.

[3] He did not seem to look on socialism, which under the influence of Harriet Taylor he advocated in *Principles of Political Economy* and later, as a danger to individual liberty in the way in which democracy, for example, might be so. This is not the place to examine the very peculiar relationship of Mill's socialist to his individualist convictions. Despite his socialist professions, none of the socialist leaders of his time – neither Louis Blanc nor Proudhon nor Lassalle nor Herzen

of human life and character. He saw that this could not be obtained without protecting individuals from each other, and above all, from the terrible weight of social pressure; this led to his insistent and persistent demands for toleration.

Toleration, Herbert Butterfield has told us, implies a certain disrespect.[1] I tolerate your absurd beliefs and your foolish acts, though I know them to be absurd and foolish. Mill would, I think, have agreed. He believed that to hold an opinion deeply is to throw our feelings into it. He once declared that when we deeply care, we must dislike those who hold the opposite views.[2] He preferred this to cold temperaments and opinions. He asked us not necessarily to respect the views of others – very far from it – only to try to understand and tolerate them; only tolerate; disapprove, think ill of, if need be mock or despise, but tolerate; for without conviction, without some antipathetic feeling, there was, he thought, no deep conviction; and without deep conviction there were no ends of life, and then the awful abyss on the edge of which he had himself once stood would yawn before us. But without tolerance the conditions for rational criticism, rational condemnation, are destroyed. He therefore pleads for reason and toleration at all costs. To understand is not necessarily to forgive. We may argue, attack, reject, condemn with passion and hatred. But we may not suppress or stifle: for that is to destroy the bad and the good, and is tantamount to collective moral and intellectual suicide. Sceptical respect for the opinions of our opponents seems to him preferable to indifference or cynicism. But even these attitudes are less harmful than intolerance, or an imposed orthodoxy that kills rational discussion.

This is Mill's faith. It obtained its classical formulation in the tract On Liberty, which he began writing in 1855 in collaboration with his wife, who, after his father, was the dominant figure in his life. Until his dying day he believed her to be endowed with a genius vastly superior to his own. He published the essay after her death in 1859 without those improvements which he was sure that her unique gifts would have brought to it.

(not to speak of Marx) appears to have regarded him even as a fellow-traveller. He was to them the very embodiment of a mild reformist liberal or bourgeois radical. Only the Fabians claimed him as an ancestor.

[1] Historical Development of the Principle of Toleration in British Life, Robert Waley Cohen Memorial Lecture 1956 (London, 1957), p. 16.

[2] Autobiography, chapter 2: CW i 51, 53.

II

I shall not give a full abstract of Mill's argument, but rather recapitulate only those salient ideas to which Mill attached the greatest importance – beliefs which his opponents attacked in his lifetime, and attack even more vehemently today. These propositions are still far from self-evident; time has not turned them to platitudes; they are not even now undisputed assumptions of a civilised outlook. Let me attempt to consider them briefly.

Men want to curtail the liberties of other men, either (*a*) because they wish to impose their power on others; or (*b*) because they want conformity – they do not wish to think differently from others, or others to think differently from themselves; or, finally, (*c*) because they believe that to the question of how one should live there can be (as with any genuine question) one true answer and one only: this answer is discoverable by means of reason, or intuition, or direct revelation, or a form of life or 'unity of theory and practice';[1] its authority is identifiable with one of these avenues to final knowledge; all deviation from it is error that

---

[1] For this fundamental Marxist formula (not apparently expressed in exactly these terms by Marx himself, nor by Engels) see Georg Lukács, 'What is Orthodox Marxism?' (1919): pp. 2–3 in *History and Class Consciousness: Studies in Marxist Dialectics* [1923], trans. Rodney Livingstone (London, 1971). Leszek Kolakowski offers as a gloss 'the understanding and transformation of reality are not two separate processes, but one and the same phenomenon': *Main Currents of Marxism: Its Origins, Growth and Dissolution* (Oxford, 1978: Oxford University Press), vol. 3, *The Breakdown*, p. 270. For Soviet philosophy, in which it is repeated *ad nauseam*, it meant roughly 'Physical sciences should work for Soviet industry; social and human sciences are instruments of political propaganda.' Similar locutions (which should not, however, be regarded as equivalent in meaning, even *mutatis mutandis*) are used by Marx's contemporaries. For example, Mill himself attributes the 'union of theory and practice' to the ancient Greeks in 'On Genius' (1832) at CW i 336; there are also references by Auguste Comte to 'harmonie entre la théorie et la pratique' ('harmony between theory and practice') in *Système de politique positive* (see p. 81 above, note 1), vol. 4 (1854), pp. 7, 172. More generally, of course, discussion of the relationship of theory and practice goes back to antiquity, perhaps originating in Socrates' doctrine that virtue is knowledge; see also Diogenes Laertius 7.125 on the Stoic view that 'the virtuous man is both a theorist, and a practitioner of things doable'. Especially well known is Leibniz's recommendation in 1700 'Theoriam cum praxi zu vereinigen' ('to combine theory with practice') in his proposal to establish a Brandenburg Academy in Berlin: see Hans-Stephan Brather, *Leibniz und seine Akademie: Ausgewählte Quellen zur Geschichte der Berliner Sozietät der Wissenschaften 1697–1716* (Berlin, 1993), p. 72. Ed.

imperils human salvation; this justifies legislation against, or even extirpation of, those who lead away from the truth, whatever their character or intentions.

Mill dismisses the first two motives as being irrational, since they stake out no intellectually argued claim, and are therefore incapable of being answered by rational argument. The only motive which he is prepared to take seriously is the last, namely, that if the true ends of life can be discovered, those who oppose these truths are spreading pernicious falsehood, and must be repressed. To this he replies that men are not infallible; that the supposedly pernicious view might turn out to be true after all; that those who killed Socrates and Christ sincerely believed them to be purveyors of wicked falsehoods, and were themselves men as worthy of respect as any to be found today; that Marcus Aurelius, 'the gentlest and most amiable of philosophers and rulers',[1] known as the most enlightened man of his time and one of the noblest, nevertheless authorised the persecution of Christianity as a moral and social danger, and that no argument ever used by any other persecutor had not been equally open to him. We cannot suppose that persecution never kills the truth. 'It is a piece of idle sentimentality', Mill observes, 'that truth, merely as truth, has an inherent power denied to error, of prevailing against the dungeon and the stake.'[2] Persecution is historically only too effective.

> To speak only of religious opinions: the Reformation broke out at least twenty times before Luther, and was put down. Arnold of Brescia was put down. Fra Dolcino was put down. Savonarola was put down. The Albigeois were put down. The Vaudois were put down. The Lollards were put down. The Hussites were put down ... In Spain, Italy, Flanders, the Austrian empire, Protestantism was rooted out; and, most likely, would have been so in England, had Queen Mary lived, or Queen Elizabeth died ... No reasonable person can doubt that Christianity might have been extirpated in the Roman Empire.[3]

And what if it be said against this that, just because we have erred in the past, it is mere cowardice to refrain from striking down evil when we see it in the present in case we may be mistaken again; or, to put it in another way, that, even if we are not infallible, yet, if we are to live at all, we must make decisions and act, and must do so

[1] L 2/237.   [2] L 2/238.   [3] ibid.

on nothing better than probability, according to our lights, with constant risk of error; for all living involves risk, and what alternative have we? Mill answers that 'There is the greatest difference between presuming an opinion to be true, because, with every opportunity for contesting it, it has not been refuted, and assuming its truth for the purpose of not permitting its refutation.'[1] You can indeed stop 'bad men' from perverting society with 'false and pernicious' views,[2] but only if you give men liberty to deny that what you yourself call bad, or pernicious, or perverted, or false, is such; otherwise your conviction is founded on mere dogma and is not rational, and cannot be analysed or altered in the light of any new facts and ideas. Without infallibility how can truth emerge save in discussion? There is no a priori road towards it; a new experience, a new argument, can in principle always alter our views, no matter how strongly held. To shut doors is to blind yourself to the truth deliberately, to condemn yourself to incorrigible error.

Mill had a strong and subtle brain and his arguments are never negligible. But it is, in this case, plain that his conclusion only follows from premises which he does not make explicit. He was an empiricist; that is, he believed that no truths are – or could be – rationally established, except on the evidence of observation. New observations could in principle always upset a conclusion founded on earlier ones. He believed this rule to be true of the laws of physics, even of the laws of logic and mathematics; how much more, therefore, in 'ideological' fields where no scientific certainty prevailed – in ethics, politics, religion, history, the entire field of human affairs, where only probability reigns; here, unless full liberty of opinion and argument is permitted, nothing can ever be rationally established. But those who disagree with him, and believe in intuited truths, in principle not corrigible by experience, will disregard this argument. Mill can write them off as obscurantists, dogmatists, irrationalists. Yet something more is needed than mere contemptuous dismissal if their views, more powerful today, perhaps, than even in Mill's own century, are to be rationally contested. Again, it may well be that without full freedom of discussion the truth cannot emerge. But this may be only a necessary, not a sufficient, condition of its discovery; the truth

[1] L 2/231.   [2] ibid.

may, for all our efforts, remain at the bottom of a well, and in the meantime the worse cause may win, and do enormous damage to mankind. Is it so clear that we must permit opinions advocating, say, race hatred to be uttered freely, because Milton has said that 'though all the winds of doctrine were let loose to play upon the earth ... who ever knew Truth put to the worse, in a free and open encounter?'[1] These are brave and optimistic judgements, but how good is the empirical evidence for them today? Are demagogues and liars, scoundrels and blind fanatics always, in liberal societies, stopped in time, or refuted in the end? How high a price is it right to pay for the great boon of freedom of discussion? A very high one, no doubt; but is it limitless? And if not, who shall say what sacrifice is, or is not, too great? Mill goes on to say that an opinion believed to be false may yet be partially true; for there is no absolute truth, only different roads towards it; the suppression of an apparent falsehood may also suppress what is true in it, to the loss of mankind. This argument, again, will not tell with those who believe that absolute truth is discoverable once and for all, whether by metaphysical or theological argument, or by some direct insight, or by leading a certain kind of life, or, as Mill's own mentors believed, by scientific or empirical methods.

His argument is plausible only on the assumption which, whether he knew it or not, Mill all too obviously made, that human knowledge was in principle never complete, and always fallible; that there was no single, universally visible, truth; that each man, each nation, each civilisation might take its own road towards its own goal, not necessarily harmonious with those of others; that men are altered, and the truths in which they believe are altered, by new experiences and their own actions – what he calls 'experiments in living;'[2] that consequently the conviction, common to Aristotelians and a good many Christian scholastics and atheistical materialists alike, that there exists a basic knowable human nature, one and the same, at all times, in all places, in all men – a static, unchanging substance underneath the altering appearances, with permanent needs, dictated by a single, discoverable goal, or pattern of goals, the same for all mankind – is mistaken; and so, too, is the

---

[1] *Aereopagita* (1644): vol. 2, p. 561, in *Complete Prose Works of John Milton* (New Haven and London, 1953–82); Milton's spelling has been modernised in the quotation.

[2] loc. cit. (p. 225 above, note 2).

notion that is bound up with it, of a single true doctrine carrying salvation to all men everywhere, contained in natural law, or the revelation of a sacred book, or the insight of a man of genius, or the natural wisdom of ordinary men, or the calculations made by an élite of Utilitarian scientists set up to govern mankind.

Mill – bravely for a professed Utilitarian – observes that the human (that is the social) sciences are too confused and uncertain to be properly called sciences at all. There are in them no valid generalisations, no laws, and therefore no predictions or rules of action can properly be deduced from them. He honoured the memory of his father, whose whole philosophy was based on the opposite assumption; he respected August Comte, and subsidised Herbert Spencer, both of whom claimed to have laid the foundations for just such a science of society. Yet his own half-articulate assumption contradicts this. Mill believes that man is spontaneous, that he has freedom of choice, that he moulds his own character, that as a result of the interplay of men with nature and with other men something novel continually arises, and that this novelty is precisely what is most characteristic and most human in men. Because Mill's entire view of human nature turns out to rest not on the notion of the repetition of an identical pattern, but on his perception of human lives as subject to perpetual incompleteness, self-transformation and novelty, his words are today alive and relevant to our own problems; whereas the works of James Mill, and of Buckle and Comte and Spencer, remain huge half-forgotten hulks in the river of nineteenth-century thought. He does not demand or predict ideal conditions for the final solution of human problems or for obtaining universal agreement on all crucial issues. He assumes that finality is impossible, and implies that it is undesirable too. He does not demonstrate this. Rigour in argument is not among his accomplishments. Yet it is this belief, which undermines the foundations on which Helvétius, Bentham and James Mill built their doctrines – a system never formally repudiated by him – that gives his case both its plausibility and its humanity.

His remaining arguments are weaker still. He says that unless it is contested, truth is liable to degenerate into dogma or prejudice; men would no longer feel it as a living truth; opposition is needed to keep it alive. 'Both teachers and learners go to sleep at their post, as soon as there is no enemy in the field', overcome as they are by

' "the deep slumber of a decided opinion" '.[1] So deeply did Mill believe this, that he declared that if there were no genuine dissenters, we had an obligation to invent arguments against ourselves, in order to keep ourselves in a state of intellectual fitness. This resembles nothing so much as Hegel's argument for war as keeping human society from stagnation. Yet if the truth about human affairs were in principle demonstrable, as it is, say, in arithmetic, the invention of false propositions in order for them to be knocked down would scarcely be needed to preserve our understanding of it. What Mill seems really to be asking for is diversity of opinion for its own sake. He speaks of the need for 'fair play to all sides of the truth'[2] – a phrase that a man would scarcely employ if he believed in simple, complete truths as the earlier Utilitarians did; and he makes use of bad arguments to conceal this scepticism, perhaps even from himself. '[I]n an imperfect state of the human mind,' he says, 'the interests of truth require a diversity of opinions.'[3] And he asks whether we are 'willing to adopt the logic of persecutors, and to say that we may persecute others because we are right, and that they must not persecute us because they are wrong'.[4] Catholics, Protestants, Jews, Muslims have all justified persecution by this argument in their day; and on their premises there may be nothing logically amiss with it.

It is these premises that Mill rejects, and rejects not, it seems to me, as a result of a chain of reasoning, but because he believes – even if he never, so far as I know, admits this explicitly – that there are no final truths not corrigible by experience, at any rate in what is now called the ideological sphere – that of value judgements and of general outlook and attitude to life. Yet within this framework of ideas and values, despite all the stress on the value of 'experiments in living' and what they may reveal, Mill is ready to stake a very great deal on the truth of his convictions about what he thinks to be the deepest and most permanent interests of men. Although his reasons are drawn from experience and not from a priori knowledge, the propositions themselves are very like those defended on metaphysical grounds by the traditional upholders of the doctrine of natural rights. Mill believes in liberty, that is, the rigid limitation of the right to coerce, because he is sure that men

---

[1] L 2/250. The concluding phrase is quoted from 'a cotemporary [sic] author' identified neither by Mill nor by the editor of CW xviii, J. M. Robson.

[2] L 2/254.   [3] L 2/257.   [4] L 4/285.

cannot develop and flourish and become fully human unless they are left free from interference by other men within a certain minimum area of their lives, which he regards as – or wishes to make – inviolable. This is his view of what men are, and therefore of their basic moral and intellectual needs, and he formulates his conclusions in the celebrated maxims according to which 'the individual is not accountable to society for his actions, in so far as these concern the interests of no person but himself',[1] and 'the only purpose for which power can be rightfully exercised over any member of a civilised community, against his will, is to prevent harm to others. His own good, either physical or moral, is not a sufficient warrant. He cannot rightfully be compelled to do or forbear ... because, in the opinions of others, to do so would be wise, or even right.'[2] This is Mill's profession of faith, and the ultimate basis of political liberalism, and therefore the proper target of attack – both on psychological and moral (and social) grounds – by its opponents during Mill's lifetime and after. Carlyle reacted with characteristic fury in a letter to his brother Alexander: 'As if it were a sin to control, or coerce into better methods, human swine in any way ... *Ach Gott im Himmel!*'[3]

Milder and more rational critics have not failed to point out that the limits of the private and public domains are difficult to demarcate; that anything a man does could, in principle, frustrate others; that no man is an island; that the social and the individual aspects of human beings often cannot, in practice, be disentangled. Mill was told that when men look upon forms of worship in which other men persist as being not merely 'abominable'[4] in themselves, but as an offence to them or to their God, they may be irrational and bigoted, but they are not necessarily lying; and that when he asks rhetorically why Muslims should not forbid the eating of pork to everyone, since they are genuinely disgusted by it, the answer, on Utilitarian premises, is by no means self-evident. It might be argued that there is no a priori reason for supposing that most men would not be happier – if that is the goal – in a wholly socialised world where private life and personal freedom are reduced to vanishing-point than in Mill's individualist order; and that whether this is so or not is a matter for experimental

[1] L 5/292.   [2] L 1/233–4.
[3] Letter of 4 May 1859 (No 287), *New Letters of Thomas Carlyle*, ed. Alexander Carlyle (London and New York, 1904), vol. 2, p. 196.
[4] L 4/283.

verification. Mill constantly protests against the fact that social and legal rules are too often determined merely by the 'likings and dislikings of society',[1] and correctly points out that these are often irrational or are founded on ignorance. But if damage to others is what concerns him most (as he professes), then the fact that their resistance to this or that belief is instinctive, or intuitive, or founded on no rational ground, does not make it the less painful, and, to that extent, damaging to them. Why should rational men be entitled to the satisfaction of their ends more than the irrational? Why not the irrational, if the greatest happiness of the greatest number (and the greatest number are seldom rational) is the sole justified purpose of action? Only a competent social psychologist can tell what will make a given society happiest. If happiness is the sole criterion, then human sacrifice, or the burning of witches, at times when such practices had strong public feeling behind them, did doubtless, in their day, contribute to the happiness of the majority. If there is no other moral criterion, then the question whether a higher balance of happiness was yielded by the slaughter of innocent old women (together with the ignorance and prejudice which made this acceptable), or by the advance in knowledge and rationality which ended such abominations but robbed men of comforting illusions, is to be answered by mere actuarial calculation.

Mill paid no attention to such considerations: nothing could go more violently against all that he felt and believed. At the centre of Mill's thought and feeling lies, not his Utilitarianism, nor the concern about enlightenment, nor about dividing the private from the public domain – for he himself at times concedes that the State may invade the private domain, in order to promote education, hygiene, or social security or justice – but his passionate belief that men are made human by their capacity for choice – choice of evil and good equally. Fallibility, the right to err, as a corollary of the capacity for self-improvement; distrust of symmetry and finality as enemies of freedom – these are the principles which Mill never abandons. He is acutely aware of the many-sidedness of the truth and of the irreducible complexity of life, which rules out the very possibility of any simple solution, or the idea of a final answer to any concrete problem. Greatly daring, and without looking back at the stern intellectual puritanism in which he was brought up, he preaches the necessity of understanding and gaining illumination

[1] L 1/222.

from doctrines that are incompatible with one another – say those of Coleridge and Bentham; he explained in his autobiography, and in his essays on these two writers, the need to understand and learn from both.

III

Kant once remarked that 'Out of the crooked timber of humanity no straight thing was ever made.'[1] Mill believed this deeply. This, and his almost Hegelian refusal to trust simple models and cut and dried formulae to cover complex, contradictory and changing situations, made him a very hesitant and uncertain adherent of organised parties and programmes. Despite his father's advocacy, despite Harriet Taylor's passionate faith in the ultimate solution of all social evils by some great institutional change (in her case that of socialism), he could not rest in the notion of a clearly discernible final goal, because he saw that men differed and evolved, not merely as a result of natural causes, but also because of what they themselves did to alter their own characters, at times in unintended ways. This alone makes their conduct unpredictable, and renders laws or theories, whether inspired by analogies with mechanics or with biology, nevertheless incapable of embracing the complexity and qualitative properties of even an individual character, let alone of a group of men. Hence the imposition of any such construction upon a living society is bound, in his favourite words of warning, to 'dwarf', 'maim', 'cramp', 'wither' human faculties.[2]

His greatest break with his father was brought about by this conviction: by his belief (which he never explicitly admitted) that particular predicaments required each its own specific treatment; that the application of correct judgement in curing a social malady mattered at least as much as knowledge of the laws of anatomy or pharmacology. He was a British empiricist and not a French rationalist, or a German metaphysician, sensitive to day-to-day play of circumstances, differences of 'climate',[3] as well as to the individual nature of each case, as Helvétius or Saint-Simon or Fichte, concerned as they were with the *grandes lignes* of development, were not. Hence his increasing anxiety, as great as Tocqueville's and greater than Montesquieu's, to preserve variety, to keep doors open to change, to resist the dangers of social pressure; and above all his hatred of the human pack in full cry against a victim,

---

[1] loc. cit. (p. 92 above, note 1).   [2] L 3/265, 271 ('maim').   [3] L 3/270.

his desire to protect dissidents and heretics as such. The whole burden of his charge against the progressives (he means Utilitarians and perhaps socialists) is that, as a rule, they do no more than try to alter social opinion in order to make it more favourable to this or that scheme or reform, instead of assailing the monstrous principle itself which says that social opinion 'should be a law to individuals'.[1]

Mill's overmastering desire for variety and individuality for their own sakes emerges in many shapes. He notes that 'Mankind are greater gainers by suffering each other to live as seems good to themselves, than by compelling each to live as seems good to the rest' – an apparent 'truism' which nevertheless, he declares, 'stands ... opposed to the general tendency of existing opinion and practice'.[2] At other times he speaks in sharper terms. He remarks that it is the habit of his time to impose conformity to an 'approved standard', namely 'to desire nothing strongly. Its ideal of character is to be without any marked character; to maim by compression, like a Chinese lady's foot, every part of human nature which stands out prominently, and tends to make the person markedly dissimilar in outline to commonplace humanity.'[3] And again, 'The greatness of England is now all collective: individually small, we only appear capable of anything great by our habit of combining; and with this our moral and religious philanthropists are perfectly contented. But it was men of another stamp than this that made England what it has been; and men of another stamp will be needed to prevent its decline.'[4]

The tone of this, if not the content, would have shocked Bentham; so indeed would this bitter echo of Tocqueville: 'Comparatively speaking, they now read the same things, listen to the same things, see the same things, go to the same places, have their hopes and fears directed to the same objects, have the same rights and liberties, and the same means of asserting them ... All the political changes of the age promote [this assimilation], since they all tend to raise the low and to lower the high. Every extension of education promotes it, because education brings people under common influences ... Improvements in the means of communication promote it', as does 'the ascendancy of public opinion'. There is 'so great a mass of influences hostile to Individuality' that 'In this age, the mere example of nonconformity, the mere refusal to bend

[1] L 1/222.   [2] L 1/226.   [3] L 3/271-2.   [4] L 3/272.

the knee to custom, is itself a service.'[1] We have come to such a pass that mere differences, resistance for its own sake, protest as such, is now enough. Conformity, and the intolerance which is its offensive and defensive arm, are for Mill always detestable, and peculiarly horrifying in an age which thinks itself enlightened; in which, nevertheless, a man can be sent to prison for twenty-one months for atheism; jurymen are rejected and foreigners denied justice because they hold no recognised religious beliefs; no public money is given for Hindu or Muslim schools because an 'imbecile display'[2] is made by an Under-Secretary who declares that toleration is desirable only among Christians but not for unbelievers. It is no better when workers employ 'a moral police'[3] to prevent some members of their trade union being paid higher wages earned by superior skill or industry than the wages paid to those who lack these attributes.

Such conduct is even more loathsome when it interferes with private relations between individuals. He declared that 'what any persons may freely do with respect to sexual relations should be deemed to be an unimportant and purely private matter, which concerns no one but themselves'; that 'to have held any human being responsible to other people and to the world for the fact itself' (apart from such of its consequences as the birth of children, which clearly created duties which should be socially enforced) 'will one day be thought one of the superstitions and barbarisms of the infancy of the human race'.[4] The same seemed to him to apply to the enforcement of temperance or Sabbath observance, or any of the matters on which 'intrusively pious members of society' should be told 'to mind their own business'.[5] No doubt the gossip to which Mill was exposed during his relationship with Harriet Taylor before his marriage to her – the relationship which Carlyle mocked as platonic – made him peculiarly sensitive to this form of social persecution. But what he was to say about it is of a piece with his deepest and most permanent convictions.

Mill's suspicion of democracy as the only just, and yet potentially the most oppressive, form of government springs from the same roots. He wondered uneasily whether centralisation of authority and the inevitable dependence of each on all and

---

[1] L 3/274–5, 269 ('In this age . . . ').   [2] L 2/240 note.   [3] L 4/287.
[4] Diary, 26 March 1854: CW xxvii 664.
[5] L 4/286.

'surveillance of each by all' would not end by grinding all down into 'a tame uniformity of thought, dealings and actions',[1] and produce 'automatons in human form'[2] and *'liberticide'*.[3] Tocqueville had written pessimistically about the moral and intellectual effects of democracy in America: 'Such a power does not destroy,' to quote the passage alluded to earlier, 'but it prevents existence ... it compresses, enervates, extinguishes and stupefies a people'; and turns it into 'a flock of timid and industrious animals, of which the government is the shepherd'.[4] Mill agreed. Yet the only cure for this, as Tocqueville himself maintained (it may be a little half-heartedly), is more democracy,[5] which can alone educate a sufficient number of individuals to independence, resistance and strength. Men's disposition to impose their own views on others is so strong that, in Mill's view, only want of power restricts it; this power is growing; hence unless further barriers are erected it will increase, leading to a proliferation of 'conformers', 'time-servers',[6] hypocrites, created by silencing opinion,[7] and finally to a society where timidity has killed independent thought, and men confine themselves to safe subjects.

Yet if we make the barriers too high, and do not interfere with opinion at all, will this not end, as Burke or the Hegelians have warned, in the dissolution of the social texture, atomisation of society – anarchy? To this Mill replies that the 'inconvenience' arising from 'conduct which neither violates any specific duty to the public, nor occasions perceptible hurt to any assignable individual except himself ... is one which society can afford to bear, for the sake of the greater good of human freedom'.[8] This is tantamount to saying that if society, despite the need for social cohesion, has itself failed to educate its citizens to be civilised men, it has no right to punish them for irritating others, or being misfits, or not conforming to some standard which the majority accepts. A smooth and harmonious society could perhaps be created, at any rate for a time, but it would be purchased at too high a price. Plato saw correctly that if a frictionless society is to emerge the poets

---

[1] *Principles of Political Economy*, book 2, chapter 1: CW ii 209.

[2] L 3/263.

[3] Letter to his wife Harriet, 15 January 1855 (Mill's emphasis): CW xiv 294.

[4] loc. cit. (p. 228 above, note 1).

[5] Which in any case he regarded as inevitable and also, perhaps, to a vision wider than his own time-bound one, ultimately more just and more generous.

[6] L 2/242.   [7] L 2/229.   [8] L 4/282.

must be driven out; what horrifies those who revolt against this policy is not so much the expulsion of the fantasy-mongering poets as such, but the underlying desire for an end to variety, movement, individuality of any kind; a craving for a fixed pattern of life and thought, timeless, changeless and uniform. Without the right of protest, and the capacity for it, there is for Mill no justice, there are no ends worth pursuing. 'If all mankind minus one, were of one opinion, and only one person were of the contrary opinion, mankind would be no more justified in silencing that one person, than he, if he had the power, would be justified in silencing mankind.'[1]

In his lecture in this series, to which I have already referred, R. W. Livingstone, whose sympathy with Mill is not in doubt, charges him with attributing too much rationality to human beings: the ideal of untrammelled freedom may be the right of those who have reached the maturity of their faculties, but of how many men today, or at most times, is this true? Surely Mill asks far too much and is far too optimistic?[2] There is certainly an important sense in which Livingstone is right: Mill was no prophet. Many social developments caused him grief, but he had no inkling of the mounting strength of the irrational forces that have moulded the history of the twentieth century. Burckhardt and Marx, Pareto and Freud were more sensitive to the deeper currents of their own times, and saw a good deal more deeply into the springs of individual and social behaviour. But I know of no evidence that Mill overestimated the enlightenment of his own age, or that he supposed that the majority of men of his own time were mature or rational or likely soon to become so. What he did see before him was the spectacle of some men, civilised by any standards, who were kept down, or discriminated against, or persecuted by prejudice, stupidity, 'collective mediocrity';[3] he saw such men deprived of what he regarded as their most essential rights, and he protested. He believed that all human progress, all human greatness and virtue and freedom, depended chiefly on the preservation of such men and the clearing of paths before them. But he did not want them appointed Platonic Guardians.[4] He thought that

[1] L 2/229.

[2] op. cit. (p. 218 above, note 3), pp. 8–9.

[3] L 3/268.

[4] This is the line which divides him from Saint-Simon and Comte, and from H. G. Wells and the technocrats.

others like them could be educated, and, when they were educated, would be entitled to make choices, and that these choices must not, within certain limits, be blocked or directed by others. He did not merely advocate education and forget the freedom to which it would entitle the educated (as Communists have), or press for total freedom of choice, and forget that without adequate education it would lead to chaos and, as a reaction to it, a new slavery (as anarchists do). He demanded both. But he did not think that this process would be rapid, or easy, or universal: he was on the whole a pessimistic man, and consequently at once defended and distrusted democracy, for which he has been duly attacked, and is still sharply criticised.

Livingstone observed that Mill was acutely conscious of the circumstances of his age, and saw no further than that. This seems to me a just comment. The disease of Victorian England was claustrophobia – there was a sense of suffocation, and the best and most gifted men of the period, Mill and Carlyle, Nietzsche and Ibsen, men both of the left and of the right – demanded more air and more light. The mass neurosis of our age is agoraphobia; men are terrified of disintegration and of too little direction: they ask, like Hobbes's masterless men in a state of nature, for walls to keep out the raging ocean, for order, security, organisation, clear and recognisable authority, and are alarmed by the prospect of too much freedom, which leaves them lost in a vast, friendless vacuum, a desert without paths or landmarks or goals. Our situation is different from that of the nineteenth century, and so are our problems: the area of irrationality is seen to be vaster and more complex than any that Mill had dreamed of. Mill's psychology has become antiquated and grows more so with every discovery that is made. He is justly criticised for paying too much attention to purely spiritual obstacles to the fruitful use of freedom – lack of moral and intellectual light – and too little (although nothing like as little as his detractors have maintained) to poverty, disease and their causes, and to the common sources and the interaction of both; and for concentrating too narrowly on freedom of thought and expression. All this is true. Yet what solutions have we found, with all our new technological and psychological knowledge and great new powers, save the ancient prescription advocated by the creators of humanism – Erasmus and Spinoza, Locke and Montesquieu, Lessing and Diderot – reason, education, self-knowledge, responsibility; above all, self-knowledge? What other hope is there for men, or has there ever been?

IV

Mill's ideal is not original. It is an attempt to fuse rationalism and romanticism: the aim of Goethe and Wilhelm Humboldt; a rich, spontaneous, many-sided, fearless, free, and yet rational, self-directed character. Mill notes that Europeans owe much to 'plurality of paths'.[1] From sheer differences and disagreements sprang toleration, variety, humanity. In a sudden outburst of anti-egalitarian feeling he praises the Middle Ages because men were then more individual and more responsible: men died for ideas, and women were equal to men. He quotes Michelet with approval: 'The poor Middle Ages, its Papacy, its chivalry, its feudality, under what hands did they perish? Under those of the attorney, the fraudulent bankrupt, the false coiner.'[2] This is the language not of a philosophical radical, but of Burke, or Carlyle, or Chesterton. In his passion for the colour and the texture of life Mill has forgotten his list of martyrs, he has forgotten the teachings of his father, of Bentham, or Condorcet. He remembers only Coleridge, only the horrors of a levelling, middle-class society – the grey, conformist congregation that worships the wicked principle that 'it is the absolute social right of every individual, that every other individual shall act in every respect exactly as he ought',[3] or, worse still, 'that it is one man's duty that another should be religious', for 'God not only abominates the act of the misbeliever, but will not hold us guiltless if we leave him unmolested'.[4] These are the shibboleths of Victorian England, and if that is its conception of social justice, it were better dead. In a similar, earlier, moment of acute indignation with the self-righteous defences of the exploitation of the poor, Mill had expressed his enthusiasm for revolution and slaughter, since justice was more precious than life.[5] He was

---

[1] L 3/274.

[2] Translated by Mill from Jules Michelet, *Histoire de France*, vols 1–5 (Paris, 1833–41), book 5, chapter 3 (vol. 3, p. 32), in Mill's review of these volumes: CW xx 252.

[3] L 4/289.　　[4] ibid.

[5] Probably a reference to remarks in a letter to John Sterling, 20–22 October 1831: CW xii 84. These remarks are referred to more directly on p. 224 above: 'a

twenty-five years old when he wrote that. A quarter of a century later, he declared that a civilisation which had not the inner strength to resist barbarism had better succumb.[1] This may not be the voice of Kant, but it is not that of Utilitarianism; rather that of Rousseau or Mazzini.

But Mill seldom continues in this tone. His solution is not revolutionary. If human life is to be made tolerable, information must be centralised and power disseminated. If everyone knows as much as possible, and has not too much power, then we may yet avoid a State which 'dwarfs its men',[2] in which there is 'the absolute rule of the head of the executive over a congregation of isolated individuals, all equals but all slaves';[3] 'with small men no great thing can really be accomplished'.[4] There is a terrible danger in creeds and forms of life which 'cramp', 'stunt', 'dwarf' men.[5] The acute consciousness in our day of the dehumanising effect of mass culture; of the destruction of genuine purposes, both individual and communal, by the treatment of men as irrational creatures to be deluded and manipulated by the media of mass advertising and mass communication – and so 'alienated' from the basic purposes of human beings by being left exposed to the play of the forces of nature interacting with human ignorance, vice, stupidity, tradition, and above all self-deception and institutional blindness – all this was as deeply and painfully felt by Mill as by Ruskin or William Morris. In this matter he differs from them only in his clearer awareness of the dilemma created by the simultaneous needs for individual self-expression and for human community. It is on this theme that the tract on liberty was composed. 'And it is to be feared', Mill added gloomily, that the 'teachings' of his essay 'will retain [their] value a long time'.[6]

Bertrand Russell – Mill's godson – once remarked that the deepest convictions of philosophers are seldom contained in their formal arguments; fundamental beliefs, comprehensive views of life

revolution that would kill all men with an income of more than £500 per annum might improve things greatly'. Ed.

[1] L 4/291.   [2] L 5/310.

[3] *Autobiography*, chapter 6: CW i 201.

[4] L 5/310.

[5] L 3/266, except 'stunt', which is in *Autobiography*, chapter 7 (CW i 260), and *Considerations on Representative Government*, chapter 3 (CW xix 400).

[6] *Autobiography*, chapter 7: CW i 260.

are like citadels which must be guarded against the enemy.[1] Philosophers expend their intellectual power in arguments against actual and possible objections to their doctrines, and although the reasons they find, and the logic that they use, may be complex, ingenious and formidable, they are defensive weapons; the inner fortress itself – the vision of life for the sake of which the war is being waged – will, as a rule, turn out to be relatively simple and unsophisticated. Mill's defence of his position in the tract on liberty is not, as has often been pointed out, of the highest intellectual quality: most of his arguments can be turned against him; certainly none is conclusive, or such as would convince a determined or unsympathetic opponent. From the days of James Stephen, whose powerful attack on Mill's position appeared in the year of Mill's death, to the conservatives and socialists and authoritarians and totalitarians of our day, the critics of Mill have, on the whole, exceeded the number of his defenders. Nevertheless, the inner citadel – the central thesis – has stood the test. It may need elaboration or qualification, but it is still the clearest, most candid, persuasive, and moving exposition of the point of view of those who desire an open and tolerant society. The reason for this is not merely the honesty of Mill's mind, or the moral and intellectual charm of his prose, but the fact that he is saying something true and important about some of the most fundamental characteristics and aspirations of human beings.

Mill is not merely uttering a string of clear propositions (each of which, viewed by itself, is of doubtful plausibility) connected by such logical links as he can supply. He perceived something profound and essential about the destructive effect of man's most successful efforts at self-improvement in modern society; about the unintended consequences of modern democracy, and the fallaciousness and practical dangers of the theories by which some of the worst of these consequences were (and still are) defended. That is why, despite the weakness of the argument, the loose ends, the dated examples, the touch of the finishing governess that Disraeli so maliciously noted, despite the total lack of that boldness of conception which only men of original genius possess, his essay educated his generation, and is controversial still. Mill's central propositions are not truisms, they are not at all self-evident. They are statements of a position which has been resisted and rejected by

[1] loc. cit. (p. xxx above, note 1).

the modern descendants of his most notable contemporaries, Marx, Carlyle, Dostoevsky, Newman, Comte, and they are still assailed because they are still contemporary. *On Liberty* deals with specific social issues in terms of examples drawn from genuine and disturbing issues of its day, and its principles and conclusions are alive in part because they spring from acute moral crises in a man's life, and thereafter from a life spent in working for concrete causes and taking genuine – and therefore at times dangerous – decisions. Mill looked at the questions that puzzled him directly, and not through spectacles provided by any orthodoxy. His revolt against his father's education, his bold avowal of the values of Coleridge and the romantics, was the liberating act that dashed these spectacles to the ground. From these half-truths, too, he liberated himself in turn, and became a thinker in his own right. For this reason, while Spencer and Comte, Taine and Buckle, even Carlyle and Ruskin – figures who loomed very large in their generation – are fast receding into (or have been swallowed by) the shadows of the past, Mill himself remains real.

One of the symptoms of this kind of three-dimensional, rounded, authentic quality is that we feel sure that we can tell where he would have stood on the issues of our own day. Can anyone doubt what position he would have taken on the Dreyfus case, or the Boer War, or Fascism, or Communism? Or, for that matter, on Munich, or Suez, or Budapest, or apartheid, or colonialism, or the Wolfenden report? Can we be so certain with regard to other eminent Victorian moralists? Carlyle or Ruskin or Dickens? Or even Kingsley or Wilberforce or Newman? Surely that alone is some evidence of the permanence of the issues with which Mill dealt and the degree of his insight into them.

V

Mill is usually represented as a just and high-souled Victorian schoolmaster, honourable, sensitive, humane, but 'sober, censorious and sad';[1] something of a goose, something of a prig; a good and noble man, but bleak, sententious and desiccated; a waxwork among other waxworks in an age now dead and gone and stiff with such effigies. His autobiography – one of the most moving accounts of a human life – modifies this impression. Mill was

---

[1] Michael St John Packe, *The Life of John Stuart Mill* (London, 1954), p. 504.

certainly an intellectual, and was well aware, and not at all ashamed, of this fact. He knew that his main interest lay in general ideas in a society largely distrustful of them: 'Englishmen', he wrote to his friend Gustave d'Eichthal, 'habitually distrust the most obvious truths, if the person who advances them is suspected of having any general views.'[1] He was excited by ideas and wanted them to be as interesting as possible. He admired the French for respecting intellectuals as the English did not. He noted that there was a good deal of talk in England about the march of intellect at home, but he remained sceptical. He wondered whether 'our "march of intellect" be not rather a march towards doing without intellect, and supplying our deficiency of giants by the united efforts of a constantly increasing multitude of dwarfs'.[2] The word 'dwarf', and the fear of smallness, pervades all his writings.

Because he believed in the importance of ideas, he was prepared to change his own if others could convince him of their inadequacy, or when a new vision was revealed to him, as it was by Coleridge or Saint-Simon, or, as he believed, by the transcendent genius of Harriet Taylor. He liked criticism for its own sake. He detested adulation, even praise of his own work. He attacked dogmatism in others and was genuinely free from it himself. Despite the efforts of his father and his mentors, he retained an unusually open mind, and his 'still and even cold appearance' and 'a head that reasons as a great Steam-Engine works' were united (to quote his friend Sterling) with 'a warm, upright and really lofty soul'[3] and a touching and pure-hearted readiness to learn from anyone, at any time. He lacked vanity and cared little for his reputation, and therefore did not cling to consistency for its own sake, nor to his own personal dignity, if a human issue was at stake. He was loyal to movements, to causes and to parties, but could not

[1] Letter of 9 February 1830: CW xii 48.

[2] 'On Genius' (1832): CW i 330. [Mill's 'On Genius' is a reply to an anonymous two-part article in the *Monthly Repository* NS 6 (1832), 556–64, 627–34, where the notion of an 'onward march' (556) of intellect is omnipresent. The exact phrase 'march of intellect' does not appear, but 'march of mind' does (557; cf. 558).]

[3] Letter from John Sterling to his son Edward, 29 July 1844, quoted in Anne Kimball Tuell, *John Sterling: A Representative Victorian* (New York, 1941), p. 69 [where 'reasons' is followed by '(?)', perhaps to indicate uncertainty on Tuell's part as to her reading of the preceding word].

be prevailed upon to support them at the price of saying what he did not think to be true.

A characteristic instance of this is his attitude to religion. His father brought him up in the strictest and narrowest atheist dogma. He rebelled against it. He embraced no recognised faith, but he did not dismiss religion, as the French encyclopaedists or the Benthamites had done, as a tissue of childish fantasies and emotions, comforting illusions, mystical gibberish and deliberate lies. He held that the existence of God was possible, indeed probable, but unproven, but that if God was good he could not be omnipotent, since he permitted evil to exist. He would not hear of a being at once wholly good and omnipotent whose nature defied the canons of human logic, since he rejected belief in mysteries as mere attempts to evade agonising issues. If he did not understand (this must have happened often), he did not pretend to understand. Although he was prepared to fight for the rights of others to hold a faith detached from logic, he rejected it himself. He revered Christ as the best man who ever lived, and regarded theism as a noble, though to him unintelligible, set of beliefs. He regarded immortality as possible, but rated its probability very low. He was in fact, a Victorian agnostic who was uncomfortable with atheism and regarded religion as something that was exclusively the individual's own affair. When he was invited to stand for Parliament, to which he was duly elected, he declared that he was prepared to answer any questions that the electors of Westminster might choose to put to him, save those on his religious views. This was not cowardice – his behaviour throughout the election was so candid and imprudently fearless that someone remarked that on Mill's platform God Almighty himself could not expect to be elected. His reason was that a man had an indefeasible right to keep his private life to himself and to fight for this right, if need be. When, at a later date, his stepdaughter Helen Taylor and others upbraided him for not aligning himself more firmly with the atheists, and accused him of temporising and shilly-shallying, he remained unshaken. His doubts were his own property: no one was entitled to extort a confession of faith from him, unless it could be shown that his silence harmed others; since this could not be shown, he saw no reason for publicly committing himself. Like Acton after him, he regarded liberty and religious toleration as the indispensable protection of all true religion, and the distinction made by the Church between spiritual and temporal realms as one of the great achievements of Christianity, inasmuch as it had made possible freedom of opinion. This last he valued beyond all things, and he defended Bradlaugh passionately, although, and because, he did not agree with his opinions.

He was the teacher of a generation, of a nation, but still no more than a teacher, not a creator or an innovator. He is known for no lasting discovery or invention. He made scarcely any significant advance in logic or philosophy or economics or political thought. Yet his range and his capacity for applying ideas to fields in which they would bear fruit were unexampled. He was not original, yet he transformed the structure of the human knowledge of his age.

Because he had an exceptionally honest, open and civilised mind, which found natural expression in lucid and admirable prose; because he combined an unswerving pursuit of the truth with the belief that its house had many mansions, so that even 'one-eyed men' like Bentham might see what men with normal vision would not;[1] because, despite his inhibited emotions and his over-developed intellect, despite his humourless, cerebral, solemn character, his conception of man was deeper, and his vision of history and life wider and less simple, than that of his Utilitarian predecessors or liberal followers, he has emerged as a major political thinker in our own day. He broke with the pseudo-scientific model, inherited from the classical world and the age of reason, of a determined human nature, endowed at all times, everywhere, with the same unaltering needs, emotions, motives, responding differently only to differences of situation and stimulus, or evolving according to some unaltering pattern. For this he substituted (not altogether consciously) the image of man as creative, incapable of self-completion, and therefore never wholly predictable: fallible, a complex combination of opposites, some reconcilable, others incapable of being resolved or harmonised; unable to cease from his search for truth, happiness, novelty, freedom, but with no guarantee, theological or logical or scientific, of being able to attain them; a free, imperfect being, capable of determining his own destiny in circumstances favourable to the development of his reason and his gifts. He was tormented by the problem of free will, and found no better solution for it than anyone else, although at times he thought he had solved it. He believed that it is neither

---

[1] 'Bentham': CW x 94. He goes on: 'Almost all rich veins of original and striking speculation have been opened by systematic half-thinkers.'

rational thought, nor domination over nature, but freedom to choose and to experiment that distinguishes men from the rest of nature; of all his ideas it is this view that has ensured his lasting fame.[1] By freedom he meant a condition in which men were not prevented from choosing both the object and the manner of their worship. For him only a society in which this condition was realised could be called fully human. Its realisation was an ideal which Mill regarded as more precious than life itself.

[1] It will be seen from the general tenor of this essay that I am not in agreement with those who wish to represent Mill as favouring some kind of hegemony of right-minded intellectuals. I do not see how this can be regarded as Mill's considered conclusion; not merely in view of the considerations that I have urged, but of his own warnings against Comtian despotism, which contemplated precisely such a hierarchy. At the same time, he was, in common with a good many other liberals in the nineteenth century both in England and elsewhere, not merely hostile to the influence of uncriticised traditionalism, or the sheer power of inertia, but apprehensive of the rule of the uneducated democratic majority; consequently he tried to insert into his system some guarantees against the vices of uncontrolled democracy, plainly hoping that, at any rate while ignorance and irrationality were still widespread (he was not over-optimistic about the rate of the growth of education), authority would tend to be exercised by the more rational, just and well-informed persons in the community. It is, however, one thing to say that Mill was nervous of majorities as such, and another to accuse him of authoritarian tendencies, of favouring the rule of a rational élite, whatever the Fabians may or may not have derived from him. He was not responsible for the views of his disciples, particularly of those whom he himself had not chosen and never knew. Mill was the last man to be guilty of advocating what Bakunin, in the course of an attack on Marx, described as *la pédantocratie*, the government by professors, which he regarded as one of the most oppressive of all forms of despotism.

[It was in fact Mill who coined the term 'pédantocratie', in a letter of 25 February 1842 to Auguste Comte: CW xiii 502. Comte liked it and adopted it, with Mill's approval (xiii 524): see for example *Catéchisme positiviste* (Paris, 1852), p. 377. Mill used the term again later, in English, at L 5/308 and in *Considerations on Representative Government*, chapter 6: CW xix 439. I have not yet found the term in Bakunin, though he does say in *Gosudarstvennost' i anarkhiya*: 'To be the slaves of pedants – what a fate for humanity!' See p. 112 in *Archives Bakounine*, vol. 3, *Étatisme et anarchie, 1873* (Leiden, 1967), and p. 134 in Michael Bakunin, *Statism and Anarchy*, ed. and trans. Marshall Shatz (Cambridge etc., 1990). Ed.]

FROM HOPE AND FEAR SET FREE

I

DOES knowledge always liberate? The view of the classical Greek philosophers, shared by much, though perhaps not all, Christian theology, is that it does. 'And ye shall know the truth, and the truth shall make you free.'[1] Ancient Stoics and most modern rationalists are at one with Christian teaching on this issue. According to this view freedom is the unimpeded fulfilment of my true nature – unimpeded by obstacles whether external or internal. In the case of the passage from which I have quoted, the freedom in question (I follow Festugière's interpretation on this point) is freedom from sin, that is, from false beliefs about God, nature and myself, which obstruct my understanding. The freedom is that of self-realisation or self-direction – the realisation by the individual's own activity of the true purposes of his nature (however such purposes or such natures are denied), which is frustrated by his misconceptions about the world and man's place in it. If to this I add the corollary that I am rational – that is, that I can understand or know (or at least form a correct belief about) why I do what I do, that is, distinguish between acting (which entails making choices, forming intentions, pursuing goals) and merely behaving (that is, being acted upon by causes the operations of which may be unknown to me or unlikely to be affected by my wishes or attitudes) – then it will follow that knowledge of the relevant facts – about the external world, other persons and my own nature – will remove impediments to my policies that are due to ignorance and delusion.

Philosophers (and theologians, dramatists, poets) have differed widely about the character of man's nature and its ends; what kind and degree of control of the external world is needed in order to achieve fulfilment, complete or partial, of this nature and its ends; whether such a general nature or objective ends exist at all; and

[1] Gospel according to St John, chapter 8, verse 32.

where the frontier dividing the external world of matter and non-rational creatures from active agents is to be found. Some thinkers have supposed that such fulfilment was (or had once been, or would one day be) possible on earth, others have denied this. Some maintained that the ends of men were objective and capable of being discovered by special methods of enquiry, but disagreed on what these were: empirical or a priori; intuitive or discursive; scientific or purely reflective; public or private; confined to specially gifted or fortunate enquirers, or in principle open to any man. Others believed that such ends were subjective, or determined by physical or psychological or social factors, which differed widely. Again, Aristotle, for example, supposed that if external conditions were too unfavourable – if a man suffered Priam's misfortunes – this made self-fulfilment, the proper realisation of one's nature, impossible. On the other hand the Stoics and Epicureans held that complete rational self-control could be achieved by a man whatever his external circumstances, since all that he needed was a sufficient degree of detachment from human society and the external world; to this they added the optimistic belief that the degree sufficient for self-fulfilment was in principle perfectly attainable by anyone who consciously sought independence and autonomy, that is, escape from being the plaything of external forces which he could not control.

Among the assumptions that are common to all these views are:

(i) that things and persons possess natures – definite structures independent of whether or not they are known;
(ii) that these natures or structures are governed by universal and unalterable laws;
(iii) that these structures and laws are, at least in principle, all knowable; and that knowledge of them will automatically keep men from stumbling in the dark and dissipating effort on policies which, given the facts – the nature of things and persons and the laws that govern them – are doomed to failure.

According to this doctrine men are not self-directed and therefore not free when their behaviour is caused by misdirected emotions – for example, fears of non-existent entities, or hatreds due not to a rational perception of the true state of affairs but to illusions, fantasies, results of unconscious memories and forgotten wounds. Rationalisations and ideologies, on this view, are false explanations of behaviour the true roots of which are unknown or ignored or misunderstood; and these in their turn breed further illusions, fantasies and forms of irrational and compulsive behaviour. True liberty consists, therefore, in self-direction: a man is free to the degree that the true explanation of his activity lies in the intentions and motives of which he is conscious, and not in some hidden psychological or physiological condition that would have produced the same effect, that is, the same behaviour (posing as choice), whatever explanation or justification the agent attempted to produce. A rational man is free if his behaviour is not mechanical, and springs from motives and is intended to fulfil purposes of which he is, or can at will be, aware; so that it is true to say that having these intentions and purposes is a necessary, if not sufficient, condition for his behaviour. The unfree man is like someone who is drugged or hypnotised: whatever explanations he may himself advance for his behaviour, it remains unaltered by any change in his ostensible, overt motives and policies; we consider him to be in the grip of forces over which he has no control, not free, when it is plain that his behaviour will be predictably the same whatever reasons he advances for it.

To put matters in this way is to identify rationality and freedom, or at least to go a long way towards it. Rational thought is thought the content or, at least, the conclusions of which obey rules and principles and are not merely items in a causal or random sequence; rational behaviour is behaviour which (at least in principle) can be explained by the actor or observer in terms of motives, intentions, choices, reasons, rules, and not solely of natural laws – causal or statistical, or 'organic' or others of the same logical type (whether explanations in terms of motives, reasons and the like and those in terms of causes, probabilities and so on are 'categorially' different and cannot in principle clash or indeed be relevant to one another is of course a crucial question; but I do not wish to raise it here). To call a man a thief is *pro tanto* to attribute rationality to him: to call him a kleptomaniac is to deny it of him. If degrees of a man's freedom directly depend on (or are identical with) the extent of his knowledge of the roots of his behaviour, then a kleptomaniac who knows himself to be one is, to that extent, free; he may be unable to stop stealing or even to try to do so; but his recognition of this, because he is now – so it is maintained – in a position to choose whether to try to resist this compulsion (even if he is bound to fail) or to let it take its course, renders him not merely more rational (which seems indisputable), but more free.

But is this always so? Is awareness of a disposition or causal characteristic on my part identical with – or does it necessarily provide me with – the power to manipulate or alter it? There is, of course, a clear but platitudinous sense in which all knowledge increases freedom in some respect: if I know that I am liable to epileptic fits, or feelings of class consciousness, or the spellbinding effect of certain kinds of music, I can – in some sense of 'can' – plan my life accordingly; whereas if I do not know this, I cannot do so; I gain some increase in power and, to that extent, in freedom. But this knowledge may also decrease my power in some other respect: if I anticipate an epileptic fit or the onset of some painful, or even agreeable, emotion, I may be inhibited from some other free exercise of my power, or be precluded from some other experience – I may be unable to continue to write poetry, or understand the Greek text which I am reading, or think about philosophy, or get up from my chair: I may, in other words, pay for an increase of power and freedom in one region by a loss of them in another. (I propose to return to this point later, in a slightly different context.)[1] Nor am I necessarily rendered able to control my fits of epilepsy or of class consciousness or addiction to Indian music by recognising their incidence. If by knowledge is meant what the classical authors meant by it – knowledge of facts (not knowledge of 'what to do', which may be a disguised way of stating not that something is the case, but a commitment to certain ends or values, or of expressing, not describing, a decision to act in a certain fashion); if, in other words, I claim to have the kind of knowledge about myself that I might have about others, then even though my sources may be better or my certainty greater, such self-knowledge, it seems to me, may or may not add to the sum total of my freedom. The question is empirical: and the answer depends on specific circumstances. From the fact that every gain in knowledge liberates me in some respect, it does not follow, for the reasons given above, that it will necessarily add to the total sum of freedom that I enjoy: it may, by taking with one hand more than it gives with the other, decrease it. But there is a more radical criticism of this view to be considered. To say that one is free only if one understands oneself (even if this is not a sufficient condition of freedom) presupposes that we have a self to be understood – that there is a structure correctly described as human nature which is

[1] See p. 274 below.

what it is, obeys the laws that it does, and is an object of natural study. This has itself been questioned, notably by certain existentialist philosophers. By these it is maintained that far more is a matter of human choice than has usually and complacently been supposed. Since choice involves responsibility, and some human beings at most times, and most human beings at some times, wish to avoid this burden, there is a tendency to look for excuses and alibis. For this reason men tend to attribute too much to the unavoidable operations of natural or social laws – for instance, to the workings of the unconscious mind, or unalterable psychological reflexes, or the laws of social evolution. Critics who belong to this school (which owes much both to Hegel and Marx and to Kierkegaard) say that some notorious impediments to liberty – say, the social pressures of which J. S. Mill made so much – are not objective forces the existence and effects of which are independent of human wishes or activities or alterable only by means not open to isolated individuals – by revolutions or radical reforms that cannot be engineered at the individual's will. What is maintained is the contrary: that I need not be bullied by others or pressed into conformity by schoolmasters or friends or parents; need never be affected in some way that I cannot help by what priests or colleagues or critics or social groups or classes think or do. If I am so affected, it is because I choose it. I am insulted when I am mocked as a hunchback, a Jew, a black, or unnerved by the feeling that I am suspected of being a traitor, only if I choose to accept the opinion – the valuation – of hunchbacks or race or treason of those by whose views and attitudes I am dominated. But I can always choose to ignore or resist this – to snap my fingers at such views and codes and outlooks; and then I am free.

This is the very doctrine, though built on different premises, of those who drew the portrait of the Stoic sage. If I choose to knuckle under to public sentiment or the values of this or that group or person, the responsibility is mine and not that of outside forces – forces, personal or impersonal, to whose allegedly irresistible influence I attribute my behaviour, attribute it only too eagerly in order to escape blame or self-blame. My behaviour, my character, my personality, according to these critics, is not a mysterious substance or the referent of a pattern of hypothetical general (causal) propositions, but a pattern of choices or of failures to choose which themselves represent a kind of choice to let events take their course, not to assert myself as an active agent. If I am self-critical and face the facts, I may find that I shuffle off my responsibilities too easily.

This applies both in the realms of theory and in those of practical affairs. Thus, if I am a historian, my view of the factors significant in history may well be profoundly affected by my desire to glorify or detract from the reputation of individuals or classes – an act, so it is argued, of free valuation on my part. Once I am aware of this, I can select and judge as I will: 'the facts' never speak – only I, the chooser, the evaluator, the judge, can do so, and do so according to my own sweet will, in accordance with principles, rules, ideals, prejudices, feelings which I can freely view, examine, accept, reject. If I minimise the human cost of a given political or economic policy, in the past or present or future, I shall upon examination often find that I do so because I disapprove of or bear a grudge against the critics or opponents of those who conduct the policy. If I seek to explain away, whether to others or to myself, some unworthy act on my part, on the ground that something – the political or military situation, or my emotion or inner state – was 'too much for me', then I am cheating myself, or others, or both. Action is choice; choice is free commitment to this or that way of behaving, living, and so on; the possibilities are never fewer than two: to do or not to do; be or not be. Hence, to attribute conduct to the unalterable laws of nature is to misdescribe reality: it is not true to experience, verifiably false; and to perpetrate such falsification – as most philosophers and ordinary men have done and are constantly doing – is to choose to evade responsibility for making choices or failing to make them, to choose to deny that to drift down a current of accepted opinion and behave semi-mechanically is itself a kind of choice – a free act of surrender; this is so because it is always possible, though sometimes painful, to ask myself what it is that I really believe, want, value, what it is that I am doing, living for; and having answered as well as I am able, to continue to act in a given fashion or alter my behaviour.

I do not wish to deny that all this needs saying: that to look on the future as already structured, solid with future facts, is conceptually fallacious; that the tendency to account both for the whole of our own behaviour and that of others in terms of forces regarded as being too powerful to resist is empirically mistaken, in that it goes beyond what is warranted by the facts. In its extreme form this doctrine does away with determination at one blow: I am determined by my own choices; to believe otherwise – say, in determinism or fatalism or chance – is itself a choice, and a particularly craven one at that. Yet it is surely arguable that this very tendency itself is a symptom of man's specific nature. Such tendencies as looking on the future as unalterable – a symmetrical analogue of the past – or the quest for excuses, escapist fantasies, flights from responsibility, are themselves psychological data. To be self-deceived is *ex hypothesi* something that I cannot have chosen consciously, although I may have consciously chosen to act in a manner likely to produce this result, without shrinking from this consequence. There is a difference between choices and compulsive behaviour, even if the compulsion is itself the result of an earlier uncompelled choice. The illusions from which I suffer determine the field of my choice; self-knowledge – destruction of the illusions – will alter this field, make it more possible for me to choose genuinely rather than suppose that I have chosen something when, in fact, it has (as it were) chosen me. But in the course of distinguishing between true and counterfeit acts of choice (however this is done – however I discover that I have seen through illusions), I nevertheless discover that I have an ineluctable nature. There are certain things that I cannot do. I cannot (logically) remain rational or sane and believe no general propositions, or remain sane and use no general terms; I cannot retain a body and cease to gravitate. I can perhaps in some sense try to do these things, but to be rational entails knowing that I shall fail. My knowledge of my own nature and that of other things and persons, and of the laws that govern them and me, saves my energies from dissipation or misapplication; it exposes bogus claims and excuses; it fixes responsibilities where they belong and dismisses false pleas of impotence as well as false charges against the truly innocent; but it cannot widen the scope of my liberty beyond frontiers determined by factors genuinely and permanently outside my control. To explain these factors is not to explain them away. Increase of knowledge will increase my rationality, and infinite knowledge would make me infinitely rational; it might increase my powers and my freedom: but it cannot make me infinitely free.

To return to the main theme: How does knowledge liberate me? Let me state the traditional position once again. On the view that I am trying to examine, the classical view which descends to us from Aristotle, from the Stoics, from a great part of Christian theology, and finds its rationalist formulation in the doctrines of Spinoza and his followers both among the German idealists and modern psychologists, knowledge, by uncovering little-recognised and therefore uncontrolled forces that affect my conduct, emancipates me from their despotic force, the greater when they have been concealed and therefore misinterpreted. Why is this so? Because once I have uncovered them, I can seek to direct them, or resist them, or create conditions in which they will be canalised into harmless channels, or turned to use – that is, for the fulfilment of my purposes. Freedom is self-government – whether in politics or in individual life – and anything that increases the control of the self over forces external to it contributes to liberty. Although the frontiers that divide self and personality from 'external' forces, whether in the individual-moral or in the public-social field, are still exceedingly vague – perhaps necessarily so – this Baconian thesis seems valid enough so far as it goes. But its claims are too great. In its classical form it is called the doctrine of self-determination. According to this, freedom consists in playing a part in determining one's own conduct; the greater this part, the greater the freedom. Servitude, or lack of freedom, is being determined by 'external' forces – whether these be physical or psychological; the greater the part played by these forces, the smaller the freedom of the individual. So far, so good. But if it be asked whether the part that I play – my choices, purposes, intentions – might not themselves be determined – caused – to be as they are by 'external' causes, the classical reply seems to be that this does not greatly matter; I am free if and only if I can do as I intended. Whether my state of mind is itself the causal product of something else – physical or psychological, of climate, or blood pressure, or my character – is neither here nor there; it may or may not be so: this, if it is so, may be known or unknown; all that matters, all that those worried about whether a man's acts are free or not wish to know, is whether my behaviour has as a necessary condition my own conscious choice. If it has, I am free in the only sense that any rational being can ask for: whether the choice itself – like the rest of me – is caused or uncaused is not what is at stake; even if it is wholly caused by natural factors, I am no less free.

Anti-determinists have naturally retorted that this merely pushed the problem a step backwards: the 'self' played its part, indeed, but was itself hopelessly 'determined'. It may be worth going back to the origins of this controversy, for, as often happens,

its earliest form is also the clearest. It came up, so far as I can tell, as
a consequence of the interest taken by the early Greek Stoics in
two, at first unconnected, ideas: that of causation, that is, the
conception, new in the fourth century BC, of unbreakable chains of
events in which each earlier event acts as a necessary and sufficient
cause of the later; and the much older notion of individual moral
responsibility. It was perceived as early as the beginning of the next
century that there was something paradoxical, and indeed incoherent, in maintaining that men's states of mind, feeling and will as
well as their actions were links in unbreakable causal chains, and at
the same time that men were responsible, that is, that they could
have acted otherwise than in fact they did.

Chrysippus was the first thinker to face this dilemma, which did
not seem to trouble Plato or Aristotle, and he invented the solution
known as self-determination – the view that so long as men were
conceived of as being acted upon by outside forces without being
able to resist them, they were as stocks and stones, unfree, and the
concept of responsibility was plainly inapplicable to them; if,
however, among the factors that determined behaviour was the
bending of the will to certain purposes, and if, moreover, such a
bending of the will was a necessary (whether or not it was a
sufficient) condition of a given action, then they were free: for the
act depended on the occurrence of a volition and could not happen
without it. Men's acts of will and the characters and dispositions
from which, whether or not they were fully aware of it, such acts
issued, were intrinsic to action: this is what being free meant.

Critics of this position, Epicureans and sceptics, were not slow
to point out that this was but a half-solution. We are told that they
maintained that although it might be that the operations of the will
were a necessary condition of what could properly be called acts,
yet if these operations were themselves links in causal chains,
themselves effects of causes 'external' to the choices, decisions and
so on, then the notion of responsibility remained as inapplicable as
before. One critic[1] called such modified determination *hemidoulia*
– 'half-slavery'. I am only half free if I can correctly maintain that I
should not have done *x* if I had not chosen it, but add that I could
not have chosen differently. Given that I have decided on *x*, my
action has a motive and not merely a cause; my 'volition' is itself
among the causes – indeed, one of the necessary conditions – of my

---

[1] The Cynic Oenamaus.

behaviour, and it is this that is meant by calling me or it free. But if the choice or decision is itself determined, and cannot, causally, be other than what it is, then the chain of causality remains unbroken, and, the critics asserted, I should be no more truly free than I am on the most rigidly determinist assumptions.

It is over this issue that the immense discussion about free will that has preoccupied philosophers ever since originally arose. Chrysippus' answer, that all that I can reasonably ask for is that my own character should be among the factors influencing behaviour, is the central core of the classical doctrine of freedom as self-determination. Its proponents stretch in unbroken line from Chrysippus and Cicero to Aquinas, Spinoza, Locke and Leibniz, Hume, Mill, Schopenhauer, Russell, Schlick, Ayer, Nowell-Smith and the majority of the contributors to the subject in our own day. Thus when a recent writer in this chronological order, Richard Hare, in one of his books[1] distinguishes free acts from mere behaviour by saying that a pointer to whether I am free to do x is provided by asking myself whether it makes sense to ask 'Shall I do x?' or 'Ought I to do x?', he is restating the classical thesis. Hare correctly says that one can ask 'Will I make a mistake?' or 'Will I be wrecked on the sea-shore?' but not 'Shall I make a mistake?' or 'Ought I to be wrecked?'; for to be wrecked or make a mistake cannot be part of a conscious choice or purpose – cannot, in the logical or conceptual sense of the word. And from this he concludes that we distinguish free from unfree behaviour by the presence or absence of whatever it is that makes it intelligible to ask 'Shall I climb the mountain?' but not 'Shall I misunderstand you?' But if, following Carneades, I were to say 'I can indeed ask "Shall I climb the mountain?", but if the answer – and the action – are determined by factors beyond my control, then how does the fact that I pursue purposes, make decisions and so forth liberate me from the causal chain?', this would be regarded as a misconceived enquiry by the Stoics and the entire classical tradition. For if my choice is indispensable to the production of a given effect, then I am not causally determined as, say, a stone or a tree that has no purposes and makes no choices is determined, and that is all that any libertarian can wish to establish.

But no libertarian can in fact accept this. No one genuinely

[1] R. M. Hare, *Freedom and Reason* (Oxford, 1963), chapter 4.

concerned by the problem constituted by the prima facie incompatibility between determinism and freedom to choose between alternatives will settle for saying 'I can do what I choose, but I cannot choose otherwise than as I do.' Self-determination is clearly not the same as mechanical determination. If the determinists are right (and it may well be that they are) then the sort of determination in terms of which human behaviour should be described is not behaviouristic, but precisely Chrysippus' *hemidoulia*. But half a loaf is not the bread that libertarians crave. For if my decisions are wholly determined by antecedent causes, then the mere fact that they are decisions, and the fact that my acts have motives and not only antecedents, do not of themselves provide that line of demarcation between freedom and necessitation, or freedom and its absence, which the ordinary notion of responsibility seems, at least for libertarians, so clearly to entail. It is in this sense that Bacon's followers claim too much.

This may be seen from another angle which will bring us back to the relations of knowledge and liberty. The growth of knowledge increases the range of predictable events, and predictability – inductive or intuitive – despite all that has been said against this position, does not seem compatible with liberty of choice. I may be told that if I say to someone 'I always knew that you would behave with wonderful courage in this situation' the person so complimented will not suppose that his capacity for freedom of choice is being impugned. But that seems to be so only because the word 'knew' is being used, as it were, in a conventionally exaggerated way. When one man says to another 'I know you well: you simply cannot help behaving generously; you could not help it if you tried', the man so addressed may be thought susceptible to flattery, because of the element of complimentary hyperbole in the words 'cannot help' and 'could not ... if you tried'. If the words were intended to be taken literally – if the flatterer meant to be understood as saying 'You can no more help being generous than being old, or ugly, or thinking in English and not in Chinese' – the notion of merit or desert would evaporate, and the compliment would be transformed from a moral into a quasi-aesthetic one.

This may be made clearer if we take a pejorative example: if I were to say of x, 'x can no more help being cruel and malicious than a volcano can help erupting – one should not blame him, only deplore his existence or seek to tame him or restrain him as one would a dangerous animal', x might well feel more deeply insulted than if we lectured him on his habits on the assumption that he was free to choose between acting and refraining from acting as he did, free to choose to listen to our homily or pay no attention to it. The mere fact that it is my character that determines my choices and actions does not, if my character itself and its effects are due to ineluctable causes, render me free in the sense that appears to be required by the notions of responsibility or of moral praise and blame. Knowledge of the causes and conditions that determine my choice – knowledge, indeed, that there are such conditions and causes, knowledge that choice is not free (without analysis of this proposition), knowledge that shows that the notion of moral responsibility is wholly compatible with rigorous determinism, and exposes libertarianism as a confusion due to ignorance or error – that kind of knowledge would assimilate our moral views to aesthetic ones, and would lead us to look on heroism or honesty or justice as we now do on beauty or kindness or strength or genius: we praise or congratulate the possessors of the latter qualities with no implication that they could have chosen to own a different set of characteristics.

This world view, if it became generally accepted, would mark a radical shift of categories. If this ever occurs, it will tend to make us think of much of our present moral and legal outlook, and of a great deal of our penal legislation, as so much barbarism founded on ignorance; it will enlarge the scope and depth of our sympathy; it will substitute knowledge and understanding for attribution of responsibility; it will render indignation, and the kind of admiration that is its opposite, irrational and obsolete; it will expose such notions as desert, merit, responsibility, remorse, and perhaps right and wrong too, as incoherent or, at the very least, inapplicable; it will turn praise and blame into purely corrective or educational instruments, or confine them to aesthetic approval or disapproval. All this it will do, and if truth is on its side, it will benefit mankind thereby. But it will not increase the range of our freedom. Knowledge will render us freer only if in fact there is freedom of choice – if on the basis of our knowledge we can behave differently from the way in which we would have behaved without it – can, not must or do – if, that is to say, we can and do behave differently on the basis of our new knowledge, but need not. Where there is no antecedent freedom – and no possibility of it – it cannot be increased. Our new knowledge will increase our rationality, our grasp of truth will deepen our understanding, add to our power, inner harmony, wisdom, effectiveness, but not, necessarily, to our liberty. If we are free to choose, then an increase in our knowledge may tell us what are the limits of this freedom and what expands or contracts it. But only to know that there are facts and laws that I cannot alter does not itself render me able to alter anything: if I have no freedom to begin with, knowledge will not increase it. If everything is governed by natural laws, then it is difficult to see what could be meant by saying that I can 'use' them better on the basis of my knowledge, unless 'can' is not the 'can' of choice – not the 'can' which applies only to situations in which I am correctly described as being able to choose between alternatives, and am not rigorously determined to choose one rather than the other. In other words, if classical determinism is a true view (and the fact that it does not square with our present usage is no argument against it), knowledge of it will not increase liberty – if liberty does not exist, the discovery that it does not exist will not create it. This goes for self-determinism no less than for its most full-blown mechanistic-behaviourist variety.

The clearest exposition of classical self-determinism is probably that given in his *Ethics* by Spinoza. Stuart Hampshire represents him,[1] it seems to me correctly, as maintaining that the fully rational man does not choose his ends, for his ends are given. The better he understands the nature of men and of the world, the more harmonious and successful will his actions be, but no serious problem of choice between equally acceptable alternatives can ever present itself to him, any more than to a mathematician reasoning correctly from true premises to logically unavoidable conclusions. His freedom consists in the fact that he will not be acted upon by causes whose existence he does not know or the nature of whose influence he does not correctly understand. But that is all. Given Spinoza's premises – that the universe is a rational order, and that to understand the rationality of a proposition or an act or an order is, for a rational being, equivalent to accepting or identifying oneself with it (as in the old Stoic notion) – the notion of choice itself turns out to depend upon the deficiencies of knowledge, the degree of ignorance. There is only one correct answer to any problem of conduct, as to any problem of theory. The correct answer having been discovered, the rational man logically cannot

---

[1] Stuart Hampshire, 'Spinoza and the Idea of Freedom', *Proceedings of the British Academy* 46 (1960), 195–215.

but act in accordance with it: the notion of free choice between alternatives no longer has application. He who understands everything understands the reasons which make it as it is and not otherwise, and being rational cannot wish it to be otherwise than as it is. This may be an unattainable (and perhaps even, when thought through, an incoherent) ideal, but it is this conception that underlies the notion that an increase in knowledge is *eo ipso* always an increase in freedom, that is, an escape from being at the mercy of what is not understood. Once something is understood or known (and only then), it is, on this view, conceptually impossible to describe oneself as being at the mercy of it. Unless this maximal rationalist assumption is made, it does not seem to me to follow that more knowledge necessarily entails an increase in the total sum of freedom; it may or may not – this, as I hope to show, is largely an empirical question. To discover that I cannot do what I once believed that I could will render me more rational – I shall not beat my head against stone walls – but it will not necessarily make me freer; there may be stone walls wherever I look; I may myself be a portion of one; a stone myself, only dreaming of being free.

There are two further points to be noted with regard to the relationship of freedom and knowledge:

(*a*) There is the well-known objection, urged principally by Karl Popper, that the idea of total self-knowledge is in principle incoherent, because if I can predict what I shall do in the future, this knowledge itself is an added factor in the situation that may cause me to alter my behaviour accordingly; and the knowledge that this is so is itself an added factor, which may cause me to alter that, and so on *ad infinitum*. Therefore total self-prediction is logically impossible. This may be so: but it is not an argument against determinism as such (nor does Popper so represent it) – only against self-prediction. If *x* can predict the total behaviour of *y*, and *y* predict the total behaviour of *x* (and they do not impart their prophecies to one another), that is all that determinism needs. I cannot be self-consciously spontaneous; therefore I cannot be self-consciously aware of all my states if spontaneity is among them. It does not follow that I can never be spontaneous; nor that, if I am, this state cannot be known to exist while it is occurring, although it cannot be so known to me. For this reason I conclude that, in principle, Popper's argument does not (and is not meant to) refute determinism.

(*b*) Stuart Hampshire, in the course of some recent remarks,[1] advances the view that self-prediction is (logically) impossible. When I say 'I know that I shall do *x*' (as against, for instance, '*x* will happen to me', or 'You will do *x*'), I am not contemplating myself, as I might someone else, and giving tongue to a conjecture about myself and my future acts, as I might be doing about someone else or about the behaviour of an animal – for that would be tantamount (if I understand him rightly) to looking upon myself from outside, as it were, and treating my own acts as mere caused events. In saying that I know that I shall do *x*, I am, on this view, saying that I have decided to do *x*: for to predict that I shall in certain circumstances in fact do *x* or decide to do *x*, with no reference to whether or not I have already decided to do it – to say 'I can tell you now that I shall in fact act in manner *x*, although I am, as a matter of fact, determined to do the very opposite' – does not make sense. Any man who says 'I know myself too well to believe that, whatever I now decide, I shall do anything other than *x* when the circumstances actually arise' is in fact, if I interpret Hampshire's views correctly, saying that he does not really, that is, seriously, propose to set himself against doing *x*, that he does not propose even to try to act otherwise, that he has in fact decided to let events take their course. For no man who has truly decided to try to avoid *x* can, in good faith, predict his own failure to act as he has decided. He may fail to avoid *x*, and he may predict this; but he cannot both decide to try to avoid *x* and predict that he will not even try to do this; for he can always try; and he knows this: he knows that this is what distinguishes him from non-human creatures in nature. To say that he will fail even to try is tantamount to saying that he has decided not to try. In this sense 'I know' means 'I have decided' and cannot in principle be predictive.

That, if I have understood it, is Hampshire's position, and I have a good deal of sympathy with it, for I can see that self-prediction is often an evasive way of disclaiming responsibility for difficult decisions, while deciding in fact to let events take their course, disguising this by attributing responsibility for what occurs to my own allegedly unalterable nature. But I agree with Hampshire's critics in the debate, whom I take to be maintaining that, although

---

[1] Iris Murdoch, S. N. Hampshire, P. L. Gardiner and D. F. Pears, 'Freedom and Knowledge', in D. F. Pears (ed.), *Freedom and the Will* (London, 1963), pp. 80–104.

the situation he describes may often occur, yet circumstances may exist in which it is possible for me both to say that I am, at this moment, resolved not to do x, and at the same time to predict that I shall do x, because I am not hopeful that, when the time comes, I shall in fact even so much as try to resist doing x. I can, in effect, say 'I know myself well. When the crisis comes, do not rely on me to help you. I may well run away; although I am at this moment genuinely resolved not to be cowardly and to do all I can to stay at your side. My prediction that my resolution will not in fact hold up is based on knowledge of my own character, and not on my present state of mind; my prophecy is not a symptom of bad faith (for I am not, at this moment, vacillating) but, on the contrary, of good faith, of a wish to face the facts. I assure you in all sincerity that my present intention is to be brave and resist. Yet you would run a great risk if you relied too much on my present decision; it would not be fair to conceal my past failures of nerve from you.' I can say this about others, despite the most sincere resolutions on their part, for I can foretell how in fact they will behave; they can equally predict this about me. Despite Hampshire's plausible and tempting argument, I believe that such objective self-knowledge is possible and occurs; and his argument does not therefore appear to me to lessen the force of the determinist thesis. It seems to me that I can, at times, though perhaps not always, place myself, as it were, at an outside vantage-point, and contemplate myself as if I were another human being, and calculate the chances of my sticking to my present resolution with almost the same degree of detachment and reliability as I should have if I were judging the case of someone else with all the impartiality that I could muster. If this is so, then 'I know how I shall act' is not necessarily a statement of decision: it can be purely descriptive. Self-prediction of this kind, provided that it does not claim to be too exact or infallible, and meets Popper's objection, cited above, by remaining tentative, allowing for possible alterations of conduct as a result of the self-prediction itself – seems possible and compatible with determinism.

In other words, I see no reason to suppose that a deterministic doctrine, whether about one's own behaviour or that of others, is in principle incoherent, or incompatible with making choices, provided that these choices are regarded as being themselves no less determined than other phenomena. Such knowledge, or well-founded belief, seems to me to increase the degree of rationality, efficiency, power; the only freedom to which it necessarily contributes is freedom from illusions. But this is not the basic sense of the term about which controversy has been boiling for twenty-two centuries.

I have no wish to enter into the waters of the freewill problem more deeply than I already have. But I should like to repeat what I have indeed said elsewhere, and for which I have been severely taken to task by determinists: that if a great advance were made in psychophysiology; if, let us suppose, a scientific expert were to hand me a sealed envelope, and ask me to note all my experiences – both introspective and others – for a limited period – say half-an-hour – and write them down as accurately as I could; and if I then did this to the best of my ability, and after this opened the envelope and read the account, which turned out to tally to a striking degree with my log-book of my experience during the last half-hour, I should certainly be shaken; and so I think would others. We should then have to admit, with or without pleasure, that aspects of human behaviour which had been believed to be within the area of the agent's free choice turned out to be subject to discovered causal laws. Our recognition of this might itself alter our behaviour, perhaps for the happier and more harmonious; but this welcome result itself would be a causal product of our new awareness. I cannot see why such discoveries should be considered impossible, or even particularly improbable; they would bring about a major transformation of psychology and sociology; after all, great revolutions have occurred in other sciences in our own day.

The principal difference, however, between previous advances and this imaginary breakthrough (and it is with this surmise that most of my critics have disagreed) is that besides effecting a vast alteration in our empirical knowledge, it would alter our conceptual framework far more radically than the discoveries of the physicists of the seventeenth or twentieth century, or of the biologists of the nineteenth, have changed it. Such a break with the past, in psychology alone, would do great violence to our present concepts and usages. The entire vocabulary of human relations would suffer radical change. Such expressions as 'I should not have done x', 'How could you have chosen x?' and so on, indeed the entire language of the criticism and assessment of one's own and others' conduct, would undergo a sharp transformation, and the expressions we needed both for descriptive and for practical – corrective, deterrent, hortatory – purposes (what others would be open to a consistent determinist?) would necessarily be vastly different from the language which we now use.

It seems to me that we should be unwise to underestimate the effect of robbing praise, blame, a good many counterfactual propositions, and the entire network of concepts concerned with freedom, choice, responsibility of much of their present function and meaning. But it is equally important to insist that the fact that such a transformation could occur – or would, at any rate, be required – does not, of course, have any tendency to show that determinism is either true or false; it is merely a consequence which those who accept it as true tend not to recognise sufficiently. I only wish to add that the further issue, whether the truth of determinism is or is not an empirical question, is itself unclear. If so revolutionary an advance in psychophysiological knowledge were achieved, the need of new concepts to formulate it, and of the consequent modification (to say the least) of concepts in other fields, would itself demonstrate the relative vagueness of the frontiers between the empirical and the conceptual. If these empirical discoveries were made, they might mark a greater revolution in human thought than any that has gone before.

It is idle to speculate on the transformation of language – or of ideas (these are but alternative ways of saying the same thing) – that would be brought about by the triumph of exact knowledge in this field. But would such an advance in knowledge necessarily constitute an overall increase in freedom? Freedom from error, from illusion, fantasy, misdirection of emotions – certainly all these. But is this the central meaning of the word as we commonly use it in philosophy or common speech?

II

I do not, of course, wish to deny that when we say that a man is free – or freer than he was before – we may be using the word to denote moral freedom, or independence, or self-determination. This concept, as has often been pointed out, is far from clear: the central terms – willing, intention, action, and the related notions – conscience, remorse, guilt, inner versus outer compulsion, and so on – stand in need of analysis, which itself entails a moral psychology that remains unprovided; and in the meanwhile the notion of moral independence – of what is, or should be, independent of what, and how this independence is achieved –

remains obscure. Moreover, it seems doubtful whether we should describe a man as being free if his conduct displayed unswerving regularities, issuing (however this is established) from his own thoughts, feelings, acts of will, so that we should be inclined to say that he could not behave otherwise than as he did. Predictability may or may not entail determinism; but if we were in a position to be so well acquainted with a man's character, reactions, outlook that, given a specific situation, we felt sure that we could predict how he would act, better perhaps than he could himself, should we be tempted to describe him as being a typical example of a man morally – or otherwise – free? Should we not think that a phrase used by Patrick Gardiner, a 'prisoner of his personality', described him better?[1] So aptly, indeed, that he might, in certain cases, come to accept it – with regret or satisfaction – himself? A man so hidebound by his own habits and outlook is not the paradigm of human freedom.

The central assumption of common thought and speech seems to me to be that freedom is the principal characteristic that distinguishes man from all that is non-human; that there are degrees of freedom, degrees constituted by the absence of obstacles to the exercise of choice; the choice being regarded as not itself determined by antecedent conditions, at least not as being wholly so determined. It may be that common sense is mistaken in this matter, as in others; but the onus of refutation is on those who disagree. Common sense may not be too well aware of the full variety of such obstacles: they may be physical or psychical, 'inner' and 'outer', or complexes compounded of both elements, difficult and perhaps conceptually impossible to unravel, due to social factors and/or individual ones. Common opinion may oversimplify the issue; but it seems to me to be right about its essence: freedom is to do with the absence of obstacles to action. These obstacles may consist of physical power, whether of nature or of men, that prevents our intentions from being realised: geographical conditions or prison walls, armed men or the threat (deliberately used as a weapon or unintended) of lack of food or shelter or other necessities of life; or again they may be psychological: fears and 'complexes', ignorance, error, prejudice, illusions, fantasies, compulsions, neuroses and psychoses – irrational factors of many kinds. Moral freedom – rational self-control – knowledge of what

[1] op. cit. (p. 266 above, note 1), p. 92.

is at stake, and of what is one's motive in acting as one does; independence of the unrecognised influence of other persons or of one's known personal past or that of one's group or culture; destruction of hopes, fears, desires, loves, hatreds, ideals, which will be seen to be groundless once they are inspected and rationally examined – these indeed bring liberation from obstacles, some of the most formidable and insidious in the path of human beings; their full effect, despite the acute but scattered insights of moralists from Plato to Marx and Schopenhauer, is beginning to be understood adequately only in the present century, with the rise of psychoanalysis and the perception of its philosophical implications. It would be absurd to deny the validity of this sense of the concept of freedom, or of its intimate logical dependence on rationality and knowledge. Like all freedom it consists of, or depends on, the removal of obstacles, in this case of psychological impediments to the full use of human powers to whatever ends men choose; but these constitute only one category of such obstacles, however important and hitherto inadequately analysed. To emphasise these to the exclusion of other classes of obstacles, and other better recognised forms of freedom, leads to distortion. Yet it is this, it seems to me, that has been done by those who, from the Stoics to Spinoza, Bradley and Stuart Hampshire, have confined freedom to self-determination.

To be free is to be able to make an unforced choice; and choice entails competing possibilities – at the very least two 'open', unimpeded alternatives. And this, in its turn, may well depend on external circumstances which leave only some paths unblocked. When we speak of the extent of freedom enjoyed by a man or a society, we have in mind, it seems to me, the width or extent of the paths before them, the number of open doors, as it were, and the extent to which they are open. The metaphor is imperfect, for 'number' and 'extent' will not really do. Some doors are much more important than others – the goods to which they lead are far more central in an individual's or society's life. Some doors lead to other open doors, some to closed ones; there is actual and there is potential freedom – depending on how easily some closed doors can be opened, given existing or potential resources, physical or mental. How is one to measure one situation against another? How is one to decide whether a man who is obstructed neither by other persons nor by circumstances from, let us say, the acquisition of adequate security or of material necessities and comforts, but is

debarred from free speech and association, is less or more free than
one who finds it impossible, because of, let us say, the economic
policies of his government, to obtain more than the necessities of
life, but who possesses greater opportunities of education or of free
communication or association with others? Problems of this type
will always arise – they are familiar enough in Utilitarian literature,
and indeed in all forms of non-totalitarian practical politics. Even if
no hard and fast rule can be provided, it still remains the case that
the measure of the liberty of a man or a group is, to a large degree,
determined by the range of choosable possibilities.

If a man's area of choice, whether 'physical' or 'mental', is
narrow, then however contented with it he may be, and however
true it may be that the more rational a man is, the clearer the one
and only rational path will be to him and the less likely will he be
to vacillate between alternatives (a proposition which seems to me
to be fallacious), neither of these situations will necessarily make
him more free than a man whose range of choice is wider. To
remove obstacles by removing desire to enter upon, or even
awareness of, the path on which the obstacles lie, may contribute to
serenity, contentment, perhaps even wisdom, but not to liberty.
Independence of mind – sanity and integration of personality,
health and inner harmony – are highly desirable conditions, and
they entail the removal of a sufficient number of obstacles to
qualify for being regarded, for that reason alone, as a species of
freedom – but only one species among others. Someone may say
that it is at least unique in this: that this kind of freedom is a
necessary condition for all other kinds of freedom – for if I am
ignorant, obsessed, irrational, I am thereby blinded to the facts, and
a man so blinded is, in effect, as unfree as a man whose possibilities
are objectively blocked. But this does not seem to me to be true. If
I am ignorant of my rights, or too neurotic (or too poor) to benefit
by them, that makes them useless to me; but it does not make them
non-existent; a door is closed to a path that leads to other, open,
doors. To destroy or lack a condition for freedom (knowledge,
money) is not to destroy that freedom itself; for its essence does
not lie in its accessibility, although its value may do so. The more
avenues men can enter, the broader those avenues, the more
avenues that each opens into, the freer they are; the better men
know what avenues lie before them, and how open they are, the
freer they will know themselves to be. To be free without knowing
it may be a bitter irony, but if a man subsequently discovers that

doors were open although he did not know it, he will reflect bitterly not about his lack of freedom but about his ignorance. The extent of freedom depends on opportunities of action, not on knowledge of them, although such knowledge may well be an indispensable condition for the use of freedom, and although impediments in the path to it are themselves a deprivation of freedom – of freedom to know. Ignorance blocks paths, and knowledge opens them. But this truism does not entail that freedom implies awareness of freedom, still less that they are identical.

It is worth noting that it is the actual doors that are open that determine the extent of someone's freedom, and not his own preferences. A man is not free merely when there are no obstacles, psychological or otherwise, in the way of his wishes – when he can do as he likes – for in that case a man might be rendered free by altering not his opportunities of action, but his desires and dispositions. If a master can condition his slaves to love their chains he does not thereby prima facie increase their liberty, although he may increase their contentment or at least decrease their misery. Some unscrupulous managers of men have, in the course of history, used religious teachings to make men less discontented with brutal and iniquitous treatment. If such measures work, and there is reason to think that they do so only too often, and if the victims have learnt not to mind their pains and indignities (like Epictetus, for example), then some despotic systems should presumably be described as creators of liberty; for by eliminating distracting temptations, and 'enslaving' wishes and passions, they create (on these assumptions) more liberty than institutions that expand the area of individual or democratic choice and thereby produce the worrying need to select, to determine oneself in one direction rather than another – the terrible burden of the *embarras de choix* (which has itself been taken to be a symptom of irrationality by some thinkers in the rationalist tradition). This ancient fallacy is by now too familiar to need refutation. I only cite it in order to emphasise the crucial distinction between the definition of liberty as nothing but the absence of obstacles to doing as I like (which could presumably be compatible with a very narrow life, narrowed by the influence upon me of personal or impersonal forces, education or law, friend or foe, religious teacher or parent, or even consciously contracted by myself), and liberty as a range of objectively open possibilities, whether these are desired or not, even though it is difficult or impossible to give rules for measuring or comparing degrees of it, or for assessing different situations with regard to it.

There is, of course, a sense, with which all moral philosophers are well acquainted, in which the slave Epictetus is more free than his master or the Emperor who forced him to die in exile; or that in which stone walls do not a prison make. Nevertheless, such statements derive their rhetorical force from the fact that there is a more familiar sense in which a slave is the least free of men, and stone walls and iron bars are serious impediments to freedom; nor are moral and physical or political or legal freedoms mere homonyms. Unless some kernel of common meaning – whether a single common characteristic or a 'family resemblance' – is kept in mind, there is the danger that one or other of these senses will be represented as fundamental, and the others will be tortured into conformity with it, or dismissed as trivial or superficial. The most notorious examples of this process are the sophistries whereby various types of compulsion and thought-control are represented as means to, or even as constitutive of, 'true' freedom, or, conversely, liberal political or legal systems are regarded as sufficient means of ensuring not only the freedom of, but opportunities for the use of such freedom by, persons who are too irrational or immature, owing to lack of education or other means of mental development, to understand or benefit by such rules or laws. It is therefore the central meaning of the term, if there is one, that it is important to establish.

There is yet another consideration regarding knowledge and liberty to which I should like to return.[1] It is true that knowledge always, of necessity, opens some doors, but does it never close others? If I am a poet, may it not be that some forms of knowledge will curtail my powers and thereby my liberty too? Let us suppose that I require as a stimulus to my imagination illusions and myths of a certain kind which are provided by the religion in which I have been brought up or to which I have been converted. Let us assume that some honourable rationalist refutes these beliefs, shatters my illusions, dissipates the myths; may it not be that my clear gain in knowledge and rationality is paid for by the diminution or destruction of my powers as a poet? It is easy enough to say that what I have lost is a power that fed on illusions or irrational states

---

[1] See p. 255 above.

and attitudes which the advance of knowledge has destroyed; that some powers are undesirable (like the power of self-deception) and that, in any case, powers are powers and not liberties. It may be said that an increase in knowledge cannot (this would, I think, be claimed as an analytic truth) diminish my freedom; for to know the roots of my activity is to be rescued from servitude to the unknown – from stumbling in a darkness populated with figments which breed fears and irrational conduct. Moreover, it will be said that as a result of the destruction of my idols I have clearly gained in freedom of self-determination; for I can now give a rational justification of my beliefs, and the motives of my actions are clearer to me. But if I am less free to write the kind of poetry that I used to write, is there not now a new obstacle before me? Have not some doors been closed by the opening of others? Whether ignorance is or is not bliss in these circumstances is another question. The question I wish to ask – and one to which I do not know the answer – is whether such absence of knowledge may not be a necessary condition for certain states of mind or emotion in which alone certain impediments to some forms of creative labour are absent. This is an empirical question, but on the answer to it the answer to a larger question depends: whether knowledge never impedes, always increases, the sum total of human freedom.

Again, if I am a singer, self-consciousness – the child of knowledge – may inhibit the spontaneity that may be a necessary condition of my performance, as the growth of culture was thought by Rousseau and others to inhibit the joys of barbarian innocence. It does not matter greatly whether this particular belief is true; the simple uncivilised savage may have known fewer joys than Rousseau supposed; barbarism may not be a state of innocence at all. It is enough to allow that there are certain forms of knowledge that have the psychological effect of preventing kinds of self-expression which, on any showing, must be considered as forms of free activity. Reflection may ruin my painting if this depends on not thinking; my knowledge that a disease, for which no cure has been discovered, is destroying me or my friend, may well sap my particular creative capacity, and inhibit me in this or that way; and to be inhibited – whatever its long-term advantages – is not to be rendered more free. It may be replied to this that if I am suffering from a disease and do not know it, I am less free than one who knows, and can at least try to take steps to check it, even if the disease has so far proved to be incurable; that not to diagnose it will certainly lead to dissipation of effort in mistaken directions, and will curtail my freedom by putting me at the mercy of natural forces the character of which, because I do not recognise it, I cannot rationally discount or cope with. This is indeed so. Such knowledge cannot decrease my freedom as a rational being, but it may finish me as an artist. One door opens, and as a result of this another shuts.

Let me take another example. Resistance against vast odds may work only if the odds are not fully known; otherwise it may seem irrational to fight against what, even if it is not known to be irresistible, can be believed with a high degree of probability to be so. For it may be my very ignorance of the odds that creates a situation in which alone I resist successfully. If David had known more about Goliath, if the majority of the inhabitants of Britain had known more about Germany in 1940, if historical probabilities could be reduced to something approaching a reliable guide to action, some achievements might never have taken place. I discover that I suffer from a fatal disease. This discovery makes it possible for me to try to find a cure – which was not possible so long as I was ignorant of the causes of my condition. But supposing that I satisfy myself that the weight of probability is against the discovery of an antidote, that once the poison has entered into the system death must follow; that the pollution of the atmosphere as the result of the discharge of a nuclear weapon cannot be undone. Then what is it that I am now more free to do? I may seek to reconcile myself to what has occurred, not kick against the pricks, arrange my affairs, make my will, refrain from a display of sorrow or indignation inappropriate when facing the inevitable – this is what 'stoicism' or 'taking things philosophically' has historically come to mean. But even if I believe that reality is a rational whole (whatever this may mean), and that any other view of it – for instance, as being equally capable of realising various incompatible possibilities – is an error caused by ignorance, and if I therefore regard everything in it as being necessitated by reason – what I myself should necessarily will it to be as a wholly rational being – the discovery of its structure will not increase my freedom of choice. It will merely set me beyond hope and fear – for these are symptoms of ignorance or fantasy – and beyond choices too, since choosing entails the reality of at least two alternatives, say action and inaction. We are told that the Stoic Posidonius said to the pain that was tormenting him 'Do your worst, pain; no matter what you do, you cannot make me hate you.'[1] But Posidonius was a rationalistic determinist: whatever truly is, is as it should be; to wish it to be otherwise is a sign of irrationality; rationality implies that choice – and the freedom defined in terms of its possibility – is an illusion, not widened but killed by true knowledge.

Knowledge increases autonomy both in the sense of Kant, and in that of Spinoza and his followers. I should like to ask once more: is all liberty just that? The advance of knowledge stops men from wasting their resources upon delusive projects. It has stopped us from burning witches or flogging lunatics or predicting the future by listening to oracles or looking at the entrails of animals or the flight of birds. It may yet render many institutions and decisions of the present – legal, political, moral, social – obsolete, by showing them to be as cruel and stupid and incompatible with the pursuit of justice or reason or happiness or truth as we now think the burning of widows or eating the flesh of an enemy to acquire skills. If our powers of prediction, and so our knowledge of the future, become much greater, then, even if they are never complete, this may radically alter our view of what constitutes a person, an act, a choice; and *eo ipso* our language and our picture of the world. This may make our conduct more rational, perhaps more tolerant, charitable, civilised, it may improve it in many ways, but will it increase the area of free choice? For individuals or groups? It will certainly kill some realms of the imagination founded upon non-rational beliefs, and for this it may compensate us by making some of our ends more easily or harmoniously attainable. But who shall say if the balance will necessarily be on the side of wider freedom? Unless one establishes logical equivalences between the notions of freedom, self-determination and self-knowledge in some a priori fashion – as Spinoza and Hegel and their modern followers seek to do – why need this be true? Stuart Hampshire and E. F. Carritt, in dealing with the topic, maintain that, faced with any situation, one can always choose at least between trying to do something and letting things take their course. Always? If it makes sense to say that there is an external world, then to know it, in the descriptive sense of 'know', is not to alter it. As for the other sense of 'know' – the pragmatic, in which 'I know what I shall do' is akin to 'I know what to do', and registers not a piece of information but a decision to alter things in a certain way – would it not wither if psycho-

---

[1] loc. cit. (p. 31 above, note 1).

physiology advanced far enough? For, in that event, may not my resolution to act or not to act resemble more and more the recommendation of Canute's courtiers?

Knowledge, we are told, extends the boundaries of freedom, and this is an a priori proposition. Is it inconceivable that the growth of knowledge will tend more and more successfully to establish the determinist thesis as an empirical truth, and explain our thoughts and feelings, wishes and decisions, our actions and choices, in terms of invariant, regular, natural successions, to seek to alter which will seem almost as irrational as entertaining a logical fallacy? This was, after all, the programme and the belief of many respected philosophers, as different in their outlooks as Spinoza, Holbach, Schopenhauer, Comte, the behaviourists. Would such a consummation extend the area of freedom? In what sense? Would it not rather render this notion, for want of a contrasting one, altogether otiose, and would not this constitute a novel situation? The 'dissolution' of the concept of freedom would be accompanied by the demise of that sense of 'know' in which we speak not of knowing that, but of knowing what to do, to which Hampshire and Hart have drawn attention;[1] for if all is determined, there is nothing to choose between, and so nothing to decide. Perhaps those who have said of freedom that it is the recognition of necessity were contemplating this very situation. If so, their notion of freedom is radically different from those who define it in terms of conscious choice and decision.

I wish to make no judgement of value: only to suggest that to say that knowledge is a good is one thing; to say that it is necessarily, in all situations, compatible with, still more that it is on terms of mutual entailment with (or even, as some seem to suppose, is literally identical with), freedom, in most of the senses in which this word is used, is something very different. Perhaps the second assertion is rooted in the optimistic view – which seems to be at the heart of much metaphysical rationalism – that all good things must be compatible, and that therefore freedom, order, knowledge, happiness, a closed future (and an open one?) must be at least compatible, and perhaps even entail one another in a systematic

---

[1] Stuart Hampshire and H. L. A. Hart, 'Decision, Intention and Certainty', *Mind* 67 (1958), 1–12.

fashion. But this proposition is not self-evidently true, if only on empirical grounds. Indeed, it is perhaps one of the least plausible beliefs ever entertained by profound and influential thinkers.

OTHER WRITINGS ON LIBERTY

My intellectual path

1. Topics & issues:

2. Freedom

3.

4.

5.

6.

7.

Berlin's notes for 'My Intellectual Path'

LIBERTY

WHAT IS political liberty? In the ancient world, particularly among the Greeks, to be free was to be able to participate in the government of one's city. The laws were valid only if one had had the right to take part in making and unmaking them. To be free was not to be forced to obey laws made by others *for* one, but not *by* one. This kind of democracy entailed that government and laws could penetrate into every province of life. Man was not free, nor did he claim freedom, from such supervision. All democrats claimed was that every man was equally liable to criticism, investigation, and if need be arraignment before the laws, or other arrangements, in the establishing and maintaining of which all the citizens had the right to participate.

In the modern world, a new idea – most clearly formulated by Benjamin Constant – makes itself felt, namely that there is a province of life – private life – with which it is thought undesirable, save in exceptional circumstances, for public authority to interfere. The central question posed by the ancient world is 'Who shall govern me?' Some said a monarch, some said the best, or the richest, or the bravest, or the majority, or the law courts, or the unanimous vote of all. In the modern world, an equally important question is 'How much government should there be?' The ancient world assumed that life was one, and that laws and the government covered the whole of it – there was no reason to protect any corner of it from such supervision. In the modern world, whether historically because of struggles of the Churches against intervention by the secular State, or of the State against the Church, or as a result of the growth of private enterprise, industry, commerce, and its desire for protection against State interference, or for whatever reason, we proceed on the assumption that there is a frontier between public and private life; and that, however small the private sphere may be, within it I can do as I please – live as I like, believe what I want, say what I please – provided this does not interfere with the similar rights of others, or undermine the order which makes this kind of arrangement possible. This is the classical liberal view, in whole or part expressed in various declarations of the rights of man in America and France, and in the writings of men like Locke, Voltaire, Tom Paine, Constant and John Stuart Mill. When we speak of civil liberties or civilised values, this is part of what is meant.

The assumption that men need protection against each other and against the government is something which has never been fully accepted in any part of the world, and what I have called the ancient Greek or classical point of view comes back in the form of arguments such as this: 'You say that an individual has the right to choose the kind of life he prefers. But does this apply to everyone? If the individual is ignorant, immature, uneducated, mentally crippled, denied adequate opportunities of health and development, he will not know how to choose. Such a person will never truly know what it is he really wants. If there are people who understand what human nature is and what it craves, and if they do for others, perhaps by some measure of control, what these others would be doing for themselves if they were wiser, better informed, maturer, more developed, are they curtailing their freedom? They are interfering with people as they are, but only in order to enable them to do what they would do if they knew enough, or were always at their best, instead of yielding to irrational motives, or behaving childishly, or allowing the animal side of their nature the upper hand. Is this then interference at all? If parents or teachers compel unwilling children to go to school or to work hard, in the name of what those children must really want, even though they may not know it, since that is what all men as such must want because they are human, then are they curtailing the liberty of the children? Surely not. Teachers and parents are bringing out their submerged or real selves, and catering to their needs, as against the transient demands of the more superficial self which greater maturity will slough off like a skin.'

If you substitute for parents a Church or a Party or a State, you get a theory on which much modern authority is based. We are told that to obey these institutions is but to obey ourselves, and therefore no slavery, for these institutions embody ourselves at our best and wisest, and self-restraint is not restraint, self-control is not slavery.

The battle between these two views, in all kinds of versions, has been one of the cardinal political issues of modern times. One side says that to put the bottle beyond the dipsomaniac's reach is not to curtail his liberties; if he is prevented from drinking, even by force, he will be healthier and therefore better capable of playing his part as man and citizen, will be more himself, and therefore freer, than if he reaches the bottle and destroys his health and sanity. The fact that he does not know this is merely a symptom of his disease, or ignorance of his own true wishes. The other side does not deny that anti-social behaviour must be restrained, or that there is a case for preventing men from harming themselves or from harming the welfare of their children or of others, but denies that such a restraint, though justified, is liberty. Liberty may have to be curtailed to make room for other good things, security or peace or health; or liberty today may have to be curtailed to make possible wider liberty tomorrow; but to curtail freedom is not to provide it, and compulsion, no matter how well justified, is compulsion and not liberty. Freedom, such people say, is only one value among many, and if it is an obstacle to the securing of other equally important ends, or interferes with other people's opportunities of reaching these ends, it must make way.

To this the other side replies that this presupposes a division of life into private and public – it assumes that men may wish in their private lives to do what others may not like, and therefore need protection from these others – but that this view of human nature rests on a fundamental mistake. The human being is one, and in the ideal society, when everyone's faculties are developed, nobody will ever want to do anything that others may resent or wish to stop. The proper purpose of reformers and revolutionaries is to knock down walls between men, bring everything into the open, make men live together without partitions, so that what one wants all want. The desire to be left alone, to be allowed to do what one wishes without needing to account for it to some tribunal – one's family or one's employers, or one's party, or one's government, or indeed the whole of one's society – this desire is a symptom of maladjustment. To ask for freedom from society is to ask for freedom from oneself. This must be cured by altering property relations as socialists desire to do, or by eliminating critical reason as some religious sects and, for that matter, Communist and Fascist regimes seek to do.

In one view – which might be called organic – all separateness is bad, and the notion of human rights which must not be trampled on is that of dams – walls demanded by human beings to separate them from one another, needed perhaps in a bad society, but with no place in a justly organised world in which all human streams flow into one undivided human river. On the second or liberal view, human rights, and the idea of a private sphere in which I am free from scrutiny, is indispensable to that minimum of independence which everyone needs if he is to develop, each on his own lines; for variety is of the essence of the human race, not a passing condition. Proponents of this view think that destruction of such rights in order to build one universal self-directing human society – of everyone marching towards the same rational ends – destroys that area for individual choice, however small, without which life does not seem worth living.

In a crude and, some have maintained, a distorted form, totalitarian and authoritarian regimes have stood for one of these views: while liberal democracies incline to the other. And, of course, varieties and combinations of these views, and compromises between them, are possible. They are the two cardinal ideas that have faced one another and dominated the world since, say, the Renaissance.

THE BIRTH OF GREEK INDIVIDUALISM

A Turning-Point in the History of Political Thought

I

Preliminary platitudes

I OUGHT first to say something about what I consider a turning-point to be. I do not know how it is in the natural sciences – empirical ones like physics and biology, or formal ones like logic and mathematics. There, perhaps, revolutions occur when a central hypothesis or system of hypotheses is undermined or exploded by a discovery that leads to new hypotheses or laws which account for the new discovery and are incompatible with the central doctrines of the old system. The method is one of clean refutation: Galileo, Newton, Lavoisier, Darwin, Einstein, Planck and perhaps Bertrand Russell and Freud literally refuted earlier theories, made them obsolete, altered the methods by which new knowledge was gained, so that the interest of the superseded methods and theories is now largely historical, and those who persist in adhering to them are regarded as eccentric and are left out of account in serious circles of recognised experts.

This is conspicuously not the case in the great fields of imprecise knowledge – history, philosophy, scholarship, criticism – ideas about the arts and about the lives of men. Plato's physics or his mathematics may be obsolete, but both Plato's and Aristotle's moral and political ideas are still capable of stirring men to violent partisanship. Karl Popper would not attack Plato's social theories with such fury and indignation if these ideas had no more life to them than, say, Plato's conception of the sun and the fixed stars, or Aristotle's doctrine that some bodies have weight and other bodies have lightness. I know of no one who feels outraged by medieval notions of cosmology or chemistry, or Descartes' physics, or phlogiston theory. But St Augustine's views on the treatment of heretics or on slavery, or St Thomas's view of political authority, or the doctrines of Rousseau or Hegel cause violent reactions, intellectual and emotional, in those who look on the empirical or logical theories of these thinkers with comparative equanimity.

There is obviously some sense in which the criteria of truth and falsehood, tenability and untenability, operate in the case of certain disciplines, and do not operate so obviously or gain such universal assent in the case of other regions of thought. There is a sense in which some studies, such as the empirical sciences and mathematics and logic, progress by parricide, by killing off their ancestors to general satisfaction, and in which some subjects do not progress, at least in the same sense, so that it is difficult to enumerate, say, philosophical propositions or systems which are by universal consensus either dead beyond recall or established on firm foundations, at any rate so far as modern knowledge is concerned.

This is a paradox which I cannot investigate more deeply at present – it is a crucial and obscure subject in itself and deserves greater attention than has been lavished upon it. But I should like to say something about these imprecise disciplines, where we are dealing not so much with specific propositions, or great systems of them, as with what nowadays are called ideologies: attitudes, more exactly conceptual systems, frameworks that consist of interrelated categories through which and by means of which we judge periods. Perhaps it is best to describe them as central models, models drawn from some field that seems to a thinker clear and well-established, and which he applies in a manner which seems to him to explain and illuminate a field that is less clear. Bertrand Russell once observed that to understand a thinker one must understand and grasp the basic pattern, the central idea which he is defending.[1] The thinker's cleverness is usually expended in inventing arguments with which to fortify this central idea, or, still more, to repel attacks, refute objections; but to understand all this reasoning, however cogent and ingenious, will not lead one to grasp the thought of a philosopher, a historian, a critic unless one penetrates through these sophisticated defences upon his bastions to what he is really defending – the inner citadel itself, which is usually comparatively simple, a fundamental perception which dominates his thought and has formed his view of the world. Plato's application of a geometrical pattern to the life of society, eternal a priori axioms obtained by intuitive means from which all know-

---

[1] loc. cit. (p. xxx above, note 1).

ledge and all rules of life can be deduced; Aristotle's biological model of every entity as developing towards its own perfection and inner goal, in terms of which alone it can be defined or understood; the great medieval pyramid that stretches from God to the lowest amoeba; the mechanical structure of Hobbes; the image of the family and its natural relationships that runs through the political structures of Bodin, Burke, the Christian socialists of the West, and the Russian Slavophils; the genetic, biological and physical patterns that are the heart of nineteenth- and twentieth-century sociological doctrines; the legal notion of the social contract: these central models are not refuted by mere aspects of experience which are altered by some historical change or intellectual discovery. New models appear, throw light over dark areas, liberate men from the chains of the old constricting framework, and either extrude them completely or sometimes half blend with them into a new pattern. These new models in their turn fail to explain and answer questions which they themselves bring into being. The concept of man as an atom at first offered liberation from a constricting a priori theocratic model, and then in its turn proved inadequate. Man as an organic cell, man as a creator, man as a producer, as a creature seeking union with nature, or as a Promethean hero-martyr seeking to subdue her – these are all models that obscure and illuminate.

II

The great moments are those when one world dies and another succeeds it. This is marked by a change in the central model. Great moments of transformation occurred, for example, when the cyclical laws of the Greeks were succeeded by the ascending straight line, the historical teleology, of the Jews and Christians; or when teleology, in its turn, was overthrown by the causal-mathematical model of the seventeenth century; or when a priori constructions yielded to methods of empirical discovery and verification. There are those who, like Condorcet or Hegel, Buckle or Marx, Spengler or Toynbee, claim to be able to perceive a single pattern of development in this succession of human perspectives. I do not wish to maintain that such ambitious efforts to reduce the vast variety of conscious human experience to one enormous dominant pattern are necessarily doomed to failure; I confine myself to saying merely that the three great crises which I shall discuss are not satisfactorily explained by the hypotheses of any of

these thinkers, and that this naturally reduces the value of these
hypotheses in my eyes. I do not wish to condemn those who
answer their own questions for failing to answer mine, but I cannot
help having a certain prejudice in favour of those writers who are
more modest and cautious, whose reflections attempt a good deal
less and, whether or not for this reason, achieve, for me, a good
deal more. History, Tolstoy once remarked, is like a deaf man who
answers questions no one has asked. I do not think that this is true
of historical writers, but it may not be entirely unjust about a good
many philosophers of history who, in the name of science, seek to
squeeze the multiplicity of phenomena into one simple cosmic
scheme – the 'terrible simplifiers' in matters of both theory and
practice against whom Montesquieu warned us more than two
centuries ago.[1]

III

The three crises in Western political theory, when at least one
central category was transformed beyond redemption, so that all
subsequent thought was altered, occurred in the fourth century BC,
during the Renaissance in Italy, and towards the end of the
eighteenth century in Germany.

Classical Western political theory may be likened to a tripod –
that is, it rests on three central assumptions. These, of course, do
not represent the totality of beliefs on which this central tradition
rests, but they are amongst its most powerful pillars, so that the
collapse or weakening of any of them is bound to affect the
tradition and, indeed, change it to a considerable degree.

1. The first assumption is that questions about values, about ends
or worth, about the rightness or desirability of human action,
including political action, are genuine questions; genuine questions
being those to which true answers exist, whether they are known
or not. These answers are objective, universal, eternally valid and in
principle knowable. To every genuine question only one answer
can be true, all the other answers being necessarily false – either
false in varying degrees, at various distances from the truth, or false
absolutely, according to the logical doctrine adopted. The route to
the truth has historically been a subject on which there have been
the most profound disagreements among men. Some have believed
that solutions were to be discovered by reason, others by faith or

[1] *De l'esprit des lois*, book 24, chapter 18: see also p. 20 above, note 2.

revelation, or empirical observation, or metaphysical intuition. Some have thought that the truth was, at least in principle, open to all if only they pursued the correct method – by reading sacred books, or communion with nature, or rational calculation, or looking within their own innermost heart; others have thought that only experts could discover the answer, or persons in certain privileged states of mind, or at certain times and in certain places. Some have thought that these truths could be discovered in this world; to others they would be revealed fully only in some future life. Some have supposed that these truths were known in a golden age in the remote past, or would be known in a golden age in the future; according to some they are timeless, according to others revealed progressively; according to some they can in principle be known to men, according to others to God alone.

Profound though these differences are, and the source at times of violent conflict, not only intellectual but social and political, they are differences within the agreed belief that the questions are genuine questions, and the answers to them, like hidden treasure, exist whether they have been found or not; so that the problem is not whether these answers exist at all, but only what is the best means of finding them. Values may differ from facts or from necessary truths in the way that Aristotle or the Fathers of the Church, or Hume or Kant or Mill, thought that they differed; but the propositions that assert or describe them are no less objective, and obey a logical structure no less coherent and rigorous, than propositions asserting facts – whether empirical or a priori or logical – and mathematical truths. This is the first and deepest assumption that underlies the classical form of political theory.

2. The second assumption is that the answers, if they are true, to the various questions raised in political theory do not clash. This follows from the simple logical rule that one truth cannot be incompatible with another. Many questions of value are bound to arise in the course of political enquiry: questions such as 'What is justice and should it be pursued?', 'Is liberty an end to be sought after for its own sake?', 'What are rights, and under what circumstances may they be ignored or, to the contrary, asserted against the claims of utility or security or truth or happiness?' The answers to these questions, if they are true, cannot collide with each other. According to some views they harmonise with one another; according to other views they form an interrelated single whole, and mutually entail and are entailed by one another, so that

denial of any one of them leads to incoherence or contradictions within the system. Whichever of these views is correct, the minimum assumption is that one truth cannot possibly logically conflict with another. Hence it follows that, if all our questions were answered, the collection or pattern or logically connected system of the true answers would constitute a total solution of all problems of value – of the questions of what to do, how to live, what to believe. This would be, in short, the description of the ideal state of which all actual human conditions fall short.

This may be called the jigsaw-puzzle view of ethics and politics and aesthetics. Since all true answers fit with one another, the problem is merely to arrange the fragments with which we are presented in everyday experience, or in moments of illumination, or at the end of some strenuous, but successful, intellectual investigation – to arrange these fragments in the unique way in which they compose the total pattern that is the answer to all our wants and perplexities.

Again the problem arises whether any man can do this, or only some – the experts or the spiritually privileged or those who happen to be in the right place for the completion of the solution to the puzzle. Is the answer vouchsafed to any man who uses correct methods, or only to a particular group in a peculiar favourable position – a particular Church or culture or class? Is the answer static, unaltered wherever and whenever it may be discovered, or dynamic – that is, once it is discovered by the progressive, perfecting searcher after the truth, who has made every serious effort to find it, then although it may not be final in the form in which he gives it, does it facilitate the process of transformation required by the continuing search for the final solution? The assumption here is that there is a final solution, that if all the answers to all the questions could *per impossibile* be found and properly related to one another, this would be a total answer – the necessary acceptance of which by those who had found it would solve all questions, both of theory and of practice, once and for all. Whether this answer is discoverable on earth or not, all attempts to answer such questions can then be represented as being so many paths towards this central totality, adequate or inadequate, in direct proportion to the inner coherence and the comprehensiveness of the answers proposed.

3. The third assumption is that man has a discoverable, describable nature, and that this nature is essentially, and not merely

contingently, social. There are certain attributes which belong to man as such, for example, the capacity for thought or communication; for a creature who does not think or communicate could not be called a man. Communication is by definition a relationship with others, and therefore relationship with other men of a systematic kind is not merely a contingent fact about men, but part of what we mean by men, a part of the definition of human beings as a species. If this is so, then political theory, which is the theory of how men do or should behave towards one another, and especially why anyone should obey anyone else rather than do as he likes (this raises all the questions of authority and sovereignty, of types of government and the foundations of obligation – these questions are necessarily raised whenever any questions about the nature or purposes of men are brought up) – political theory is not a doctrine or a particular technique that men can use or not use, like the theory of navigation (men need not, after all, use ships if they do not wish to), but rather more like theories of thinking (which they cannot help doing), or theories of growth or history, or theories that deal with other inalienable attributes of human beings. Hence the traditional divisions of philosophy which deal with permanent, irremovable characteristics of human life: logic, metaphysics, epistemology, ethics, politics, aesthetics.

Each of these pillars on which political theory rests has been attacked. They have been attacked, historically, in order of mounting importance, in the reverse order from that in which I have stated them. The view of man as an intrinsically social being, and of political theory as consisting of questions that penetrate to the heart of what human beings are, was attacked at the end of the fourth century. The proposition that all values are compatible with one another, and that in principle there is a total solution of human problems, if only we could discover it – there must, at any rate, be a method of searching for it – was questioned by Machiavelli, questioned to such effect that the old confidence which had lasted for more than two thousand years never returned. The proposition that there may, in principle, exist no final solution to human problems, and that some values may be incompatible with others, entails considerations which few men are capable of facing without growing altogether too upset. Finally, the claim that questions of value are genuine questions and capable of solution, at least in principle, and that politics is a branch of intellectual enquiry capable of yielding propositions which can be true or false, was compromised by the German romantics toward the end of the eighteenth century with results of a very violent, revolutionary kind. The consequences are with us still; they have destroyed the foundations of the old beliefs and, whether as causes or as symptoms, they mark the most violent political and moral upheavals of our own day.

I shall discuss these three great crises one by one.[1] I begin with the first – the question of man as a social being.

IV

It is by now a well-worn commonplace that the Greeks of the classical period, and in particular Athens and Sparta in the fifth century BC, conceived of human beings in essentially social terms. The evidence for this need scarcely be adduced. Attic tragedy and comedy in the fifth century, and the historians Herodotus and Thucydides, take for granted that the natural life of men is the institutionalised life of the *polis*. The notion of resistance to it – in the name of individual liberty or even peaceful retreat from the market-place into private life – is scarcely conceived. *Idiotes* means just 'private citizen', but in so far as such a person is concerned with his own private affairs at the expense of those of the city, it can be a pejorative term, like the modern word etymologically related to it. As for the philosophers – those who consciously examined the presuppositions of commonly accepted notions and enquired about the ends of life – if we are to take the two great masters whose works dominate Greek, and all subsequent, thought – Plato and Aristotle – the emphasis on social values is overwhelming in their works. 'One should say not that a citizen belongs to himself,' says Aristotle, 'but that all belong to the *polis*: for the individual is a part of the *polis*.'[2]

This simple statement could stand as a formula that summarises the attitude of all major thinkers of classical Athens. Aristotle cautiously qualifies this thesis: there can be such a thing as too much uniformity in the city. The citizens must not be crushed, differences of character and attitude must always be given adequate room in which to realise themselves. The virtues that Aristotle discusses are largely the characteristics of human beings in their

---

[1] Only the first crisis is treated here: see p. xxvii above.

[2] *Politics* 1337a27; compare also *Nicomachean Ethics* 1180a24–9 and *Metaphysics* 1075a19.

intercourse with each other within a social context: the ideal figure of the generous, distinguished, rich, public-spirited man with a wide liberal outlook, great dignity and sweep, raised above the heads of the ordinary middle-class citizen, is not conceivable save in terms of a well-organised, ordered society. 'Man has been created by nature to live in a *polis*.'[1] This sentiment is central in the classical texts of Greek art and thought that have survived. No argument seems needed to establish this proposition, for it is evidently something that all sane men believe without question, it is part of the general notion of man. Solitude can be endured only by a god or a beast: it is subhuman or superhuman.

This too is the general attitude of Plato, for all his disgust with Athenian democracy. Some Platonists suppose him to be more interested in the well-ordered individual soul or mind than in social and political organisation. Occasionally he makes remarks to the effect that 'no evil can befall a good man either in his lifetime or after his death'[2] – and this is, in effect, repeated in the *Republic*.[3] Both Plato and Aristotle speak of the contemplative life as the highest that a man can lead. Their vision is of the ultimate goal which all things seek, the answer to the question why things are as they are and seek to be what they seek to be: *that* is the fulfilment of the quest for truth, both in theory and practice. To return to the cave and the world of illusion, where men pursue false ends, and struggle and squabble and fret and lead foolish and vicious lives – this return is to be viewed only with extreme reluctance. Still, return they must. Why? Because they must create a society in which the wise man – Socrates – will not be put to death? Or because only the State can give that education which makes men capable of virtue and wisdom, and the grasp of reality which alone gives moral and intellectual security and satisfaction? These are different answers and not consistent with one another: but what they have in common is the view that men cannot and should not live outside the State.

It is true that Socrates kept out of things, on the whole: he obeyed the laws and performed his military service with exceptional distinction, but he kept out of politics, if we are to believe those who wrote about him, because Athenian democracy was too corrupt and no man who knew where the truth lay would seek the

---

[1] *Politics* 1253a–3. [2] *Apology* 41d1. [3] 613a.

tawdry prizes which a vicious society offered. Nevertheless, one of the charges against him was that he was too close to Critias, chief of the tyrants who seized power and instituted a reign of terror and butchered a good many democrats. Socrates was accused not of turning his back upon civic life, but of 'corrupting the young men'[1] and of sowing scepticism about the values that preserved the social texture, and, no doubt, of being a friend of Alcibiades, who was a traitor, and of other young men of good birth who looked down upon the grocers and tanners who formed the bulk of the Athenian electorate; in other words, of preaching doctrines which made for the rule by an élite, a rational élite perhaps, but still, superior persons raised above the ordinary citizenry, oligarchs who believed in their own superior values and not in equality or majority votes.

This is not political detachment but active subversion of a particular type of political life. In the *Crito*, where the laws are speaking to Socrates before his approaching death, they tell him that he is a child and slave of the laws. He was among those who passed the laws. Once they are set up it is the duty of the citizen to obey – there is no question of opting out of such a commitment. The citizen owes more to the laws than to his physical parents.[2] Socrates takes this for granted; he does not dispute it: morality integrates you into society, and above all you must not destroy the laws by disobeying them because they are unjust, because you suffer unjustly under them. The claims of the social texture are supreme. The proposition that Plato was interested solely or even principally in creating conditions in which the minority gifted enough to discover the truth would have conditions in which they could pursue their studies is not really tenable. However the *Republic* may be interpreted, the *Politicus* is a treatise not about means, but about ends – how the only life which, according to him, men can lead while remaining men, namely the life of the city, should be conducted by those who are responsible. Virtue for Plato is the fruit of State-directed education. A bad State must be reformed or abolished, but not in favour of a loose association of individuals. There is nothing which Plato is more bitterly opposed to than 'a society in which men are allowed to do whatever they like'.[3] The most violent statement of this is in the famous passage

---

[1] *Apology* 24b–c.   [2] 50c–51c, esp. 51a.   [3] *Republic* 557b5.

in the *Laws* where, after earlier criticising Sparta as a militarist State – a mere 'army camp'[1] – he declares, a good many pages later:

> the principal thing is that none, man or woman, should ever be without an officer set over him, and that none should get the mental habit of taking any step, whether in earnest or jest, on his own individual responsibility. In peace and in war he must live always with his eye on his superior officer, following his lead and guided by him in his smallest actions ... In a word, he must train the mind not even to consider acting as an individual or to know how to do it.[2]

No doubt this was written in his embittered old age, after the failure of the Sicilian experiment, when his passionate belief in human reason may have been weakened by his experience of human vice and folly. Still, in a milder version, this is the note struck by Plato whenever the question of political organisation arises. The reduction of social life to a single rigorous pattern inspired by logic or mathematics may argue a latent hatred of human association as such and of the problems of reconciling the variety of men and purposes, or blending them into some viable form of life worthy of human beings, in which the art or science of politics may be held to consist. Be that as it may, Plato clearly thinks of men in a social context. In his image man is among other men. His morality is a social morality, even though not to the extent of Aristotle's – for whom morals were deducible from politics. We discover what men should do by asking ourselves what functions nature has designed them to perform in the pattern for which they were created. The Greek city is derived from this pattern. Where the association is too big, as, say, in Persia, or too crude, as it is among the barbarians, or does not exist at all – when disintegration sets in and men find themselves on their own – that causes degeneration, abnormality. The norm is the equilibrium of forces and characteristics embodied in the city. The worst and most corrosive of vices – injustice – is the upsetting of this equilibrium. The best constitutions are those which keep things in balance, preserve the pattern, and create the framework within which men can socially – and, therefore, morally and intellectually – realise themselves. Men's characters are defined in terms of the kind of society for which they were created by nature. There are the

[1] 666e. [2] 942a–c.

democratic, the oligarchic, the plutocratic man: bricks defined in terms of the building into which they naturally fit. This is a celebrated Greek ideal of life at its most articulate.

Is there no opposition to this? What about Antigone, who defied the laws of the State in order to bury her brother? She defies Creon's laws, but not in the name of some individual conviction or the values of private life: she appeals to the unwritten laws, not of today or yesterday, to which all mankind is subject, laws valid for any human society, but not for individuals unrelated by social links. It is an appeal from one social morality to another, not from a social morality to an individual one.

And the Sophists? Here we reach an important, but unfortunately insoluble, problem. For we do not know too much about what the Sophists taught. Perhaps they did not write books on any large scale; or perhaps what they wrote perished – for we know at least some titles of books by the opponents of Socrates and Plato that have not survived. But our main authority for what Protagoras, Prodicus, Hippias, Thrasymachus believed is what Plato and Aristotle tell us. We know a little more about other figures, for example Antiphon. But the bulk of what we know comes from enemy sources, the caricatures of a man who hated them as much as Aristophanes – except that Aristophanes included Socrates as well – and painted satirical portraits of genius. The true facts about those he described are for ever obliterated. To this point I intend to revert later, for it is highly relevant to my entire argument. But for the moment let me say only that the Sophists, like the orators and the dramatists, give evidence of sharp disagreements about what kind of State is the best, but not of opposition to the supremacy of the social institutions.

Lycophron thought that the division into classes was artificial, a work not of nature but of the human will or prejudice. Alcidamas (and in some degree Euripides) thought the institution of slavery artificial, for nature meant all men to be alike – and likewise the distinction between Greeks and barbarians. Antiphon said: 'None of us is by definition barbarian or Greek, for we all breathe out into the air by mouth and nostrils.'[1] Being barbarian or Greek is a human arrangement which, presumably, humans could at will undo. Archelaus thought the distinctions between justice and crookedness were the results of human arrangements, not of

---

[1] Diels–Kranz, 6th ed., 87 B 44, B 2. 24–34 (ii 353).

nature; Phaleas thought this about the qualities of property. Critias thought God an invention for the purpose of keeping men in order, for unless they were taught that there was an ever-watchful eye upon them, even when no men saw them, marking their conduct and prepared to punish for transgressions, they would behave badly when they thought no one was looking, and society would be subverted.

The Sophists are relativists, egalitarians, pragmatists, atheists, but for the most part, at any rate towards the end of the fifth century, they are not individualists. They want to alter society, not concentrate attention upon the individual and his character and needs. They differ about what kind of society is the most rational. They wish to eliminate mere traditional survivals. They criticise institutions for which they see no good reason, but not institutional life as such. Some appear to be democrats, some are not. It is one of the great paradoxes of history that the democracy that is Athens' greatest political glory was defended by so few that almost every writer who has survived is in some degree an enemy or a critic of it. The ideal is *isonomia*, equality before the laws – 'the most beautiful of all names', as Herodotus makes Otanes call it[1] – or *eunomia*, good order, a conservative slogan. Equality is defended against tyranny and arbitrary rule. Aristotle thinks that a State is satisfactory in which men rule and are ruled in turn,[2] while the cynical Antiphon wonders whether any man would not prefer to rule unjustly rather than be ruled justly by others.

There is no trace here of genuine individualism, the doctrine that there are personal values – pleasure, or knowledge, or friendship, or virtue, or self-expression in art or life – to which political and social arrangements should be subordinated: for which they create a pedestal, a means however indispensable, but still only a means. The assumption is, on the contrary, that all these values can be realised only within and as part of the life of the Greek *polis*. To ignore social arrangements, to profit by them, is not a normal frame of mind. Even Thrasymachus, who thinks that justice is the interest of the stronger, does not imply that life outside the intimate association of masters and slaves is conceivable. Callicles in Plato's *Gorgias* speaks for the bold, unscrupulous, self-seeking, gifted egoist who sweeps aside the institutions of the city like cobwebs and tramples on them and does as he likes – that is, might

[1] 3. 80. 6.   [2] *Politics* 1317b2.

is right: nature demands despotism, not individualism. Lactantius is
right in thinking Socrates does not win the argument against
Thrasymachus and his like; the common opinion which he mar-
shalls against him is not enough against violent individualism of
this type. But Plato evidently thought that he had refuted the
claims of these egomaniacs, with their distorted view of the facts,
which would cost them dear in the end.

At this point it may be asked whether I have forgotten the
greatest of all professions of political faith, the funeral speech of
Pericles as reported by Thucydides, incomparably the greatest
statement of its kind in the whole of our history. Certainly,
Pericles says, Athens differs from Sparta in that 'we live as free
citizens, both in our public life and in our attitude to one another
in the affairs of daily life; we are not angry with our neighbour if
he behaves as he pleases, we do not cast sour looks at him, which if
they can do no harm nevertheless can cause pain'.[1] There is a
similar remark, less nobly expressed, in the speech of Nikias to the
dispirited, defeated Athenian troops in Sicily in 416 BC.[2] Euripides
also speaks up for freedom of speech,[3] and Demosthenes says: 'In
Sparta you are not allowed to praise the laws of Athens, or of this
State or that; far from it, you have to praise what agrees with their
constitution';[4] whereas in Athens free criticism of constitutions is
evidently permitted.

What does this come to? Pericles says that some States are more
liberal than others: not, as he has all too often been interpreted, that
in Athens individuals have rights, natural or State-conferred, to
speak as they please or act as they please within certain limits, with
which the State has no right to interfere. This is the view advanced
by Gomme, but he seems to be mistaken. No doubt the individual
did 'have ample freedom in private life',[5] no doubt there were
protests from the conservatives, such as Aristotle's disapproval of
men 'who live as they please' – as Euripides says, 'each according
to his fancy'[6] – or Plato's disgust with the city that has so much
variety, so many foreigners, women and slaves who get above

---

[1] 2. 37.

[2] 7. 69 (Nikias 'reminded them of their fatherland with all its great freedom
and the uncommanded liberty of lifestyle for all').

[3] *Hippolytus* 421–2; *Ion* 672–5; *Phoenissae* 390–3; *Temenidae* fr. 737 Nauck.

[4] *Against Leptines*, 20. 106.

[5] Herbert J. Muller, *Freedom in the Ancient World* (London, 1962), p. 168.

[6] Aristotle, *Politics* 1310a33; Euripides, fr. 883 Nauck.

themselves and presume to behave almost like citizens. The pseudo-Xenophontic *Constitution of Athens* launches a diatribe against resident foreigners and slaves. Isocrates complains that there is not enough moral control over private lives, that the Areopagus should reassert its ancient authority in these matters. All this implies that life in Athens was a good deal freer, that there was more variety, perhaps more chaos than in totalitarian Sparta or perhaps other more tightly organised, more militarised States. But what Pericles is saying, in effect, is what any headmaster proud of the spirit of his school, any commander proud of the spirit of his army, might well say: We do not need compulsion. What other States have to force their citizens to do, ours perform because they are truly devoted to their city, because they are spontaneously loyal, because their lives are bound up with their city, in which they all have faith and pride.

It is a far cry from this to the assertion of the rights of the individual. Schoolboys, however lightly ruled, have no rights against the masters. The school may take pride in the fact that it does not need to threaten or bully, punish or intimidate, but it is the collective spirit of the school, the solidarity of its members, that is being praised: the Athenian State was the object of its own worship and upon its altar men were, if Pericles is to be believed, ready to sacrifice themselves. But to sacrifice oneself freely is still to sacrifice oneself, uncoerced surrender is still surrender; and vice and error are still defined in terms of each man pulling in his own direction, satisfying his own individual nature. Thucydides likes Pericles and does not like Cleon. Demosthenes believes in political freedom, freedom from rule by other States – say, Macedon – and so does Pericles, and all the great Athenians. Some believe in a loose texture, some in a tight one, but there is no note of individualism here, of the value of the State consisting in what it contributes to the individual satisfactions of its individual members. They are to lay down their lives for it; it has no duties, only claims; they have no claims against it, only duties. But in a well-organised, harmonious State, such as Pericles tries to represent Athens as being, claims are not pressed; they are satisfied spontaneously, and no one scowls at his neighbour for being different from himself. Variety versus uniformity, spontaneity versus coercion, loyalty versus tyranny, love instead of fear: these are the Periclean ideals. However attractive they may be found, they are not identical either with individualism or (a much later stage of human development) with the notion of the right of the individual against encroachment by the State – the staking out of a claim to the sacrosanct area within which he literally can do as he pleases, however foolish, eccentric, outrageous his conduct.

That is the testimony of the major authors. There are some dissident voices; they are few and far between, and I shall have occasion to mention them later. Aristotle may have been an old-fashioned conservative towards the end of his life, but it is his view of the nature of society – the harmonious social whole, pursuing goals implanted in it by nature herself, to which every element must be subordinated, so that ethics and politics are wholly social and educational, as explained in his treatises on what the relationships are between the natural purposes of the various constituents of society, and how they may be made to perform their functions, their natural functions, as effectively and richly as possible – it is that vision that has bound its spell on the ancient world, the middle ages, and on a good many modern societies since his day.

At this point there is a most surprising development. Aristotle died in 322 BC. Some sixteen years or so later, Epicurus began to teach in Athens, and after him Zeno, a Phoenician from Kition in Cyprus. Within a few years theirs are the dominant philosophical schools in Athens. It is as if political philosophy had suddenly vanished away. There is nothing about the city, the education of citizens to perform their tasks within it, bad and good constitutions – nothing at all about this.[1] Nothing about the need for hierarchies or their dangers; nothing about the value of small organised communities, of extrovert social life as the mark and criterion of human nature; nothing about how to train specialists in governing men, or about the organisation of life so that unequal gifts are appropriately rewarded, with the explanation that different constitutions place different emphasis on different types of gift and character. Personal ethics are no longer deduced from social morality, ethics are no longer a branch of politics, the whole no longer precedes the parts, the notion of fulfilment as necessarily social and public disappears without a trace. Within twenty years or less we find, in place of hierarchy, equality; in place of emphasis on the superiority of specialists, the doctrine that any man can

---

[1] It is possible that Berlin might have wished to qualify this to some degree to take account of Zeno's *Republic*, a response (of which only fragments survive) to Plato's work of the same title. See Malcolm Schofield, *The Stoic Idea of the City* (Cambridge etc., 1991). Ed.

discover the truth for himself and live the good life as well as any other man, at least in principle; in place of emphasis on intellectual gifts, ability, skill, there is now stress upon the will, moral qualities, character; in place of loyalty, which holds small groups together, groups moulded by tradition and memories, and the organic fitting-in of all their parts and functions, there is a world without national or city frontiers; in place of the outer life, the inner life; in place of political commitment, taken for granted by all the major thinkers of the previous age, sermons recommending total detachment. In place of the pursuit of grandeur, glory, immortal fame, nobility, public spirit, self-realisation in harmonious social action, gentlemanly ideals, we now have a notion of individual self-sufficiency, praise of austerity, a puritanical emphasis on duty, above all constant stress on the fact that the highest of all values is peace of soul, individual salvation, obtained not by knowledge of an accumulating kind, not by the gradual increase of scientific information (as Aristotle taught), nor by the use of sensible judgement in practical affairs, but by sudden conversion – a shining of the inner light. Men are distinguished into the converted and the unconverted. There are to be no intermediate types – they are either saved or not saved, either wise or stupid. One either knows how to save one's soul or one does not. One can be drowned as easily in a foot of water as in many fathoms, said the Stoics. One is either in Canopus or outside it: to be an inch outside and many miles outside are equally not to be in Canopus – all or nothing. It is something like the sudden puritanism following the Elizabethan Age.

For the older of the two teachers, Epicurus, the State hardly exists. The problem is how to avoid being hurt, how to escape misery. Reality – nature – is governed by iron laws which men cannot possibly alter. You cannot destroy or avoid nature, but you can avoid colliding with it unnecessarily. What makes men unhappy? Fear of the gods, superstition, fear of death, fear of pain – whence all the elaborate ritual, propitiation, obedience to the infernal powers that is called religion. But what if the gods, even if they do exist, take no interest in men, but live blissfully in their own remote world, unconcerned with affairs on earth? If fear of the gods goes, the burden is much lightened. As for pain, skilful management will diminish that too, both for me and for my neighbours. If the pain is intolerably intense it will not last long and death will release me; if it lasts it cannot be intense, and by living carefully, following the prescriptions of nature, one can avoid pain and disease. What remains of life? Happiness, peace, inner harmony. How may it be obtained? Not by seeking wealth, power, recognition, for these expose you to competition and all the sweat and toil of the arena. Public life brings more pains than pleasures; its rewards are not worth having, for they merely multiply your anxieties. Avoid situations in which you become liable to pain. All men are vulnerable: they must contract the vulnerable surface that may be wounded by other men or by things and events. This must be done by avoiding all forms of commitment. Epicurus preaches passionately, as a man who wishes to suppress all passions as sources of pain and trouble, against what today is called an *engagé* attitude to politics. *Lathe biosas:*[1] get through life as obscurely as you can. Seek to avoid notice and you will not be hurt. Public life holds out rewards that are only a painful delusion. Be like an actor.[2] Play the part that has been set up for you, but do not identify yourself with it. Above all, no enthusiasm, *pas trop de zèle*. Pay taxes, vote, obey orders, but withdraw into yourself. 'Man is not by nature adapted for living in civic communities.'[3] 'Confront every desire with the question: What do I gain by gratifying it, and what shall I lose by crushing it?'[4]

Should one be just? Yes, because if you cheat – break rules – you may be discovered, and others may, because they are not dispassionate sages like you, punish you or at least hate you; and if you are haunted by the fear of being exposed, this will ruin your pleasures. There is no value in justice as such; justice is only a means of avoiding too much friction with others, of getting along. The reason for it is utility: all society is founded upon a social contract whereby arrangements are made which make it possible for human beings not to get in each other's way too much.

And knowledge? Is that desirable? Certainly, for only in this way will you know what to do and what to avoid if you are to attain to peace and contentment. 'Vain is the word of the philosopher which heals not the suffering of man.'[5] This might well be the motto of the Rockefeller Foundation today. Knowledge is not

---

[1] Fr. 551 Usener: literally 'Escape notice having lived.'
[2] Bion fr. 16A Kindstrand.
[3] See under Epicurus fr. 551 Usener (p. 327, lines 9–10).
[4] Epicurus fr. 6. 71 Arrighetti.
[5] ibid. fr. 247.

an end in itself; nothing is an end in itself except individual happiness, and this is to be obtained by reliable goods – the love of friends, which is a positive source of pleasure, the joys of private life.

Should wealth be sought? Not as such, for that leads to fears, conflicts, but if it comes your way it is unreasonable to reject it. The wise man should be able to do with bread and water, but if luxuries come his way, why should he not accept them too? Public life is a snare and a delusion, and you should participate in it only if you need to – to avoid pain – or if you happen to have a restless temperament, or enjoy it: that is, if it offers some kind of opiate to you which other things do not. You cannot obtain all that you want: to want and not to get is to be a slave to desires, to be tossed about by forces stronger than yourself. Since you cannot get what you want, you must try to want only what you can get – you cannot manipulate the universe, but you can manipulate your own psychological states, within limits. Try not to want something that may easily be taken away from you. 'There is but one way to freedom: to despise what is not in our power.'[1] What you cannot get is not worth striving for.

There are two ways of being happy – by satisfying desires and by eliminating them. The first can be achieved only on a modest scale, since we are neither omniscient nor omnipotent, and facts are as they are and cannot be changed much; the second way is the only way to peace and independence. Independence is everything: the two great Epicurean words are *autarkeia* and *ataraxia* – self-sufficiency and imperturbability. And social life? And the glory of the city? And great dangers bravely faced? And Alexander in his plumed helmet mowing down the slaves of the King of Persia? These are not roads to permanent happiness. They merely excite the desires and make you seek for more and more, and enslave you more and more hopelessly to vast unfulfillable ambitions, and expose you to hopes and fears which do not let you rest. The greatest achievement of a man is to teach himself not to mind. That is the lesson to be drawn from the life of Socrates, not social arrangements or the value of mathematics as a path to metaphysical truth. You have not long to live and might as well arrange yourself as comfortably as possible in your own corner of the world. If you

[1] *Encheiridion* 19. 2.

do not interfere with others, or envy or hate them, or seek to alter their lives against their wishes, or try for power, you will get by.

This combination of belief in rationalism, which liberates one from fanaticism and anxiety, and belief in utilitarianism and personal relationships as the supreme good in life is a doctrine familiar whenever the stresses of life become too much for distinguished and sensitive persons. It is a form of retreat in depth, retreat into the inner citadel of the inviolable individual soul, so protected by fortitude and reason that nothing can upset it, or wound it, or throw it off its balance. Godwin believed something of the kind and imparted it to Shelley, in whose Platonism it plays a part. In our own day it constituted the morality of a good many English and, perhaps, some French and American intellectuals before and after 1914 – rationalist, anti-clerical, pacifist, contemptuous of the pursuit of reputation or wealth – who believed above all in personal relationships and aesthetic enjoyment, friendship and the production and enjoyment of beauty, and the pursuit of the unvarnished truth as alone worthy of human beings. Virginia Woolf, Roger Fry, the philosopher G. E. Moore, in his earlier years Maynard Keynes believed something of this kind. When E. M. Forster declared shortly before the last war, 'if I had to choose between betraying my country and betraying my friend, I hope I should have the guts to betray my country',[1] this was a militant expression of the Epicurean creed – a total reversal of previous Greek beliefs. 'A study of the laws of nature creates men of haughty independence of mind [*sobroi* and *autarkeis*] who pride themselves on the goods proper to man [*idioi agathoi*], not to circumstances.'[2] Public life is part of circumstances, not of the individual. The State is an instrument and not an end. Personal salvation is all that matters. The doctrine is one of liberation through self-sufficiency. This is indeed a transvaluation of values.

The Stoics were, of course, more influential than the Epicureans. Zeno, who established himself in Athens at the turn of the fourth century, was a foreigner, a Phoenician from Cyprus who taught that wisdom consisted of inner freedom, which could be obtained only by eliminating the passions from one's constitution. The world was a rational pattern and order, and since man by nature was a rational creature, to understand this order was to recognise

---

[1] *Two Cheers for Democracy* (London, 1951), 'What I Believe', p. 78.
[2] Epicurus fr. 6. 45 Arrighetti.

its beauty and its necessity – the laws of reason were graven in deathless letters upon our deathless reason.[1] If only you could rid yourself of the influences that ruined you – errors about the world, induced by stupidity or ignorance or a bad and corrupt condition – you would become invulnerable to that which made other men vicious and unhappy. To understand the world truly is to understand that everything in it is necessary, and what you call evil is an indispensable element in a larger harmony. To achieve this understanding is to cease to feel the common desires, fears, hopes of mankind, and dedicate yourself to a life led in accordance with reason or nature – which to Zeno are the same, for nature is the embodiment of the laws of universal reason. The Stoic sage observes that reason governs the world. If pain is part of the design, it must be embraced; your will must be adjusted to it. 'Do your worst, pain,' exclaimed the Stoic Posidonius when racked by mortal disease; 'no matter what you do, you cannot make me hate you.'[2]

Since any man can grasp the rational necessity of whatever occurs, there is no need to achieve harmony, stability, peace of mind for that minimum of material health and wealth that Aristotle admitted to be necessary for happiness. King Priam, however brave and good, could not achieve happiness, according to Aristotle, because his misfortunes were too great; according to the Stoics, he could. The only thing that is real is the basic reason that goes through nature and men. Why collect details of 257 constitutions in order to find out what suits what kinds of men, where, in what climates, with what traditions – when all men are fundamentally the same, and we can discover a priori, by training the reason within us to grasp the eternal laws of the world, what we must do to be at harmony with ourselves and the external world, rather than learn this by the uncertain inductive path chosen by the Peripatetics? How do we know what is certain? Because sometimes something 'almost takes hold of us by the hair . . . and drags us to assent'.[3] Some truths are incorrigible and irresistible. It is easier to be harmonious and at peace in some circumstances than in others: if gold had not been dug up or luxuries brought by ships from abroad, there would be more simplicity and peace, but even in the

---

[1] *Stoicorum veterum fragmenta* (hereafter *SVF*) iii 360.
[2] loc. cit. (p. 31 above, note 1) = Edelstein–Kidd T38.
[3] Sextus Empiricus, *Adversus mathematicos* 7 (*Adversus logicos* 1). 257.

sophisticated and corrupt Athens of the beginning of the third
century, discipline over emotion can be obtained, and one can
make oneself impervious to the evil will of men or the blows of
fortune. The ship must be wholly sealed from leaking – allow the
faintest crack through which feelings might seep and you are sunk.

The ideal is *apathia* – passionlessness. The Stoic sage is impass-
ive, dry, detached, invulnerable; he alone is king, priest, master,
god. Like the Pharisees to whom Josephus compares them, the
Stoic sages were accused of coldness, hypocrisy, pride, disdain,
pretentiousness. The movement had its martyrs: since misery
resulted only from deviation from reason, from over-attachment to
persons or things, if circumstances became too evil or the tyrant
too brutal and menacing, you could always escape the consequences by freely taking your own life. The Stoics did not
advocate suicide, but neither did they preach against it. A rational
man dies when life according to reason becomes impossible,
because his faculties have decayed too far or life can be bought at
too irrational a price. Man is a dog tied to a cart; if he is wise he will
run with it. (That is called following nature – being rational and
wise. If he is unwise it will drag him and he will run with it willy-
nilly.)

What are the political doctrines of the early Stoics? Only the
wise can live in peace and concord. They can live in any city; it
doesn't matter where, for being passionless they will feel no special
attachment to any body of men. The ideal dwelling-place will have
no temples to the gods, no statues of them, no law courts, no
gymnasia, no armies or warships or money, for the wise do not
need these things; if you live in the light of reason, the conflicts, the
fears and hopes that lead to the erection of these institutions will
melt away. Zeno advocates total sexual freedom: all children shall
be children of all the inhabitants. In the proper human life,
according to Zeno, 'We should not live by cities or demes,
severally divided according to our own idea of what is just, but
should consider that all men are demesmen and fellow citizens;
there should be one life and one world, just as of a herd feeding
together, nurtured by a common pasture.'[1] This is the world of
good men; only they can enjoy love, friendship, inner and outer
harmony.

---

[1] *SVF* i 262. The Greek word for 'pasture' also means 'law'.

This is what Zeno preached; and, Plutarch exclaimed enthusiastically, Alexander of Macedon achieved it. Tarn complains that, just as Aristotle divided men into those who are free and those who are slaves by nature, so Zeno divided them into the good and wicked, the saved and the sinners. But this is not just. Any man can be saved, but not any man can transform his Aristotelian, fixed nature from that of a slave to that of a free man. What is plain is that while Plato and Aristotle desired to organise, to create and preserve an order, Plato's communism is, principally, a means of breeding suitable citizens. Zeno wishes to abolish this; both Zeno and his disciples Cleanthes and Chrysippus advocated social freedom of the most extreme kind: sexual promiscuity, homosexuality, incest, the eating of human flesh, permission to do anything that is not forbidden by *physis* – nature – for all contrary rules and traditions and habits, when examined, will be found to be artificial and irrational. When you look into yourself, and only into yourself – for there is nowhere else to look (you should certainly not look at social institutions, which are a mere external, adventitious aid to living) – then you will find that some rules are graven upon your heart by nature herself, while others are mere human inventions, ephemeral and directed to irrational ends, nothing to the wise man.

Later Stoicism absorbed a much more Aristotelian doctrine into itself and adapted itself to the uses of the Roman Empire, abandoning its sharp anti-political tone and content – for in principle Stoicism is as anti-political as Epicureanism. True, Zeno impressed the Macedonian ruler of Athens, Antigonus Gonatas, as a teacher of civic virtue. He would not serve him himself, but supplied pupils who became court chaplains and personal advisers to Hellenistic kings, and sometimes generals and practical social reformers (as in Sparta). Nevertheless the king, for the Stoics, is not a divine creature as he is for the Pythagoreans and even for Aristotle; he is a human being, and since it is desirable that life should be as rational as possible, the Stoic sage can give him advice and influence him in the right direction, which, although not the most essential duty – which is to put oneself in the right frame of mind and nothing else – creates conditions in which men can more easily save themselves by Stoic introspection, self-examination of the tasks that reason lays upon them.

It is sometimes said that Zeno believed in a world State, but this is a misinterpretation of Plutarch's text: he has no interest in the State at all. In sharp contradiction to Plato and Aristotle, he believes that wisdom is to be learned and exercised not in the ideal *polis*, but in a world filled with wise men. Society is fundamentally a hindrance to self-sufficiency. It is evident that men cannot avoid society altogether, and must make the best of it, but so far from ethics being deducible from politics, the private from the public, the proper route is the other way about: to regulate public affairs in accordance with the rules of private morality. The virtuous or wise man must learn not to mind the storms of public life, to escape into himself, to ignore that which, being public, is ultimately of small importance. The distance between the Epicurean *ataraxia* – imperturbability – and the Stoic *apathia* – passionlessness – is not great. Pleasure or duty, happiness or rational self-realisation, these were the opposed ideals of the Hellenistic world. Whatever their differences, they were as one against the public world of Plato and Aristotle and the major Sophists. The break is immense and its consequences great. For the first time the idea gains ground that politics is a squalid occupation, not worthy of the wise and the good. The division of ethics and politics is made absolute; men are defined in individual terms, and politics, at best, becomes the application of certain ethical principles to human groups, instead of the other way around. Not public order, but personal salvation is all that matters. To sacrifice salvation to public needs is the greatest, most fatal error a man can commit; the betrayal of all that makes him human, of the reason within him, that which alone confers dignity and value upon men. There is no need to speak of the influence of this conception in Christianity, particularly in its Augustinian and quietist traditions.

It is very odd. How could so sharp a break occur within two decades? At one moment all the major thinkers appear to be discussing social and political questions; less than twenty years later no one at all is doing so. The Aristotelians are collecting plants, accumulating information about planets, animals and geographical formations; the Platonists are occupied with mathematics; no one speaks of social or political issues at all – it suddenly becomes a subject beneath the notice of serious men.

The official explanation which almost all historians adopt is, of course, the destruction of the city-state by Philip and Alexander of Macedon. The conventional view, adopted by almost all historians on the subject (there are some honorable exceptions), is that the writings of the major thinkers reflect political conditions directly and unambiguously. Sophocles, the Thucydidean Pericles, Aeschylus, Herodotus are spokesmen for Athens during the highest peak of her power and creative achievement. Plato, Isocrates, Thucydides himself reflect the internal stress and strain of the beginning of decadence. Demosthenes is the last desperate stand of independent democracy. Then comes the battle of Chaeronea in 338 BC. The *polis* is destroyed by the Macedonian phalanx. Aristotle – like Hegel's owl of Minerva[1] – speaks for the past, not the future, and is out of date by the time that he escapes from Athens in 323. The *polis* becomes insignificant. A great new world is opened by Alexander's armies, and the average Greek or Athenian (as the author chooses), deprived of the sense of intimacy and security provided by the walls of the small self-contained city, feels puny and insignificant in the vast new empire which stretches out to the East. There is no natural unit to which to give his loyalty, and in which he can huddle for security.

The bleak new atmosphere, with familiar landmarks gone, makes him feel frightened and solitary, and concerned with his own personal salvation. Public life decays. Public concerns seem irrelevant. Menander, the fellow citizen and contemporary of Epicurus, writes comedies about domestic personal issues. Naturalism succeeds the idealised painting and sculpture which represented common ideals of the entire *polis* – noble objects of social worship and admiration and emulation. Superstition fills the vacuum left by the disappearance of State religion. Men retreat into themselves. The social fabric disintegrates. All men are equal before the remote despot in Pella or Alexandria or Antioch. The organic community has been pulverised into dissociated atoms. Stoicism and Epicureanism are natural forms of faith for men in this condition.

What is unplausible about this account is that the catastrophic change – for it is nothing less – occurs too rapidly. Athens was of small account before Chaeronea, and did not cease to be a city-state in 337 BC. It was defeated, but it had been defeated by the Spartans before, and yet it led a sufficiently intense life as a city-state in the fourth century, as the speeches of the orators, if nothing else, convey. There was a Macedonian garrison in the Acropolis; it was expelled. True, it returned to subdue the rebellious city. Still,

---

[1] Mentioned at the end of Hegel's foreword to *Grundlinien der Philosophie des Rechts*: see Georg Wilhelm Friedrich Hegel, *Sämtliche Werke*, ed. Hermann Glockner (Stuttgart, 1927–51), vol. 7, p. 37.

civic feeling continued; men continued to vote, to elect to public office, to bear liturgies. The *poleis* were not dissolved by Alexander or his successors: on the contrary, new ones were created. The inscriptions do not show a slackening of public spirit. There was no real collapse until Romans appear on the scene. No doubt the cities did lose their independent character, especially in the field of foreign policy. It would, of course, be absurd to deny that Alexander had transformed the Mediterranean world. Yet however firmly you may believe that the ideological superstructure faithfully follows changes in the social or economic substructure – in this case, political organisation – there was certainly no break in the history of the *polis* so sharp, to judge from the subjective experiences of the citizens, as to explain so abrupt, swift and total a transformation of political outlook.

That Alexander's conquests were a pertinent factor in the development is, of course, true; but it is difficult to suppose that it is alone sufficient to explain what occurred. It is as if one were to say that Napoleon's conquest of Europe totally transformed social and political thought; it did not. It modified it deeply, but there is not that gap between the writings of, say, Hume and James Mill, or Kant and Hegel, which marks the break between Aristotle and Zeno. Men do not say to themselves: 'My old world is crumbling, I must turn my attention to other aspects of experience. The outer life has become dreary, frightening and flat – it is time to turn to the inner life.' (And if the unconscious is, at this point, called to our aid, it is only reasonable to say that it does not work quite so fast underground.) Men did not say this, especially in the ancient world, where changes seem to have taken less abrupt and catastrophic turns than in our own time. It is only reasonable to assume, therefore, that Stoic and Epicurean individualism did not spring quite so fully armed from the head of this now defeated and humiliated Athena. And, indeed, the new thinkers had some predecessors, occasionally mentioned by the ancient historians of philosophy. Zeno was a pupil of Crates, who was a Cynic, and he, in his turn, belonged to the school of Diogenes, who flourished, if that is the proper term for his peculiar life, in the middle of the fourth century BC. We know that behind him stand the figures of Antisthenes and Aristippus. Antisthenes, who was a personal pupil of Socrates and was known not to have taken an interest in public life or the State, who believed in independence, whose hero was Herakles, performer of great labours for the benefit of men, followed the narrow path of principle. Aristippus, who proclaimed himself a stranger everywhere, said that he wished 'neither to rule nor to be ruled',[1] and therefore went too far for Socrates. His device was *ekho all' oukh ekhomai* ('I possess but am not possessed'):[2] I enjoy pleasures and seek them but they cannot make me their slave; I can detach myself from them at will. Antisthenes agreed with Plato about one thing, at any rate, that victory over oneself was the most difficult and most important of all victories. Aristippus was a Cyrenaic who came to Athens from a very different climate; he may have believed that pleasure, provided one is not enslaved by it, is the natural end of man, whereas the Stoics believed that it was the enemy and clouded the passions and obscured the truth and so made men stumble and lose their way and become enslaved by forces they could not control; but the ideal of both was the same – independence, self-possession, individual self-assertion. So far as most men were blind, enslaved, prey to irrational feelings, the sage was likely to be unpopular and in some danger; hence his interest in swaying the rulers to his own way of thought.

Behind Antisthenes, behind Socrates even, stands the enigmatic figure of Antiphon, the Sophist of the end of the fifth century, of whom at least we possess independent evidence in a papyrus. He believed that you can cheat men, but not nature. If you eat a poisonous food, you die; but if you commit what is called an injustice, then, if no one has seen it, you will not suffer for it. It pays you to practise justice only if there are witnesses of your act – human beings upon whom you can make an impression, if need be a false one. Anarchy is a painful state of affairs, so there is a reason to teach children to obey, but if you can get away with something condemned by the human rules which particular human beings have established, then why not do so? He was against lawsuits because in claiming justice you made enemies of those against whom you witnessed, however truthfully, and this might prove a source of grave disadvantage to you later. From what we gather, Antiphon was a pessimistic quietist who preached the need for self-protection. The world was full of violent, dangerous men ready to make the innocent suffer. He gives advice to the victims on how to

---

[1] Socrates' formulation of Aristippus' position. Xenophon, *Memorabilia* 2. 1. 12.

[2] Diogenes Laertius 2. 75.

keep out of trouble. This is the first audible voice in ancient Greece which says – what Epicurus and his followers later echoed down the centuries – that the only satisfactory life is lived by keeping out of the sight of those who can do you damage, by creeping into a corner of your own choosing and constructing a private life which alone can satisfy the deepest needs of man. This is what Plato set himself to refute – the view that justice, participation in public life, does not pay but leads to wounds and misery and frustrated ambition. How well he accomplished his task is an issue that is still argued to this day.

Diogenes went further than this. He declared that he had to alter the currency – to destroy the old values and substitute new ones. He boasted that he belonged to no city – for that is what the claim to be cosmopolitan means – in the sense in which the *Communist Manifesto* of 1847 declared that 'The workers have no country' and 'The proletarians have nothing to lose but their chains.'[1] Only the independent man was free, and freedom alone makes happy, by making invulnerable. He inveighed against the arts, the sciences and all external graces with deliberate rudeness to Alexander. The rough jokes attributed to him create an image of a man who deliberately set out to shock public opinion in order to call attention to the gratuitous falsity and conventional hypocrisies of civilised life. He advocated, so we are told, total disregard of the proprieties: sexual intercourse and every intimate function may be performed in public. What deters one from it? The fact that people are shocked? What of it? Why should one respect the reactions of fools or hypocrites, slaves of convention, men who do not understand that men can attain to happiness and dignity only by following nature, that is by ignoring artificial arrangements when all their instincts urge them in the opposite direction? This is full-blown individualism, but represented by our authorities as eccentric and a little deranged.

Crates, a rich man, gave up his wealth and took a few possessions in a knapsack and became the missionary and the saint of life according to nature. He called on families made unhappy by fears or jealousies or hatreds, reconciled enemies, created harmony and happiness, and, pauper and hunchback that he was, won the love of a beautiful and aristocratic lady, who married him against all

---

[1] Karl Marx, Friedrich Engels, op. cit. (p. 85 above, note 1), vol. 4, pp. 479, 493; cf. eid., *Collected Works* (London, 1975–), vol. 2, pp. 502, 519.

protestations and became his fellow missionary. Man must be free, his possessions must be few enough to be carried in a sack slung across his shoulders, the *pera* which became the symbol of itinerant preachers of the Cynic sect. Here are Crates' words:

> There is a city, Knapsack is its name, in the midst of the wine-coloured sea of Typhos [illusion]. Fair and fruitful it is, exceedingly beggarly, owning nothing. Thither sails no fool nor parasite nor lecher delighting in harlots, but it bears thyme and garlic and figs and bread. For such men fight not one another, nor yet do they take up arms for petty gain, nor for glory ... Free are they from lust, the enslaver of men, they are not twisted by it: rather do they take pleasures in freedom and immortal kinghood.[1]

And again:

> I am a citizen of the lands Obscurity and Poverty, impregnable to fortune, a fellow citizen of Diogenes, who defied all the plots of envy.[2]

These are the true predecessors of the new individualism – not many; and represented by our major authorities as somewhat marginal figures in the development of Greek culture. But were they indeed marginal? We cannot tell, for the principal, the fatal difficulty of this entire account is that we simply do not know what doctrines and opinions were held either by ordinary Greeks or by the thinkers among them. The vast bulk of our information comes from the writings of Plato and Aristotle, and they do not trouble to conceal their bias. Aristotle is perhaps a little more detached, scholarly and objective than Plato, but his own views are very positive and he shows little charity to his opponents, neither more nor less than other philosophers have since the beginning of the activity. What we know about the Sophists of the fifth century, and the Cynics and Sceptics and other so-called minor sects, is about as accurate as it would be if all we knew about, say, the writings of Bertrand Russell and modern linguistic analysis came to us from Soviet histories of philosophy; or if our only source for medieval thought was Russell's own history of Western thought. It

---

[1] Lloyd-Jones–Parsons, *Supplementum Hellenisticum*, frr. 351, 352. 4–5.
[2] Diogenes Laertius 6. 93.

is difficult to represent one's opponents fairly, and Plato plainly did not even try, unless they were positively sympathetic to him, like Parmenides or, in part, Protagoras – while the thinkers of whom we speak were plainly bitter enemies, whose views were to be put down at all costs.

The only point I wish to stress is that it is intrinsically unlikely that Zeno and Epicurus, Carneades and the new academy sprang up fully fledged to take over ethics and politics from the failing hands of degenerate Aristotelians and Platonists. Other scholars have felt this and have made gallant efforts to derive Stoicism, at least, from oriental sources. They point out, quite accurately, that every Stoic teacher of any note came from Asia or Africa. Grant and Zeller, Pohlenz and Bevan and a host of others think it no accident that Zeno and Persaeus came from the Phoenician colony in Cyprus; Herillus came from Carthage; Athenodorus came from Tarsus; Cleanthes from the Troad; Chrysippus from Cilicia; Diogenes the Stoic from Babylon; Posidonius from Syria; Panaetius from Rhodes; others from Sidon and Seleucia, Ascalon and the Bosphorus – alas, not a single Stoic was born in old Greece. It is implied that these men brought oriental ideas for personal salvation, black-and-white conceptions of good and evil, duty and sin, the desirability of dissolution in the eternal fire, the attractiveness of suicide. And perhaps it is hinted that this is echoed, in however vague a form, in the Jewish Bible: in the notion of individual responsibility to God that is no longer communal in Jeremiah, in Ezekiel and in the Psalms.[1] Who knows? Perhaps Philo of Alexandria, who was always trying to persuade people that Plato was acquainted with the teachings of Moses, was saying something that had some substance in it.

These theories are more interesting as indications that there is something inexplicable in this situation than because they are intrinsically plausible. Epicurus, whose doctrines for these purposes come close to those of the Stoics, was of pure Athenian blood, even though he grew up in Samos. Diogenes had come from Sinope, but Crates came from Elis, and no one suspected Antiphon of foreign origin. There is nothing inherently un-Greek in Zeno's doctrines: the belief in universal reason, in nature, in peace and inner harmony, self-mastery and independence, liberty and a calm detachment are not Hebraic values. He did speak of duty in terms

[1] Jeremiah 31: 29–34; Ezekiel 18: 20, 14: 12–20, 33: 1–20; Psalms 40, 50, 51.

of absolute rules, but this sprang from his conception of reason as providing ends, as in Plato – as a rigorous category admitting of no degree. There are no voices that thunder at human beings, no sublime and mysterious and terrifying divine presence whose nature it is impious to enquire into: on the contrary, everything is nearly too rational, too systematic, too neat and cut-and-dried, too positivistic. There is no element of mysticism in either Zeno or Epicurus. Cleanthes' profoundly religious hymn is not the utterance of a mystic but of a rationalist, a believer in cosmic reason. If these men were, indeed, foreign in origin and habits and appearance, they assimilated, if anything, too eagerly to the Greek model, like many a colonial in Imperial Rome or natives of the Levant or India in France or England in the nineteenth century. The movements are Greek through and through. Indeed Dodds complains that they were too rationalistic, so that the irrational impulses of the Greeks forced a return to superstition.

Yet the revolution is very great, and if it is not sudden – because the names of the thinkers who preceded it or the opposition to the philosophies of Plato and Aristotle has simply been suppressed or forgotten – that is no more than a conjecture, and rests on considerations of general plausibility, not on any hard evidence that we possess.

What did the revolution come to? Let me attempt to summarise it.

(*a*) Politics and ethics are divorced. The natural unit is now no longer the group, in terms of which men are defined as natural members of it, even if not limbs of an organism, but the individual. His needs, his purposes, his solutions, his fate are what matter. Social institutions may be natural ways of satisfying the individual's needs; however, they are not ends in themselves, but means. And politics, the discipline that deals with the nature and purpose of such institutions, is not a philosophical enquiry that asks about ends and the nature of reality, but a technological discipline that tells men how to obtain what they need or deserve, or should have or make or be – questions answered by ethical or psychological enquiry, not by treatises about the State or about kingship. There are many of these latter, but they are handbooks for Hellenistic rulers or loyal tributes and justifications of their conduct by tame court philosophers.

(*b*) The only genuine life is the inner life; what is outer is expendable. A man is not a man unless his acts are dictated by himself and not forced upon him by a despot from without or by circumstances which he cannot control. The only portion of himself that is within his control is his inner consciousness. If he trains that consciousness to ignore and reject what it cannot control, he acquires independence from the external world. Only the independent are free, and only the free can satisfy their desires, that is, attain to peace and happiness. Such independence can be obtained only by understanding the nature of reality. But whereas for Plato and Aristotle this reality contains public life – the State – as intrinsic parts of it, for the Hellenistic philosophers it does not; hence the decay of political philosophy until Roman needs and Roman practice cause a specious revival in it.

(c) The ethics are the ethics of the individual, but this is not the same – and this point is of some importance – as the notion of individual rights or the sacredness of private life. Diogenes did not mind whether you were disgusted by his mode of living, his rags, his filth, his obscenity, his insulting behaviour, but he did not seek privacy as such. He merely ignored social conventions because he believed that those who knew the truth would not be horrified, but would live as he did. There is more inclination to privacy in Epicurus, but even there there is no individual to keep others out of his particular corner – a right to a room of one's own. This is a much later idea, and those writers who, like Sabine and, indeed, Pohlenz, who is a far more genuine scholar, speak of the emergence of the new value of privacy, and in the case of Sabine go so far as to talk about the rights of man, misunderstand the ancient world profoundly. Not until a force that in principle resisted the encroachments of the civil establishment – the Christian Church in its early struggles against Rome, and, perhaps, before it, Orthodox Jews who fought the secularising policies of Antiochus Epiphanes – created a conflict of authority did the idea arise that frontiers must be drawn beyond which the State is not entitled to venture. Even then it took many centuries for the notion of individual rights to emerge, the notion defended so passionately by Benjamin Constant, that men need an area, however small, within which they can do as they please, no matter how foolish or disapproved of by others. The notion of freedom from State control which his contemporary Humboldt defended, and which found its most eloquent champion in John Stuart Mill – that notion is wholly alien to the ancient world. Neither Plato nor Xenophon nor Aristotle

nor Aristophanes, who deplore the selfishness, rapacity, lawless-
ness, lack of civic sense, irresponsibility of Athenian democracy;
nor Pericles, who defends the 'open' society over which he
presides; nor the Stoics and Sceptics and their successors, who
thought of nothing but the self-preservation and self-gratification
of individuals – none of these had any notion of the rights of man,
the right to be left alone, the right not to be impinged upon within
identifiable frontiers. That comes much later, and it is a gross
anachronism to find it in the ancient world, whether Greek or
Hebraic.

(d) But what happened was dramatic enough. One of the legs of
the tripod upon which Western political philosophy rests was, if
not broken, cracked. Individual salvation, individual happiness,
individual taste, individual character emerge as the central goal, the
centre of interest and value. The State is no longer what it was for
Aristotle – a self-sufficient group of human beings united by
natural pursuit of the good (that is, satisfying) life – but 'a mass of
people living together, governed by law' (so Chrysippus at the
beginning of the third century defined it).[1] A man may serve the
State 'if nothing stops him',[2] but it is not the central function of
his life.

This is the moment that marks the birth of the idea that politics
is unworthy of a truly gifted man, and painful and degrading to a
truly good one. Of this attitude to politics there is scarcely any
earlier trace, although perhaps the life of Socrates, as perhaps of
original and interesting thinkers of earlier times of whom we know
too little, bears witness to this too. At any rate, from now on this
new scale of values haunts the European consciousness. Public and
individual values, which had not been discriminated before, now
go in different directions and, at times, clash violently. There is an
attempt to patch up the situation by the Stoics of the Roman
Republic and the Roman Empire. Panaetius regrets Zeno's violently anti-political attitude and tries to say that all this was written
on the 'dog's tail',[3] that is, when Zeno was still under the
influence of the Cynic Crates. But once the seamless whole of the
city-state in which the public and the private were not distinguished is torn, nothing can ever make it entirely whole again. In
the Renaissance, in modern times, the notion of the separateness of

[1] *SVF* iii 329.   [2] *SVF* iii 697. Cf. Zeno, *SVF* i 271.
[3] Diogenes Laertius 7. 4.

moral and political values, the ethics of resistance, of withdrawal, of personal relationships, versus those of the service of mankind, is one of the deepest and most agonising issues. This is the hour of its birth.

It seems to have come to maturity, and to have begun to possess the minds of the intellectually most influential city that ever existed, somewhere between the death of Aristotle and the rise of the Stoics and the Epicureans. We know little about this intermediate period. Theophrastus reigned in the Lyceum in the place of Aristotle, and he believed in *oikeiosis* – kinship of all life – that there was a natural bond that united men to one another, a great solidarity, not service in a common cause, or the march towards a common purpose, or perception of the same truths, or union by some reciprocally accepted convention, or the claims of utility, but the sense of the unity of life, of the value of men as men, of humanity as a single family with world-wide frontiers. This is not a political idea, but a biological and moral one. Where does it come from? Not from Aristotle, who thought that neither barbarians nor slaves were even remote cousins to free men. But it is echoed by Zeno and by Epicurus. Where does it come from? That is a question to which we may never be able to discover the answer. Antiphon? Pythagoras? We do not know. Plato and Aristotle, if they knew, chose not to tell us.

(e) The new age of individualism is usually deplored as an age of decadence. Cornford says that after Aristotle 'nothing remains but the philosophy of old age, the resignation of a twilight that deepens alike over the garden of Pleasure and the hermitage of Virtue'.[1] Sabine observes that the result of the decline of the city-state was 'a defeatist attitude, a mood of disillusionment, a disposition to withdraw and to create a private life in which public interests had a small or even a negative part'.[2] Then follows a passage in which it is suggested that 'the unfortunate and dispossessed' made themselves even more violently vocal against the city-state and its values and laid 'stress upon the seamy side of the existing social order'.[3] 'To Plato and Aristotle', the same author goes on, 'the values offered by citizenship still seemed fundamentally satisfying, or at

[1] Francis Macdonald Cornford, *Before and After Socrates* (Cambridge, 1932), p. 109.
[2] George H. Sabine, *A History of Political Thought*, 4th ed. (Fort Worth etc., 1973), p. 131.
[3] ibid.

least capable of being made so; to a few of their contemporaries and increasingly to their successors this appeared to be false.'[1] How does he know that there were few? If Greek literature does not reflect the prevalent democracy, but, on the contrary, criticism of it, why should it record a perhaps widespread desire for private values and private salvation? Why should we consider Plato and Aristotle better witnesses to the general thought of their time than Prodicus or Antiphon? Are Burke and Hegel, because they possess more genius, more reliable witnesses of the thought of their own time than Paine or Bentham? If Goethe and Comte were the only authors that survived from their age, how accurately should we be able to deduce its political and moral outlook? As for the pessimistic note struck by Cornford or Sabine, why should we assume that the decline of the 'organic' community was an unmixed disaster? Might it not have had a liberating effect? Perhaps the individuals who lived in greater and more centralised units felt a greater degree of independence, less interference. Rostovtzeff speaks of 'buoyant optimism' in the cities of the Greek diaspora.[2] The great leap forward in the sciences, and the arts as well, coincides with Cornford's theory of twilight and the disillusionment and defeatism of which Sabine and Barker speak. To every age its values: the individualism of the Hellenistic age is attributed by these thinkers to men's loneliness in the new mass society. Yet perhaps what they felt was not loneliness, but a sense of suffocation in the *polis*? First aristocrats like Heraclitus complained of it, then others. So far from being a sad, slow decline, it meant expanding horizons. The third century marks the beginning of new values, and a new conception of life; the condemnation of it by Aristotle and his modern disciples rests on assumptions which, to say the least, do not seem self-evidently valid.

---

[1] ibid., pp. 131–2.

[2] M. Rostovtzeff, *The Social and Economic History of the Hellenistic World* (Oxford, 1941), p. 1095.

FINAL RETROSPECT

Excerpts from 'My Intellectual Path'

Determinism

POLITICAL FREEDOM is a topic to which I devoted two lectures during the 1950s. The first of these was entitled 'Historical Inevitability'.[1] Here I stated that determinism was a doctrine very widely accepted among philosophers for many hundreds of years. Determinism declares that every event has a cause, from which it unavoidably follows. This is the foundation of the natural sciences: the laws of nature and all their applications – the entire body of natural science – rest upon the notion of an eternal order which the sciences investigate. But if the rest of nature is subject to these laws, can it be that man alone is not? When a man supposes, as most ordinary people do (though not most scientists and philosophers), that when he rises from the chair he need not have done so, that he did so because he chose to do so, but he need not have chosen – when he supposes this, he is told that this is an illusion, that even though the necessary work by psychologists has not yet been accomplished, one day it will be (or at any rate in principle can be), and then he will know that what he is and does is necessarily as it is, and could not be otherwise. I believe this doctrine to be false, but I do not in this essay seek to demonstrate this, or to refute determinism – indeed, I am not sure if such a demonstration or refutation is possible. My only concern is to ask myself two questions. Why do philosophers and others think that human beings are fully determined? And, if they are, is this compatible with normal moral sentiments and behaviour, as commonly understood?

My thesis is that there are two main reasons for supporting the doctrine of human determinism. The first is that, since the natural sciences are perhaps the greatest success story in the whole history

[1] Reprinted above, pp. 94–165.

of mankind, it seems absurd to suppose that man alone is not subject to the natural laws discovered by the scientists. (That, indeed, is what the eighteenth-century *philosophes* maintained.) The question is not, of course, whether man is wholly free of such laws – no one but a madman could maintain that man does not depend on his biological or psychological structure or environment, or on the laws of nature. The only question is: Is his liberty totally exhausted thereby? Is there not some corner in which he can act as he chooses, and not be determined to choose by antecedent causes? This may be a tiny corner of the realm of nature, but unless it is there, his consciousness of being free, which is undoubtedly all but universal – the fact that most people believe that, while some of their actions are mechanical, some obey their free will – is an enormous illusion, from the beginnings of mankind, ever since Adam ate the apple, although told not to do so, and did not reply, 'I could not help it, I did not do it freely, Eve forced me to do it.'

The second reason for belief in determinism is that it does devolve the responsibility for a great many things that people do on to impersonal causes, and therefore leaves them in a sense unblameworthy for what they do. When I make a mistake, or commit a wrong or a crime, or do anything else which I recognise, or which others recognise, as bad or unfortunate, I can say, 'How could I avoid it? – that was the way I was brought up' or 'That is my nature, something for which natural laws are responsible' or 'I belong to a society, a class, a Church, a nation, in which everyone does it, and nobody seems to condemn it' or 'I am psychologically conditioned by the way in which my parents behaved to each other and to me, and by the economic and social circumstances in which I was placed, or was forced into, not to be able to choose to act otherwise' or, finally, 'I was under orders.'

Against this, most people believe that everyone has at least two choices that he can make, two possibilities that he can realise. When Eichmann says 'I killed Jews because I was ordered to; if I had not done it I would have been killed myself' one can say 'I see that it is improbable that you would have chosen to be killed, but in principle you could have done it if you had decided to do it – there was no literal compulsion, as there is in nature, which caused you to act as you did.' You may say it is unreasonable to expect people to behave like that when facing great dangers: so it is, but however unlikely it may be that they should decide to do so, in the literal sense of the word they *could* have chosen to do so. Martyrdom cannot be expected, but can be accepted, against whatever odds – indeed, that is why it is so greatly admired.

So much for the reasons for which men choose to embrace determinism in history. But if they do, there is a difficult logical consequence, to say the least. It means that we cannot say to anyone, 'Did you have to do that? Why need you have done that?' – the assumption behind which is that he could have refrained, or done something else. The whole of our common morality, in which we speak of obligation and duty, right and wrong, moral praise and blame – the way in which people are praised or condemned, rewarded or punished, for behaving in a way in which they were not forced to behave, when they could have behaved otherwise – this network of beliefs and practices, on which all current morality seems to me to depend, presupposes the notion of responsibility, and responsibility entails the ability to choose between black and white, right and wrong, pleasure and duty; as well as, in a wider sense, between forms of life, forms of government, and the whole constellations of moral values in terms of which most people, however much they may or may not be aware of it, do in fact live.

If determinism were accepted, our vocabulary would have to be very, very radically changed. I do not say that this is impossible in principle, but it goes further than what most people are prepared to face. At best, aesthetics would have to replace morality. You can admire or praise people for being handsome, or generous or musical – but that is not a matter of their choice, that is 'how they are made'. Moral praise would have to take the same form: if I praise you for saving my life at your own risk, I mean that it is wonderful that you are so made that you could not avoid doing this, and I am glad that I encountered someone literally determined to save my life, as opposed to someone else who was determined to look the other way. Honourable or dishonourable conduct, pleasure-seeking and heroic martyrdom, courage and cowardice, deceitfulness and truthfulness, doing right against temptation – these would become like being good-looking or ugly, tall or short, old or young, black or white, born of English or Italian parents: something that we cannot alter, for everything is determined. We can hope that things will go as we should like, but we cannot do anything towards this – we are so made that we cannot help but act in a particular fashion. Indeed, the very notion of an act denotes choice; but if choice is itself determined, what is the difference between action and mere behaviour?

It seems to me paradoxical that some political movements demand sacrifices and yet are determinist in belief. Marxism, for example, which is founded on historical determinism – the inevitable stages through which society must pass before it reaches perfection – enjoins painful and dangerous acts, coercion and killing, equally painful at times both to the perpetrators and to the victims; but if history will inevitably bring about the perfect society, why should one sacrifice one's life for a process which will, without one's help, reach its proper, happy destination? Yet there is a curious human feeling that if the stars in their courses are fighting for you, so that your cause will triumph, then you should sacrifice yourself in order to shorten the process, to bring the birth-pangs of the new order nearer, as Marx said. But can so many people be truly persuaded to face these dangers, just to shorten a process which will end in happiness whatever they may do or fail to do? This has always puzzled me, and puzzled others.

All this I discussed in the lecture in question, which has remained controversial, and has been much discussed and disputed, and is so still.

Freedom

My other lecture on freedom was entitled 'Two Concepts of Liberty'.[1] This inaugurated my Oxford Professorship, and its gist was to distinguish between two notions of liberty, negative and positive. By negative liberty I meant the absence of obstacles which block human action. Quite apart from obstacles created by the external world, or by the biological, physiological, psychological laws which govern human beings, there is lack of political freedom – the central topic of my lecture – where the obstacles are man-made, whether deliberately or unintentionally. The extent of negative liberty depends on the degree to which such man-made obstacles are absent – on the degree to which I am free to go down this or that path without being prevented from doing so by man-made institutions or disciplines, or by the activities of specific human beings.

It is not enough to say that negative freedom simply means

[1] Reprinted above, pp. 166–217.

freedom to do what I like, for in that case I can liberate myself from obstacles to the fulfilment of desire simply by following the ancient Stoics and killing desire. But that path, the gradual elimination of the desires to which obstacles can occur, leads in the end to humans being gradually deprived of their natural, living activities: in other words, the most perfectly free human beings will be those who are dead, since then there is no desire and therefore no obstacles. What I had in mind, rather, was simply the number of paths down which a man can walk, whether or not he chooses to do so. That is the first of the two basic senses of political freedom.

Some have maintained, against me, that freedom must be a triadic relationship: I can overcome or remove or be free from obstacles only in order to do something, to be free to perform a given act or acts. But I do not accept that. The basic sense of unfreedom is that in which we ascribe it to the man in gaol, or the man tied to a tree; all that such a man seeks is the breaking of his chains, escape from the cell, without necessarily aiming at a particular activity once he is liberated. In the larger sense, of course, freedom means freedom from the rules of a society or its institutions, from the deployment against one of excessive moral or physical force, or from whatever shuts off possibilities of action which otherwise would be open. This I call 'freedom from'.

The other central sense of freedom is freedom *to*: if my negative freedom is specified by answering the question 'How far am I controlled?', the question for the second sense of freedom is 'Who controls me?' Since we are talking about man-made obstacles, I can ask myself 'Who determines my actions, my life? Do I do so, freely, in whatever way I choose? Or am I under orders from some other source of control? Is my activity determined by parents, schoolmasters, priests, policemen? Am I under the discipline of a legal system, the capitalist order, a slave-owner, the government (monarchical, oligarchic, democratic)? In what sense am I master of my fate? My possibilities of action may be limited, but how are they limited? Who are those who stand in my way, how much power can they wield?'

These are the two central senses of 'liberty' which I set myself to investigate. I realised that they differed, that they were answers to two different questions; but, although cognate, they did not in my view clash – the answer to one did not necessarily determine the answer to the other. Both freedoms were ultimate human ends, both were necessarily limited, and both concepts could be perverted in the course of human history. Negative liberty could be interpreted as economic *laissez-faire*, whereby in the name of freedom owners are allowed to destroy the lives of children in mines, or factory-owners to destroy the health and character of workers in industry. But that was a perversion, not what the concept basically means to human beings, in my view. Equally it was said that it is a mockery to inform a poor man that he is perfectly free to occupy a room in an expensive hotel, although he may not be able to pay for it. But that, too, is a confusion. He is indeed free to rent a room there, but has not the means of using this freedom. He has not the means, perhaps, because he has been prevented from earning more than he does by a man-made economic system – but that is a deprivation of freedom to earn money, not of freedom to rent the room. This may sound a pedantic distinction, but it is central to discussions of economic versus political freedom.

The notion of positive freedom has led, historically, to even more frightful perversions. Who orders my life? I do. I? Ignorant, confused, driven hither and thither by uncontrolled passions and drives – is that all there is to me? Is there not within me a higher, more rational, freer self, able to understand and dominate passions, ignorance and other defects, which I can attain to only by a process of education or understanding, a process which can be managed only by those who are wiser than myself, who make me aware of my true, 'real', deepest self, of what I am at my best? This is a well-known metaphysical view, according to which I can be truly free and self-controlled only if I am truly rational – a belief which goes back to Plato – and since I am not perhaps sufficiently rational myself, I must obey those who are indeed rational, and who therefore know what is best not only for themselves but also for me, and who can guide me along lines which will ultimately awaken my true rational self and put it in charge, where it truly belongs. I may feel hemmed in – indeed, crushed – by these authorities, but that is an illusion: when I have grown up and have attained to a fully mature, 'real' self, I shall understand that I would have done for myself what has been done for me if I had been as wise, when I was in an inferior condition, as they are now.

In short, they are acting on my behalf, in the interests of my higher self, in controlling my lower self; so that true liberty for the lower self consists in total obedience to them, the wise, those who know the truth, the élite of sages; or perhaps my obedience must be to those who understand how human destiny is made – for if Marx is right, then it is a Party (which alone grasps the demands of the rational goals of history) which must shape and guide me, whichever way my poor empirical self may wish to go; and the Party itself must be guided by its far-seeing leaders, and in the end by the greatest and wisest leader of all.

There is no despot in the world who cannot use this method of argument for the vilest oppression, in the name of an ideal self which he is seeking to bring to fruition by his own, perhaps somewhat brutal and prima facie morally odious means (prima facie only for the lower empirical self). The 'engineer of human souls', to use Stalin's phrase,[1] knows best; he does what he does not simply in order to do his best for his nation, but in the name of the nation itself, in the name of what the nation would be doing itself if only it had attained to this level of historical understanding. That is the great perversion which the positive notion of liberty has been liable to: whether the tyranny issues from a Marxist leader, a king, a Fascist dictator, the masters of an authoritarian Church or class or State, it seeks for the imprisoned, 'real' self within men, and 'liberates' it, so that this self can attain to the level of those who give the orders.

This goes back to the naïve notion that there is only one true answer to every question: if I know the true answer and you do not, and you disagree with me, it is because you are ignorant; if you knew the truth, you would necessarily believe what I believe; if you seek to disobey me, this can be so only because you are wrong, because the truth has not been revealed to you as it has been to me. This justifies some of the most frightful forms of oppression and enslavement in human history, and it is truly the most dangerous, and, in our century in particular, the most violent, interpretation of the notion of positive liberty.

This notion of two kinds of liberty and their distortions then formed the centre of much discussion and dispute in Western and other universities, and does so to this day.

---

[1] See p. 82 above, note 1.

AUTOBIOGRAPHICAL APPENDICES

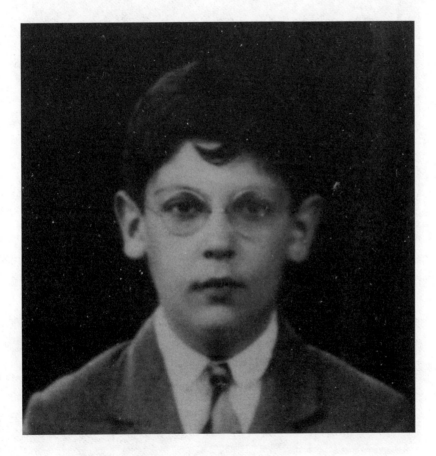

Berlin aged twelve, Arundel House School, July 1921

I

I. Berlin. February 1922.

(author being 12½ yr)

The story of which I am going to tell is about of the murder of Uritzky minister of justice of soviet Russia in the 1919. yet (in the year 1918 the people in Russia and its Capital Petrograd especially, were very depressed by the Bolsheviks, who absolutely terrorized the people. One of the most depressed noble families in Petrograd was the family of the Ivanovs. It consisted of Andrew Ivanov an old man aged 64, his son Peter a handsome and brave young man, and an old servant named Vasily. although They were very depressed they it did not They had a so cozy little home until in which they lived in which freedom and peace and friendship reigned undisturbed until a sudden shock came about to destroy

The first page of the manuscript of 'The Purpose Justifies the Ways' (1922)

THE PURPOSE JUSTIFIES THE WAYS

I

THE STORY of which I am going to tell is about the murder of Uritsky, Minister of Justice of Soviet Russia in the year 1919.

Already in the year 1918 the people in Russia, and its capital Petrograd especially, were very depressed by the Bolsheviks, who terrorised the people to the utmost. One of the most noble families in Petrograd was the family of the Ivanovs. It consisted of Andrew Ivanov, an old man aged sixty-four, his son Peter, a handsome and brave young man, and an old servant named Vasily. Although very depressed, they had a cosy little home in which peace and friendships reigned undisturbed, until a sudden shock came about to destroy their well-earned happiness.

It was a bright cold winter morning. The sun appeared as a little red disc on the clear sky. All nature seemed to be enjoying itself, lapped by the bright rays of the sun. A sudden knock at the door was heard and the next moment an officer and two soldiers entered the Ivanovs' little hall.

'Is Andrew Ivanov living here?' asked the officer curtly.

'I am Andrew Ivanov, and am at your service,' answered the old man quietly.

'Take him away,' ordered the officer, signing to his soldiers. 'This man is guilty before the law for hiding some diamonds in his house. Search the house instantly and if you find any precious stones you will give them to me.'[1]

Peter, who looked at the scene with bewilderment and anger, suddenly dealt the officer a blow that sent him on to the floor, while himself, quick as a lightning, jumped out of the window and soon was out of sight. The soldiers followed the example of their commander, who rose from the ground and went for Peter. But the blow over his head made him fall over the first stone that lay in his

---

[1] Once when the Berlins' flat in Petrograd was searched the maid successfully hid the family jewels in the snow on the balcony.

way and thus stopped him. In his fall a sheet of paper fell out of his hip pocket. Old Vasily the servant, who followed him remarkably quickly for a man of sixty, picked up the paper unnoticed by the officer.

II

Meanwhile Peter decided to go to his cousin Leonid. Leonid, a young man himself, five years elder than his cousin, was dining when Peter rushed in. His burning black eyes, waving dark hair and the bewildered expression on his countenance made Leonid stunned to his place, amazed and bewildered.

'Where do you come from, cousin?' he asked when he recovered his breath, 'And what does that wild look of yours mean?'

Peter, full of hatred, told everything briefly to Leonid, when a knock on the door interrupted him. 'The soldiers!' exclaimed Peter, who looked through the keyhole.

'This way,' pointed Leonid shortly, pointing at the cupboard in the room.

Peter jumped into it without any noise. Leonid, who opened the door to the soldiers, let them in and, as if amazed, asked: 'What made you enter my quiet house, my worthy friends?'

The deceived soldiers asked in loud voices: 'Leonid Ivanov, confess that your cousin is hiding here. You will not be remembered in the court as a guilty man (for we know all your little faults for which you deserve to be punished).'

Peter trembled in his hiding place when he heard this.

'No, my worthy friends, you are on the wrong path, and very much mistaken in thinking that Peter my cousin is here. He never entered my house since his last visit two weeks ago.' Leonid played his part so well that the soldiers were ready to believe that they made mistake.

'But we saw Peter enter this house . . . In any case you would not mind if we would search the house instantly.'

'But my friends,' protested Leonid, 'surely you would not mind a glass of good wine before you start!

'Ahoy! Gregory, bring some of my best wine for these worthy veterans,' cried Leonid, not waiting for the answer of the soldiers. 'Now then friends, let us be merry.'

Leonid all the time added more and more wine to the cups of the 'comrades' while himself hardly touched his own cup. Two hours passed and the drunken soldiers were carried off to unconscious. Meanwhile Peter thanked Leonid for his narrow escape, when suddenly Vasily the old servant of the Ivanovs rushed in.

'Your father is murdered by the wretches,' exclaimed the man, 'by the order of Uritsky, and there is the evidence,' said Vasily, hastily pulling out of his pocket the document he picked up when the officer dropped it. It run like this: 'By the hand of Uritsky minister of justice in the Republic of the Soldiers', Peasants' and Workmen's deputies: allowance given to Captain B. to arrest Andrew Ivanov and if necessary also Peter Ivanov. Uritsky.'

When Peter had read this he found a bit of paper between the folds of the document: 'Andrew Ivanov to be shot 3.15 p.m. at Gorohovaya 3. Peter Ivanov to be executed at 5.30 the same day. Uritsky.'

Peter looked at his watch. It showed 3.10 p.m. Without telling a word he darted from the house in the direction of Gorohovaya 3. He entered the gate at 3.14½. Thirty seconds remained. Not looking where he went, he slipped and fell down. When he got up he heard a horrible scream. Death and life fought in this scream. 'Boom!' Twelve guns sounded, and Peter knew the fate of his father.

He wandered on the streets like a madman. At last, when he came back to Leonid's house, he fainted on the doorstep. Leonid at once understood what had happened. He tried to keep himself up but failed, and burst into bitter tears.

After Peter came to his senses again the old Vasily said to him: 'Peter! Thy enemies the Bolshevist wretches have executed thy father! Therefore swear that thou wilt revenge for thy father!'

In that minute a shot was fired through the window by the officer which came to know how his soldiers were treated. He fired to revenge himself for the blow he received. His shot hit Vasily in his back.

'I swear!' said Peter. Meanwhile the old man's eyes for a moment closed, opened, and had that clear look that people only get in their last moments.

'Revenge!' he murmured, and fell heavily on Peter's hands, unconscious. A minute elapsed, and he opened his eyes for the last time. 'I'm going to meet you, my Master ... Andr...'. He did not finish for death cut his bounds on the earth.

'As long as I live I shall try to revenge upon Uritsky,' called Peter loudly.

'And I am with you, O Peter!' cried Leonid, taking a step forward and raising his hand.

'Death to Uritsky!' they cried both.

III

It was the year 1919. A dark November night. The wind blew outside and the soft armchair before the burning stove seemed so warm and comfortable. In this deep armchair sat a man about forty years old with long flowing hair which showed a big white forehead, two deep little black eyes covered with long eyebrows grown together (which gave his face a somewhat severe look), a sharp nose, a carnivorous mouth and a sharp chin covered with a little French beard. This was the famous Uritsky.

He possessed a clever but also cruel look and all his countenance bore an expression of a fanatic. He signed death verdicts without moving his eyebrow. His leading motto in life was 'The purpose justifies the ways.' He did not stop before anything for bringing out his plans.

He made a good impression at first, but if one looked at the man with his little burning eyes, the man felt that Uritsky read all his thoughts. His eyes made an impression of a thousand little spears shooting through one's brains.

His look hypnotised people whom he wanted to obey him. This was once a famous man, 'comrade' Uritsky, the man of action and one of the greatest Bolshevist factors.

He divided manhood in two classes: first class, people that stood in his way; second, the people who obeyed him. The former, according to Uritsky's understanding, did not deserve to live at all.

'Tzin! tzin!' sounded the bell rung by Uritsky. A moment later Uritsky's young secretary appeared. His name was Michael Sereveev. He wore a big black beard and a black curling moustache. Had he not the moustache and the beard, which at a careful examination would be recognised as false, you would see our old friend Peter Ivanov.

'Sit down Michael,' said Uritsky to him in a weak voice. After Michael alias Peter sat, Uritsky continued his talk. 'Come here,' he said melancholically, 'and tell me a story that would quieten my nerves, for I am tired of the day's work, you know, Michael. Tell me a story that a nurse told you when you were a baby. It is foolish, but it will quieten my nerves. Go on and tell me your tale.'

'I see, sir,' answered Peter, and began.

'Thousands of years ago and thousands of miles away there lived a folk of good people. The people were kind and noble and enjoyed their life thoroughly until a great disaster came along. A new not worthy government ruled the country and destroyed it. It shed the blood of the people. At the head of it stood an ex-murderer, a cruel and clever villain.

'Between others, also one of the most honourable citizens was executed. His son also was to be executed. But he escaped and swore to revenge his father's death upon the villain who signed the death verdict.

'And now', finished Peter loudly, pulling out his automatic, 'the hour come! Hands up!' he shouted, levelling his pistol with Uritsky's forehead. 'Boom!' sounded the pistol, and Uritsky without a groan fell heavily on the floor.

'Ho! Ahoy! Soldiers!' shouted Peter, and when the soldiers appeared he faced them with his pistol. The soldiers moved back in alarm. 'I killed your master,' he cried, 'and now my mission on earth is finished. My father is executed, so is Leonid, both without a trial, and I have not got anybody to live for! O Father, I am going to join you!' 'Boom!' fired Peter and fell heavily over the body of his dead enemy.

When the soldiers came near they found that both were dead.

A LETTER TO GEORGE KENNAN

New College, Oxford
13 February 1951

Dear George,

I have ill rewarded your wonderful letter by leaving it so long unanswered. I received it towards the end of term here when I was genuinely worn out by teaching and examining, and scarcely capable of taking anything in, but even then it moved me profoundly. I took it off with me to Italy and read it and re-read it, and kept putting off the day on which I would write an answer worthy of it, but no such day ever came. I began many letters but each seemed trivial, and what the Russians call 'suetlivo'[1] – full of hurrying sentences, scattered and moving in all directions at once, inappropriate either to the theme or to your words about it; but I cannot bear (if only because of the feelings which your letter excited in me) to say nothing merely because I am not sure how much I have to say. So you must forgive me if what I write is chaotic, not merely in form but in substance, and does little justice to your thesis. I shall simply go on and hope for the best, and beg you to pardon me if I am wasting your time.

I must begin by saying that you have put in words something which I believe not only to be the centre of the subject but something which, perhaps because of a certain reluctance to face the fundamental moral issue on which everything turns, I failed to say; but once forced to face it, I realise both that it is craven to sail round it as I have done, and moreover that it is, in fact, what I myself believe, and deeply believe, to be true; and more than this: that upon one's attitude to this issue which you have put very

---

[1] 'In a fussy or bustling manner.' (All notes to this letter are editorial.)

plainly, and very, if I may say so, poignantly, depends one's entire moral outlook, i.e. everything one believes.

Let me try and say what I think it is; you say (and I am not quoting) that every man possesses a point of weakness, an Achilles' heel, and by exploiting this a man may be made a hero or a martyr or a rag. Again, if I understand you correctly, you think that Western civilisation has rested upon the principle that, whatever else was permitted or forbidden, the one heinous act which would destroy the world was to do precisely this – the deliberate act of tampering with human beings so as to make them behave in a way which, if they knew what they were doing, or what its consequences were likely to be, would make them recoil with horror and disgust. The whole of the Kantian morality (and I don't know about Catholics, but Protestants, Jews, Muslims and high-minded atheists believe it) lies in this; the mysterious phrase about men being 'ends in themselves' to which much lip-service has been paid, with not much attempt to explain it, seems to lie in this: that every human being is assumed to possess the capacity to choose what to do, and what to be, however narrow the limits within which his choice may lie, however hemmed in by circumstances beyond his control; that all human love and respect rests upon the attribution of conscious motives in this sense; that all the categories, the concepts, in terms of which we think about and act towards one another – goodness, badness, integrity and lack of it, the attribution of dignity or honour to others which we must not insult or exploit, the entire cluster of ideas such as honesty, purity of motive, courage, sense of truth, sensibility, compassion, justice; and, on the other side, brutality, falseness, wickedness, ruthlessness, lack of scruple, corruption, lack of feelings, emptiness – all these notions in terms of which we think of others and ourselves, in terms of which conduct is assessed, purposes adopted – all this becomes meaningless unless we think of human beings as capable of pursuing ends for their own sakes by deliberate acts of choice – which alone makes nobility noble and sacrifices sacrifices.

The whole of that morality, which is most prominent in the nineteenth century, in particular in the romantic period, but implicit in both Christian and Jewish writings, and far less present in the pagan world, rests on the view that it is a marvellous thing in itself when a man pits himself against the world, and sacrifices himself to an ideal without reckoning the consequences, even when we consider his ideal false and its consequences disastrous. We

admire purity of motive as such, and think it a wonderful thing –
or at any rate deeply impressive, perhaps to be fought but never
despised – when somebody throws away material advantage,
reputation etc. for the sake of bearing witness to something which
he believes to be true, however mistaken and fanatical we may
think him to be. I do not say that we worship passionate self-
abandonment or automatically prefer a desperate fanaticism to
moderation and enlightened self-interest. Of course not; yet
nevertheless we do think such conduct deeply moving even when
misdirected. We admire it *always* more than calculation; we at least
understand the kind of aesthetic splendour which all defiance has
for some people – Carlyle, Nietzsche, Leontiev and Fascists
generally. We think that only those human beings are a credit to
their kind who do not let themselves be pushed too far by the
forces of nature or history, either passively or by glorying in their
own impotence; and we idealise only those who have purposes for
which they accept responsibility, on which they stake something,
and at times everything; living consciously and bravely for whatever they think good, i.e. worth living and, in the last resort, dying
for.

All this may seem an enormous platitude, but, if it is true, this is,
of course, what ultimately refutes utilitarianism and what makes
Hegel and Marx such monstrous traitors to our civilisation. When,
in the famous passage,[1] Ivan Karamazov rejects the worlds upon
worlds of happiness which may be bought at the price of the
torture to death of one innocent child, what can utilitarians, even
the most civilised and humane, say to him? After all, it is in a sense
unreasonable to throw away so much human bliss purchased at so
small a price as *one* – only one – innocent victim, done to death
however horribly – what after all is one soul against the happiness
of so many? Nevertheless, when Ivan says he would rather return
the ticket, no reader of Dostoevsky thinks this cold-hearted or mad
or irresponsible; and although a long course of Bentham or Hegel
might turn one into a supporter of the Grand Inquisitor, qualms
remain.

Ivan Karamazov cannot be totally exorcised; he speaks for us all,
and this I take to be your point, and the foundation of your

---

[1] Dostoevsky, *The Brothers Karamazov*, book 5, chapter 4: vol. 1, p. 287, in
the Penguin Classics edition, trans. David Magarshack (Harmondsworth, 1958):
'too high a price has been placed on harmony. We cannot afford to pay so much
for admission. And therefore I hasten to return my ticket of admission.'

optimism. What I take you to say, and what I should have said myself if I had had the wit or the depth, is that the one thing which no utilitarian paradise, no promise of eternal harmony in the future within some vast organic whole will make us accept is the use of human beings as mere means – the doctoring of them until they are made to do what they do, not for the sake of the purposes which are their purposes, fulfilment of hopes which however foolish or desperate are at least their own, but for reasons which only we, the manipulators, who freely twist them for our purposes, can understand. What horrifies one about Soviet or Nazi practice is not merely the suffering and the cruelty, since although that is bad enough, it is something which history has produced too often, and to ignore its apparent inevitability is perhaps real Utopianism – no; what turns one inside out, and is indescribable, is the spectacle of one set of persons who so tamper and 'get at' others that the others do their will without knowing what they are doing; and in this lose their status as free human beings, indeed as human beings at all.

When armies were slaughtered by other armies in the course of history, we might be appalled by the carnage and turn pacifist; but our horror acquires a new dimension when we read about children, or for that matter grown-up men and women, whom the Nazis loaded into trains bound for gas chambers, telling them that they were going to emigrate to some happier place. Why does this deception, which may in fact have diminished the anguish of the victims, arouse a really unutterable kind of horror in us? The spectacle, I mean, of the victims marching off in happy ignorance of their doom amid the smiling faces of their tormentors? Surely because we cannot bear the thought of human beings denied their last rights – of knowing the truth, of acting with at least the freedom of the condemned, of being able to face their destruction with fear or courage, according to their temperaments, but at least as human beings, armed with the power of choice. It is the denial to human beings of the possibility of choice, the getting them into one's power, the twisting them this way and that in accordance with one's whim, the destruction of their personality by creating unequal moral terms between the gaoler and the victim, whereby the gaoler knows what he is doing, and why, and plays upon the victim, i.e. treats him as a mere object and not as a subject whose motives, views, intentions have any intrinsic weight whatever – by destroying the very possibility of his having views, notions of a relevant kind – that is what cannot be borne at all.

What else horrifies us about unscrupulousness if not this? Why is the thought of someone twisting someone else round his little finger, even in innocent contexts, so beastly (for instance in Dostoevsky's *Dyadyushkin Son*[1] which the Moscow Arts Theatre used to act so well and so cruelly)? After all, the victim may prefer to have no responsibility; the slave be happier in his slavery. Certainly we do not detest this kind of destruction of liberty *merely* because it denies liberty of action; there is a far greater horror in depriving men of the very capacity for freedom – that is the real sin against the Holy Ghost. Everything else is bearable so long as the possibility of goodness – of a state of affairs in which men freely choose, disinterestedly seek ends for their own sake – is still open, however much suffering they may have gone through. Their souls are destroyed only when this is no longer possible. It is when the desire for choice is broken that what men do thereby loses all moral value, and actions lose all significance (in terms of good and evil) in their own eyes; that is what is meant by destroying people's self-respect, by turning them, in your words, into rags. This is the ultimate horror because in such a situation there are no worthwhile motives left: nothing is worth doing or avoiding, the reasons for existing are gone. We admire Don Quixote, if we do, because he has a pure-hearted desire to do what is good, and he is pathetic because he is mad and his attempts are ludicrous.

For Hegel and for Marx (and possibly for Bentham, although he would have been horrified by the juxtaposition) Don Quixote is not merely absurd but immoral. Morality consists in doing what is good. Goodness is that which will satisfy one's nature. Only that will satisfy one's nature which is part of the historical stream along which one is carried willy-nilly, i.e. that which 'the future' in any case holds in store. In some ultimate sense, failure is proof of a misunderstanding of history, of having chosen what is doomed to destruction, in preference to that which is destined to succeed. But to choose the former is 'irrational', and since morality is rational choice, to seek that which will not come off is immoral. This doctrine that the moral and the good is the successful, and that failure is not only unfortunate but wicked, is at the heart of all that is most horrifying both in utilitarianism and in 'historicism' of the Hegelian, Marxist type. For if only that were best which made one

[1] 'Uncle's Dream', a novella published in 1859.

happiest in the long run, or that which accorded with some mysterious plan of history, there really would be no reason to 'return the ticket'. Provided that there was a reasonable probability that the new Soviet man might either be happier, even in some very long run, than his predecessors, or that history would be bound sooner or later to produce someone like him whether we liked it or not, to protest against him would be mere silly romanticism, 'subjective', 'idealistic', ultimately irresponsible. At most we would argue that the Russians were factually wrong and the Soviet method not the best for producing this desirable or inevitable type of man. But of course what we violently reject is not these questions of fact, but the very idea that there are any circumstances in which one has a right to get at, and shape, the characters and souls of other men for purposes which these men, if they realised what we were doing, might reject.

We distinguish to this extent between factual and value judgement – that we deny the right to tamper with human beings to an unlimited extent, *whatever* the truth about the laws of history; we might go further and deny the notion that 'history' in some mysterious way 'confers' upon us 'rights' to do this or that; that some men or bodies of men can morally claim a right to our obedience because they, in some sense, carry out the behests of 'history', are its chosen instrument, its medicine or scourge or in some important sense 'Welthistorisch'[1] – great, irresistible, riding the waves of the future, beyond our petty, subjective, not rationally bolsterable ideas of right and wrong. Many a German and I daresay many a Russian or Mongol or Chinese today feels that it is more adult to recognise the sheer immensity of the great events that shake the world, and play a part in history worthy of men by abandoning themselves to them, than by praising or damning and indulging in [bourgeois][2] moralisings: the notion that history must be applauded as such is the horrible German way out of the burden of moral choice.

If pushed to the extreme, this doctrine would, of course, do away with all education, since when we send children to school or influence them in other ways without obtaining their approval for what we are doing, are we not 'tampering' with them, 'moulding' them like pieces of clay with no purpose of their own? Our answer

---

[1] 'World-historical.'
[2] Conjectural restoration of word omitted by typist.

has to be that certainly all 'moulding' is evil, and that if human beings at birth had the power of choice and the means of understanding the world, it would be criminal; since they have not, we temporarily enslave them, for fear that, otherwise, they will suffer worse misfortunes from nature and from men, and this 'temporary enslavement' is a necessary evil until such time as they are able to choose for themselves – the 'enslavement' having as its purpose not an inculcation of obedience but its contrary, the development of power of free judgement and choice; still, evil it remains even if necessary.

Communists and Fascists maintain that this kind of 'education' is needed not only for children but for entire nations for long periods, the slow withering away of the State corresponding to immaturity in the lives of individuals. The analogy is specious because peoples, nations are not individuals and still less children; moreover in promising maturity their practice belies their professions; that is to say, they are lying, and for the most part know that they are. From a necessary evil in the case of the education of helpless children, this kind of practice becomes an evil on a much larger scale, and quite gratuitous, based either on utilitarianism, which misrepresents our moral values, or again on metaphors which misdescribe both what we call good and bad, and the nature of the world, the facts themselves. For we, i.e. those who join with us, are more concerned with making people free than making them happy; we would rather that they chose badly than not at all; because we believe that unless they choose they cannot be either happy or unhappy in any sense in which these conditions are worth having; the very notion of 'worth having' presupposes the choice of ends, a system of free preferences; and an undermining of *them* is what strikes us with such cold terror, worse than the most unjust sufferings, which nevertheless leave the possibility of knowing them for what they are – of free judgement, which makes it possible to condemn them – still open.

You say that men who in this way undermine the lives of other men will end by undermining themselves, and the whole evil system is therefore doomed to collapse. In the long run I am sure you are right, because open-eyed cynicism, the exploitation of others by men who avoid being exploited themselves, is an attitude difficult for human beings to keep up for very long. It needs too much discipline and appalling strain in an atmosphere of such mutual hatred and distrust as cannot last because there is not enough moral intensity or general fanaticism to keep it going. But still the run can be very long before it is over, and I do not believe that the corrosive force from inside will work away at the rate which perhaps you, more hopefully, anticipate. I feel that we must avoid being inverted Marxists. Marx and Hegel observed the economic corrosion in their lifetime, and so the revolution seemed to be always round the corner. They died without seeing it, and perhaps it would have taken centuries if Lenin had not given history a sharp jolt. Without the jolt, are moral forces alone sufficient to bury the Soviet grave-diggers? I doubt it. But that in the end the worm would eat them I doubt no more than you; but whereas you say that is an isolated evil, a monstrous scourge sent to try us, not connected with what goes on elsewhere, I cannot help seeing it as an extreme and distorted but only too typical form of some general attitude of mind from which our own countries are not exempt.

For saying this, E. H. Carr has attacked me with some violence, in a leading article in *The Times Literary Supplement* last June.[1] This makes me believe I must be even more right than I thought, since his writings are among the more obvious symptoms of what I tried to analyse, and he rightly interprets my articles as an attack on all he stands for. All this comes out particularly in his last oeuvre – on the Russian Revolution – in which the opposition and the victims are not allowed to testify – feeble flotsam adequately taken care of by history, which has swept them away as, being against the current, they, *eo ipso*, deserve. Only the victors deserve to be heard; the rest – Pascal, Pierre Bezukhov, all Chekhov's people, all the critics and casualties of Deutschtom or White Man's Burdens, or the American Century, or the Common Man on the March – these are historical dust, *lishnye lyudi*,[2] those who have missed the bus of history, poor little rats inferior to Ibsenite rebels who are all potential Catilines and dictators. Surely there never was a time when more homage was paid to bullies as such: and the weaker the victim the louder (and sincerer) his paeans – *vide* E. H. Carr,

[1] 'The New Scepticism' (unsigned), *The Times Literary Supplement*, 9 June 1950, 357.

[2] 'Superfluous men'. The concept of the 'superfluous man' was given its familiar name by Turgenev in *Dnevnik lishnego cheloveka* ('Diary of a superfluous man'): see entry for 23 March 1850. The term was also used as a catchphrase by Dostoevsky in *Zapiski iz podpol'ya* ('Notes from Underground', 1864).

Koestler, Burnham, Laski, *passim*? But I must not waste your time any further.

Once more I should like to say how deeply moved I was by your formulation of what it is that excites in us the unparalleled horror which we feel when we read of what goes on in Soviet territories, and [to record] my admiration and unbounded moral respect for the insight and scruple with which you set it forth. These qualities seem to me unique at present; more than this I cannot say.

Yours ever,
[Isaiah][1]

---

[1] This letter has been transcribed (with some additional paragraph breaks) from a carbon typescript which does not bear a signature. I have not been able to trace the top copy.

NOTES ON PREJUDICE

FEW THINGS have done more harm than the belief on the part of individuals or groups (or tribes or states or nations or churches) that he or she or they are in *sole* possession of the truth: especially about how to live, what to be & do – & that those who differ from them are not merely mistaken, but wicked or mad: & need restraining or suppressing. It is a terrible and dangerous arrogance to believe that you alone are right: have a magical eye which sees *the* truth: & that others cannot be right if they disagree. This makes one certain that there is *one* goal & one only for one's nation or church or the whole of humanity, & that it is worth any amount of suffering (particularly on the part of other people) if only the goal is attained – 'through an ocean of blood to the Kingdom of Love' (or something like this) said Robespierre:[1] & Hitler, Lenin, Stalin, & I daresay leaders in the religious wars of Christian v. Moslem or Catholics v. Protestants sincerely believed this: the belief that there is one & only one true answer to the central questions which have agonized mankind & that one has it oneself – or one's Leader has it – was responsible for the oceans of blood: but no Kingdom of Love sprang from it – or could: there are many ways of living, believing, behaving: mere *knowledge* provided by history, anthropology, literature, art, *law* makes clear that the differences of cultures & characters are as deep as the similarities (which make men human) & that we are none the poorer for this rich variety: *knowledge* of it opens the windows of the mind (and soul) and makes people wiser, nicer, & more civilized: absence of it breeds

---

[1] Berlin may be referring to the passage where Robespierre writes that 'en scellant notre ouvrage de notre sang, nous puissons voir au moins briller l'aurore de la félicité universelle' ('by sealing our work with blood, we may see at least the bright dawn of universal happiness'). *Rapport sur les principes de morale politique qui doivent guider la Convention nationale dans l'administration intérieure de la République* [Paris, 1794], p. 4.

irrational prejudice, hatreds, ghastly extermination of heretics and those who are different: if the two great wars, plus Hitler's genocides haven't taught us that, we are incurable.

The most valuable – or one of the most valuable – elements in the British tradition is precisely the relative freedom from political, racial, religious fanaticism & monomania: Compromising with people with whom you don't sympathize or altogether understand is indispensable to any decent society: nothing is more destructive than a happy sense of one's own – or one's nation's – infallibility which lets you destroy others with a quiet conscience because you are doing God's (e.g. the Spanish Inquisition or the Ayatollas) or the superior race's (e.g. Hitler) or History's (e.g. Lenin–Stalin) work. The only cure is *understanding* how other societies – in space or time, live: and that it is *possible* to lead lives different from one's own, & yet to be fully human, worthy of love, respect or at least *curiosity*. Jesus, Socrates, John Hus of Bohemia, the great chemist Lavoisier, socialists and liberals (as well as conservatives) in Russia, Jews in Germany, all perished at the hands of 'infallible' ideologues: intuitive certainty is no substitute for carefully tested empirical knowledge based on observation and experiment and free discussion between men: the first people totalitarians destroy or silence are men of ideas & free minds.

II

Another source of avoidable conflict is stereotypes. Tribes hate neighbouring tribes by whom they feel threatened, & then rationalize their fears by representing them as wicked or inferior, or absurd or despicable in some way. Yet these stereotypes alter sometimes quite rapidly: Take the 19th century alone: In, say, 1840 the French are thought of as swashbuckling, gallant, immoral, militarized, men with curly moustachios, dangerous to women, likely to invade England in revenge for Waterloo; & the Germans are beer drinking, rather ludicrous provincials, musical, full of misty metaphysics, harmless but somewhat absurd. By 1871 the Germans are Uhlans storming through France incited by the terrible Bismarck – terrifying Prussian militarists filled with national pride etc. France is a poor, crushed, civilized land, in need of protection from all good men, lest its art & literature are crushed underheel by the terrible invaders.

The Russians in the 19th century are crushed serfs, + darkly brooding semi-religious Slav mystics who write deep novels + a huge horde of cossacks loyal to the Tsar, who sing beautifully. In our times all this has dramatically altered: crushed population, yes, but technology, tanks, godless materialism, crusade against capitalism, etc etc. – the English are ruthless imperialists lording it over fuzzy wuzzies, looking down their long noses at the rest of the world – & then impoverished, liberal, decent welfare state beneficiaries in need of allies. And so on. All these stereotypes are substitutes for real knowledge – which is never of anything so simple or permanent as a particular generalized image of foreigners, – & are stimuli to national self satisfaction & disdain of other nations. It is a prop to nationalism.

III

Nationalism – which everybody in the 19th century thought was *ebbing* – is the strongest & most dangerous force at large to-day. It is usually the product of a wound inflicted by one nation on the pride or territory of another: if Louis XIV had not attacked & devastated the Germans, & humiliated them for years – the Sun King whose state gave laws to everybody – in politics, warfare, art, philosophy, science – the Germans would not, perhaps, have become quite so aggressive by, say, the early 19th century when they became fiercely nationalistic against Napoleon. If the Russians, similarly, had not been treated as a barbarous mass by the West in the 19th century, or the Chinese humiliated by opium wars or general exploitation, neither would have fallen so easily to a doctrine which promised *them* to inherit the earth after they had – with the help of historic forces which none may stop – crushed all the capitalist unbelievers. If the Indians had not been patronized etc. etc. – Conquest, enslavement of peoples, imperialism etc are not fed by just greed or desire for glory, but have to justify themselves to themselves by some central idea: French as the only true culture: the white man's burden: communism: & the stereotypes of others as inferior or wicked. Only knowledge, careful & not short cuts – can dispel this: even that won't dispel human aggressiveness or dislike for the dissimilar (in skin, culture, religion) by itself: still, education in history, anthropology, law (especially if they are 'comparative' & not just of one's own country as they usually are) helps.

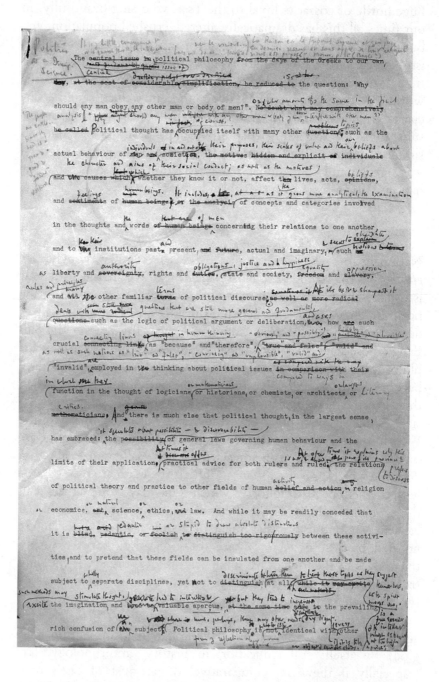

The central issue in political philosophy from the days of the Greeks to our own,
may, at the cost of considerable simplification, be reduced to the question: "Why
should any man obey any other man or body of men?". No doubt what may comprehensively
be called political thought has occupied itself with many other questions, such as the
actual behaviour of men and societies, the motives hidden and explicit of individuals
and the causes which whether they know it or not, affect their lives, acts, opinions,
and sentiments of human beings, or the analysis of concepts and categories involved
in the thoughts and words of human beings concerning their relations to one another
and to their institutions past, present, and future, actual and imaginary, such
as liberty and sovereignty, rights and duties, state and society, freedom and slavery,
and all the other familiar terms of political discourse, as well as more radical
questions such as the logic of political argument or deliberation, how are such
crucial connecting links as "because" and "therefore", "true and false", "valid" and
"invalid", employed in the thinking about political issues in comparison with their
function in the thought of logicians, or historians, or chemists, or architects or
mathematicians. And there is much else that political thought, in the largest sense,
has embraced: the possibility of general laws governing human behaviour and the
limits of their application, practical advice for both rulers and ruled, the relations
of political theory and practice to other fields of human belief and action, religion
economics, and science, ethics, and law. And while it may be readily conceded that
it is blind, pedantic, or foolish, to distinguish too rigorously between these activities, and to pretend that these fields can be insulated from one another and be made
subject to separate disciplines, yet not to distinguish at all, while it may excite
excite the imagination, and yield valuable aperçus, at the same time to the prevailing
rich confusion of the subjects. Political philosophy is not identical with other

The first page of the typescript of 'Political Ideas in the Romantic Age'

BERLIN AND HIS CRITICS

Ian Harris

THE ESSAYS collected in *Liberty* are mostly attempts to develop the general position that Isaiah Berlin had adopted by the late 1940s and early 1950s. That position had three aspects. It applied Berlin's philosophical views to the intellectual history of Europe in the eighteenth and nineteenth centuries; it attributed to that history practical consequences for the middle years of the twentieth century; and it responded to those consequences by outlining a liberal political theory.

Berlin's view of knowledge suggested that experience alters conceptual frameworks. Thus, for instance, since political theories address the experience of an epoch, and experience varies over time, such theories cannot cumulate progressively in the manner attributed to the natural sciences. The distinction this suggests took two, not unfamiliar, forms. One distinguished types of knowledge: between the natural sciences and the humanities. The other was an ontological distinction between their respective subject-matters, with on one side the notions that the facts of nature were consistent with one another and admitted of deterministic explanations, and on the other side that the features of a distinctively human life, including values, were inconsistent with each other and the products of free choice.

Berlin complemented these, neo-Kantian, views with a trajectory of intellectual history, seen in its most complete form in a typescript as yet unpublished, prepared initially at the beginning of the 1950s, 'Political Ideas in the Romantic Age'.[1] He identified

---

[1] For details of this typescript see Berlin's *Freedom and its Betrayal: Six Enemies of Human Liberty* (London, 2002: Chatto and Windus; Princeton, 2002: Princeton University Press), pp. xii–xiii, xv. (Subsequent page references are by number alone.) *Freedom and its Betrayal* is a reworking and selective expansion of some of the material from 'Political Ideas in the Romantic Age', broadcast as a

Kant as the inventor of the distinction between the realm of value and the facts of nature. Before Kant, it was understood that mankind belonged to a realm of fact, that facts were consistent with each other, and that all values, including moral values, were in some sense natural. These presuppositions issued during the (French) Enlightenment in the view that human conduct was determined, could be seen in a way analogous to that in which we view physical nature, and was properly a subject of modification in order to conform with nature rightly understood. If Rousseau translated such views into a political idiom, Kant, by rejecting them, gave a cue to such movements as romanticism and nationalism. These emphasised instead humanity's capacity to determine its own conduct, its capacity for invention, and its ability to multiply values.

This interpretation illuminated *The Age of Enlightenment*,[1] evaluated *Three Critics of the Enlightenment*,[2] and fertilised *The Roots of Romanticism*,[3] but Berlin also found difficulties in the romantic legacy as much as in the 'scientific' one: he linked Maistre with the origins of Fascism and implied that the legacy of Marxism was more ambiguous than was made plain in Berlin's 1939 intellectual biography of its founder. Though the romantic legacy emphasised freedom, it might involve also a personification that located agency with groups, and subordinated individuals and minorities to their will; and whereas enlightened thought implied determinism, it might also include toleration and reason. Berlin's intellectual history suggested a need to clarify and to criticise traditions, as well as to express them, a general procedure not dissimilar from that of his contemporary Michael Oakeshott in *The Politics of Faith and the Politics of Scepticism*[4] and *On Human Conduct*.[5] The two men differed (as in other particulars) in that Berlin's preoccupations in the 1940s and 1950s had a more obviously practical reference than Oakeshott's after the *Cambridge Journal*.[6]

series of lectures in 1952. See in particular Berlin's treatment of Kant, 57–62.

[1] New York, 1956: New American Library.

[2] London, 2000: Pimlico; Princeton, 2000: Princeton University Press.

[3] London, 1999: Chatto and Windus; Princeton, 1999: Princeton University Press.

[4] New Haven, 1996: Yale University Press.

[5] Oxford, 1975: Clarendon Press.

[6] Edited by Oakeshott from 1948 to 1954.

These preoccupations found expression from 1947 partly in Berlin's broadcasts, lectures and writings about Russia, which suggested that the pre-1917 intelligentsia contained a great many elements that did not point to Soviet destinations, besides a few that did.[1] Berlin also began to work out a liberal alternative to totalitarianism. This was a more common project than the Russian one. F. A. Hayek's *The Road to Serfdom*,[2] Karl Popper's *The Open Society and its Enemies*,[3] J. L. Talmon's *Origins of Totalitarian Democracy*[4] and George Sabine's 'The Two Democratic Traditions'[5] all in their different ways suggested or implied that there should be spheres within which the individual should be free from social and political interference, and constructed genealogies for totalitarianism, whilst the notion that the domestic function of the State is not to pattern the whole of society, but instead to provide a basic structure of order consistent with many different types of life and thought, is found, along with associated motifs, in many later works. Berlin's account, however, was worked out in his own manner.

Berlin's earliest surviving piece of writing, reprinted here, is the story 'The Purpose Justifies the Ways'. Whilst we certainly would do badly to read conceptual opinions into the mind of this twelve-year-old author, the piece reveals the disposition which found expression in Berlin's mature work. The tale shows how the lives situated within an area of negative freedom ('a cosy little home') are first threatened and then destroyed by the crude consequentialism of Berlin's Commissar Uritsky, and by the belief this implied in his own intellectual sufficiency (not to mention his extreme personal nastiness). Though the tale is also about how Peter Ivanov revenged himself against Uritsky, this act vindicated a way of life against oppression. Berlin's own 'inner citadel'[6] developed concep-

---

[1] For assessments of Berlin's writings on Russia, see Aileen Kelly, *Toward Another Shore* (New Haven and London, 1998: Yale University Press), introduction and chapter 1, and her 'A Revolutionary Without Fanaticism', in Mark Lilla, Ronald Dworkin and Robert B. Silvers (eds), *The Legacy of Isaiah Berlin* (New York, 2001: New York Review Books), 3–30.

[2] London, 1944: Routledge; Chicago, 1944: University of Chicago Press.

[3] London, 1945: Routledge; Princeton, 1950: Princeton University Press.

[4] London, 1952: Secker and Warburg; published in the USA as *The Rise of Totalitarian Democracy* (Boston, 1952: Beacon Press).

[5] *Philosophical Review* 61 (1952), 451–74.

[6] See pp. xxx, 246, 288 above.

tual protection against the same threat. He became preoccupied by the contrast between a settled, civilised life and its disturbance by the intrusive claims of intellectual monopolists. This was elaborated in many versions, of which perhaps the least formal, and certainly one of the most passionate, is his claim in 'Notes on Prejudice' (included here) that 'the belief that there is one & only one true answer to the central questions which have agonized mankind ... was responsible for ... oceans of blood: but no Kingdom of Love sprang from it'.[1] The main essays in this volume show Berlin identifying conceptual intruders, demarcating the civil area into which they should not venture, and sketching a view of reality and knowledge that indicated just how mistaken their claims were.

The earliest item Berlin included in *Four Essays on Liberty* – 'Political Ideas in the Twentieth Century' (1950) – examined the origins of Communism, Fascism and Marxism, and dwelt on the belief that human life tended in 'one and only one direction',[2] on the general prevalence of instrumentality and on 'the artificial stilling of doubts',[3] the last by treating people as properly subjects of science; to these it preferred 'more room' to differ,[4] and suggested very briefly that human goals were really various, and 'at times incompatible'.[5] It attracted little published notice beyond an unsigned leading article by E. H. Carr.[6] This implied that Berlin's attitude was nostalgic rather than practical; but Berlin's piece also occasioned a notable exchange of letters between George Kennan and Berlin, which identified a need for development and the role of 'the Kantian morality' within it.[7] Berlin's letter is published for the first time in the present volume.

By reprinting 'Political Ideas', Berlin placed it as a preface to two of his more substantial lectures, 'Historical Inevitability' (1954) and 'Two Concepts of Liberty' (1958).

Berlin needed at least to make space for free choice if he was to give conceptual strength to his preferences. 'Historical Inevitability' accordingly was more philosophical than historical in method, and devoted itself to this task, albeit negatively. It connected determinism with the view that 'the world has a direction and is

---

[1] p. 345 above.   [2] 85.   [3] 88.   [4] 92.   [5] 93.
[6] 'The New Scepticism', *Times Literary Supplement*, 9 June 1950, 357.
[7] 337.

governed by laws',[1] that these laws could be known, and provided grounds for understanding humanity (and not just nature) specifically in terms of groups rather than individuals; that this view undermined individual responsibility; that determinism would require radical changes in 'our moral and psychological categories';[2] and that moral judgement remained possible. The lecture, which was printed as a short book by Oxford University Press,[3] stimulated much comment, including high praise from Pieter Geyl in *Debates with Historians*,[4] and less high praise from E. H. Carr in *What is History?*[5] Popper's *The Poverty of Historicism*[6] is in some respects comparable with 'Historical Inevitability'. Philosophical commentators included J. A. Passmore in 'History, the Individual, and Inevitability';[7] Ernest Nagel in 'Determinism in History';[8] Amartya Sen in 'Determinism and Historical Predictions';[9] and Morton White in *Foundations of Historical Knowledge*.[10] The piece also stimulated a most perceptive brief treatment of Berlin by D. M. Mackinnon in *A Study in Ethical Theory*.[11]

Christopher Dawson, reviewing 'Historical Inevitability', remarked that Berlin's 'thesis is a simple one that will enlist the sympathy of all good citizens', and added that 'he attacks the enemies of freedom ... with such indiscriminate enthusiasm, that ... he has made a clean sweep of science and metaphysics and theology, and stands alone on the stricken field'.[12] Berlin did indeed need to make at least two further steps towards being constructive.

One was to insist upon negative freedom as a complement to a capacity for free choice, the other to explain that neither metaphysics nor, in particular, value, properly understood, admitted the viewpoint Berlin rejected. His classic statement of these claims was his inaugural lecture at Oxford as Chichele Professor of Social and Political Theory, 'Two Concepts of Liberty'. 'Two Concepts'

[1] 114. [2] 123. [3] London, 1954.

[4] Gröningen/The Hague, 1955: Wolters/Nijhoff; London, 1955: Batsford.

[5] London/New York, 1961: Macmillan/St Martin's Press.

[6] London, 1957: Routledge; Boston, 1957: Beacon Press.

[7] *Philosophical Review* 68 (1959), 93–102.

[8] *Philosophy and Phenomenological Research* 20 (1959–60), 291–317, at 311–6; compare his *The Structure of Science* (London, 1961: Routledge; New York, 1961: Harcourt, Brace and World), 599–605.

[9] *Enquiry* (Delhi) 2 (1959), 99–115, at 113–14.

[10] New York, 1965: Harper and Row, 265 ff.

[11] London, 1957: A. and C. Black; New York, 1962: Collier, 207–17.

[12] *Harvard Law Journal* 70 (1957), 584–8, at 585.

indicated that though the concepts of negative and positive freedom were 'at no great logical distance'[1] from each other, yet over
time they had been developed in very inconsistent ways. Berlin
gave an account of the distortion of the positive concept from its
original form of collective control over external nature to group
control over, and modification of, the individual; he connected it
with the metaphysical view that society and nature alike disclose a
harmonious order, discoverable by reason, towards which political
authority might direct people; and he concluded the lecture by
suggesting quite briefly a contrary view, 'that not all good things
are compatible, still less all the ideals of mankind',[2] that choice
amongst them was necessary and therefore so was the freedom to
exercise choice that the provision of negative freedom would
facilitate.

'Two Concepts' excited much comment in the years immediately succeeding publication, including an unsigned review by
Richard Wollheim, at once friendly and critical,[3] and a eulogy by
Noel Annan.[4] There was a variety of further responses. These
included Marshall Cohen, 'Berlin and the Liberal Tradition',[5]
which found 'Two Concepts' 'fundamentally obscure',[6] and
criticised especially its reading of positive liberty; David Spitz, 'The
Nature and Limits of Freedom',[7] which suggested that Berlin's
'central thesis'[8] had been argued by Dorothy Fosdick's *What is
Liberty?*;[9] and A. S. Kaufman, 'Professor Berlin on "Negative
Freedom"',[10] which found confusion.

Fuller commentary began with Alan Ryan, 'Freedom',[11] which
discussed both Berlin and his critics. It was carried forward by L. J.
Macfarlane, 'On Two Concepts of Liberty',[12] which remains the
most penetrating general discussion of Berlin's treatment of liberty.

[1] 178.   [2] 213.

[3] 'A Hundred Years After', *Times Literary Supplement*, 20 February 1959,
89–90.

[4] 'Misconceptions of Freedom', *Listener*, 19 February 1959, 323–4.

[5] *Philosophical Quarterly* 10 (1960), 216–27.

[6] 217.

[7] *Dissent* 8 No 1 (Winter 1961), 78–85, at 79–82.

[8] 79.

[9] London and New York, 1939: Harper.

[10] *Mind* 71 (1962), 241–3.

[11] *Philosophy* 40 (1965), 93–112.

[12] *Political Studies* 14 (1966), 293–305.

H. J. McCloskey, 'A Critique of the Ideals of Liberty',[1] doubted that much of what Berlin had discussed, whether negative or positive, was liberty properly so called. Better known is the essay by Gerald C. MacCallum, Jr., 'Negative and Positive Freedom',[2] which, however, does not transparently understand positive freedom; MacCallum also wrote 'Berlin on the Compatibility of Values, Ideals and "Ends"'.[3] On these, see respectively Tom Baldwin, 'MacCallum and the Two Concepts of Freedom',[4] and G. A. Cohen, 'A Note on Values and Sacrifices'.[5] 'Berlin's Division of Liberty' was questioned in C. B. Macpherson, *Democratic Theory: Essays in Retrieval.*[6] Bernard Crick advanced another view again in *Freedom as Politics.*[7] G. W. Smith argued against Berlin that the genuinely contented slave has social freedom in 'Slavery, Contentment, and Social Freedom'.[8] Hans Blokland examined 'Isaiah Berlin on Positive and Negative Freedom'.[9] Of especial importance is Charles Taylor's 'What's Wrong with Negative Liberty', in Alan Ryan (ed.), *The Idea of Freedom,*[10] which suggested quite a different account of positive freedom. Christopher Megone sharply criticised both Berlin and Taylor in 'One Concept of Liberty'.[11] Ronald Dworkin's attempt to develop 'Two Concepts of Liberty' in a characteristic way is in Avishai and Edna Margalit (eds.), *Isaiah Berlin: A Celebration.*[12] The suggestion that negative and positive freedom had supported each other in at least one country was developed powerfully by Judith Shklar, 'Positive Liberty, Negative

---

[1] *Mind* 74 (1965), 483–508.

[2] *Philosophical Review* 76 (1967), 312–34; later anthologised.

[3] *Ethics,* 77 (1966–7), 139–45.

[4] *Ratio* 26 (1984), 125–42.

[5] *Ethics* 79 (1968–9), 159–62.

[6] Oxford, 1973: Clarendon Press, chapter 5. See also his *The Rise and Fall of Economic Justice* (Oxford, 1985: Oxford University Press), 92–100.

[7] Sheffield, 1966: University of Sheffield; repr. in Crick's *Political Theory and Practice* (London, [1972]: Allen Lane).

[8] *Philosophical Quarterly* 27 (1977), 236–48.

[9] In his *Freedom and Culture in Western Society* (London and New York, 1997: Routledge), chapter 2.

[10] Oxford, 1979: Clarendon Press, 175–93; repr. in Taylor's *Philosophy and the Human Sciences: Philosophical Papers* (Cambridge and New York, 1985: Cambridge University Press), vol. 2, 211–29, amongst other places.

[11] *Political Studies* 35 (1987), 611–22.

[12] London, 1991: Hogarth Press; Chicago, 1991: University of Chicago Press, 100–9.

Liberty in the United States'.[1] 'Two Concepts' is often mentioned briefly in extended philosophical discussions of political freedom, for instance, Carl J. Friedrich, 'Rights, Liberties, Freedoms: A Reappraisal',[2] and Hillel Steiner, *An Essay on Rights*.[3]

Criticism of the intellectual history implied in 'Two Concepts' has included David Nicholls, 'Positive Liberty, 1880–1914';[4] a decidedly sceptical treatment of its illustrative examples in Anthony Arblaster, 'Vision and Revision: A Note on the Text of Isaiah Berlin's *Four Essays on Liberty*';[5] a criticism of its account of Green in Avital Simhony, 'On Forcing Individuals to be Free: T. H. Green's Liberal Theory of Positive Freedom';[6] and of its view of Spinoza in David West, 'Spinoza on Positive Freedom',[7] to which Berlin responded with 'A Reply to David West'.[8] The reader may judge how adequately the history of political thought can be understood via the negative/positive distinction by consulting Z. A. Pelczynski and John Gray (eds.), *Conceptions of Liberty in Political Philosophy*.[9] The phase of thought in which 'Two Concepts' was written is itself considered in Noel O'Sullivan, 'Visions of Freedom: The Response to Totalitarianism', in Jack Hayward, Brian Barry and Archie Brown (eds.), *The British Study of Politics in the Twentieth Century*, a volume of general relevance to Berlin's life.[10]

The possibility that Berlin's pluralism involved relativism did not escape the vigilance of Leo Strauss. His essay 'Relativism' appeared in Helmut Schoeck and James W. Wiggins (eds.), *Relativism and the Study of Man*.[11] Other important reflections on the

---

[1] First published in French in 1980; translated by Stanley Hoffman in Shklar's *Redeeming American Political Thought*, ed. Stanley Hoffman and Dennis F. Thompson (Chicago and London, 1998: University of Chicago Press), 110–26.

[2] *American Political Science Review* 57 No 4 (1963), 841–54.

[3] Oxford and Cambridge, Mass., 1994: Blackwell.

[4] *American Political Science Review* 56 No 1 (1962), 114–28, at 114 note 8.

[5] *Political Studies* 19 (1971), 81–6.

[6] ibid. 29 (1991), 303–20.

[7] ibid. 41 (1993), 284–96.

[8] ibid., 297–8.

[9] London, 1984: Athlone Press; New York, 1984: St Martin's Press.

[10] Oxford, 1999: Clarendon Press/The British Academy.

[11] Princeton, 1961: Van Nostrand, 137–57. It was reprinted in his *The Rebirth of Classical Political Rationalism*, ed. Thomas L. Pangle (Chicago and London, 1989: University of Chicago Press).

theme are Arnaldo Momigliano, 'On the Pioneer Trail';[1] Hilary Putnam, 'Pragmatism and Relativism: Universal Values and Traditional Ways of Life';[2] and Steven Lukes, 'Berlin's Dilemma'.[3] Berlin addressed the question in 'Alleged Relativism in Eighteenth-Century European Thought' (1980) and 'The Pursuit of the Ideal' (1988), both reprinted in his *The Crooked Timber of Humanity*.[4]

The energy of its prose, the width of its reference and the sharpness of its distinction between negative and positive freedom have made 'Two Concepts of Liberty' pedagogically irresistible, whether for works of reference – as Chandran Kukuthas, 'Liberty', in Robert E. Goodin and Philip Pettit, (eds.), *A Companion to Contemporary Political Philosophy*[5] – for textbooks – such as Tim Gray, *Freedom*,[6] Raymond Plant, *Modern Political Thought*,[7] and Peter Lassman and Steve Buckler, *Political Thinkers of the Twentieth Century*[8] – and for brief discussions on the way to other destinations – as in Philip Pettit, *Republicanism*.[9] The lecture has been reprinted frequently as a whole or in part. Examples include Robert E. Goodin and Philip Pettit (eds.), *Contemporary Political Philosophy: An Anthology*;[10] David Miller (ed.), *Liberty*;[11] Michael Sandel (ed.), *Liberalism and its Critics*;[12] and Anthony Quinton (ed.), *Political Philosophy*.[13] Berlin himself obligingly provided a digest of 'Two Concepts', 'Liberty' (1995), reprinted here. Ian Harris, 'Isaiah Berlin: *Two Concepts of Liberty*',[14] attempted to clarify what Berlin had said.

Berlin's reading of the distinction between negative and positive

[1] *New York Review of Books*, 11 November 1976, 33–8.

[2] In his *Words and Life* (Cambridge, Mass., and London, 1995: Harvard University Press), 182–97 at 192–3.

[3] *Times Literary Supplement*, 27 March 1998, 8–10.

[4] London, 1990: John Murray; New York, 1991: Knopf.

[5] Oxford and Cambridge, Mass., 1993: Blackwell, 534–47, at 534–8.

[6] Basingstoke, 1990: Macmillan; Atlantic Highlands, NJ, 1991: Humanities Press International, chapter 1.

[7] Oxford, 1991: Blackwell, 235–8, 247–8

[8] London, 1999: Routledge, chapter 5.

[9] Oxford, 1997: Clarendon Press, 17–18, 21–2, 27.

[10] Oxford and Cambridge, Mass., 1997: Blackwell.

[11] Oxford, 1991: Oxford University Press (with other relevant items).

[12] Oxford, 1984: Blackwell; New York, 1984: New York University Press.

[13] Oxford, 1967: Oxford University Press.

[14] In Murray Forsyth and Maurice Keens-Soper (eds.), *The Political Classics: Green to Dworkin* (Oxford, 1996: Oxford University Press), 121–42.

freedom has been put to use in various ways. See, for example, Sandra Farganis, 'Liberty: Two Perspectives on the Women's Movement';[1] Partha Dasgupta, *An Inquiry into Well-Being and Destitution*;[2] Ronald Dworkin, *Freedom's Law*;[3] and Robert Grant, 'Morality, Social Policy and Berlin's Two Concepts'.[4]

The brief account of conflicts of value at the end of 'Two Concepts' applied to politics a staple of moral philosophy that Oxford had made its own, being one of the few points on which Ross and Ayer could converge.[5] It was also welcome to those who distinguished the right and the good in political philosophy, and John Rawls has endorsed Berlin's theses about it as much as those about negative and positive freedom.[6] Further treatments of value pluralism include Thomas Nagel, 'The Fragmentation of Value', in his *Mortal Questions*;[7] Bernard Williams, 'Conflicts of Value';[8] Charles Taylor, 'The Diversity of Goods';[9] Michael Walzer, *Spheres of Justice*;[10] Joseph Raz, *The Morality of Freedom*;[11] Michael Stocker, *Plural and Conflicting Values*;[12] and Steven Lukes, *Moral Conflict and Politics*.[13] A useful anthology of essays on this topic is

[1] *Ethics* 88 (1977–8), 67–73.

[2] Oxford and New York, 1993: Clarendon Press, chapter 2, section 5.

[3] Cambridge, Mass, 1996: Harvard University Press; Oxford, 1996: Oxford University Press, 214–17.

[4] In Arien Mack (ed.), *Liberty and Pluralism* [*Social Research* 66 No 4 (1999)], 1217–44.

[5] See, amongst earlier examples, James Fitzjames Stephen, *Liberty Equality, Fraternity* (1873, 1874), ed. Stuart D. Warner (Indianapolis, 1993: Liberty Press), 93 ff., 118, 169, 172, 174, 180, 206, 225, etc., and Franz Brentano, *The Origin of Our Knowledge of Right and Wrong* (1889), ed. Oskar Kraus and Roderick M. Chisholm, trans. Roderick M. Chisholm and Elizabeth H. Schneewind (London, 1969: Routledge; New York, 1969: Humanities Press), para. 32.

[6] See most recently his *Political Liberalism* (New York, 1993: Columbia University Press), 57, 197, 198n, 299n, 303n, 332, and *Justice as Fairness: A Restatement* (Cambridge, Mass., 2001: Harvard University Press), 177 note 61.

[7] Cambridge and New York, 1979: Cambridge University Press.

[8] In *The Idea of Freedom*, 221–32, and in his *Moral Luck* (Cambridge and New York, 1981: Cambridge University Press).

[9] In Amartya Sen and Bernard Williams (eds.), *Utilitarianism and Beyond* (Cambridge and New York, 1982: Cambridge University Press), and in his *Philosophical Papers*, vol. 2, 230–47.

[10] New York, 1983: Basic Books; Oxford, 1983: Martin Robertson.

[11] Oxford and New York, 1986: Clarendon Press.

[12] Oxford and New York, 1990: Clarendon Press.

[13] Oxford, 1991: Clarendon Press, esp. part 1.

Christopher W. Gowans (ed.), *Moral Dilemmas*.[1] This view and its congeners, of course, attract criticism from utilitarians, as for example James Griffin, *Well-Being*.[2] The whole topic is treated in Ruth Chang (ed.), *Incommensurability, Incomparability, and Practical Reason*,[3] which is dedicated to Berlin's memory, and is discussed with special reference to him by Dworkin, Williams, Nagel and Taylor in part 2 of *The Legacy of Isaiah Berlin*.[4] Broader philosophical considerations of Berlinian themes include Bernard Williams's 'Introduction' to Berlin's *Concepts and Categories*,[5] and Richard Wollheim, 'The Idea of a Common Human Nature'.[6]

Value pluralism, not least because of Berlin's account of it, has given birth to a number of recent debates. Roger Hausheer, 'Berlin and the Emergence of Liberal Pluralism'[7] was one of the earliest treatments. The implications of Berlin's views are examined searchingly by Eric Mack in 'Isaiah Berlin and the Quest for Liberal Pluralism',[8] and in 'The Limits of Diversity: The New Counter-Enlightenment and Isaiah Berlin's Liberal Pluralism'.[9] George Crowder questioned the relationship between 'Pluralism and Liberalism',[10] which attracted a response from Berlin and Bernard Williams, 'Pluralism and Liberalism: A Reply',[11] with further remarks from Crowder.[12] For a significantly revised view from Crowder see, for example, his *Liberalism and Value Pluralism*.[13]

The attempt to disconnect liberalism and pluralism owes much to the vigorous midwifery of John Gray. In his *Isaiah Berlin*[14] he produced a fully rounded view, hinted at previously in his 'On

---

[1] New York, 1987: Oxford University Press.

[2] Oxford and New York, 1986: Clarendon Press, chapter 5.

[3] Cambridge, Mass., and London, 1997: Harvard University Press.

[4] See p. 355 above, note 1.

[5] London, 1978: Hogarth Press; New York, 1979: Viking, xi–xviii.

[6] In *Isaiah Berlin: A Celebration*, 67–79.

[7] In Pierre Manent and others, *European Liberty* (The Hague, 1983: Nijhoff), 49–81.

[8] *Public Affairs Quarterly* 7 No 3 (1993), 215–30.

[9] In Howard Dickman (ed.), *The Imperiled Academy* (New Brunswick, 1993: Transaction Books), 97–126.

[10] *Political Studies* 42 (1994), 293–305.

[11] ibid., 306–9.

[12] ibid. 44 (1996), 649–51.

[13] London and New York, 2002: Continuum.

[14] London, 1995: HarperCollins; Princeton, 1996: Princeton University Press.

Negative and Positive Liberty'[1] and again in 'Berlin's Agonistic Liberalism'.[2] He has taken his views further in 'Where Pluralists and Liberals Part Company',[3] and in *Two Faces of Liberalism*.[4] Gray's interpretation of Berlin has been reviewed by Michael Walzer, 'Are There Limits to Liberalism?',[5] and examined closely by Hans Blokland, 'Berlin on Pluralism and Liberalism: A Defence'.[6] It provided a cue for further accounts of the matter by Amy Gutmann, 'Liberty and Pluralism in Pursuit of the Non-Ideal',[7] and by Jonathan Riley, 'Crooked Timber and Liberal Culture'.[8]

Steven Lukes provided a robust defence of Berlin's approach to politics in 'The Singular and the Plural: On the Distinctive Liberalism of Isaiah Berlin',[9] and again in 'An Unfashionable Fox'.[10] As the literature on pluralism has assumed very extensive proportions in the last decade – for instance, a whole number of *Social Research* is devoted to *Liberty and Pluralism*, as we have seen[11] – it cannot be discussed here: but two items that demand mention are the study of the relations of liberalism and pluralism in Charles Larmore, 'Pluralism and Reasonable Disagreement',[12] and the question posed by George Kateb, 'Can Cultures be Judged? Two Defenses of Cultural Pluralism in Isaiah Berlin's Work'.[13]

Berlin's treatment of nationalism, or something like it, in 'Two Concepts' is less critical than of other manifestations of positive liberty, and is more puzzled too. Berlin's own commitment to Zionism was expressed practically (see Michael Ignatieff, *Isaiah*

---

[1] *Political Studies* 28 (1980), reprinted in his *Liberalisms* (London and New York, 1989: Routledge), chapter 4.

[2] In his *Post-Liberalism* (London and New York, 1993: Routledge), 64–9.

[3] *International Journal of Philosophical Studies* 6 (1998), 17–36; also in Maria Baghramian and Attracta Ingram (eds.), *Pluralism: The Philosophy and Politics of Diversity* (London and New York, 2000: Routledge), chapter 4.

[4] Cambridge, 2000: Polity; New York, 2000: New Press.

[5] *New York Review of Books*, 19 October 1995, 28–31.

[6] *The European Legacy*, 4 No 4 (1999), 1–23.

[7] *Liberty and Pluralism*, 1039–62.

[8] In *Pluralism*, 120–155.

[9] *Social Research* 61 (1994), 698–718.

[10] In *The Legacy of Isaiah Berlin*, 43–57.

[11] See p. 358 above, note 4.

[12] *Social Philosophy and Practice* 11 No 1 (1994), 61–79.

[13] *Liberty and Pluralism*, 1009–38.

Berlin: A Life)[1] and on paper in a number of essays, including 'Jewish Slavery and Emancipation' (1951), reprinted in his posthumous collection *The Power of Ideas*.[2] Considerations of his views include Stuart Hampshire, 'Nationalism';[3] Joan Cocks, 'Individuality, Nationality, and the Jewish Question';[4] and Avishai Margalit, 'The Crooked Timber of Humanity', Richard Wollheim, 'Berlin and Zionism' and Michael Walzer, 'Liberalism, Nationalism, Reform'.[5] Berlin's views are sometimes discussed in broader treatments, as by David Miller in *On Nationality*.[6]

'Two Concepts' left at least one important gap in Berlin's conceptual wall against totalitarianism. If to be free implied knowledge and the exercise of reason, then the distinction between the concepts of negative and positive freedom might be less radical than he had insisted in 1958. 'From Hope and Fear Set Free' (1964) correspondingly suggested that knowledge did not always liberate, and this presidential address to the Aristotelian Society finds its proper home in the present volume as a complement to the Chichele inaugural.

The tension between one view of knowledge and freedom was exemplified in 'John Stuart Mill and the Ends of Life'. This suggested that the younger Mill's thought embodied two very different strands of opinion. The first, deriving from Bentham and the Enlightenment, accented reason but also the determinism that went with man as part of nature;[7] yet, on the other hand, Mill's own open-mindedness made him recognise that this did not fit the facts of experience, and led him to tease out another strand, in which free choice and the importance of realising negative freedom in society were prominent. This interpretation, as well as expressing Oxonian distrust of the utilitarian tradition, portrayed a Mill who was a well-disposed but confused thinker. Though, as Berlin noted, this lecture attracted little attention, it contrasted with

[1] London, 1998: Chatto and Windus; New York, 1998: Metropolitan, esp. chapter 9.

[2] London, 2000: Chatto and Windus; Princeton, 2000: Princeton University Press.

[3] In *Isaiah Berlin: A Celebration*, 127–34.

[4] *Liberty and Pluralism*, 1191–1216.

[5] All in part 3 of *The Legacy of Isaiah Berlin*.

[6] Oxford and New York, 1995: Clarendon Press, 7–8.

[7] For a fuller statement of Berlin's rejection of this sort of utilitarianism, see *Freedom and its Betrayal*, 'Helvétius'.

another view. The footnote appended near the end of the piece in *Four Essays* briefly criticises, without naming, Maurice Cowling, *Mill and Liberalism*,[1] and Shirley Robin Letwin, *The Pursuit of Certainty*.[2] These gave a higher estimate of Mill's competence and a less flattering view of his intentions. Though in the latter respect they have never won general adherence, and perhaps did not mean to do so, in the former they presaged a change in direction for the literature about Mill. This has included Alan Ryan, *The Philosophy of J. S. Mill*;[3] John Gray, *Mill on Liberty*;[4] Dennis F. Thompson, *John Stuart Mill and Representative Government*,[5] William Thomas, *Mill*,[6] Ann P. Robson, John M. Robson and Bruce L. Kinzer, *A Moralist In and Out of Parliament*,[7] and the number of the *Political Science Reviewer* devoted to Mill.[8] Of especial relevance here is Richard Wollheim, 'John Stuart Mill and Isaiah Berlin',[9] which implies that Mill, properly interpreted, was both more coherent and closer to Berlin than Berlin had thought. Berlin and Mill are examined together with Green by Richard Bellamy, 'T. H. Green, J. S. Mill, and Isaiah Berlin on the Nature of Liberty and Liberalism'.[10]

Berlin devoted his intellectual energies in the years after 1959 partly to working out further the intellectual history that his published essays had adumbrated and his unpublished lectures had treated more fully. 'The Birth of Greek Individualism' of 1962, reprinted here, identified the fourth century BC, the Renaissance and Romanticism as crucial stages in his historical interpretation, and a number of Berlin's essays and lectures sought to give further substance to the two latter, especially 'The Originality of Machiavelli', in his *Against the Current*,[11] and *The Roots of Romanticism*.

[1] Cambridge, 1963, 1990: Cambridge University Press.

[2] Cambridge, 1965: Cambridge University Press; repr. Indianapolis, 1998: Liberty Press.

[3] London, 1970, 1987: Macmillan; repr. Atlantic Highlands, NJ, 1990: Humanities Press International.

[4] London, 1983, Basingstoke, 1995: Routledge.

[5] Princeton, 1976: Princeton University Press.

[6] Oxford and New York, 1985: Oxford University Press.

[7] Toronto and London, 1992: University of Toronto Press.

[8] 24 (1995).

[9] In *The Idea of Freedom*, 153–69.

[10] In Hyman Gross and Ross Harrison (eds.), *Jurisprudence: Cambridge Essays* (Oxford and New York, 1992: Clarendon Press), 257–85.

[11] London, 1979: Hogarth Press; New York, 1980: Viking.

Berlin's view of intellectual history was subjected to a searching examination by Hans Aarsleff, 'Vico and Berlin';[1] was treated critically by P. N. Furbank, 'On Pluralism';[2] and was connected to Berlin's liberalism by Graeme Garrard, 'The Counter-Enlightenment Liberalism of Isaiah Berlin'.[3] It was subjected more recently to an uncompromising criticism by Mark Lilla in 'Wolves and Lambs'.[4] Berlin's view of Herder was developed by Charles Taylor, 'The Importance of Herder'.[5] It is considered by Hans Aarsleff, 'Herder's Cartesian *Ursprung* vs. Condillac's Expressivist *Essai*',[6] and placed on a larger canvas in his 'Facts, Fiction, and Opinion in the History of Linguistics: Language and Thought in the 17th and 18th Centuries'.[7] A topic relevant to Berlin's concerns was addressed in Larry Siedentop, 'Two Liberal Traditions'.[8] Assessments of Berlin's own present relevance will be found in Jonny Steinberg, 'The Burdens of Berlin's Modernity',[9] and Ira Katznelson, 'Isaiah Berlin's Modernity',[10] whilst some contemporary currents of thought are surveyed in Raymond Tallis, *Enemies of Hope*.[11]

Extended treatments of Berlin's thought include Robert A. Kocis, *A Critical Appraisal of Isaiah Berlin's Political Philosophy*,[12] and Claude J. Galipeau, *Isaiah Berlin's Liberalism*,[13] as well as John Gray's enterprising *Isaiah Berlin*, whilst there is a running commentary on some of Berlin's writings in Ignatieff, *Isaiah Berlin*. Briefer synoptic views of varying perspective appear in Perry

---

[1] *London Review of Books*, 5–18 November 1981, 6–7 (with Berlin's response in the same number, 7–8, and correspondence, 3–16 June 1982, 5).

[2] *Raritan* 17 (1997), 83–95.

[3] *Journal of Political Ideologies* 2 (1997), 281–96.

[4] In *The Legacy of Isaiah Berlin*, 31–42.

[5] In *Isaiah Berlin: A Celebration*, 40–63; reprinted in Taylor's *Philosophical Arguments* (Cambridge, Mass., and London, 1995: Harvard University Press), chapter 5.

[6] In D. Gambarara, S. Gensini and A. Pennisi (eds), *Language Philosophies and the Language Sciences* (Münster, 1996: Nodus), 165–79.

[7] In Lisa McNair and others (eds), *Papers from the Parasession on Theory and Data in Linguistics* (Chicago, 1996: Chicago Linguistic Society), 1–11.

[8] In *The Idea of Freedom*, 153–74.

[9] *History of European Ideas* 22 (1996), 369–83.

[10] In *Liberalism and Pluralism*, 1079–1101.

[11] London, 1997: Macmillan; New York, 1997: St Martin's Press.

[12] Lewiston and Lampeter, 1989: Mellen Press.

[13] Oxford and New York, 1994: Clarendon Press.

Anderson, 'Components of the National Culture',[1] and 'The Pluralism of Isaiah Berlin';[2] Alan Ryan, 'A Glamorous Salon: Isaiah Berlin's Disparate Gifts',[3] and his 'Isaiah Berlin: Political Theory and Liberal Culture';[4] Bhikhu Parekh, *Contemporary Political Thinkers*;[5] Noel Annan, *Our Age*,[6] and his *The Dons*;[7] Michael Tanner, 'Isaiah: A Dissenting Voice';[8] Bernard Williams, 'Berlin, Isaiah (1909–97)';[9] Stefan Collini, 'Liberal Mind: Isaiah Berlin';[10] Michael Lessnoff, *Political Philosophers of the Twentieth Century*;[11] Michael Kenny, 'Isaiah Berlin's Contribution to Modern Political Theory';[12] and Maurice Cowling, *Religion and Public Doctrine in Modern England*.[13]

This bibliographical essay has commented on only a small selection of the literature about Berlin. A full listing of his own writings, compiled by Henry Hardy, to whom all students of Berlin are indebted, will be found in *Against the Current*.[14] This is also available in regularly updated form (see opposite) on the website of the Isaiah Berlin Literary Trust, which includes also a full secondary bibliography. Henry Hardy's own writings about Berlin include 'Confessions of an Editor'.[15]

A postscript is to be found on page 366.

[1] *New Left Review* No 50 (July–August 1968), 3–57, esp. 25–8.

[2] In his *A Zone of Engagement* (London and New York, 1992: Verso), 230–50.

[3] *Encounter* 43 No 4 (October 1974), 67–72.

[4] *Annual Review of Political Science* 2 (1999), 345–62.

[5] Oxford, 1982: Martin Robertson; Baltimore, Md, 1982: Johns Hopkins University Press, chapter 2.

[6] London, 1990: Weidenfeld and Nicolson; New York, 1990: Random House, esp. 274–9.

[7] London, 1999: HarperCollins; Chicago, 1999: University of Chicago Press, 209–32.

[8] *Spectator*, 15 November 1997, 16–17.

[9] In Edward Craig (ed.), *Routledge Encyclopaedia of Philosophy* (London and New York, 1998: Routledge), vol. 1, 750–3.

[10] In his *English Pasts* (Oxford and New York, 1999: Oxford University Press), 195–209.

[11] Oxford and Malden, Mass., 1999: Blackwell, chapter 8.

[12] *Political Studies* 48 (2000), 1026–39.

[13] Cambridge and New York, 1980–2001: Cambridge University Press, vol. 3, 646–50.

[14] This list was updated (again) in the most recent printing (Princeton, 2001: Princeton University Press).

[15] *Australian Financial Review*, 30 June 2000, 4–5; also available on the website.

1999

- 243 *The Roots of Romanticism*, the A. W. Mellon Lectures in the Fine Arts, 1965, ed. Henry Hardy (London, 1999: Chatto and Windus; Princeton, 1999: Princeton University Press; London, 2000: Pimlico); trans. Dutch, German, Greek, Hebrew, Italian, Japanese, Polish, Spanish
- 244 'La reputacion de Vico', trans. by Enrique Bocardo Crespo of review of Peter Burke, *Vico*, in Pablo Badillo O'Farrell and Enrique Bocardo Crespo (eds), *Isaiah Berlin: la mirada despierta de la historia* (Madrid, 1999: Tecnos); original English version, 'The Reputation of Vico', published in *New Vico Studies* 17 (1999), 1–5

2000

- 245 *The Power of Ideas*, ed. Henry Hardy (London, 2000: Chatto and Windus; Princeton, 2000: Princeton University Press) (reprints of 27, 43, 52, 54a, 55, 62, 63, 65, 78, 85, 102, 103, 111, 113, 115, 127, 221, 240, together with 248); trans. German, Italian, Spanish
- 246 *Three Critics of the Enlightenment: Vico, Hamann, Herder*, ed. Henry Hardy (London, 2000: Pimlico; Princeton, 2000: Princeton University Press) (reprints of 148, with revisions to the Vico material, and 212, with the English original of the Foreword to the German edition); trans. Chinese, Greek
- 247 'Herzen: A Preacher of the Truth', in Gionavva Calebich Creazza, *Aleksandr Ivanovic Herzen: profezia e tradizione* (Naples, 2000: CUEN), 39–40
- 248 'The Search for Status' (talk based on part of 71), in *POI*, 195–9
- 249 Letter to Anand Chandavarkar on Keynes and anti-Semitism, in Anand Chandavarkar, 'Was Keynes anti-Semitic?', *Economic and Political Weekly*, 6 May 2000, 1619–24, at 1623

2001

- 250 'A Visit to Leningrad' (1945), *Times Literary Supplement*, 23 March 2001, 13–15
- 250a 'A Sense of Impending Doom' (1935; original title 'Literature and the Crisis'), *Times Literary Supplement*, 27 July 2001, 11–12
- 250b 'The State of Psychology in 1936' (1936), *History and Philosophy of Psychology* 3 No 1 (2001), 76–83
- 250c 'Notes on Prejudice' (1981), *New York Review of Books*, 18 October 2001, 12; repr. in *L* and, as 'Notes on Prejudice and Fanaticism', *Australian Financial Review*, 12 October 2001, Review section, 4; trans. Swedish

2002

- 251 *Freedom and its Betrayal: Six Enemies of Human Liberty* (1952), ed. Henry Hardy (London, forthcoming 2002: Chatto & Windus; Princeton, forthcoming 2002: Princeton University Press)
- 252 *Liberty*, ed. Henry Hardy, with a critical bibliography by Ian Harris (Oxford and New York, forthcoming 2002: Oxford University Press) (253, with other writings on liberty: reprints of 221, 241a, excerpts from 240, and 241, together with 254 and 255)
- 253 'Five Essays on Liberty', ed. Henry Hardy (second edition of 112, with reprint of 93 added), in *L*
- 254 A Letter to George Kennan 1951), in *L*

The end of the bibliography from the Isaiah Berlin Virtual Library,

http://berlin.wolf.ox.ac.uk/, October 2001

Postscript

'Of making many books there is no end.' Since this essay was written, Berlin and his themes have continued to claim attention. Positive freedom has been considered by Adam Swift, who unpicks several of the strands woven together in 'Two Concepts', and finds more to say for some of these than Berlin.[1] Jonathan Riley, who is writing a book entitled *Pluralistic Liberalisms: Berlin, Rawls and Mill*, has reworked 'Crooked Timber and Liberal Culture'[2] by way of 'Interpreting Berlin's Liberalism', and has addressed George Kateb's question[4] in 'Defending Cultural Pluralism within Liberal Limits'.[5]

---

[1] *Political Philosophy: A Beginner's Guide for Students and Politicians* (Oxford etc., 2001: Polity and Blackwell), part 2, 'Liberty'.

[2] See p. 360 above.

[3] *American Political Science Review* 95 (2001), 283–95.

[4] See p. 360 above.

[5] *Political Theory* 30 No 1 (February 2002), forthcoming.

CONCORDANCE TO
FOUR ESSAYS ON LIBERTY

IN THIS concordance, whose aim is to enable readers to find references to the original page-numbering of *Four Essays on Liberty* easily in the present volume, the first column lists the pages of *Four Essays on Liberty*, the second column specifies on which page of *Liberty* the opening words of the original page (excluding subheadings) are to be found, and the third column gives those opening words as they appear in *Liberty*.

FEL	L	FEL page begins	FEL	L	FEL page begins
ix	3	The first of these four essays	xxviii	21	myself to have refuted it
x	4	The main issues between	xxix	22	but be conveyed
xi	5	and conduct	xxx	23	But this is so because
xii	5	philosophers when	xxxi	24	enter imaginatively
xiii	6	of the basic terms	xxxii	25	extreme eccentricity
xiv	7	'self-determinism'	xxxiii	26	more than this seems
xv	8	which we are then	xxxiv	26	unalterable patterns
xvi	9	Spinoza, most men	xxxv	27	and extend our liberty
xvii	10	subscribe to determinism	xxxvi	28	I recognize the fact
xviii	11	different 'levels'	xxxvii	29	no way out
xix	12	inspire Professor Passmore's	xxxviii	30	(*b*) whether the term 'liberty'
xx	13	necessarily, to each other	xxxix	31	'Nature', which
xxi	14	would not think it reasonable	xl	32	this in any quantitative
xxii	15	if we took determinism	xli	33	by 'team spirit'
xxiii	16	particular nexus between	xlii	34	eighteenth century
xxiv	17	passage that I have quoted	xliii	35	to deserve to be called
xxv	18	can only escape	xliv	36	others, if I do
xxvi	19	altogether plausible	xlv	37	have taken this 'negative'
xxvii	20	the truth	xlvi	38	thought this too obvious
			xlvii	39	form, is in far
			xlviii	40	strong – a situation

FEL	L	FEL page begins	FEL	L	FEL page begins
xlix	41	hard-and-fast rule	27	79	old symbols
l	42	expense of efficiency	28	80	forms the obverse
li	43	there exists such a thing	29	81	continue to say
			30	82	human souls'
lii	44	everything is still	31	83	In the United States
liii	45	relativity largely derives	32	84	flourished, for instance
liv	46	give the kind of reasons	33	85	In this sinister fashion
lv	46	virtually useless	34	86	scientific enquiry
lvi	47	vision, a principle	35	87	of diagnosticians
lvii	48	exploit or dismiss	36	88	this kind – the artificial
lviii	49	enthusiasm for common	37	89	alignment of forces
lix	50	and finally to forget	38	90	eagerly today
lx	51	shown by philosophical	39	91	economic organisation
lxi	52	so critical that	40	92	more frequent *ad hoc*
lxii	53	certain evils	41	94	Writing some ten years
lxiii	54	political problems	42	95	affected the categories
1	55	Historians of ideas	43	95	so confidently prophesied
2	56	The notion of 'laws'	44	96	But whatever value
3	57	of time – was not	45	97	such as environment
4	57	economic and political	46	98	civilisations or races
5	58	Lytton Strachey	47	99	limited extent
6	59	realization of that free	48	100	There are many versions
7	60	common to all	49	101	theory, stated in
8	61	And yet to a casual	50	102	knowledge permit
9	62	even legislation	51	103	the Life-Force
10	63	a considerable degree	52	104	which puts obstacles
11	64	Marx with much	53	105	-fore no historical account
12	65	unbridled private	54	106	metaphor. To those
13	66	were the deepest	55	107	play their parts
14	67	analysis of the character	56	108	ultimate 'structure of reality'
15	68	essentially romantic	57	109	shall have laws
16	68	a doctrine which	58	109	laws' which make
17	70	a splendid disregard	59	110	necessarily empty
18	71	Diderot or Saint-Simon	60	111	demand justice from
19	72	that which divided	61	112	irresistible – which truly
20	73	slaves by nature	62	113	element; they enter
21	74	the flow of life	63	114	direction truly 'scientific'
22	75	made by such great	64	115	'responsible'. I live at
23	76	they – even Sextus	65	117	To assess degrees
24	77	psychological possibility			
25	78	Orwell and Aldous Huxley			
26	78	adjusted as to involve			

FEL	L	FEL page begins	FEL	L	FEL page begins
66	117	used, whereby history	105	154	prevent it will only
			106	155	Two powerful doctrines
67	118	known, to us			
68	119	historians and sociologists	107	155	'the unity of the knower
69	120	The proposition that	108	156	in one field than
70	121	the sense of history	109	157	invalid; and the desire
71	122	-evitable' depends on			
72	123	to convince ourselves	110	158	contemporary collapse
73	124	models, pure and unapplied	111	159	material factors – physical
74	125	to be reminded			
75	126	boundary between	112	160	there is no anxiety
76	126	everything, explain	113	161	effective younger sister
77	127	compulsion of this type	114	162	metaphysico-theological
78	128	relief from moral burdens	115	163	our task to describe
			116	164	to me to spring
79	129	see why this or that	117	165	little regard for experience
80	130	moment, as Taine			
81	131	illusion, and with it	118	166	If men never disagreed
82	132	claims masquerading			
83	133	seek to save	119	167	some cases violently
84	134	is responsible for much	120	168	It may be that
			121	168	ideas or spiritual forces
85	135	or the complexities			
86	136	For to treat what	122	169	able to do or be
87	137	cannot by definition	123	170	freedom. It is only
88	138	Pasteur as a benefactor	124	171	the interests of other
			125	172	is not some species
89	139	beliefs about the world	126	173	'economic' – is increased
90	140	inaccuracy, or stupidity	127	173	interference is to be drawn
91	140	-torians to suppress	128	175	would say of Occam
92	142	historians differ from	129	176	In the second place
93	142	are as creditable	130	177	connected with democracy
94	143	as a rule, quantitatively	131	178	is a good deal more
95	144	our historical language	132	178	and positive ways
			133	179	if they were more
96	145	and avoidable intrusion	134	180	theories of self-realisation
97	146	be based on ignorance	135	181	I am the possessor
			136	182	independent, on its
98	147	grasp these rules	137	183	creatures at the mercy
99	148	of the propositions			
100	149	with nothing to contrast	138	184	tampering with human
101	150	merited perhaps, but	139	185	men and things
102	151	martyrs and the minorities	140	186	losing their original
			141	187	who, even while
103	152	desirable to have	142	188	all other obstacles
104	153	we can never know	143	189	fallacious corollary

FEL	L	FEL page begins	FEL	L	FEL page begins
144	190	plan my life	178	222	conditioning human beings
145	191	Those who believed	179	223	whose religion breathes
146	192	order must in principle	180	224	in Jamaica
147	193	of themselves'	181	225	as a criterion of
148	194	the predisposed order	182	226	unrealized; among
149	195	follow. In the ideal case	183	227	Mill had scarcely any
150	196	understand your true goals	184	228	variety of human life
151	197	aesthetic, justification	185	229	the essay after her death
152	198	that only thus will	186	231	amiable of rulers
153	199	automatically be	187	232	always alter our views
154	200	to Sarastro's temple	188	233	great? Mill goes on
155	201	society, everything	189	234	foundations for just
156	202	taken to be	190	235	of opinion for its
157	203	human, and therefore	191	236	will, is to prevent
158	204	or nation, than	192	237	damaging to them
159	204	'organic' view	193	238	Kant once remarked that
160	205	Mill called 'Pagan	194	239	means Utilitarians and
161	206	can be substituted	195	239	the mere refusal
162	207	at any rate to believe	196	240	authority and the inevitable
163	208	of the fully qualified	197	242	revolt against this
164	209	as mercilessly as	198	242	Guardians. He thought
165	210	rights, or the word	199	243	the ancient prescription
166	211	of what I mean	200	245	that. A quarter
167	212	One belief, more than	201	246	formidable, they are
168	213	of some of our ideals	202	247	contemporary. *On Liberty*
169	214	perversity. Indeed	203	248	ashamed, of this fact
170	215	cannot be satisfied	204	249	of God was possible
171	216	-counter some unforeseen	205	250	He was the teacher
172	217	and sense of their own	206	251	over nature, but
173	218	[I must begin by]	207	69	[This is not an entirely]
174	219	the centenary of the birth			
175	219	Everyone knows the story			
176	220	went through his first			
177	221	spontaneity and uniqueness			

INDEX

Compiled by Douglas Matthews

References in *italic* are to 'Berlin and his Critics' (pages 349–66)

Aarsleff, Hans, *363*
Abramsky, Chimen, 69n
activity: and liberty, 34–5
Acton, John Emerich Edward Dalberg, 1st
  Baron, 23–4, 33, 151, 249
Aeschylus, 310
Africa: social protest in, 64n
Against the Current (IB), xxvii, *362*, *364*
Age of Enlightenment, The (IB), *350*
Agnelli Prize, xxvi
Alcibiades, 296
Alcidamas, 298
Alembert, Jean Le Rond d', 109
Alexander the Great (of Macedon), 115,
  144, 309–10, 312, 314
Ambrose, St, 182n
anarchistic nihilism, 88
Anarchists, 195
Anderson, Perry, *363–4*
animism, 19, 158
Annan, Noel, *354*, *364*
anthropomorphism, 19
Antigone, 298
Antigonus Gonatas, 309
Antiochus Epiphanes, 318
Antiphon, 33, 298–9, 313, 320–1
Antisthenes, 312–13
Aquinas, St Thomas, 135n, 261, 287
Arblaster, Anthony, *356*
Archelaus, 298
Aristippus, 312–13
Aristophanes, 298, 319
Aristotelian Society: IB's Presidential
  Address to, xix
Aristotle: and determinism, 16; and civic
  liberty, 33; leaves Athens, 49; on
  obstacles to self-fulfilment, 253; on
  knowledge as liberating, 257; on
  causation and moral responsibility, 260;
  moral and political ideas, 287, 289, 291,
  297, 299, 302–3, 309, 311–12, 315,
  317–21; on social life, 294–5; exalts
  contemplative life, 295; on King Priam,
  307; and Stoic doctrines, 310; escapes
  from Athens, 311
Armstrong, Hamilton Fish, 55n
Asia: social protest in, 64n
Assassins, 88
Associated Television company, xxvi
Athenodorus, 316
Athens, 294, 300–2, 308, 311, 319; see also
  Greece (ancient)
Attila the Hun, 115
Augustine, St, 287
authority: and liberty, 35–7, 39, 194–5,
  206; and obedience, 75, 198, 284; and
  disagreement, 88–9, 90, 92; area of, 206,
  209–12; in ancient world, 283–4; see also
  sovereignty
autonomy, 185, 277
Ayer, Alfred Jules, 116n, 131, 261, *358*
Aztecs, 102

Babeuf, François Noel ('Gracchus'), 71
Bacon, Francis, 111–12, 259
Baghramian, Maria, and Attracta Ingram,
  360n
Bain, Alexander, 223n
Bakunin, Mikhail Aleksandrovich, 113,
  251n
Baldwin, Tom, *355*
Barker, Ernest, 33, 321
Barrès, Maurice, 130
Baudelaire, Charles, 66
Beaver, Harold, xiv–xv
behaviourism, 95, 124, 278
Belinsky, Vissarion Grigorievich, 172
Bellamy, Richard, *362*
Belloc, Hilaire, 118, 138
Bentham, Jeremy: on law as infraction of

liberty, 41n, 170n, 195; on social development, 62; on utilising man's slavery to passions, 184; on liberty to do evil, 194n; on individual interests, 217n; and J. S. Mill, 220–2, 227, 234, 238–9, 244, 250; on happiness, 222–3, 225n, 226; Utilitarianism, 224; Mill's essay on, 225; influence and reputation, 321, 338; and moral goodness, 340; on reason and determinism, *361*

Berenson, Bernard, 94

Bergson, Henri: anti-rationalism, 67, 74

Bevan, Edwyn Robert, 316

Bismarck, Prince Otto von, 159

blame *see* praise and blame

Blanc, Louis, 228n

Blanqui, Louis Auguste, 71

Blok, Alexander, xxi & n

Blokland, Hans, *355, 360*

Bodin, Jean, 289

Bonald, Louis Gabriel Ambroise, vicomte de, 63

Booth, John Wilkes, 13

Bosanquet, Bernard, 196

Bossuet, Jacques Bénigne, 10, 101, 156

bourgeoisie: achievements, 81

Bowra, Maurice, xxin

Bowring, John, 223n

Boy's Herald, The, xxviiin

Bradley, Francis Herbert, 196, 271

Brandeis, Louis, 164n

Brather, Hans-Stephan, 230n

Brentano, Franz, *358n*

Brinton, Crane, 194n

Brown, John, xiii–xv

Büchner, Georg, 67, 96

Buckle, Henry Thomas, 77, 234, 247, 289

Buckroyd, Carol, xxiv

Bukharin, Nikolay Ivanovich, 184n

Burckhardt, Jacob, 20n, 64, 227, 242

Burke, Edmund: on composite society, 130, 203, 206n, 241; on individual liberties and interests, 173, 217n; on restraint, 194; on compromise, 215; and Mill, 244; on political structure, 289; reputation, 321

Burnham, James, 344

Butler, Joseph, 102n

Butler, Samuel: *Erewhon,* 15

Butterfield, Herbert, 133, 135n, 138n, 229

Cabet, Étienne, 112

Caesar, Julius, 115

Callicles, 299

Calvinism, 10, 175

Campanella, Tommaso, 112

Carlile, Richard, 223 & n

Carlyle, Alexander, 236

Carlyle, Thomas: historical view, 20, 100, 244; irrationalism, 60, 66, 197; cynicism, 78, 134; as prophet, 218; and Mill, 228, 247; on social control, 236; on Mill's relations with Harriet Taylor, 240; opposes Victorian claustrophobia, 243; influence, 247; defiance, 338

Carneades, 261, 316

Carr, Edward Hallett: criticises IB, xxi, 352–3; and IB's views on determinism, 7, 10–11; historiographical views, 19–22, 26–7, 30, 132n; moral sermonising, 24, 138n; upholds victors over victims, 343; *What is History?*, 11n

Carritt, Edgar Frederick, 277

causality: in history, 5, 27–9; and self-determination, 260–1

Chaeronea, battle of (338 BC), 311

Chamberlain, Houston Stewart, 100

Chang, Ruth, *359*

Charlemagne, 20

Chasles, Philarète, 92n

Chesterton, Gilbert Keith, 244

children: obedience to orders, 193, 195

choice: and exercise of liberty, 44–9, 53, 271–2, 278, 340; as illusion, 110; constraints on, 122–6; existentialism and, 162; and coercion, 177n; and conflict of values, 214; Mill on supremacy of, 222, 237; of belief, 257–8; and self-determination, 260–8; Kant on, 337; and deception, 339; *see also* determinism; free will

Chrysippus, 7, 260–2, 309, 316, 319

Church, the: authoritarianism, 88, 90, 283–4; and values, 291–2

Cicero, 31, 117, 261

civil liberties, 65

class (social), 68–70, 99–100

Cleanthes, 309, 316–17

Cleon, 301

Cobden, Richard, 38

Cocks, Joan, *361*

coercion: and deprivation of freedom, 168–71, 173–6, 184, 210; of the weak and ignorant, 179, 186n, 197–8; and rule by reason, 193

Cohen, Gerald Allan, *355*

Cohen, Marshall, 40n, *354*

Cole, George Douglas Howard, 166n

Coleridge, Samuel Taylor, 36, 221, 238, 244, 248

Collini, Stefan, *364*

Common Knowledge (ed. Perl), xxvi

Communards (French), 71

Communism: rise of, 60–1, 68, *352*; totalitarianism of, 77, 198; fanaticism of, 88; on education, 342

compulsion, 196–7, 274, 284

Comte, Auguste: and impersonality of history, 19–20, 109, 129; influence and reputation, 77, 94–5, 247, 321; on disagreement in ethics and social sciences, 80–1; and scientific supremacy in politics, 86; Memorial Lectures, 94; character and qualities, 95; Utopianism, 112; and generalisations in history, 141, 158; belief in universal causation, 153; as founder of sociology, 161; and human benefactors, 163; on free thinking in politics, 197; Mill's attitude to, 227, 234, 242n, 247, 251n; on harmony of theory and practice, 230n; and 'pédantocratie', 251n; and self-determination, 278

Concepts and Categories (IB), xxv

Condorcet, Marie Jean Antoine Nicolas Caritat, marquis de: on unitary nature of values, 42, 212n, 289; liberalism, 62; on history as natural science, 95, 109, 111, 129; Utopianism, 112, 212n; on individual rights in ancient world, 176; Mill and, 244; *Esquisse d'un tableau historique des progrès de l'esprit humain*, 111

conformism, 44, 239–42, 244

Conservatives, 59, 63, 66

Constant, Benjamin: quoted, 3; and State intervention, 38–9, 173; on 'sacred frontiers', 52; on liberty, 171, 209–11, 283–4; and liberalism, 207; and J. S. Mill, 227; on individual rights, 318

Constitution of Athens, 301

Cornford, Francis Macdonald, 320–1

Cowling, Maurice, *362, 364*

Craig, Edward, *364*

Crates, 312, 314–16, 319

Creighton, Mandell, Bishop of London, 23–4, 138

Crick, Bernard, 35, *355*

crimes: and blame, 14–15

Critias, 296, 299

Cromwell, Oliver, 115, 138

Crooked Timber of Humanity, The (IB), xxviii, *357*

Crowder, George, *359*

Cumberledge, Geoffrey, xii

Cushman, John, xii

Cynics, 312, 315

Darwin, Charles, 89, 142, 158, 287; *The Origin of Species*, 219

Dasgupta, Partha, *358*

David and Goliath, 276

Davin, Dan, xiii

Dawson, Christopher, 27n, *353*

democracy: and individual liberty, 42, 176–8, 211; Mill mistrusts, 240–1, 243, 251n; in USA, 241, 284; in ancient Greece, 283, 295–6, 299, 321; in France, 284

Demosthenes, 300–1, 311

Denmark, 90

Descartes, René, 141, 287

desires: and freedom, 31–2, 326

despotism: and individual liberty, 49–50; *see also* tyranny

determinism: concept of, 4–12, 16–18, 29–30, 116n, 122, 124, 155; and blame, 14–16, 111, 116n; and historicism, 19–21, 28, 113–14, 120, 124; and knowledge, 139, 154, 264, 278; social, 160–1; belief in, 161, 257, 322–4; and search for causes, 188; and self-prediction, 265–70; and rationality, 277; Marxism and, 325; *see also* self-determination

Dickens, Charles, 247

Dickman, Howard, *359*n

Diderot, Denis, 71, 243

Diogenes of Babylon (Stoic), 316

Diogenes Laertius, 230n

Diogenes of Sinope (Cynic), 312, 314, 318–19

Disraeli, Benjamin (Earl of Beaconsfield), 246

Dodds, Eric Robertson, 317

domination, 192

Dostoevsky, Fedor Mikhailovich, 47, 66, 79, 171, 247; *The Brothers Karamazov*, 86, 338 & n; *The Devils*, 71; *Dyadyushkin Son* ('Uncle's Dream'), 340; *Zapiski iz podpol'ya* ('Notes from Underground'), 343n

Durham, John George Lambton, 1st Earl of, 224

Durkheim, Émile, 158n

Dworkin, Ronald, *355, 358, 359*

East India Company, 224

education: and political ideals, 61–2, 195; and obedience, 195–8, 214, 284, 342; Mill on effects of, 242–3; as moulding, 341–2

Eichmann, Adolf, 323
Eichthal, Gustave d', 248
Einstein, Albert, 287
Eliot, Thomas Stearns: quoted, 94
empiricism: opposes impersonal forces, 27; and the real, 123n; Mill's, 232, 238
Engels, Friedrich, 71, 85, 101n, 130, 166, 230n
England: trade unions in, 84; self-confidence in, 187n; see also Great Britain
Epictetus, 31, 182n, 186, 273–4
Epicureans, 253, 260, 306, 309–12, 320
Epicurus, 33, 189, 302–4, 311, 314, 316–18, 320
equality: and freedom, 180n, 200
Erasmus, Desiderius, 175, 243
ethics: and determinism, 16; and attaining truth, 75
Euripides, 298, 300
evil: freedom to perform, 194 & n
existentialism, 162
Eyre, Edward John, 224

Fabianism, 68, 227, 229n
Faguet, Émile, 51n
fanaticism, 345–7
Farganis, Sandra, 358
Fascism: rise of, 60, 352 ; totalitarianism, 77; rejects old values, 79; reliance on instinct, 83; ideology, 158; defiance, 338; on education, 342; Maistre and, 350
fatalism, 10, 116n
Festugière, André Jean, 252
Feuerbach, Ludwig, 87
Fichte, Johann Gottlieb, 51n, 167, 191, 195–7, 238
'Final Retrospect' (IB), xxv, xxxi
Floud, Jean Esther, xxviii
Foreign Affairs (journal), 3, 55n
Forster, Edward Morgan, 129, 306
Fosdick, Dorothy, 354
Four Essays on Liberty (IB): literature on, xxxi, 362; publishing history, ix–x, xiii, xv–xxv
Four Freedoms, The (TV series), xxvi
Fourier, François Charles Marie, 87, 112
Fox, William Johnson, 223n
France: anti-clerical governments, 84; trade unions in, 84; self-confidence in, 187n; democracy in, 284
France, Anatole, 112
Franco, General Francisco, 148
Franklin, Benjamin, 20n
fraternity: and liberty, 201

Frederick II (the Great), King of Prussia, 116, 176n
free will: and determinism, 5, 7, 116n, 124–5; and Stoics, 34; and differing values, 43–4; Mill on problem of, 250
freedom see liberty
Freedom and its Betrayal (IB), xi, xxv, 349n
French Revolution: as historical landmark, 61; historical representation of, 142, 144; and desire for freedom, 208
Freud, Sigmund, 74, 78, 88, 130, 158, 242, 287
Friedrich, Carl Joachim, 356
'From Hope and Fear Set Free' (IB), xx–xxi, xxiv, xxv, 361
Fromm, Erich, 34–5
Fry, Roger, 306
Furbank, Philip Nicholas, 363

Galileo Galilei, 287
Galipeau, Claude J., 363
Gambarara, Daniele, Stefano Gensini and Antonino Pennisi, 363n
Garden of Eden see paradise
Gardiner, Patrick Lancaster, 4n, 270
Garrard, Graeme, 363
Gascoigne, Bamber, xxvi
Genghis Khan, 20, 131, 143, 163
Germany: trade unions in, 84; anti-liberalism in, 167; inner freedom in, 186; political theory in, 290, 294; nationalism, 347
Geyl, Pieter, 353
Gibbon, Edward, 118, 134
Gilgamesh, epic of, 105
Gladstone, William Ewart, 84
Gnosticism, 130, 158
Gobineau, Joseph Arthur, comte de, 100
God: existence of, 75
Godwin, William, 14, 129, 306
Goethe, Johann Wolfgang von, 244, 321
Gomme, Arnold Wycombe, 34n
Goodin, Robert Edward, and Philip Pettit, 357
Gorky, Maxim, 82n
government see authority
Gowans, Christopher W., 359
Gracchi, the, 117
Grant, Robert, 316, 358
Gray, John Nicholas, x–xin, 359–60, 362, 363
Gray, Tim, 357
Great Britain: tolerance in, 90; see also England
Greece (ancient): and individual liberty, 32–4, 176, 186, 283–4; influence on

modern liberalism, 62; social life and individualism in, 287, 294–321; gods in, 299, 303

Green, Thomas Hill, 41n, 53, 180n, 196, 356, 362

Griffin, James P., 359

Gross, Hyman, and Ross Harrison, 362n

Grotius, Hugo, 62

Gutmann, Amy, 360

Hague Court, the, 61

Halévy, Élie, 138

Hampshire, Stuart Newton: xvi, xxi & n, 4n, 16, 18n; and determinism, 116n; on Spinoza, 264 & n; on self-prediction, 266–7; and self-determination, 271, 277; on IB's Jewish views, 361

happiness: as product of rational organisation, 112; increase in, 154; compulsion to, 183; Mill's belief in, 221–3, 225–7, 237; Bentham on, 225n, 226; as alternative to freedom, 342

Hardy, Henry Robert Dugdale, 364

Hare, Richard Mervyn, 261

Harris, Ian Colin, xxxi, 357

Hart, Herbert Lionel Adolphus, xvi, 4n, 278

Hausheer, Roger N., 359

Hayek, Friedrich August von, 101n, 351

Hayward, Jack, Brian Barry and Archie Brown, 356

Hayward, Max, xxin

Hazlitt, William, ix

Hegel, Georg Wilhelm Friedrich: and Plekhanov, 19; and historiography, 20, 56n, 99, 101, 112–13, 156; and rationalism, 188; on understanding as freedom, 189; and controlling domination, 192; on obedience, 196; on social conditioning, 206n; and harmony of values, 213, 289; argument for war, 235; and impediments to liberty, 256; and self-determination, 277, 338; reactions to, 288; on owl of Minerva, 311; and Kant, 312; influence and reputation, 321; and moral goodness, 340; on economic corrosion, 343

Heine, Heinrich, 167

Helen of Troy, 8

Helvétius, Claude Adrien: rationalism, 20; liberalism, 62; on freedom, 169n; on slavery to passions, 184; belief in finality, 234, 238

Heraclitus, 321

Herakles, 312

Herder, Johann Gottfried, 20, 95, 100, 140n, 189, 363

Herillus, 316

Herodotus, 33, 294, 299, 310

Herzen, Alexander Ivanovich, 51n, 64, 228n

'Herzen and Bakunin on Individual Liberty' (IB), xxv

heteronomy, 179, 183–4, 185, 195–6, 202n

Hilbert, David, 142

Himmler, Heinrich, 23

Hippias, 298

'Historical Inevitability' (IB), xxv, 352–3

history: causality in, 5, 27–9; E. H. Carr on impersonality of, 19–20, 26; and biography, 20; and judgement, 21–5, 115–20, 125–6, 129–35, 138, 141, 145–53, 163–4; motives and intentions in, 26–7, 98, 159–60; and factual integrity, 55–8, 118–19, 157, 162–3; bias and objectivity in, 56, 134, 136–7, 139–40, 145–8, 150, 152; and growth of institutions, 56, 98–9, 128; and conflicting forces, 61; and natural laws, 95–6, 104, 108–10, 126, 139–41; and individual human behaviour, 96–8, 125; 'march of' and mission in, 101–10, 113–15, 119, 126–8; and progress, 112; responsibility and choice in, 121–6, 128, 157; impersonal factors in, 125; and human imperfection, 133–6; as science, 139–40; generalisations in, 141–2; structure and unification in, 156–61, 290; moral categories and concepts in, 163–5; conflicts of ideas in, 168; Tolstoy on, 290

Hitler, Adolf: judgements on, 20, 22, 116, 131, 138, 144, 163; nationalism, 100; dogmatism, 345; genocides, 346

Hobbes, Thomas: on determinism, 9, 116n; pessimistic view of life, 60 & n; on seeking security, 73; on reality as knowable, 130; on free man, 170n; on desirability of controls, 173; on sovereigns, 210; desire for security, 243; basic ideas, 289; Leviathan, 60n

Holbach, Paul Heinrich Dietrich, Baron von, 109, 278; System of Nature, 116

Honderich, Edgar Dawn Ross (Ted), xxvi

humanitarian liberalism: doctrine of, 59, 68, 79, 185, 199n, 236–7, 239; in ancient Greece, 287, 294–321

Humboldt, Wilhelm von, 227, 244, 318

Hume, David: on fact and value, 6n, 291; on determinism, 9, 116n; doubts final solutions, 76; and self-determination, 261; beliefs and ideas, 312

Hus, John, 346
Huxley, Aldous, 44, 78, 143
hypnosis, 184n

Ibsen, Henrik, 89, 243
Idealist metaphysicians, 37
ideas: power of, 167–8
Ignatieff, Michael, *360*, *363*
imperialism, 91
individual: definition and recognition of,
   201–5; social behaviour, 236
individualism *see* humanitarian
   individualism
Isaiah Berlin Literary Trust, xxxi, *364*
Isocrates, 311

Jacobinism, 49, 73–4, 194 & n, 208
James, William, 7–8, 11, 181
Jefferson, Thomas, 173
Jellinek, Georg, 33
Jesus Christ, 231, 249, 346
Johnson, Samuel, 117n
Jones, Arnold Hugh Martin, xxv
Joseph II, Emperor of Austria, 176n
Josephus, 308
justice: and determinism, 15; Mill on
   importance of, 244
Justinian, 23n

Kannegiesser, Leonid, xxix
Kant, Immanuel: on determinism, 7, 12,
   16; maxims, 14; on men as natural
   objects, 18n; on laws of morality, 28; on
   Holy Will, 44; rationalism, 88; on
   'crooked timber of humanity', 92, 216,
   237; on freedom and obligation, 117n,
   182n, 183–5, 202n; on real and ideal,
   123n; on human autonomy, 162, 198–9,
   277; on compulsion to happiness, 183;
   on human values, 184, 291;
   individualism, 191, 198; on political
   liberty, 194; and 'negative' liberty, 199n;
   on paternalism, 203; Mill and, 245; and
   Hegel, 312; on human choice, 337;
   distinguishes realm of value and facts of
   nature, *350* & n; *Critique of Pure
   Reason*, 167
Kateb, George, *360*, *366*
Katznelson, Ira, x, *363*
Kaufman, Arnold Saul, 40n, *354*
Kelly, Aileen M., *351*n
Kemp-Welch, Anthony, 82n
Kennan, George: IB's letter to, xxix–xxx,
   336–44, *352*
Kenny, Michael, *364*

Kepler, Johannes, 162
Keynes, John Maynard, 306
Kierkegaard, Søren, 60, 67, 256
Kingsley, Charles, 247
Knapheis, Baillie, xvi
knowledge: as liberating, 130–1, 190, 252,
   255–9, 263–5, 272–3, 277–8; in history,
   132–6; and determinism, 139; sociology
   of, 158; and predictability, 262; negative
   effects of, 274–6; advancement of, 277;
   Epicurus on, 304–5
Kocis, Robert Albert, *363*
Koestler, Arthur, 344
Kolakowski, Leszek, 230n
Kraus, Oskar, and Roderick M. Chisholm,
   *358*n
Kropotkin, Prince Peter, 71
Kukuthas, Chandran, *357*

Lactantius, 300
laissez-faire, 213, 327
La Mettrie, Julien Offray de, 96
Laplace, Pierre Simon, marquis de, 12, 120
Larmore, Charles, *360*
Laski, Harold Joseph, 344
Laslett, Peter, and others, 36n
Lassalle, Ferdinand Johann Gottlieb, 228n
Lassman, Peter, and Steve Buckler, *357*
Lavoisier, Antoine Laurent, 287
law: as infraction of liberty, 41n, 170n,
   195; and exercise of freedom, 174,
   193–5, 198–9; obedience to, 183; natural,
   210; restraints and curbs in, 215; in
   ancient Greece, 296, 299
League of Nations, 61, 84
Leff, Gordon, 27n
Leibniz, Gottfried Wilhelm, 109, 230n,
   261, 343
Lenin, Vladimir Il'ich: and irrationalism,
   68, 72–3; authoritarianism, 69, 71–3;
   Utopianism, 73; on reality as knowable,
   130; achievements, 159; dogmatism, 345
Léon, Xavier, 51n
Leontiev, Konstantin, 67, 338
Lessing, Gotthold Ephraim, 89, 112, 243
Lessnoff, Michael, *364*
'Letter to George Kennan' (IB), xxix–xxx
Letwin, Shirley Robin, *362*
Lewis, Clarence Irving, 20n
liberal individualism *see* humanitarian
   liberalism
liberalism: in IB's philosophical outlook, x;
   beliefs, 59, 62, 65; and historicism, 65;
   and irrationalists, 67; and freedom,
   175, 286

liberty (freedom): IB's views on, xxvi;
'positive' and 'negative', 4, 30–1, 35,
37–43, 48–50, 53, 169, 175, 177 & n,
178–9, 181, 186–7, 199n, 204, 207–8,
273, 325–7, 354, 358 ; in ancient Greece,
32–4, 294–321; and activity, 34–5; and
authority, 35–7, 39, 49–50; and
individualism, 38, 60, 201–3; and State
intervention, 38–9, 173; and choice,
44–9, 53, 272; conditions for exercise of,
45–7, 50; and security, 46; from
domination, 48; value of, 50–2; frontiers
of, 52–3; and self-realisation, 53; and
sovereignty, 75, 208–12; and economic
strength, 80; as illusion, 110, 131; and
causal laws, 124–5; influenced by
knowledge, 130–1, 190, 252, 255–9,
263–5, 272–8; and coercion, 168–71,
174–5, 179, 210, 274; Mill on, 171,
174–6, 186, 206, 208, 211, 215, 224–5,
235–6, 243, 246, 251; nature and
varieties of, 171–3, 177n; and socio-
economic conditions, 172; and law, 174,
193–5; political, 176, 283–6; and
democracy, 177; and equality, 180n; and
frustration of goals and desires, 181–3,
186–7; and concept of self, 182; for
others, 191–3; and reason, 192–4; and
social recognition, 202–6; and conflict
and harmony of values, 212–13;
restraints and curbs on, 214–15, 285; and
self-determination, 259–61, 269–71, 275;
as human attribute, 270–1
'Liberty' (IB), xxv, xxvi
Lilla, Mark, 363
Lincoln, Abraham, 13
Linnet, Catherine, x, xiv–xv, xxii
Livingstone, Richard Winn, 218, 242–3
Lloyd George, David, 84
Locke, John: influence, 62, 73; and
determinism, 116n; on freedom, 171;
optimism, 173; on law and freedom, 193,
284; humanism, 243; and self-
determination, 261
Louis XIV, King of France, 347
Lukács, Georg, 230n
Lukes, Steven, 357, 358, 360
Lycophron, 298

Macaulay, Thomas Babington, Baron, 118,
134, 138, 218–19
MacCallum, Gerald Cushing, jr, 36n, 355
McCloskey, Henry John, 355
Macfarlane, Leslie John, 32n, 52, 53n, 354
Machiavelli, Niccolò, 293

Mack, Arien, xin, 358n
Mack, Eric, 359
Mackinnon, Donald Mackenzie, 353
MacLennan, Bud, xv
McNair, Lisa, 363n
Macpherson, Crawford Brough, 355
Maistre, Joseph de, 51n, 73–4, 78, 350
Mandel'berg, Viktor Evseevich (pseud.
Posadovsky), 69, 70n, 71
Manent, Pierre, and others, 359n
Marcus Aurelius, Roman Emperor, 231
Margalit, Avishai, 355, 361
Margalit, Edna, 355
Marmontel, Jean François, 221
Marx, Karl: historicism, 20, 56n, 99, 101,
112–13, 132, 137n, 158, 325; and
speaking for oppressed, 64; recoils from
despotism, 71; and class, 72; élitism, 73;
on 'superstructure', 73; influence, 77;
and totalitarianism, 78; and oppressive
institutions, 87; morality, 130; and new
animism, 158n; on understanding as key
to freedom, 189–90; and controlling
domination, 192, 328; and harmony of
values, 213, 289; as prophet, 218, 227,
242; view of Mill, 229n, 247; and unity
of theory and practice, 230n; Bakunin
attacks, 251n; and impediments to
liberty, 256; and self-determination, 271,
338; and moral goodness, 340; on
economic corrosion, 343; Communist
Manifesto (with Friedrich Engels), 314;
A Contribution to the Critique of
Political Economy, 219
Marxism: and determinism, 10; historicism,
19, 26, 57, 99, 158; and application of
reason, 66–9; revolutionary principles,
70; on withering away of State, 166; on
individual freedom, 170n; attraction of,
205; and unity of theory and practice,
230n; and historical determinism, 325;
origins of, 352
Masaryk, Thomas, 62
Maurras, Charles, 73
Mazzini, Giuseppe, 245
Megone, Christopher, 355
Menander, 311
metaphors, 106 & n
methodology, 149n
Meyer, Sheldon, xv
Michelet, Jules, 57, 95, 134, 244
Middle Ages, 151, 244
Mill, Harriet see Taylor, Harriet
Mill, James, 219–22, 227, 234, 238, 244,
247

Mill, John Stuart: IB writes on, xiii–xiv, 3;
  and determinism, 11; and significance of
  human lives, 24; and State intervention,
  38–9, 174, 318; on value judgements, 43,
  291; quotes Comte, 81n; ideals, 84, 89,
  227; rationalism, 88; influence, 89; on
  freedom, 171, 174–6, 186, 206, 208, 211,
  215, 224–5, 235–6, 243, 251; optimism,
  173; critics and opponents, 175, 246; and
  necessary constraint, 196; on private and
  social life, 201, 236–7; and deprivation
  of human rights, 204; on social
  recognition, 205; and liberalism, 207,
  236; on government by the people,
  208–9; on 'permanent interests of man',
  210n; advocates 'experiments in living',
  215, 225n; background and upbringing,
  219–22, 247; character, 220–2, 248;
  search for ends of life, 220–1, 226,
  230–1; beliefs and values, 221–4, 226,
  228–34, 236–8, 242–5, 247, 250–1, 284,
  312, 361–2; on happiness, 221–3, 225–6,
  237; lack of prophetic vision, 227–8,
  242; encourages dissent and diversity,
  228, 235, 239–42, 244; marriage, 229,
  240; on toleration, 229; empiricism, 232,
  238; and individualism, 236–7, 239; on
  effects of democracy, 240–1, 243, 251n;
  reputation and influence, 247–8, 250;
  values intellect and ideas, 247–8; attitude
  to religion, 249–50; on social
  impediments to liberty, 256; and self-
  determination, 261; On Liberty, 218–19,
  229, 246–7
Miller, David, 357, 361
Milton, John, 233
Momigliano, Arnaldo, 357
monism, 4, 216
Montaigne, Michel Eyquem, seigneur de,
  62, 76
Montesquieu, Charles Louis de Secondat,
  baron de: opposes tyranny, 53; historical
  interpretations, 158; on political liberty,
  193; belief in variety, 238, 290;
  humanism, 243
Moore, George Edward, 306
morality: judgements, 4, 21–5, 110, 118,
  126, 136, 139; scientific explanations of,
  129; and responsibility, 131; in history,
  163–5; and human choice, 337
Morris, William, 245
Moses, 316
Mozart, Wolfgang Amadeus: The Magic
  Flute, 200
Muhammad the Prophet, 115

Muller, Herbert Joseph, 300n
Mussolini, Benito, 164n
'My Intellectual Path' (IB), xxv, xxviii–xxix

Nagel, Ernest, 8, 10 & n, 28, 30, 353
Nagel, Thomas, 4n, 358, 359
Namier, Lewis Bernstein, 121
Napoleon I (Bonaparte), Emperor of
  France, 20, 144, 159, 163, 197, 347
nationalism: compatibility with
  internationalism, 65; fanaticism, 88;
  dangers of, 347; see also romantic
  nationalism
natural sciences: and search for causes, 17;
  as model for political theory, 67; and
  attaining truth, 75; Comte on, 95;
  history as, 95–6, 108–9, 126; neutrality
  of view in, 141–2; generalisations in,
  143, 144n; and unification theories, 156;
  nature and methods of, 165; and
  determinism, 322
Nazism, 339
Neoplatonism, 158
New Deal (USA), 84, 91
New York Review of Books, xxvin, xxviii,
  xxx
Newman, John Henry, Cardinal, 247
Newton, Isaac, 108, 142, 287
Nicholls, David, 41n, 356
Nietzsche, Friedrich: and social struggle,
  64; irrationalism, 66; élitism, 73; and
  cosmic force, 113; opposes Victorian
  claustrophobia, 243; defiance, 338
Nikias, 33, 300
'Notes on Prejudice' (IB), xxx, 352
Nowell-Smith, Patrick Horace, 116n, 261

Oakeshott, Michael, 350
obedience, 75, 168, 183, 195–8, 327–8
'objective reason', 196
objectivity, 147–9
Occam, William, 175, 176n
Oenamaus, 260n
'On the Pursuit of the Ideal' (IB), xxvi
oppression, 192, 328
Origen, 141n
original sin, 128
'Originality of Machiavelli, The' (IB), xxvii
Orwell, George, 78
O'Sullivan, Noel, 356
Otanes, 33
Ouyang Kang, xxvii
Owen, Robert, 112

Oxford Companion to Philosophy (ed. Honderich), xxvi

Packe, Michael St John, 247n
Paine, Thomas, 173, 284, 321
Palmerston, Henry John Temple, 3rd Viscount, 224
Panaetius, 316, 319
paradise (Garden of Eden): as original human state, 155–6, 192
Parekh, Bhikhu, *364*
Pareto, Vilfredo, 73, 158, 242
Parkes, Joseph, 223n
Parmenides, 315
Passmore, John Arthur, 12, 27n, *353*
Pasteur, Louis, 22, 138
paternalism, 47, 183, 203
'pédantrocratie, la', 251n
Pelczynski, Zbigniew Andrzej, and John Gray, *356*
Pericles, 33, 300–1, 310, 319
Peripatetics, 307
Perl, Jeffrey, xxvi–xvii
Persaeus, 316
persecution, 231, 235
pessimism, 154
Pettit, Philip, *357*
Phaleas, 299
philanthropy, 87
Philip of Macedon, 310
Philo of Alexandria, 316
philosophes, 158, 198, 216, 323
Planck, Max, 287
Plant, Raymond, *357*
Plato: pessimism, 78; and authoritarianism, 88; on Sophocles, 185; on harmony of values, 213; moral and political ideas, 215, 287–8, 296–7, 309, 311–12, 315–18, 321; on causation and moral responsibility, 260; and self-determination, 271; on social life, 294–7, 300, 309, 314; and Sophists, 298, 300; and Stoic doctrines, 310; and Moses, 316; and rationalism, 327; *Apology*, 296; *Crito*, 296; *Gorgias*, 299; *Laws*, 296; *Politicus*, 296; *Republic*, 295, 302n
Platonism, 306
Plekhanov, Georgy Valentinovich, 19, 70, 130
pluralism: centrality to IB, x, xxvii, *356*; and differing goals, 151; and conflict of values and aims, 212–17, *358–60*; Mill and, 233, 235, 238, 244
Plutarch, 309
Pohlenz, Max, 316, 318
'Political Ideas in the Romantic Age' (IB), *349* & n

'Political Ideas in the Twentieth Century' (IB), xx, xxx, *352*
political theory: nature of, 168; changes in, 290–2
Pollard, Sydney, 10n
Popper, Karl Raimund, x, 100n, 101n, 265, 267, 287, *351*, *353*
Posadovsky (*pseud.*) *see* Mandel'berg, Viktor Evseevich
Posidonius, 31, 276–7, 307, 316
positivism, 20, 80
power: control of, 54; and compromise, 64; *see also* authority
Power of Ideas, The (IB), xxviii, *361*
praise and blame: determinism and, 9–10, 13–16, 122, 269, 324; effect of, 28; and historical inevitability, 115, 122, 146; and knowledge, 131–2, 150; and self-determination, 263
Preen, Friedrich von, 20n
prejudice, 345–7
Priam, King, 307
privacy, 176
Procrustes, 216
Prodicus, 298, 321
progress: and human improvement, 62–4; concept of, 89; technological, 91; in ideas, 287–8
Proper Study of Mankind, The (IB), xxv, xxvin, xxvii
Protagoras, 298, 315
Protestantism, 185
Proudhon, Pierre Joseph, 228n
Proust, Marcel, 142
psychology: laws of, 108–9
'Purpose Justifies the Ways, The' (IB), xxiv, xxviii
Pushkin, Alexander Sergeevich, 171
Putnam, Hilary, *357*
Pythagoras, 320

quietism, 186n, 187n
Quinton, Anthony Meredith, *357*
Quixote, Don, 340

Racine, Jean, 142
Rainborow, Thomas, 202n
Ranke, Leopold von, 57, 95, 138
rationalism: and political solutions, 62, 66–7, 74–5, 76, 191–3; and obstacles to self-realisation, 188; and natural laws, 190; and behaviour, 253–4, 256, 264–5; in ancient Greece, 306; and exercise of freedom, 327; *see also* reason
Rawls, John, *358*

Raz, Joseph, *358*
reason: and irrational influences, 61;
     Marxist belief in, 66–9; and liberation,
     130–1, 190; and unification theories, 156,
     290–1; and individualism, 185, 190,
     198–9; and coercion, 197; *see also*
     rationalism
Reformation, 176
relativism, 152, 155
religion: persecution of, 231; Mill's attitude
     to, 249–50; in ancient Greece, 298–9,
     303
Renaissance, Italian, 62, 112, 176, 290, 319
Renouvier, Charles Bernard, 11
representation (political), 3; *see also*
     democracy
responsibility: and determinism, 6, 28–9,
     116n, 117, 121–2, 128, 131, 136, 163,
     164, 323; and conscience, 48n; moral,
     260, 338; and self-prediction, 266–7
revolutions: and individual responsibility,
     163; causes and aims, 207
Rickman, Hans Peter, 28n
rights: natural, 72, 210; and society, 191; as
     absolute, 211; and freedom, 285–6;
     unconsidered in ancient Greece, 319
Riley, Jonathan, *360, 366*
Robert Waley Cohen Memorial Lecture
     (1959), xii
Roberts, Colin, xiii, xvin
Robespierre, Maximilien, 92, 144, 167, 345
     & n
Robson, Ann Provost, John Mercel
     Robson and Bruce L. Kinzer, *362*
romantic nationalism, 59–61, 80
'Romantic Revolution, The' (IB), xxvii
romanticism, 88; and history, 113; and
     political theory, 294; IB's views on, *350*
Rome (ancient), 102, 117–18, 176, 186,
     309, 312, 319
Roosevelt, Franklin Delano, 84
Roots of Romanticism, The (IB), xxvii, *350,*
     362
Ross, William David, *358*
Rostovtzeff, Michael I., 321
Rousseau, Jean-Jacques: on human chains,
     32, 51n; Heine on, 167; on ill will, 170;
     on obedience to laws, 183; influence on
     liberal humanism, 185; on true freedom,
     185; individualism, 191, 198; on
     harmonious society, 194; on austerity of
     laws of liberty, 208; Constant opposes,
     209; Mill and, 245; on barbarian
     innocence, 275; reactions to, 288; on
     human conduct, *350*

Ruskin, John, 245, 247
Russell, Bertrand: on understanding, xxix,
     288; and determinism, 116n; on
     fundamental beliefs, 245; and self-
     determination, 261; revolutionary ideas,
     287; knowledge of, 315
Russian Social Democratic Party, 2nd
     Congress (1903), 69
Russian Thinkers (IB), xxv
Ryan, Alan James, *354, 355, 362, 364*

Sabine, George Holland., 318, 320n, 321,
     351
Saint-Simon, Claude-Henri, comte de: on
     human fulfilment, 71; prophesies
     materialist government, 85–6, 166;
     Utopianism, 112, 238; on obedience to
     general laws, 129; and finality, 227; Mill
     and, 242n, 248
Sainte-Beuve, Charles-Augustin, 20, 92n
Sandel, Michael, *357*
Santayana, George, xxx
Savigny, Friedrich Karl von, 57
Sceptics (Greek sect), 315, 319
Schelling, Friedrich Wilhelm Joseph von,
     99, 158, 167, 219
Schlick, Moritz, 9, 116n, 261
Schoeck, Helmut, and James Wilhelm
     Wiggins, *356*
Schofield, Malcolm, 302n
Schopenhauer, Arthur, 66, 123n, 154, 187,
     261, 271, 278
Schumpeter, Joseph Alois, 217n
science *see* natural sciences
self: and attainment of freedom, 184–5; *see*
     also individual
self-denial, 186
self-determination, 259–71, 275
self-fulfilment, 253–4
self-government, 177
self-knowledge, 244
self-mastery, 178–82
self-prediction, 265–7
self-realisation, 187–91
Sen, Amartya Kumar, 7n, 8–9, 15, *353,*
     *358*n
Seneca, 62
Sense of Reality, The (IB), xxvii
Sextus Empiricus, 76, 307n
Shackleton, Robert, 225n
Shaw, George Bernard, 112
Sheldon, Olive, xiii
Shelley, Percy Bysshe, 306
Shklar, Judith, *355, 356*n
Siedentop, Larry, *363*
Simhony, Avital, *356*

Simon, Richard, xv
slavery, 179, 184, 210–11, 273–4
Slavophils, 289
Smerdis, pseudo-, 33
Smith, Adam, 79, 173
Smith, Geoffrey W., *355*
social Darwinism, 37
social democracy, 68, 91
socialism: beliefs, 59, 65; and irrationalists, 67; Mill and, 228n
sociology: laws of, 108–9, 124, 159, 161–2
Socrates: disciples, 33, 312; accepts Athenian law, 49, 295; on virtue and knowledge, 200; killed, 231, 295, 346; accused of corrupting young men, 296; Sophist opponents, 298; on learning not to mind, 305; Antisthenes and, 312; opposes Aristippus, 313; and unworthiness of political participation, 319
Sophists, 298–9, 310, 315
Sophocles, 185, 311
Sorel, Georges, 67, 158
sovereignty: and liberty, 75, 208–12
Soviet Union: and central plan, 82
Sparta, 207, 294, 296, 300–1
Spencer, Herbert, 20, 38, 234, 247
Spengler, Oswald, 99, 101, 130, 289
Spinoza, Benedictus de: on determinism, 9, 13, 15, 129, 278; influence, 62; rationalism, 88, 188; on reality as knowable, 130; and controlling domination, 192; on children's obedience, 193; humanism, 243; on knowledge, 259; on self-determinism, 264, 271, 277; and positive freedom, *356*; *Ethics*, 264
Spitz, David, xiiin, 43, 46, *354*
Stalin, Josef Vissarionovich: historical statements on, 20, 148; regime, 55n; on creative artists as 'engineers of human soul', 82 & n, 328; judgements on, 163; dogmatism, 345
Stallworthy, Jon, xi, xv–xvii, xix–xxii, xxiv
State, the: intervention by, 38–9, 65, 76, 90, 171, 283–4, 318; growth in responsibilities, 80; withering away of, 166, 342; authoritarianism, 198; service to, 206; Mill on stultifying effects of, 245; social life in, 295; in ancient Greece, 300–3, 306, 318–19
Steinberg, Jonny, *363*
Steiner, Hillel, *356*
Stendhal (*pseudonym of* Marie-Henri Beyle), 143

Stephen, James Fitzjames, 175, 246, *358*n
stereotypes (national), 346–7
Sterling, Edward, 248n
Sterling, John, 174n, 205n, 244n, 248
Stirner, Max, 60
Stocker, Michael, *358*
Stoics: and determinism, 5, 7, 16, 29, 154; and security against conditioning, 18n; and freedom, 31–2, 34, 186, 198; and acceptance, 154, 276; and harmony of theory and practice, 230n; on knowledge as liberating, 252–3, 256–7; on causation, 260; and self-determination, 261, 271; and rationality, 264, 306–7; on saving the soul, 303; doctrines and influence, 306–13, 316, 319–20; on pleasure as enemy, 313; oriental origins, 316; and suppression of desire, 326
Storrs Lectures (Yale University, 1962), xv, xxvii
Strauss, Leo, *356*
suffering: caused by ignorance, 111
superstition: philosophical, 16–18
surrealism, 88
Sutcliffe, Peter H., xv
Swift, Adam, *366*
Swift, Jonathan, 78
Swinburne, Algernon Charles, xxiv
Switzerland, 90
syndicalism, 68

Tacitus, 57
Taine, Hippolyte, 130, 134, 247
Talleyrand, Charles Maurice de, 92
Tallis, Raymond, *363*
Talmon, Jacob Leib, *351*
Tanner, Michael, *364*
Tarn, William Woodthorpe, 309
Tawney, Richard Henry, 171n, 215
Taylor, Charles, *355*, *358*, *359*, *363*
Taylor, Harriet (*later* wife of J. S. Mill), 228n, 229, 238, 240, 248
Taylor, Helen, 249
technocrats, 216, 242n
teleology, 105, 107–9, 118
Tennyson, Alfred, 1st Baron, 62
theocrats, 216
theology: and attaining truth, 75
Theophrastes, 320
theory and practice: unity of, 230 & n
Thomas, William, *362*
Thompson, Dennis Frank, *362*
thought: as human attribute, 292–3
Thrasymachus, 298–300
Three Critics of the Enlightenment (IB), xin, *350*

'Three Turning-Points in the History of Political Thought' (IB), xxvii

Thucydides, 57, 148, 294, 300–1, 311

Times Higher Educational Supplement, ix

Times Literary Supplement, 30n, 343

Tkachev, Petr Nikitich, 71

Tocqueville, Alexis de: and State intervention, 38; and social struggle, 64; rationalism, 88; on freedom, 171, 211–19; death, 219; prophecies, 227; Mill admires, 228; belief in variety, 238; on American democracy, 241

toleration, 90, 92, 218–19, 229, 240

Tolstoy, Count Lev Nikolaevich, 72, 129, 133, 135n, 290

totalitarianism, 78, 83, 286, *351*

Toynbee, Arnold Joseph, 99, 105, 158, 289

trade unionism, 68, 84

Treitschke, Heinrich von, 118

Trotsky, Leon, 55, 134

truth: theology and, 75; in political theory, 290–2; and deliberate deception, 339

Tuell, Anne Kimball, 248n

Turgenev, Ivan Sergeevich: *Dnevnik lishnego cheloveka* ('Diary of a superfluous man'), 343n; *Fathers and Children*, 86

Turgot, Anne Jacques Robert, baron de l'Aulne, 153

'Two Concepts of Liberty' (IB), x, xii, xvin, xxv, xxxi, 30, 50n, *352, 354, 356, 357, 358*, 360–1

tyranny, 53–4, 208–9, 214

Ulam, Adam, xiv

understanding: and historical process, 153–4; as key to freedom, 189–90, 265; of basic ideas, 288; *see also* knowledge

United Nations, 84

United States of America: and State responsibilities, 80; political issues in, 83–4; materialism, 88; self-confidence in, 187n; democracy in, 241, 284

Uritsky, Moise Solomonovich, xxix, 333–5, *351*

Utilitarianism: on moulding human material, 184; on morality, 198, 342; Mill's attitude to, 221–2, 226–7, 239, 245, 250; Bentham advocates, 224; belief in simple truths, 235, 250; refuted by human achievers, 338

Utopianism, 112, 153, 166

Vaihinger, Hans, 123n

value judgements: and determinism, 4, 8–9, 13, 21–5, 28, 116–19, 136–7; Mill on, 43; varieties of, 44–6

values: harmonisation of, 212–14, 216–17, 292

Vico, Giambattista, 95, 140n

Vico and Herder (IB), x

Villey, Michel: *Leçons d'histoire de la philosophie du droit*, 176n

Voltaire, François Marie Arouet de: rationalism, 20; historical sense, 57; influence, 89; and toleration, 117; on liberty, 284

Waelder, Robert, 31n

Walzer, Michael, *358, 360, 361*

Warner, Stuart D., *358n*

Weber, Max, 20, 48n, 158n

Wells, Herbert George, 20, 112, 143, 242n

West, David, *356*

White, Morton, 13 & n, 14–15, 29–30, *353*

Wilberforce, William, 247

Wilbur, George B., and Warner Muensterberger, 31n

Williams, Bernard Arthur Owen, *358, 359*, 364

Wilson, Woodrow, 62, 84

Wollheim, Richard, 30n, *354, 359, 361, 362*

Woolf, Virginia, 306

Wordsworth, William, 221

World Spirit, 98

Xenophon, 313n, 318

Zeitgeist, 130

Zelinsky, Kornely L., 82n

Zeller, Eduard, 316

Zeno, 130, 302, 306–10, 312, 316–17, 319–20

Zionism, *360*

Zola, Émile, 143